The History
of a Crime

The History of a Crime

of a Crime

Victor Hugo

MINT EDITIONS

The History of a Crime was first published in 1877.

This edition published by Mint Editions 2021.

ISBN 9781513211947 | E-ISBN 9781513210742

Published by Mint Editions®

MINT
EDITIONS

minteditionbooks.com

Publishing Director: Jennifer Newens
Design & Production: Rachel Lopez Metzger
Project Manager: Micaela Clark
Translated by T.H. Joyce and Arthur Locker
Typesetting: Westchester Publishing Services

Contents

THE FOURTH DAY—THE VICTORY

THE FIRST DAY
THE AMBUSH

I

"Security"

On December 1, 1851, Charras[1] shrugged his shoulder and unloaded his pistols. In truth, the belief in the possibility of a *coup d'état* had become humiliating. The supposition of such illegal violence on the part of M. Louis Bonaparte vanished upon serious consideration. The great question of the day was manifestly the Devincq election; it was clear that the Government was only thinking of that matter. As to a conspiracy against the Republic and against the People, how could anyone premeditate such a plot? Where was the man capable of entertaining such a dream? For a tragedy there must be an actor, and here assuredly the actor was wanting. To outrage Right, to suppress the Assembly, to abolish the Constitution, to strangle the Republic, to overthrow the Nation, to sully the Flag, to dishonor the Army, to suborn the Clergy and the Magistracy, to succeed, to triumph, to govern, to administer, to exile, to banish, to transport, to ruin, to assassinate, to reign, with such complicities that the law at last resembles a foul bed of corruption. What! All these enormities were to be committed! And by whom? By a Colossus? No, by a dwarf. People laughed at the notion. They no longer said "What a crime!" but "What a farce!" For after all they reflected; heinous crimes require stature. Certain crimes are too lofty for certain hands. A man who would achieve an 18th Brumaire must have Arcola in his past and Austerlitz in his future. The art of becoming a great scoundrel is not accorded to the first comer. People said to themselves, Who is this son of Hortense? He has Strasbourg behind him instead of Arcola, and Boulogne in place of Austerlitz. He is a Frenchman, born a Dutchman, and naturalized a Swiss; he is a Bonaparte crossed with a Verhuell; he is only celebrated for the ludicrousness of his imperial attitude, and he who would pluck a feather from his eagle would risk finding a goose's quill in his hand. This Bonaparte does not pass currency in the array, he is a counterfeit image less of gold than of lead, and assuredly French soldiers will not give us the change for this

---

1. Colonel Charras was Under-Secretary of State in 1848, and Acting Secretary of War under the Provisional Government.

false Napoleon in rebellion, in atrocities, in massacres, in outrages, in treason. If he should attempt roguery it would miscarry. Not a regiment would stir. Besides, why should he make such an attempt? Doubtless he has his suspicious side, but why suppose him an absolute villain? Such extreme outrages are beyond him; he is incapable of them physically, why judge him capable of them morally? Has he not pledged honor? Has he not said, "No one in Europe doubts my word?" Let us fear nothing. To this could be answered, Crimes are committed either on a grand or on a mean scale. In the first category there is Caesar; in the second there is Mandrin. Caesar passes the Rubicon, Mandrin bestrides the gutter. But wise men interposed, "Are we not prejudiced by offensive conjectures? This man has been exiled and unfortunate. Exile enlightens, misfortune corrects."

For his part Louis Bonaparte protested energetically. Facts abounded in his favor. Why should he not act in good faith? He had made remarkable promises. Towards the end of October, 1848, then a candidate for the Presidency, he was calling at No. 37, Rue de la Tour d'Auvergne, on a certain personage, to whom he remarked, "I wish to have an explanation with you. They slander me. Do I give you the impression of a madman? They think that I wish to revivify Napoleon. There are two men whom a great ambition can take for its models, Napoleon and Washington. The one is a man of Genius, the other is a man of Virtue. It is ridiculous to say, 'I will be a man of Genius;' it is honest to say, 'I will be a man of Virtue.' Which of these depends upon ourselves? Which can we accomplish by our will? To be Genius? No. To be Probity? Yes. The attainment of Genius is not possible; the attainment of Probity is a possibility. And what could I revive of Napoleon? One sole thing—a crime. Truly a worthy ambition! Why should I be considered man? The Republic being established, I am not a great man, I shall not copy Napoleon; but I am an honest man. I shall imitate Washington. My name, the name of Bonaparte, will be inscribed on two pages of the history of France: on the first there will be crime and glory, on the second probity and honor. And the second will perhaps be worth the first. Why? Because if Napoleon is the greater, Washington is the better man. Between the guilty hero and the good citizen I choose the good citizen. Such is my ambition."

From 1848 to 1851 three years elapsed. People had long suspected Louis Bonaparte; but long-continued suspicion blunts the intellect and wears itself out by fruitless alarms. Louis Bonaparte had had dissimulating ministers such as Magne and Rouher; but he had also had straightforward ministers such as Léon Faucher and Odilon Barrot; and these last had affirmed that he was upright and sincere. He had been seen to beat his breast before the doors of Ham; his foster sister, Madame Hortense Cornu, wrote to Mieroslawsky, "I am a good Republican, and I can answer for him." His friend of Ham, Peauger, a loyal man, declared, "Louis Bonaparte is incapable of treason." Had not Louis Bonaparte written the work entitled "Pauperism"? In the intimate circles of the Elysée Count Potocki was a Republican and Count d'Orsay was a Liberal; Louis Bonaparte said to Potocki, "I am a man of the Democracy," and to D'Orsay, "I am a man of Liberty." The Marquis du Hallays opposed the *coup d'état*, while the Marquise du Hallays was in its favor. Louis Bonaparte said to the Marquis, "Fear nothing" (it is true that he whispered to the Marquise, "Make your mind easy"). The Assembly, after having shown here and there some symptoms of uneasiness, had grown calm. There was General Neumayer, "who was to be depended upon," and who from his position at Lyons would at need march upon Paris. Changarnier exclaimed, "Representatives of the people, deliberate in peace." Even Louis Bonaparte himself had pronounced these famous words, "I should see an enemy of my country in anyone who would change by force that which has been established by law," and, moreover, the Army was "force," and the Army possessed leaders, leaders who were beloved and victorious. Lamoricière, Changarnier, Cavaignac, Leflô, Bedeau, Charras; how could anyone imagine the Army of Africa arresting the Generals of Africa? On Friday, November 28, 1851, Louis Bonaparte said to Michel de Bourges, "If I wanted to do wrong, I could not. Yesterday, Thursday, I invited to my table five Colonels of the garrison of Paris, and the whim seized me to question each one by himself. All five declared to me that the Army would never lend itself to a *coup de force*, nor attack the inviolability of the Assembly. You can tell your friends this."—"He smiled," said Michel de Bourges, reassured, "and I also smiled." After this, Michel de Bourges declared in the Tribune, "this is the man for me." In that same month of November a satirical journal, charged with calumniating the President of the Republic, was sentenced to fine and imprisonment for a caricature depicting a shooting-gallery and Louis Bonaparte using the Constitution as a target. Morigny, Minister of the Interior, declared in the Council before the President "that a Guardian of Public Power ought never to violate the law as otherwise he would be—" "a dishonest man," interposed the President. All these words and all these facts were notorious. The material and moral impossibility of the *coup d'état* was manifest to all. To outrage the National Assembly! To arrest the Representatives! What madness! As we have seen, Charras, who had long remained on his guard, unloaded his pistols. The feeling of security was complete and unanimous. Nevertheless there were some of us in the Assembly who still retained a few doubts, and who occasionally shook our heads, but we were looked upon as fools.

II

Paris Sleeps—The Bell Rings

On the 2d December, 1851, Representative Versigny, of the Haute-Saône, who resided at Paris, at No. 4, Rue Léonie, was asleep. He slept soundly; he had been working till late at night. Versigny was a young man of thirty-two, soft-featured and fair-complexioned, of a courageous spirit, and a mind tending towards social and economical studies. He had passed the first hours of the night in the perusal of a book by Bastiat, in which he was making marginal notes, and, leaving the book open on the table, he had fallen asleep. Suddenly he awoke with a start at the sound of a sharp ring at the bell. He sprang up in surprise. It was dawn. It was about seven o'clock in the morning.

Never dreaming what could be the motive for so early a visit, and thinking that someone had mistaken the door, he again lay down, and was about to resume his slumber, when a second ring at the bell, still louder than the first, completely aroused him. He got up in his nightshirt and opened the door.

Michel de Bourges and Théodore Bac entered. Michel de Bourges was the neighbor of Versigny; he lived at No. 16, Rue de Milan.

Théodore Bac and Michel were pale, and appeared greatly agitated.

"Versigny," said Michel, "dress yourself at once—Baune has just been arrested."

"Bah!" exclaimed Versigny. "Is the Mauguin business beginning again?"

"It is more than that," replied Michel. "Baune's wife and daughter came to me half-an-hour ago. They awoke me. Baune was arrested in bed at six o'clock this morning."

"What does that mean?" asked Versigny.

The bell rang again.

"This will probably tell us," answered Michel de Bourges.

Versigny opened the door. It was the Representative Pierre Lefranc. He brought, in truth, the solution of the enigma.

"Do you know what is happening?" said he.

"Yes," answered Michel. "Baune is in prison."

"It is the Republic who is a prisoner," said Pierre Lefranc. "Have you read the placards?"

"No."

Pierre Lefranc explained to them that the walls at that moment were covered with placards which the curious crowd were thronging to read, that he had glanced over one of them at the corner of his street, and that the blow had fallen.

"The blow!" exclaimed Michel. "Say rather the crime."

Pierre Lefranc added that there were three placards—one decree and two proclamations—all three on white paper, and pasted close together.

The decree was printed in large letters.

The ex-Constituent Laissac, who lodged, like Michel de Bourges, in the neighborhood (No. 4, Cité Gaillard), then came in. He brought the same news, and announced further arrests which had been made during the night.

There was not a minute to lose.

They went to impart the news to Yvan, the Secretary of the Assembly, who had been appointed by the Left, and who lived in the Rue de Boursault.

An immediate meeting was necessary. Those Republican Representatives who were still at liberty must be warned and brought together without delay.

Versigny said, "I will go and find Victor Hugo."

It was eight o'clock in the morning. I was awake and was working in bed. My servant entered and said, with an air of alarm,—

"A Representative of the people is outside who wishes to speak to you, sir."

"Who is it?"

"Monsieur Versigny:"

"Show him in."

Versigny entered, and told me the state of affairs. I sprang out of bed.

He told me of the "rendezvous" at the rooms of the ex-Constituent Laissac.

"Go at once and inform the other Representatives," said I.

He left me.

III

What Had Happened During the Night

P revious to the fatal days of June, 1848, the esplanade of the Invalides was divided into eight huge grass plots, surrounded by wooden railings and enclosed between two groves of trees, separated by a street running perpendicularly to the front of the Invalides. This street was traversed by three streets running parallel to the Seine. There were large lawns upon which children were wont to play. The centre of the eight grass plots was marred by a pedestal which under the Empire had borne the bronze lion of St. Mark, which had been brought from Venice; under the Restoration a white marble statue of Louis XVIII; and under Louis Philippe a plaster bust of Lafayette. Owing to the Palace of the Constituent Assembly having been nearly seized by a crowd of insurgents on the 22d of June, 1848, and there being no barracks in the neighborhood, General Cavaignac had constructed at three hundred paces from the Legislative Palace, on the grass plots of the Invalides, several rows of long huts, under which the grass was hidden. These huts, where three or four thousand men could be accommodated, lodged the troops specially appointed to keep watch over the National Assembly.

On the 1st December, 1851, the two regiments hutted on the Esplanade were the 6th and the 42d Regiments of the Line, the 6th commanded by Colonel Garderens de Boisse, who was famous before the Second of December, the 42d by Colonel Espinasse, who became famous since that date.

The ordinary night-guard of the Palace of the Assembly was composed of a battalion of Infantry and of thirty artillerymen, with a captain. The Minister of War, in addition, sent several troopers for orderly service. Two mortars and six pieces of cannon, with their ammunition wagons, were ranged in a little square courtyard situated on the right of the Cour d'Honneur, and which was called the Cour des Canons. The Major, the military commandant of the Palace, was placed under the immediate control of the Questors.[1] At nightfall the gratings and the doors were

---

1. The Questors were officers elected by the Assembly, whose special duties were to keep and audit the accounts, and who controlled all matters affecting the social economy of the House.

secured, sentinels were posted, instructions were issued to the sentries, and the Palace was closed like a fortress. The password was the same as in the Place de Paris.

The special instructions drawn up by the Questors prohibited the entrance of any armed force other than the regiment on duty.

On the night of the 1st and 2d of December the Legislative Palace was guarded by a battalion of the 42d.

The sitting of the 1st of December, which was exceedingly peaceable, and had been devoted to a discussion on the municipal law, had finished late, and was terminated by a Tribunal vote. At the moment when M. Baze, one of the Questors, ascended the Tribune to deposit his vote, a Representative, belonging to what was called "Les Bancs Elyséens" approached him, and said in a low tone, "Tonight you will be carried off." Such warnings as these were received everyday, and, as we have already explained, people had ended by paying no heed to them. Nevertheless, immediately after the sitting the Questors sent for the Special Commissary of Police of the Assembly, President Dupin being present. When interrogated, the Commissary declared that the reports of his agents indicated "dead calm"—such was his expression—and that assuredly there was no danger to be apprehended for that night. When the Questors pressed him further, President Dupin, exclaiming "Bah!" left the room.

On that same day, the 1st December, about three o'clock in the afternoon, as General Leflô's father-in-law crossed the boulevard in front of Tortoni's, someone rapidly passed by him and whispered in his ear these significant words, "Eleven o'clock—midnight." This incident excited but little attention at the Questure, and several even laughed at it. It had become customary with them. Nevertheless General Leflô would not go to bed until the hour mentioned had passed by, and remained in the Offices of the Questure until nearly one o'clock in the morning.

The shorthand department of the Assembly was done out of doors by four messengers attached to the *Moniteur*, who were employed to carry the copy of the shorthand writers to the printing-office, and to bring back the proof-sheets to the Palace of the Assembly, where M. Hippolyte Prévost corrected them. M. Hippolyte Prévost was chief of the stenographic staff, and in that capacity had apartments in the Legislative Palace. He was at the same time editor of the musical *feuilleton* of the *Moniteur*. On the 1st December he had gone to the Opéra Comique for the first representation of a new piece, and did not return till after midnight. The fourth messenger from the *Moniteur* was waiting for him with a proof of the last slip of the sitting; M. Prévost corrected the proof, and the messenger was sent off. It was then a little after one o'clock, profound quiet reigned around, and, with the exception of the guard, all in the Palace slept. Towards this hour of the night, a singular incident occurred. The Captain-Adjutant-Major of the Guard of the Assembly came to the Major and said, "The Colonel has sent for me," and he added according to military etiquette, "Will you permit me to go?" The Commandant was astonished. "Go," he said with some sharpness, "but the Colonel is wrong to disturb an officer on duty." One of the soldiers on guard, without understanding the meaning of the words, heard the Commandant pacing up and down, and muttering several times, "What the deuce can he want?"

Half an hour afterwards the Adjutant-Major returned. "Well," asked the Commandant, "what did the Colonel want with you?" "Nothing," answered the Adjutant, "he wished to give me the orders for tomorrow's duties." The night became further advanced. Towards four o'clock the Adjutant-Major came again to the Major. "Major," he said, "the Colonel has asked for me." "Again!" exclaimed the Commandant. "This is becoming strange; nevertheless, go."

The Adjutant-Major had amongst other duties that of giving out the instructions to the sentries, and consequently had the power of rescinding them.

As soon as the Adjutant-Major had gone out, the Major, becoming uneasy, thought that it was his duty to communicate with the Military Commandant of the Palace. He went upstairs to the apartment of the Commandant—Lieutenant Colonel Niols. Colonel Niols had gone to bed and the attendants had retired to their rooms in the attics. The Major, new to the Palace, groped about the corridors, and, knowing little about the various rooms, rang at a door which seemed to him that of the Military Commandant. Nobody answered, the door was not opened, and the Major returned downstairs, without having been able to speak to anybody.

On his part the Adjutant-Major re-entered the Palace, but the Major did not see him again. The Adjutant remained near the grated door of the Place Bourgogne, shrouded in his cloak, and walking up and down the courtyard as though expecting someone.

At the instant that five o'clock sounded from the great clock of the dome, the soldiers who slept in the hut-camp before the Invalides were suddenly awakened. Orders were given in a low voice in the huts to take up arms, in silence. Shortly afterwards two regiments, knapsack on back were marching upon the Palace of the Assembly; they were the 6th and the 42d.

At this same stroke of five, simultaneously in all the quarters of Paris, infantry soldiers filed out noiselessly from every barrack, with their colonels at their head. The *aides-de-camp* and orderly officers of Louis Bonaparte, who had been distributed in all the barracks, superintended this taking up of arms. The cavalry were not set in motion until three-quarters of an hour after the infantry, for fear that the ring of the horses' hoofs on the stones should wake slumbering Paris too soon.

M. de Persigny, who had brought from the Elysée to the camp of the Invalides the order to take up arms, marched at the head of the 42d, by the side of Colonel Espinasse. A story is current in the army, for at the present day, wearied as people are with dishonorable incidents, these occurrences are yet told with a species of gloomy indifference—the story is current that at the moment of setting out with his regiment one of the colonels who could be named hesitated, and that the emissary from the Elysée, taking a sealed packet from his pocket, said to him, "Colonel, I admit that we are running a great risk. Here in this envelope, which I have been charged to hand to you, are a hundred thousand francs in banknotes *for contingencies*." The envelope was accepted, and the regiment set out. On the evening of the 2d of December the colonel said to a lady, "This morning I earned a hundred thousand francs and my General's epaulets." The lady showed him the door.

Xavier Durrieu, who tells us this story, had the curiosity later on to see this lady. She confirmed the story. Yes, certainly! she had shut the door in the face of this wretch; a soldier, a traitor to his flag who dared visit her! She receive such a man? No! she could not do that, "and," states Xavier Durrieu, she added, "And yet I have no character to lose."

Another mystery was in progress at the Prefecture of Police.

Those belated inhabitants of the Cité who may have returned home at a late hour of the night might have noticed a large number of street cabs loitering in scattered groups at different points round about the Rue de Jerusalem.

From eleven o'clock in the evening, under pretext of the arrivals of refugees at Paris from Genoa and London, the Brigade of Surety and the eight hundred *sergents de ville* had been retained in the Prefecture. At three o'clock in the morning a summons had been sent to the forty-eight

Commissaries of Paris and of the suburbs, and also to the peace officers. An hour afterwards all of them arrived. They were ushered into a separate chamber, and isolated from each other as much as possible. At five o'clock a bell was sounded in the Prefect's cabinet. The Prefect Maupas called the Commissaries of Police one after another into his cabinet, revealed the plot to them, and allotted to each his portion of the crime. None refused; many thanked him.

It was a question of arresting at their own homes seventy-eight Democrats who were influential in their districts, and dreaded by the Elysée as possible chieftains of barricades. It was necessary, a still more daring outrage, to arrest at their houses sixteen Representatives of the People. For this last task were chosen among the Commissaries of Police such of those magistrates who seemed the most likely to become ruffians. Amongst these were divided the Representatives. Each had his man. Sieur Courtille had Charras, Sieur Desgranges had Nadaud, Sieur Hubaut the elder had M. Thiers, and Sieur Hubaut the younger General Bedeau, General Changarnier was allotted to Lerat, and General Cavaignac to Colin. Sieur Dourlens took Representative Valentin, Sieur Benoist Representative Miot, Sieur Allard Representative Cholat, Sieur Barlet took Roger (Du Nord), General Lamoricière fell to Commissary Blanchet, Commissary Gronfier had Representative Greppo, and Commissary Boudrot Representative Lagrange. The Questors were similarly allotted, Monsieur Baze to the Sieur Primorin, and General Leflô to Sieur Bertoglio.

Warrants with the name of the Representatives had been drawn up in the Prefect's private Cabinet. Blanks had been only left for the names of the Commissaries. These were filled in at the moment of leaving.

In addition to the armed force which was appointed to assist them, it had been decided that each Commissary should be accompanied by two escorts, one composed of *sergents de ville*, the other of police agents in plain clothes. As Prefect Maupas had told M. Bonaparte, the Captain of the Republican Guard, Baudinet, was associated with Commissary Lerat in the arrest of General Changarnier.

Towards half-past five the *fiacres* which were in waiting were called up, and all started, each with his instructions.

During this time, in another corner of Paris—the old Rue du Temple—in that ancient Soubise Mansion which had been transformed into a Royal Printing Office, and is today a National Printing Office, another section of the Crime was being organized.

Towards one in the morning a passerby who had reached the old Rue du Temple by the Rue de Vieilles-Haudriettes, noticed at the junction of these two streets several long and high windows brilliantly lighted up, These were the windows of the work-rooms of the National Printing Office. He turned to the right and entered the old Rue du Temple, and a moment afterwards paused before the crescent-shaped entrance of the front of the printing-office. The principal door was shut, two sentinels guarded the side door. Through this little door, which was ajar, he glanced into the courtyard of the printing-office, and saw it filled with soldiers. The soldiers were silent, no sound could be heard, but the glistening of their bayonets could be seen. The passer-by surprised, drew nearer. One of the sentinels thrust him rudely back, crying out, "Be off."

Like the *sergents de ville* at the Prefecture of Police, the workmen had been retained at the National Printing Office under plea of night-work. At the same time that M. Hippolyte Prévost returned to the Legislative Palace, the manager of the National Printing Office re-entered his office, also returning from the Opéra Comique, where he had been to see the new piece, which was by his brother, M. de St. Georges. Immediately on his return the manager, to whom had come an order from the Elysée during the day, took up a pair of pocket pistols, and went down into the vestibule, which communicates by means of a few steps with the courtyard. Shortly afterwards the door leading to the street opened, a *fiacre* entered, a man who carried a large portfolio alighted. The manager went up to the man, and said to him, "Is that you, Monsieur de Béville?"

"Yes," answered the man.

The *fiacre* was put up, the horses placed in a stable, and the coachman shut up in a parlor, where they gave him drink, and placed a purse in his hand. Bottles of wine and louis d'or form the groundwork of this hind of politics. The coachman drank and then went to sleep. The door of the parlor was bolted.

The large door of the courtyard of the printing-office was hardly shut than it reopened, gave passage to armed men, who entered in silence, and then reclosed. The arrivals were a company of the Gendarmerie Mobile, the fourth of the first battalion, commanded by a captain named La Roche d'Oisy. As may be remarked by the result, for all delicate expeditions the men of the *coup d'état* took care to employ the Gendarmerie Mobile and the Republican Guard, that it is to say the two corps almost entirely composed of former Municipal Guards, bearing at heart a revengeful remembrance of the events of February.

Captain La Roche d'Oisy brought a letter from the Minister of War, which placed himself and his soldiers at the disposition of the manager of the National Printing Office. The muskets were loaded without a word being spoken. Sentinels were placed in the workrooms, in the corridors, at the doors, at the windows, in fact, everywhere, two being stationed at the door leading into the street. The captain asked what instructions he should give to the sentries. "Nothing more simple," said the man who had come in the *fiacre*. "Whoever attempts to leave or to open a window, shoot him."

This man, who, in fact, was De Béville, orderly officer to M. Bonaparte, withdrew with the manager into the large cabinet on the first story, a solitary room which looked out on the garden. There he communicated to the manager what he had brought with him, the decree of the dissolution of the Assembly, the appeal to the Army, the appeal to the People, the decree convoking the electors, and in addition, the proclamation of the Prefect Maupas and his letter to the Commissaries of Police. The four first documents were entirely in the handwriting of the President, and here and there some erasures might be noticed.

The compositors were in waiting. Each man was placed between two gendarmes, and was forbidden to utter a single word, and then the documents which had to be printed were distributed throughout the room, being cut up in very small pieces, so that an entire sentence could not be read by one workman. The manager announced that he would give them an hour to compose the whole. The different fragments were finally brought to Colonel Béville, who put them together and corrected the proof sheets. The machining was conducted with the same precautions, each press being between two soldiers. Notwithstanding all possible diligence the work lasted two hours. The gendarmes watched over the workmen. Béville watched over St. Georges.

When the work was finished a suspicious incident occurred, which greatly resembled a treason within a treason. To a traitor a greater traitor. This species of crime is subject to such accidents. Béville and St. Georges, the two trusty confidants in whose hands lay the secret of the *coup d'état*, that is to say the head of the President;—that secret, which ought at no price to be allowed to transpire before the appointed hour, under risk of causing everything to miscarry, took it into their heads to confide it at once to two hundred men, in order "to test the effect," as the ex-Colonel Béville said later on, rather naïvely. They read the mysterious document which had just been printed to the Gendarmes Mobiles, who were drawn up in the courtyard. These ex-municipal guards applauded. If they had hooted, it might be asked what the two experimentalists in the *coup d'état* would have done. Perhaps M. Bonaparte would have waked up from his dream at Vincennes.

The coachman was then liberated, the *fiacre* was horsed, and at four o'clock in the morning the orderly officer and the manager of the National Printing Office, henceforward two criminals, arrived at the Prefecture of Police with the parcels of the decrees. Then began for them the brand of shame. Prefect Maupas took them by the hand.

Bands of bill-stickers, bribed for the occasion, started in every direction, carrying with them the decrees and proclamations.

This was precisely the hour at which the Palace of the National Assembly was invested. In the Rue de l'Université there is a door of the Palace which is the old entrance to the Palais Bourbon, and which opened into the avenue which leads to the house of the President of the Assembly. This door, termed the Presidency door, was according to custom guarded by a sentry. For sometime past the Adjutant-Major, who had been twice sent for during the night by Colonel Espinasse, had remained motionless and silent, close by the sentinel. Five minutes after, having left the huts of the Invalides, the 42d Regiment of the line, followed at some distance by the 6th Regiment, which had marched by the Rue de Bourgogne, emerged from the Rue de l'Université. "The regiment," says an eye-witness, "marched as one steps in a sickroom." It arrived with a stealthy step before the Presidency door. This ambuscade came to surprise the law.

The sentry, seeing these soldiers arrive, halted, but at the moment when he was going to challenge them with a *qui-vive*, the Adjutant-Major seized his arm, and, in his capacity as the officer empowered to countermand all instructions, ordered him to give free passage to the 42d, and at the same time commanded the amazed porter to open the door. The door turned upon its hinges, the soldiers spread themselves through the avenue. Persigny entered and said, "It is done."

The National Assembly was invaded.

At the noise of the footsteps the Commandant Mennier ran up. "Commandant," Colonel Espinasse cried out to him, "I come to relieve your battalion." The Commandant turned pale for a moment, and his eyes remained fixed on the ground. Then suddenly he put his hands to his shoulders, and tore off his epaulets, he drew his sword, broke it across his knee, threw the two fragments on the pavement, and, trembling with rage, exclaimed with a solemn voice, "Colonel, you disgrace the number of your regiment."

"All right, all right," said Espinasse.

The Presidency door was left open, but all the other entrances remained closed. All the guards were relieved, all the sentinels changed, and the battalion of the night guard was sent back to the camp of the Invalides, the soldiers piled their arms in the avenue, and in the Cour d'Honneur. The 42d, in profound silence, occupied the doors outside and inside, the courtyard, the reception-rooms, the galleries, the corridors, the passages, while everyone slept in the Palace.

Shortly afterwards arrived two of those little chariots which are called "forty sons," and two *fiacres*, escorted by two detachments of the Republican Guard and of the Chasseurs de Vincennes, and by several squads of police. The Commissaries Bertoglio and Primorin alighted from the two chariots.

As these carriages drove up a personage, bald, but still young, was seen to appear at the grated door of the Place de Bourgogne. This personage had all the air of a man about town, who had just come from the opera, and, in fact, he had come from thence, after having passed through a den. He came from the Elysée. It was De Morny. For an instant he watched the soldiers piling their arms, and then went on to the Presidency door. There he exchanged a few words with M. de Persigny. A quarter of an hour afterwards, accompanied by 250 Chasseurs de Vincennes, he took possession of the ministry of the Interior, startled M. de Thorigny in his bed, and handed him brusquely a letter of thanks from Monsieur Bonaparte. Some days previously honest M. De Thorigny, whose ingenuous remarks we have already cited, said to a group of men near whom M. de Morny was passing, "How these men of the Mountain calumniate the President! The man who would break his oath, who would achieve a *coup d'état* must necessarily be a worthless wretch." Awakened rudely in the middle of the night, and relieved of his post as Minister like the sentinels of the Assembly, the worthy man, astounded, and rubbing his eyes, muttered, "Eh! then the President *is* a ——."

"Yes," said Morny, with a burst of laughter.

He who writes these lines knew Morny. Morny and Walewsky held in the quasi-reigning family the positions, one of Royal bastard, the other of Imperial bastard. Who was Morny? We will say, "A noted wit, an intriguer, but in no way austere, a friend of Romieu, and a supporter of Guizot possessing the manners of the world, and the habits of the roulette table, self-satisfied, clever, combining a certain liberality of ideas with a readiness to accept useful crimes, finding means to wear a gracious smile with bad teeth, leading a life of pleasure, dissipated but reserved, ugly, good-tempered, fierce, well-dressed, intrepid, willingly leaving a brother prisoner under bolts and bars, and ready to risk his head for a brother Emperor, having the same mother as Louis Bonaparte, and like Louis Bonaparte, having some father or other, being able to call himself Beauharnais, being able to call himself Flahaut, and yet calling himself Morny, pursuing literature as far as light comedy, and politics, as far as tragedy, a deadly free liver, possessing all the frivolity consistent with assassination, capable of being sketched by Marivaux and treated of by Tacitus, without conscience, irreproachably elegant, infamous, and amiable, at need a perfect duke. Such was this malefactor."

It was not yet six o'clock in the morning. Troops began to mass themselves on the Place de la Concorde, where Leroy-Saint-Arnaud on horseback held a review.

The Commissaries of Police, Bertoglio and Primorin ranged two companies in order under the vault of the great staircase of the Questure, but did not ascend that way. They were accompanied by agents of police, who knew the most secret recesses of the Palais Bourbon, and who conducted them through various passages.

General Leflô was lodged in the Pavilion inhabited in the time of the Duc de Bourbon by Monsieur Feuchères. That night General Leflô had staying with him his sister and her husband, who were visiting Paris, and who slept in a room, the door of which led into one of the corridors of the Palace. Commissary Bertoglio knocked at the door, opened it, and together with his agents abruptly burst into the room, where a woman was in bed. The general's brother-in-out sprang out of bed, and cried out to the Questor, who slept in an adjoining room, "Adolphe, the doors are being forced, the Palace is full of soldiers. Get up!"

The General opened his eyes, he saw Commissary Bertoglio standing beside his bed.

He sprang up.

"General," said the Commissary, "I have come to fulfil a duty."

"I understand," said General Leflô, "you are a traitor."

The Commissary stammering out the words, "Plot against the safety of the State," displayed a warrant. The General, without pronouncing a word, struck this infamous paper with the back of his hand.

Then dressing himself, he put on his full uniform of Constantine and of Médéah, thinking in his imaginative, soldier-like loyalty that there were still generals of Africa for the soldiers whom he would find on his way. All the generals now remaining were brigands. His wife embraced him; his son, a child of seven years, in his nightshirt, and in tears, said to the Commissary of Police, "Mercy, Monsieur Bonaparte."

The General, while clasping his wife in his arms, whispered in her ear, "There is artillery in the courtyard, try and fire a cannon."

The Commissary and his men led him away. He regarded these policemen with contempt, and did not speak to them, but when he recognized Colonel Espinasse, his military and Breton heart swelled with indignation.

"Colonel Espinasse," said he, "you are a villain, and I hope to live long enough to tear the buttons from your uniform."

Colonel Espinasse hung his head, and stammered, "I do not know you."

A major waved his sword, and cried, "We have had enough of lawyer generals." Some soldiers crossed their bayonets before the unarmed prisoner, three *sergents de ville* pushed him into a *fiacre*, and a sub-lieutenant approaching the carriage, and looking in the face of the man who, if he were a citizen, was his Representative, and if he were a soldier was his general, flung this abominable word at him, "Canaille!"

Meanwhile Commissary Primorin had gone by a more roundabout way in order the more surely to surprise the other Questor, M. Baze.

Out of M. Baze's apartment a door led to the lobby communicating with the chamber of the Assembly. Sieur Primorin knocked at the door. "Who is there?" asked a servant, who was dressing. "The Commissary of Police," replied Primorin. The servant, thinking that he was the Commissary of Police of the Assembly, opened the door.

At this moment M. Baze, who had heard the noise, and had just awakened, put on a dressing-gown, and cried, "Do not open the door."

He had scarcely spoken these words when a man in plain clothes and three *sergents de ville* in uniform rushed into his chamber. The man, opening his coat, displayed his scarf of office, asking M. Baze, "Do you recognize this?"

"You are a worthless wretch," answered the Questor.

The police agents laid their hands on M. Baze. "You will not take me away," he said. "You, a Commissary of Police, you, who are a magistrate, and know what you are doing, you outrage the National Assembly, you violate the law, you are a criminal!" A hand-to-hand struggle ensued—four against one. Madame Baze and her two little girls giving vent to screams, the servant being thrust back with blows by the *sergents de ville*. "You are ruffians," cried out Monsieur Baze. They carried him away by main force in their arms, still struggling, naked, his dressing-gown being torn to shreds, his body being covered with blows, his wrist torn and bleeding.

The stairs, the landing, the courtyard, were full of soldiers with fixed bayonets and grounded arms. The Questor spoke to them. "Your Representatives are being arrested, you have not received your arms to break the laws!" A sergeant was wearing a brand-new cross. "Have you been given the cross for this?" The sergeant answered, "We only know one master." "I note your number," continued M. Baze. "You are a dishonored regiment." The soldiers listened with a stolid air, and seemed still asleep. Commissary Primorin said to them, "Do not answer, this has nothing to do with you." They led the Questor across the courtyard to the guard-house at the Porte Noire.

This was the name which was given to a little door contrived under the vault opposite the treasury of the Assembly, and which opened upon the Rue de Bourgogne, facing the Rue de Lille.

Several sentries were placed at the door of the guard-house, and at the top of the flight of steps which led thither, M. Baze being left there in charge of three *sergents de ville*. Several soldiers, without their weapons, and in their shirt-sleeves, came in and out. The Questor appealed to them in the name of military honor. "Do not answer," said the *sergent de ville* to the soldiers.

M. Baze's two little girls had followed him with terrified eyes, and when they lost sight of him the youngest burst into tears. "Sister," said the elder, who was seven years old, "let us say our prayers," and the two children, clasping their hands, knelt down.

Commissary Primorin, with his swarm of agents, burst into the Questor's study, and laid hands on everything. The first papers which he perceived on the middle of the table, and which he seized, were the famous decrees which had been prepared in the event of the Assembly having voted the proposal of the Questors. All the drawers were opened and searched. This overhauling of M. Baze's papers, which the

Commissary of Police termed a domiciliary visit, lasted more than an hour.

M. Baze's clothes had been taken to him, and he had dressed. When the "domiciliary visit" was over, he was taken out of the guardhouse. There was a *fiacre* in the courtyard, into which he entered, together with the three *sergents de ville*. The vehicle, in order to reach the Presidency door, passed by the Cour d'Honneur and then by the Courde Canonis. Day was breaking. M. Baze looked into the courtyard to see if the cannon were still there. He saw the ammunition wagons ranged in order with their shafts raised, but the places of the six cannon and the two mortars were vacant.

In the avenue of the Presidency the *fiacre* stopped for a moment. Two lines of soldiers, standing at ease, lined the footpaths of the avenue. At the foot of a tree were grouped three men: Colonel Espinasse, whom M. Baze knew and recognized, a species of Lieutenant-Colonel, who wore a black and orange ribbon round his neck, and a Major of Lancers, all three sword in hand, consulting together. The windows of the *fiacre* were closed; M. Baze wished to lower them to appeal to these men; the *sergents de ville* seized his arms. The Commissary Primorin then came up, and was about to re-enter the little chariot for two persons which had brought him.

"Monsieur Baze," said he, with that villainous kind of courtesy which the agents of the *coup d'état* willingly blended with their crime, "you must be uncomfortable with those three men in the *fiacre*. You are cramped; come in with me."

"Let me alone," said the prisoner. "With these three men I am cramped; with you I should be contaminated."

An escort of infantry was ranged on both sides of the *fiacre*. Colonel Espinasse called to the coachman, "Drive slowly by the Quai d'Orsay until you meet a cavalry escort. When the cavalry shall have assumed the charge, the infantry can come back." They set out.

As the *fiacre* turned into the Quai d'Orsay a picket of the 7th Lancers arrived at full speed. It was the escort: the troopers surrounded the *fiacre*, and the whole galloped off.

No incident occurred during the journey. Here and there, at the noise of the horses' hoofs, windows were opened and heads put forth; and the prisoner, who had at length succeeded in lowering a window heard startled voices saying, "What is the matter?"

The *fiacre* stopped. "Where are we?" asked M. Baze.

"At Mazas," said a *sergent de ville*.

The Questor was taken to the office of the prison. Just as he entered he saw Baune and Nadaud being brought out. There was a table in the centre, at which Commissary Primorin, who had followed the *fiacre* in his chariot, had just seated himself. While the Commissary was writing, M. Baze noticed on the table a paper which was evidently a jail register, on which were these names, written in the following order: Lamoricière, Charras, Cavaignac, Changarnier, Leflô, Thiers, Bedeau, Roger (du Nord), Chambolle. This was probably the order in which the Representatives had arrived at the prison.

When Sieur Primorin had finished writing, M. Baze said, "Now, you will be good enough to receive my protest, and add it to your official report." "It is not an official report," objected the Commissary, "it is simply an order for committal." "I intend to write my protest at once," replied M. Baze. "You will have plenty of time in your cell," remarked a man who stood by the table. M. Baze turned round. "Who are you?" "I am the governor of the prison," said the man. "In that case," replied M. Baze, "I pity you, for you are aware of the crime you are committing." The man turned pale, and stammered a few unintelligible words.

The Commissary rose from his seat; M. Baze briskly took possession of his chair, seated himself at the table, and said to Sieur Primorin, "You are a public officer; I request you to add my protest to your official report." "Very well," said the Commissary, "let it be so." Baze wrote the protest as follows:—

> "I, the undersigned, Jean-Didier Baze, Representative of the People, and Questor of the National Assembly, carried off by violence from my residence in the Palace of the National Assembly, and conducted to this prison by an armed force which it was impossible for me to resist, protest in the name of the National Assembly and in my own name against the outrage on national representation committed upon my colleagues and upon myself.
>
> "Given at Mazas on the 2d December 1851, at eight o'clock in the morning.
>
> BAZE

While this was taking place at Mazas, the soldiers were laughing and drinking in the courtyard of the Assembly. They made their coffee in the saucepans. They had lighted enormous fires in the courtyard; the flames, fanned by the wind, at times reached the walls of the Chamber. A superior official of the Questure, an officer of the National Guard, Ramond de la Croisette, ventured to say to them, "You will set the Palace on fire"; whereupon a soldier struck him a blow with his fist.

Four of the pieces taken from the Cour de Canons were ranged in battery order against the Assembly; two on the Place de Bourgogne were pointed towards the grating, and two on the Pont de la Concorde were pointed towards the grand staircase.

As side-note to this instructive tale let us mention a curious fact. The 42d Regiment of the line was the same which had arrested Louis Bonaparte at Boulogne. In 1840 this regiment lent its aid to the law against the conspirator. In 1851 it lent its aid to the conspirator against the law: such is the beauty of passive obedience.

IV

OTHER DOINGS OF THE NIGHT

During the same night in all parts of Paris acts of brigandage took place. Unknown men leading armed troops, and themselves armed with hatchets, mallets, pincers, crow-bars, life-preservers, swords hidden under their coats, pistols, of which the butts could be distinguished under the folds of their cloaks, arrived in silence before a house, occupied the street, encircled the approaches, picked the lock of the door, tied up the porter, invaded the stairs, and burst through the doors upon a sleeping man, and when that man, awakening with a start, asked of these bandits, "Who are you?" their leader answered, "A Commissary of Police." So it happened to Lamoricière who was seized by Blanchet, who threatened him with the gag; to Greppo, who was brutally treated and thrown down by Gronfier, assisted by six men carrying a dark lantern and a pole-axe; to Cavaignac, who was secured by Colin, a smooth-tongued villain, who affected to be shocked on hearing him curse and swear; to M. Thiers, who was arrested by Hubaut (the elder); who professed that he had seen him "tremble and weep," thus adding falsehood to crime; to Valentin, who was assailed in his bed by Dourlens, taken by the feet and shoulders, and thrust into a padlocked police van; to Miot, destined to the tortures of African casemates; to Roger (du Nord), who with courageous and witty irony offered sherry to the bandits. Charras and Changarnier were taken unawares.

They lived in the Rue St. Honoré, nearly opposite to each other, Changarnier at No. 3, Charras at No. 14. Ever since the 9th of September Changarnier had dismissed the fifteen men armed to the teeth by whom he had hitherto been guarded during the night, and on the 1st December, as we have said, Charras had unloaded his pistols. These empty pistols were lying on the table when they came to arrest him. The Commissary of Police threw himself upon them. "Idiot," said Charras to him, "if they had been loaded, you would have been a dead man." These pistols, we may note, had been given to Charras upon the taking of Mascara by General Renaud, who at the moment of Charras' arrest was on horseback in the street helping to carry out the *coup d'état*. If these pistols had remained loaded, and if General Renaud had had the task of arresting Charras, it would have been curious if Renaud's pistols had killed Renaud. Charras assuredly would not have hesitated. We have already mentioned the names of these police rascals. It is useless to repeat them. It was Courtille who arrested Charras, Lerat who arrested Changarnier, Desgranges who arrested Nadaud. The men thus seized in their own houses were Representatives of the people; they were inviolable, so that to the crime of the violation of their persons was added this high treason, the violation of the Constitution.

There was no lack of impudence in the perpetration of these outrages. The police agents made merry. Some of these droll fellows jested. At Mazas the under-jailors jeered at Thiers, Nadaud reprimanded them severely. The Sieur Hubaut (the younger) awoke General Bedeau. "General, you are a prisoner."—"My person is inviolable."—"Unless you are caught red-handed, in the very act."—"Well," said Bedeau, "I am caught in the act, the heinous act of being asleep." They took him by the collar and dragged him to a *fiacre*.

On meeting together at Mazas, Nadaud grasped the hand of Greppo, and Lagrange grasped the hand of Lamoricière. This made the police gentry laugh. A colonel, named Thirion, wearing a commander's cross round his neck, helped to put the Generals and the Representatives into jail. "Look me in the face," said Charras to him. Thirion moved away.

Thus, without counting other arrests which took place later on, there were imprisoned during the night of the 2d of December, sixteen Representatives and seventy-eight citizens. The two agents of the crime furnished a report of it to Louis Bonaparte. Morny wrote "Boxed up"; Maupas wrote "Quadded." The one in drawing-room slang, the other in the slang of the galleys. Subtle gradations of language.

V

The Darkness of the Crime

Versigny had just left me.

While I dressed hastily there came in a man in whom I had every confidence. He was a poor cabinet-maker out of work, named Girard, to whom I had given shelter in a room of my house, a carver of wood, and not illiterate. He came in from the street; he was trembling.

"Well," I asked, "what do the people say?"

Girard answered me,—

"People are dazed. The blow has been struck in such a manner that it is not realized. Workmen read the placards, say nothing, and go to their work. Only one in a hundred speaks. It is to say, 'Good!' This is how it appears to them. The law of the 31st May is abrogated—'Well done!' Universal suffrage is re-established—'Also well done!' The reactionary majority has been driven away—'Admirable!' Thiers is arrested—'Capital!' Changarnier is seized—'Bravo!' Round each placard there are *claqueurs*. Ratapoil explains his *coup d'état* to Jacques Bonhomme, Jacques Bonhomme takes it all in. Briefly, it is my impression that the people give their consent."

"Let it be so," said I.

"But," asked Girard of me, "what will you do, Monsieur Victor Hugo?"

I took my scarf of office from a cupboard, and showed it to him.

He understood.

We shook hands.

As he went out Carini entered.

Colonel Carini is an intrepid man. He had commanded the cavalry under Mieroslawsky in the Sicilian insurrection. He has, in a few moving and enthusiastic pages, told the story of that noble revolt. Carini is one of those Italians who love France as we Frenchmen love Italy. Every warm-hearted man in this century has two fatherlands—the Rome of yesterday and the Paris of today.

"Thank God," said Carini to me, "you are still free," and he added, "The blow has been struck in a formidable manner. The Assembly is invested. I have come from thence. The Place de la Révolution, the

Quays, the Tuileries, the boulevards, are crowded with troops. The soldiers have their knapsacks. The batteries are harnessed. If fighting takes place it will be desperate work."

I answered him, "There will be fighting."

And I added, laughing, "You have proved that the colonels write like poets; now it is the turn of the poets to fight like colonels."

I entered my wife's room; she knew nothing, and was quietly reading her paper in bed.

I had taken about me five hundred francs in gold. I put on my wife's bed a box containing nine hundred francs, all the money which remained to me, and I told her what had happened.

She turned pale, and said to me, "What are you going to do?"

"My duty."

She embraced me, and only said two words:—

"Do it."

My breakfast was ready. I ate a cutlet in two mouthfuls. As I finished, my daughter came in. She was startled by the manner in which I kissed her, and asked me, "What is the matter?"

"Your mother will explain to you."

And I left them.

The Rue de la Tour d'Auvergne was as quiet and deserted as usual. Four workmen were, however, chatting near my door; they wished me "Good morning."

I cried out to them, "You know what is going on?"

"Yes," said they.

"Well. It is treason! Louis Bonaparte is strangling the Republic. The people are attacked. The people must defend themselves."

"They will defend themselves."

"You promise me that?"

"Yes," they answered.

One of them added, "We swear it."

They kept their word. Barricades were constructed in my street (Rue de la Tour d'Auvergne), in the Rue des Martyrs, in the Cité Rodier, in the Rue Coquenard, and at Notre-Dame de Lorette.

VI

"Placards"

On leaving these brave men I could read at the corner of the Rue de la Tour d'Auvergne and the Rue des Martyrs, the three infamous placards which had been posted on the walls of Paris during the night.

Here they are.

Proclamation of the President of the Republic.
Appeal to the People.

"Frenchmen! The present situation can last no longer. Everyday which passes enhances the dangers of the country. The Assembly, which ought to be the firmest support of order, has become a focus of conspiracies. The patriotism of three hundred of its members has been unable to check its fatal tendencies. Instead of making laws in the public interest it forges arms for civil war; it attacks the power which I hold directly from the People, it encourages all bad passions, it compromises the tranquillity of France; I have dissolved it, and I constitute the whole People a judge between it and me.

"The Constitution, as you know, was constructed with the object of weakening beforehand the power which you were about to confide to me. Six millions of votes formed an emphatic protest against it, and yet I have faithfully respected it. Provocations, calumnies, outrages, have found me unmoved. Now, however, that the fundamental compact is no longer respected by those very men who incessantly invoke it, and that the men who have ruined two monarchies wish to tie my hands in order to overthrow the Republic, my duty is to frustrate their treacherous schemes, to maintain the Republic, and to save the Country by appealing to the solemn judgment of the only Sovereign whom I recognize in France—the People.

"I therefore make a loyal appeal to the whole nation, and I say to you: If you wish to continue this condition of uneasiness which degrades us and compromises our future, choose another in my place, for I will no longer retain a power which is impotent to do good, which renders me responsible for actions which I cannot prevent, and which binds me to the helm when I see the vessel driving towards the abyss.

"If on the other hand you still place confidence in me, give me the means of accomplishing the great mission which I hold from you.

"This mission consists in closing the era of revolutions, by satisfying the legitimate needs of the People, and by protecting them from subversive passions. It consists, above all, in creating institutions which survive men, and which shall in fact form the foundations on which something durable may be established.

"Persuaded that the instability of power, that the preponderance of a single Assembly, are the permanent causes of trouble and discord, I submit to your suffrage the following fundamental bases of a Constitution which will be developed by the Assemblies later on:—

"1. A responsible Chief appointed for ten years.
"2. Ministers dependent upon the Executive Power alone.
"3. A Council of State composed of the most distinguished men, who shall prepare laws and shall support them in debate before the Legislative Body.
"4. A Legislative Body which shall discuss and vote the laws, and which shall be elected by universal suffrage, without *scrutin de liste*, which falsifies the elections.
"5. A Second Assembly composed of the most illustrious men of the country, a power of equipoise the guardian of the fundamental compact, and of the public liberties.

"This system, created by the first Consul at the beginning of the century, has already given repose and prosperity to France; it would still insure them to her.

"Such is my firm conviction. If you share it, declare it by your votes. If, on the contrary, you prefer a government without strength, Monarchical or Republican, borrowed I know not from what past, or from what chimerical future, answer in the negative.

"Thus for the first time since 1804, you will vote with a full knowledge of the circumstances, knowing exactly for whom and for what.

"If I do not obtain the majority of your suffrages I shall call together a New Assembly and shall place in its hands the commission which I have received from you.

"But if you believe that the cause of which my name is the symbol,—that is to say, France regenerated by the Revolution of '89, and organized by the Emperor, is to be still your own, proclaim it by sanctioning the powers which I ask from you.

"Then France and Europe will be preserved from anarchy, obstacles will be removed, rivalries will have disappeared, for all will respect, in the decision of the People, the decree of Providence.

"Given at the Palace of the Elysée, 2d December, 1851.

Louis Napoleon Bonaparte

Proclamation of the President of the Republic to the Army.

"Soldiers! Be proud of your mission, you will save the country, for I count upon you not to violate the laws, but to enforce respect for the first law of the country, the national Sovereignty, of which I am the Legitimate Representative.

"For a long time past, like myself, you have suffered from obstacles which have opposed themselves both to the good that I wished to do and to the demonstrations of your sympathies in my favor. These obstacles have been broken down.

"The Assembly has tried to attack the authority which hold from the whole Nation. It has ceased to exist.

"I make a loyal appeal to the People and to the Army, and I say to them: Either give me the means of insuring your prosperity, or choose another in my place.

"In 1830, as in 1848, you were treated as vanquished men. After having branded your heroic disinterestedness, they disdained to consult your sympathies and your wishes, and yet you are the flower of the Nation. Today, at this solemn moment, I am resolved that the voice of the Army shall be heard.

"Vote, therefore, freely as citizens; but, as soldiers do not forget that passive obedience to the orders of the Chief of the

State is the rigorous duty of the Army, from the general to the private soldier.

"It is for me, responsible for my actions both to the People and to posterity, to take those measures which may seem to me indispensable for the public welfare.

"As for you, remain immovable within the rules of discipline and of honor. By your imposing attitude help the country to manifest its will with calmness and reflection.

"Be ready to repress every attack upon the free exercise of the sovereignty of the People.

"Soldiers, I do not speak to you of the memories which my name recalls. They are engraven in your hearts. We are united by indissoluble ties. Your history is mine. There is between us, in the past, a community of glory and of misfortune.

"There will be in the future community of sentiment and of resolutions for the repose and the greatness of France.

"Given at the Palace of the Elysée, December 2d, 1851.

(Signed) L.N. Bonaparte

In the Name of the French People.

"The President of the Republic decrees:—

"Article I. The National Assembly is dissolved.

"Article II. Universal suffrage is re-established. The law of May 31 is abrogated.

"Article III. The French People are convoked in their electoral districts from the 14th December to the 21st December following.

"Article IV. The State of Siege is decreed in the district of the first Military Division.

"Article V. The Council of State is dissolved.

"Article VI. The Minister of the Interior is charged with the execution of this decree.

"Given at the Palace of the Elysée, 2d December, 1851.

Louis Napoleon Bonaparte
De Morny, Minister of the Interior

VII

No. 70, Rue Blanche

The Cité Gaillard is somewhat difficult to find. It is a deserted alley in that new quarter which separates the Rue des Martyrs from the Rue Blanche. I found it, however. As I reached No. 4, Yvan came out of the gateway and said, "I am here to warn you. The police have an eye upon this house, Michel is waiting for you at No. 70, Rue Blanche, a few steps from here."

I knew No. 70, Rue Blanche. Manin, the celebrated President of the Venetian Republic, lived there. It was not in his rooms, however, that the meeting was to take place.

The porter of No. 70 told me to go up to the first floor. The door was opened, and a handsome, gray-haired woman of some forty summers, the Baroness Coppens, whom I recognized as having seen in society and at my own house, ushered me into a drawing-room.

Michel de Bourges and Alexander Rey were there, the latter an ex-Constituent, an eloquent writer, a brave man. At that time Alexander Rey edited the *National*.

We shook hands.

Michel said to me,—

"Hugo, what will you do?"

I answered him,—

"Everything."

"That also is my opinion," said he.

Numerous representatives arrived, and amongst others Pierre Lefranc, Labrousse, Théodore Bac, Noël Parfait, Arnauld (de l'Ariége), Demosthenes Ollivier, an ex-Constituent, and Charamaule. There was deep and unutterable indignation, but no useless words were spoken.

All were imbued with that manly anger whence issue great resolutions.

They talked. They set forth the situation. Each brought forward the news which he had learnt.

Théodore Bac came from Léon Faucher, who lived in the Rue Blanche. It was he who had awakened Léon Faucher, and had announced the news to him. The first words of Léon Faucher were, "It is an infamous deed."

From the first moment Charamaule displayed a courage which, during the four days of the struggle, never flagged for a single instant. Charamaule is a very tall man, possessed of vigorous features and convincing eloquence; he voted with the Left, but sat with the Right. In the Assembly he was the neighbor of Montalembert and of Riancey. He sometimes had warm disputes with them, which we watched from afar off, and which amused us.

Charamaule had come to the meeting at No. 70 dressed in a sort of blue cloth military cloak, and armed, as we found out later on.

The situation was grave; sixteen Representatives arrested, all the generals of the Assembly, and he who was more than a general, Charras. All the journals suppressed, all the printing offices occupied by soldiers. On the side of Bonaparte an army of 80,000 men which could be doubled in a few hours; on our side nothing. The people deceived, and moreover disarmed. The telegraph at their command. All the walls covered with their placards, and at our disposal not a single printing case, not one sheet of paper. No means of raising the protest, no means of beginning the combat. The *coup d'état* was clad with mail, the Republic was naked; the *coup d'état* had a speaking trumpet, the Republic wore a gag.

What was to be done?

The raid against the Republic, against the Assembly, against Right, against Law, against Progress, against Civilization, was commanded by African generals. These heroes had just proved that they were cowards. They had taken their precautions well. Fear alone can engender so much skill. They had arrested all the men of war of the Assembly, and all the men of action of the Left, Baune, Charles Lagrange, Miot, Valentin, Nadaud, Cholat. Add to this that all the possible chiefs of the barricades were in prison. The organizers of the ambuscade had carefully left at liberty Jules Favre, Michel de Bourges, and myself, judging us to be less men of action than of the Tribune; wishing to leave the Left men capable of resistance, but incapable of victory, hoping to dishonor us if we did not fight, and to shoot us if we did fight.

Nevertheless, no one hesitated. The deliberation began. Other representatives arrived every minute, Edgar Quinet, Doutre, Pelletier, Cassal, Bruckner, Baudin, Chauffour. The room was full, some were seated, most were standing, in confusion, but without tumult.

I was the first to speak.

I said that the struggle ought to be begun at once. Blow for blow.

That it was my opinion that the hundred and fifty Representatives of the Left should put on their scarves of office, should march in procession through the streets and the boulevards as far as the Madeleine, and crying "Vive la République! Vive la Constitution!" should appear before the troops, and alone, calm and unarmed, should summon Might to obey Right. If the soldiers yielded, they should go to the Assembly and make an end of Louis Bonaparte. If the soldiers fired upon their legislators, they should disperse throughout Paris, cry "To Arms," and resort to barricades. Resistance should be begun constitutionally, and if that failed, should be continued revolutionarily. There was no time to be lost.

"High treason," said I, "should be seized red-handed, is a great mistake to suffer such an outrage to be accepted by the hours as they elapse. Each minute which passes is an accomplice, and endorses the crime. Beware of that calamity called an 'Accomplished fact.' To arms!"

Many warmly supported this advice, among others Edgar Quinet, Pelletier, and Doutre.

Michel de Bourges seriously objected. My instinct was to begin at once, his advice was to wait and see. According to him there was danger in hastening the catastrophe. The *coup d'état* was organized, and the People were not. They had been taken unawares. We must not indulge in illusion. The masses could not stir yet. Perfect calm reigned in the faubourgs; Surprise existed, yes; Anger, no. The people of Paris, although so intelligent, did not understand.

Michel added, "We are not in 1830. Charles X, in turning out the 221, exposed himself to this blow, the re-election of the 221. We are not in the same situation. The 221 were popular. The present Assembly is not: a Chamber which has been insultingly dissolved is always sure to conquer, if the People support it. Thus the People rose in 1830. Today they wait. They are dupes until they shall be victims." Michel de Bourges concluded, "The People must be given time to understand, to grow angry, to rise. As for us, Representative, we should be rash to precipitate the situation. If we were to march immediately straight upon the troops, we should only be shot to no purpose, and the glorious insurrection for Right would thus be beforehand deprived of its natural leaders—the Representatives of the People. We should decapitate the popular army. Temporary delay, on the contrary, would be beneficial. Too much zeal must be guarded against, self-restraint is necessary, to give way would be to lose the battle before having begun it. Thus, for example, we must not attend the meeting announced by the Right for noon, all those who went there would be arrested. We must remain free, we must remain in readiness, we must remain calm, and must act waiting the advent of the People. Four days of this agitation without fighting would weary the army." Michel, however, advised a beginning, but simply by placarding Article 68 of the Constitution. But where should a printer be found?

Michel de Bourges spoke with an experience of revolutionary procedure which was wanting in me. For many years past he had acquired a certain practical knowledge of the masses. His council was wise. It must be added that all the information which came to us seconded him, and appeared conclusive against me. Paris was dejected.

The army of the *coup d'état* invaded her peaceably. Even the placards were not torn down. Nearly all the Representatives present, even the most daring, agreed with Michel's counsel, to wait and see what would happen. "At night," said they, "the agitation will begin," and they concluded, like Michel de Bourges, that the people must be given time to understand. There would be a risk of being alone in too hasty a beginning. We should not carry the people with us in the first moment. Let us leave the indignation to increase little by little in their hearts. If it were begun prematurely our manifestation would miscarry. These were the sentiments of all. For myself, while listening to them, I felt shaken. Perhaps they were right. It would be a mistake to give the signal for the combat in vain. What good is the lightning which is not followed by the thunderbolt?

To raise a voice, to give vent to a cry, to find a printer, there was the first question. But was there still a free Press?

The brave old ex-chief of the 6th Legion, Colonel Forestier, came in. He took Michel de Bourges and myself aside.

"Listen," said he to us. "I come to you. I have been dismissed. I no longer command my legion, but appoint me in the name of the Left, Colonel of the 6th. Sign me an order and I will go at once and call them to arms. In an hour the regiment will be on foot."

"Colonel," answered I, "I will do more than sign an order, I will accompany you."

And I turned towards Charamaule, who had a carriage in waiting.

"Come with us," said I.

Forestier was sure of two majors of the 6th. We decided to drive to them at once, while Michel and the other Representatives should await us at Bonvalet's, in the Boulevard du Temple, near the Café Turc. There they could consult together.

We started.

We traversed Paris, where people were already beginning to swarm in a threatening manner. The boulevards were thronged with an uneasy crowd. People walked to and fro, passers-by accosted each other without any previous acquaintance, a noteworthy sign of public anxiety; and groups talked in loud voices at the corners of the streets. The shops were being shut.

"Come, this looks better," cried Charamaule.

He had been wandering about the town since the morning, and he had noticed with sadness the apathy of the masses.

We found the two majors at home upon whom Colonel Forestier counted. They were two rich linendrapers, who received us with some embarrassment. The shopmen had gathered together at the windows, and watched us pass by. It was mere curiosity.

In the meanwhile one of the two majors countermanded a journey which he was going to undertake on that day, and promised us his co-operation.

"But," added he, "do not deceive yourselves, one can foresee that we shall be cut to pieces. Few men will march out."

Colonel Forestier said to us, "Watrin, the present colonel of the 6th, does not care for fighting; perhaps he will resign me the command amicably. I will go and find him alone, so as to startle him the less, and will join you at Bonvalet's."

Near the Porte St. Martin we left our carriage, and Charamaule and myself proceeded along the boulevard on foot, in order to observe the groups more closely, and more easily to judge the aspect of the crowd.

The recent levelling of the road had converted the boulevard of the Porte St. Martin into a deep cutting, commanded by two embankments. On the summits of these embankments were the footways, furnished with railings. The carriages drove along the cutting, the foot passengers walked along the footways.

Just as we reached the boulevard, a long column of infantry filed into this ravine with drummers at their head. The thick waves of bayonets filled the square of St. Martin, and lost themselves in the depths of the Boulevard Bonne Nouvelle.

An enormous and compact crowd covered the two pavements of the Boulevard St. Martin. Large numbers of workmen, in their blouses, were there, leaning upon the railings.

At the moment when the head of the column entered the defile before the Theatre of the Porte St. Martin a tremendous shout of "Vive la République!" came forth from every mouth as though shouted by one man. The soldiers continued to advance in silence, but it might have been said that their pace slackened, and many of them regarded the crowd with an air of indecision. What did this cry of "Vive la République!" mean? Was it a token of applause? Was it a shout of defiance?

It seemed to me at that moment that the Republic raised its brow, and that the *coup d'état* hung its head.

Meanwhile Charamaule said to me, "You are recognized."

In fact, near the Château d'Eau the crowd surrounded me. Some young men cried out, "Vive Victor Hugo!" One of them asked me, "Citizen Victor Hugo, what ought we to do?"

I answered, "Tear down the seditious placards of the *coup d'état*, and cry 'Vive la Constitution!'"

"And suppose they fire on us?" said a young workman.

"You will hasten to arms."

"Bravo!" shouted the crowd.

I added, "Louis Bonaparte is a rebel, he has steeped himself today in every crime. We, Representatives of the People, declare him an outlaw, but there is no need for our declaration, since he is an outlaw by the mere fact of his treason. Citizens, you have two hands; take in one your Right, and in the other your gun and fall upon Bonaparte."

"Bravo! Bravo!" again shouted the people.

A tradesman who was shutting up his shop said to me, "Don't speak so loud, if they heard you talking like that, they would shoot you."

"Well, then," I replied, "you would parade my body, and my death would be a boon if the justice of God could result from it."

All shouted "Long live Victor Hugo!"

"Shout 'Long live the Constitution,'" said I.

A great cry of "Vive la Constitution! Vive la République"; came forth from every breast.

Enthusiasm, indignation, anger flashed in the faces of all. I thought then, and I still think, that this, perhaps, was the supreme moment. I was tempted to carry off all that crowd, and to begin the battle.

Charamaule restrained me. He whispered to me,—

"You will bring about a useless fusillade. Everyone is unarmed. The infantry is only two paces from us, and see, here comes the artillery."

I looked round; in truth several pieces of cannon emerged at a quick trot from the Rue de Bondy, behind the Château d'Eau.

The advice to abstain, given by Charamaule, made a deep impression on me. Coming from such a man, and one so dauntless, it was certainly not to be distrusted. Besides, I felt myself bound by the deliberation which had just taken place at the meeting in the Rue Blanche.

I shrank before the responsibility which I should have incurred. To have taken advantage of such a moment might have been victory, it might also have been a massacre. Was I right? Was I wrong?

The crowd thickened around us, and it became difficult to go forward. We were anxious, however, to reach the *rendezvous* at Bonvalet's.

Suddenly someone touched me on the arm. It was Léopold Duras, of the *National*.

"Go no further," he whispered, "the Restaurant Bonvalet is surrounded. Michel de Bourges has attempted to harangue the People, but the soldiers came up. He barely succeeded in making his escape. Numerous Representatives who came to the meeting have been arrested. Retrace your steps. We are returning to the old *rendezvous* in the Rue Blanche. I have been looking for you to tell you this."

A cab was passing; Charamaule hailed the driver. We jumped in, followed by the crowd, shouting, "Vive la République! Vive Victor Hugo!"

It appears that just at that moment a squadron of *sergents de ville* arrived on the Boulevard to arrest me. The coachman drove off at full speed. A quarter of an hour afterwards we reached the Rue Blanche.

VIII

"Violation of the Chamber"

At seven o'clock in the morning the Pont de la Concorde was still free. The large grated gate of the Palace of the Assembly was closed; through the bars might be seen the flight of steps, that flight of steps whence the Republic had been proclaimed on the 4th May, 1848, covered with soldiers; and their piled arms might be distinguished upon the platform behind those high columns, which, during the time of the Constituent Assembly, after the 15th of May and the 23d June, masked small mountain mortars, loaded and pointed.

A porter with a red collar, wearing the livery of the Assembly, stood by the little door of the grated gate. From time to time Representatives arrived. The porter said, "Gentlemen, are you Representatives?" and opened the door. Sometimes he asked their names.

M. Dupin's quarters could be entered without hindrance. In the great gallery, in the dining-room, in the *salon d'honneur* of the Presidency, liveried attendants silently opened the doors as usual.

Before daylight, immediately after the arrest of the Questors MM. Baze and Leflô, M. de Panat, the only Questor who remained free, having been spared or disdained as a Legitimist, awoke M. Dupin and begged him to summon immediately the Representatives from their own homes. M. Dupin returned this unprecedented answer, "I do not see any urgency."

Almost at the same time as M. Panat, the Representative Jerôme Bonaparte had hastened thither. He had summoned M. Dupin to place himself at the head of the Assembly. M. Dupin had answered, "I cannot, I am guarded." Jerôme Bonaparte burst out laughing. In fact, no one had deigned to place a sentinel at M. Dupin's door; they knew that it was guarded by his meanness.

It was only later on, towards noon, that they took pity on him. They felt that the contempt was too great, and allotted him two sentinels.

At half-past seven, fifteen or twenty Representatives, among whom were MM. Eugène Sue, Joret, de Rességuier, and de Talhouet, met together in M. Dupin's room. They also had vainly argued with M. Dupin. In the recess of a window a clever member of the Majority,

M. Desmousseaux de Givré, who was a little deaf and exceedingly exasperated, almost quarrelled with a Representative of the Right like himself whom he wrongly supposed to be favorable to the *coup d'état*.

M. Dupin, apart from the group of Representatives, alone dressed in black, his hands behind his back, his head sunk on his breast, walked up and down before the fire-place, where a large fire was burning. In his own room, and in his very presence, they were talking loudly about himself, yet he seemed not to hear.

Two members of the Left came in, Benoît (du Rhône), and Crestin. Crestin entered the room, went straight up to M. Dupin, and said to him, "President, you know what is going on? How is it that the Assembly has not yet been convened?"

M. Dupin halted, and answered, with a shrug which was habitual with him,—

"There is nothing to be done."

And he resumed his walk.

"It is enough," said M. de Rességuier.

"It is too much," said Eugène Sue.

All the Representatives left the room.

In the meantime the Pont de la Concorde became covered with troops. Among them General Vast-Vimeux, lean, old, and little; his lank white hair plastered over his temples, in full uniform, with his laced hat on his head. He was laden with two huge epaulets, and displayed his scarf, not that of a Representative, but of a general, which scarf, being too long, trailed on the ground. He crossed the bridge on foot, shouting to the soldiers inarticulate cries of enthusiasm for the Empire and the *coup d'état*. Such figures as these were seen in 1814. Only instead of wearing a large tri-colored, cockade, they wore a large white cockade. In the main the same phenomenon; old men crying, "Long live the Past!" Almost at the same moment M. de Larochejaquelein crossed the Place de la Concorde, surrounded by a hundred men in blouses, who followed him in silence, and with an air of curiosity. Numerous regiments of cavalry were drawn up in the grand avenue of the Champs Elysées.

At eight o'clock a formidable force invested the Legislative Palace. All the approaches were guarded, all the doors were shut. Some Representatives nevertheless succeeded in penetrating into the interior of the Palace, not, as has been wrongly stated, by the passage of the President's house on the side of the Esplanade of the Invalides, but by the little door of the Rue de Bourgogne, called the Black Door. This door, by what omission or what connivance I do not know, remained open till noon on the 2d December. The Rue de Bourgogne was nevertheless full of troops. Squads of soldiers scattered here and there in the Rue de l'Université allowed passers-by, who were few and far between, to use it as a thoroughfare.

The Representatives who entered by the door in Rue de Bourgogne, penetrated as far as the Salle des Conférences, where they met their colleagues coming out from M. Dupin.

A numerous group of men, representing every shade of opinion in the Assembly, was speedily assembled in this hall, amongst whom were MM. Eugène Sue, Richardet, Fayolle, Joret, Marc Dufraisse, Benoît (du Rhône), Canet, Gambon, d'Adelsward, Créqu, Répellin, Teillard-Latérisse, Rantion, General Leydet, Paulin Durrieu, Chanay, Brilliez, Collas (de la Gironde), Monet, Gaston, Favreau, and Albert de Rességuier.

Each new-comer accosted M. de Panat.

"Where are the vice-Presidents?"

"In prison."

"And the two other Questors?"

"Also in prison. And I beg you to believe, gentlemen," added M. de Panat, "that I have had nothing to do with the insult which has been offered me, in not arresting me."

Indignation was at its height; every political shade was blended in the same sentiment of contempt and anger, and M. de Rességuier was no less energetic than Eugène Sue. For the first time the Assembly seemed only to have one heart and one voice. Each at length said what he thought of the man of the Elysée, and it was then seen that for a long time past Louis Bonaparte had imperceptibly created a profound unanimity in the Assembly—the unanimity of contempt.

M. Collas (of the Gironde) gesticulated and told his story. He came from the Ministry of the Interior. He had seen M. de Morny, he had spoken to him; and he, M. Collas, was incensed beyond measure at M. Bonaparte's crime. Since then, that Crime has made him Councillor of State.

M. de Panat went hither and thither among the groups, announcing to the Representatives that he had convened the Assembly for one o'clock. But it was impossible to wait until that hour. Time pressed. At the Palais Bourbon, as in the Rue Blanche, it was the universal feeling that each hour which passed by helped to accomplish the *coup d'état*. Everyone felt as a reproach the weight of his silence or of his inaction;

the circle of iron was closing in, the tide of soldiers rose unceasingly, and silently invaded the Palace; at each instant a sentinel the more was found at a door, which a moment before had been free. Still, the group of Representatives assembled together in the Salle des Conférences was as yet respected. It was necessary to act, to speak, to deliberate, to struggle, and not to lose a minute.

Gambon said, "Let us try Dupin once more; he is our official man, we have need of him." They went to look for him. They could not find him. He was no longer there, he had disappeared, he was away, hidden, crouching, cowering, concealed, he had vanished, he was buried. Where? No one knew. Cowardice has unknown holes.

Suddenly a man entered the hall. A man who was a stranger to the Assembly, in uniform, wearing the epaulet of a superior officer and a sword by his side. He was a major of the 42d, who came to summon the Representatives to quit their own House. All, Royalists and Republicans alike, rushed upon him. Such was the expression of an indignant eye-witness. General Leydet addressed him in language such as leaves an impression on the cheek rather than on the ear.

"I do my duty, I fulfil my instructions," stammered the officer.

"You are an idiot, if you think you are doing your duty," cried Leydet to him, "and you are a scoundrel if you know that you are committing a crime. Your name? What do you call yourself? Give me your name."

The officer refused to give his name, and replied, "So, gentlemen, you will not withdraw?"

"No."

"I shall go and obtain force."

"Do so."

He left the room, and in actual fact went to obtain orders from the Ministry of the Interior.

The Representatives waited in that kind of indescribable agitation which might be called the Strangling of Right by Violence.

In a short time one of them who had gone out came back hastily, and warned them that two companies of the *Gendarmerie Mobile* were coming with their guns in their hands.

Marc Dufraisse cried out, "Let the outrage be thorough. Let the *coup d'état* find us on our seats. Let us go to the Salle des Séances," he added. "Since things have come to such a pass, let us afford the genuine and living spectacle of an 18th Brumaire."

They all repaired to the Hall of Assembly. The passage was free. The Salle Casimir-Périer was not yet occupied by the soldiers.

They numbered about sixty. Several were girded with their scarves of office. They entered the Hall meditatively.

There, M. de Rességuier, undoubtedly with a good purpose, and in order to form a more compact group, urged that they should all install themselves on the Right side.

"No," said Marc Dufraisse, "everyone to his bench." They scattered themselves about the Hall, each in his usual place.

M. Monet, who sat on one of the lower benches of the Left Centre, held in his hand a copy of the Constitution.

Several minutes elapsed. No one spoke. It was the silence of expectation which precedes decisive deeds and final crises, and during which everyone seems respectfully to listen to the last instructions of his conscience.

Suddenly the soldiers of the *Gendarmerie Mobile*, headed by a captain with his sword drawn, appeared on the threshold. The Hall of Assembly was violated. The Representatives rose from their seats simultaneously, shouting "Vive la République!"

The Representative Monet alone remained standing, and in a loud and indignant voice, which resounded through the empty hall like a trumpet, ordered the soldiers to halt.

The soldiers halted, looking at the Representatives with a bewildered air.

The soldiers as yet only blocked up the lobby of the Left, and had not passed beyond the Tribune.

Then the Representative Monet read the Articles 36, 37, and 68 of the Constitution.

Articles 36 and 37 established the inviolability of the Representatives. Article 68 deposed the President in the event of treason.

That moment was a solemn one. The soldiers listened in silence.

The Articles having been read, Representative d'Adelsward, who sat on the first lower bench of the Left, and who was nearest to the soldiers, turned towards them and said,—

"Soldiers, you see that the President of the Republic is a traitor, and would make traitors of you. You violate the sacred precinct of rational Representation. In the name of the Constitution, in the name of the Law, we order you to withdraw."

While Adelsward was speaking, the major commanding the *Gendarmerie Mobile* had entered.

"Gentlemen," said he, "I have orders to request you to retire, and, if you do not withdraw of your own accord, to expel you."

"Orders to expel us!" exclaimed Adelsward; and all the Representatives added, "Whose orders; Let us see the orders. Who signed the orders?"

The major drew forth a paper and unfolded it. Scarcely had he unfolded it than he attempted to replace it in his pocket, but General Leydet threw himself upon him and seized his arm. Several Representatives leant forward, and read the order for the expulsion of the Assembly, signed "Fortoul, Minister of the Marine."

Marc Dufraisse turned towards the *Gendarmes Mobiles*, and cried out to them,—

"Soldiers, your very presence here is an act of treason. Leave the Hall!"

The soldiers seemed undecided. Suddenly a second column emerged from the door on the right, and at a signal from the commander, the captain shouted,—

"Forward! Turn them all out!"

Then began an indescribable hand-to-hand fight between the gendarmes and the legislators. The soldiers, with their guns in their hands, invaded the benches of the Senate. Repellin, Chanay, Rantion, were forcibly torn from their seats. Two gendarmes rushed upon Marc Dufraisse, two upon Gambon. A long struggle took place on the first bench of the Right, the same place where MM. Odilon Barrot and Abbatucci were in the habit of sitting. Paulin Durrieu resisted violence by force, it needed three men to drag him from his bench. Monet was thrown down upon the benches of the Commissaries. They seized Adelsward by the throat, and thrust him outside the Hall. Richardet, a feeble man, was thrown down and brutally treated. Some were pricked with the points of the bayonets; nearly all had their clothes torn.

The commander shouted to the soldiers, "Rake them out."

It was thus that sixty Representatives of the People were taken by the collar by the *coup d'état*, and driven from their seats. The manner in which the deed was executed completed the treason. The physical performance was worthy of the moral performance.

The three last to come out were Fayolle, Teillard-Latérisse, and Paulin Durrieu.

They were allowed to pass by the great door of the Palace, and they found themselves in the Place Bourgogne.

The Place Bourgogne was occupied by the 42d Regiment of the Line, under the orders of Colonel Garderens.

Between the Palace and the statue of the Republic, which occupied the centre of the square, a piece of artillery was pointed at the Assembly opposite the great door.

By the side of the cannon some Chasseurs de Vincennes were loading their guns and biting their cartridges.

Colonel Garderens was on horseback near a group of soldiers, which attracted the attention of the Representatives Teillard-Latérisse, Fayolle, and Paulin Durrieu.

In the middle of this group three men, who had been arrested, were struggling crying, "Long live the Constitution! Vive la République!"

Fayolle, Paulin Durrieu, and Teillard-Latérisse approached, and recognized in the three prisoners three members of the majority, Representatives Toupet-des-Vignes Radoubt, Lafosse, and Arbey.

Representative Arbey was warmly protesting. As he raised his voice, Colonel Garderens cut him short with these words, which are worthy of preservation,—

"Hold your tongue! One word more, and I will have you thrashed with the butt-end of a musket."

The three Representatives of the Left indignantly called on the Colonel to release their colleagues.

"Colonel," said Fayolle, "You break the law threefold."

"I will break it sixfold," answered the Colonel, and he arrested Fayolle, Durrieu, and Teillard-Latérisse.

The soldiery were ordered to conduct them to the guard house of the Palace then being built for the Minister of Foreign Affairs.

On the way the six prisoners, marching between a double file of bayonets, met three of their colleagues Representatives Eugène Sue, Chanay, and Benoist (du Rhône).

Eugène Sue placed himself before the officer who commanded the detachment, and said to him,—

"We summon you to set our colleagues at liberty."

"I cannot do so," answered the officer.

"In that case complete your crimes," said Eugène Sue, "We summon you to arrest us also."

The officer arrested them.

They were taken to the guard-house of the Ministry for Foreign Affairs, and, later on, to the barracks of the Quai d'Orsay. It was not till night that two companies of the line came to transfer them to this ultimate resting-place.

While placing them between his soldiers the commanding officer bowed down to the ground, politely remarking, "Gentlemen, my men's guns are loaded."

The clearance of the hall was carried out, as we have said, in a disorderly fashion, the soldiers pushing the Representatives before them through all the outlets.

Some, and amongst the number those of whom we have just spoken, wens out by the Rue de Bourgogne, others were dragged through the Salle des Pas Perdus towards the grated door opposite the Pont de la Concorde.[1]

The Salle des Pas Perdus has an ante-chamber, a sort of crossway room, upon which opened the staircase of the High Tribune, and several doors, amongst others the great glass door of the gallery which leads to the apartments of the President of the Assembly.

As soon as they had reached this crossway room which adjoins the little rotunda, where the side door of exit to the Palace is situated, the soldiers set the Representatives free.

There, in a few moments, a group was formed, in which the Representatives Canet and Favreau began to speak. One universal cry was raised, "Let us search for Dupin, let us drag him here if it is necessary."

They opened the glass door and rushed into the gallery. This time M. Dupin was at home. M. Dupin, having learnt that the gendarmes had cleared out the Hall, had come out of his hiding-place. The Assembly being thrown prostrate, Dupin stood erect. The law being made prisoner, this man felt himself set free.

The group of Representatives, led by MM. Canet and Favreau, found him in his study.

There a dialogue ensued. The Representatives summoned the President to put himself at their head, and to re-enter the Hall, he, the man of the Assembly, with them, the men of the Nation.

M. Dupin refused point-blank, maintained his ground, was very firm, and clung bravely to his nonentity.

---

1. This grated door was closed on December 2, and was not reopened until the 12th March, when M. Louis Bonaparte came to inspect the works of the Hall of the Corps Legislatif.

"What do you want me to do?" said he, mingling with his alarmed protests many law maxims and Latin quotations, an instinct of chattering jays, who pour forth all their vocabulary when they are frightened. "What do you want me to do? Who am I? What can I do? I am nothing. No one is any longer anything. *Ubi nihil, nihil.* Might is there. Where there is Might the people lose their Rights. *Novus nascitur ordo.* Shape your course accordingly. I am obliged to submit. *Dura lex, sed lex.* A law of necessity we admit, but not a law of right. But what is to be done? I ask to be let alone. I can do nothing. I do what I can. I am not wanting in good will. If I had a corporal and four men, I would have them killed."

"This man only recognizes force," said the Representatives. "Very well, let us employ force."

They used violence towards him, they girded him with a scarf like a cord round his neck, and, as they had said, they dragged him towards the Hall, begging for his "liberty," moaning, kicking—I would say wrestling, if the word were not too exalted.

Some minutes after the clearance, this Salle des Pas Perdus, which had just witnessed Representatives pass by in the clutch of gendarmes, saw M. Dupin in the clutch of the Representatives.

They did not get far. Soldiers barred the great green folding-doors. Colonel Espinasse hurried thither, the commander of the gendarmerie came up. The butt-ends of a pair of pistols were seen peeping out of the commander's pocket.

The colonel was pale, the commander was pale, M. Dupin was livid. Both sides were afraid. M. Dupin was afraid of the colonel; the colonel assuredly was not afraid of M. Dupin, but behind this laughable and miserable figure he saw a terrible phantom rise up—his crime, and he trembled. In Homer there is a scene where Nemesis appears behind Thersites.

M. Dupin remained for some moments stupefied, bewildered and speechless.

The Representative Gambon exclaimed to him,—

"Now then, speak, M. Dupin, the Left does not interrupt you."

Then, with the words of the Representatives at his back, and the bayonets of the soldiers at his breast, the unhappy man spoke. What his mouth uttered at this moment, what the President of the Sovereign Assembly of France stammered to the gendarmes at this intensely critical moment, no one could gather.

Those who heard the last gasps of this moribund cowardice, hastened to purify their ears. It appears, however, that he stuttered forth something like this:—

"You are Might, you have bayonets; I invoke Right and I leave you. I have the honor to wish you good day."

He went away.

They let him go. At the moment of leaving he turned round and let fall a few more words. We will not gather them up. History has no rag-picker's basket.

IX

An End Worse than Death

We should have been glad to have put aside, never to have spoken of him again, this man who had borne for three years this most honorable title, President of the National Assembly of France, and who had only known how to be lacquey to the majority. He contrived in his last hour to sink even lower than could have been believed possible even for him. His career in the Assembly had been that of a valet, his end was that of a scullion.

The unprecedented attitude that M. Dupin assumed before the gendarmes when uttering with a grimace his mockery of a protest, even engendered suspicion. Gambion exclaimed, "He resists like an accomplice. He knew all."

We believe these suspicions to be unjust. M. Dupin knew nothing. Who indeed amongst the organizers of the *coup d'état* would have taken the trouble to make sure of his joining them? Corrupt M. Dupin? was it possible? and, further, to what purpose? To pay him? Why? It would be money wasted when fear alone was enough. Some connivances are secured before they are sought for. Cowardice is the old fawner upon felony. The blood of the law is quickly wiped up. Behind the assassin who holds the poniard comes the trembling wretch who holds the sponge.

Dupin took refuge in his study. They followed him. "My God!" he cried, "can't they understand that I want to be left in peace."

In truth they had tortured him ever since the morning, in order to extract from him an impossible scrap of courage.

"You ill-treat me worse than the gendarmes," said he.

The Representatives installed themselves in his study, seated themselves at his table, and, while he groaned and scolded in an arm-chair, they drew up a formal report of what had just taken place, as they wished to leave an official record of the outrage in the archives.

When the official report was ended Representative Canet read it to the President, and offered him a pen.

"What do you want me to do with this?" he asked.

"You are the President," answered Canet. "This is our last sitting. It is your duty to sign the official report."

This man refused.

X

The Black Door

M. Dupin is a matchless disgrace.

Later on he had his reward. It appears that he became some sort of an Attorney-General at the Court of Appeal.

M. Dupin renders to Louis Bonaparte the service of being in his place the meanest of men.

To continue this dismal history.

The Representatives of the Right, in their first bewilderment caused by the *coup d'état*, hastened in large numbers to M. Daru, who was Vice-President of the Assembly, and at the same time one of the Presidents of the Pyramid Club. This Association had always supported the policy of the Elysée, but without believing that a *coup d'état* was premeditated. M. Daru lived at No. 75, Rue de Lille.

Towards ten o'clock in the morning about a hundred of these Representatives had assembled at M. Daru's home. They resolved to attempt to penetrate into the Hall where the Assembly held its sittings. The Rue de Lille opens out into the Rue de Bourgogne, almost opposite the little door by which the Palace is entered, and which is called the Black Door.

They turned their steps towards this door, with M. Daru at their head. They marched arm in arm and three abreast. Some of them had put on their scarves of office. They took them off later on.

The Black Door, half-open as usual, was only guarded by two sentries.

Some of the most indignant, and amongst them M. de Kerdrel, rushed towards this door and tried to pass. The door, however, was violently shut, and there ensued between the Representatives and the *sergents de ville* who hastened up, a species of struggle, in which a Representative had his wrist sprained.

At the same time a battalion which was drawn up on the Place de Bourgogne moved on, and came at the double towards the group of Representatives. M. Daru, stately and firm, signed to the commander to stop; the battalion halted, and M. Daru, in the name of the Constitution, and in his capacity as Vice-President of the Assembly, summoned the soldiers to lay down their arms, and to give free passage to the Representatives of the Sovereign People.

The commander of the battalion replied by an order to clear the street immediately, declaring that there was no longer an Assembly; that as for himself, he did not know what the Representatives of the People were, and that if those persons before him did not retire of their own accord, he would drive them back by force.

"We will only yield to violence," said M. Daru.

"You commit high treason," added M. de Kerdrel.

The officer gave the order to charge.

The soldiers advanced in close order.

There was a moment of confusion; almost a collision. The Representatives, forcibly driven back, ebbed into the Rue de Lille. Some of them fell down. Several members of the Right were rolled in the mud by the soldiers. One of them, M. Etienne, received a blow on the shoulder from the butt-end of a musket. We may here add that a week afterwards M. Etienne was a member of that concern which they styled the Consultative Committee. He found the *coup d'état* to his taste, the blow with the butt-end of a musket included.

They went back to M. Daru's house, and on the way the scattered group reunited, and was even strengthened by some new-comers.

"Gentlemen," said M. Daru, "the President has failed us, the Hall is closed against us. I am the Vice-President; my house is the Palace of the Assembly."

He opened a large room, and there the Representatives of the Right installed themselves. At first the discussions were somewhat noisy. M. Daru, however, observed that the moments were precious, and silence was restored.

The first measure to be taken was evidently the deposition of the President of the Republic by virtue of Article 68 of the Constitution. Some Representatives of the party which was called *Burgraves* sat round a table and prepared the deed of deposition.

As they were about to read it aloud a Representative who came in from out of doors appeared at the door of the room, and announced to the Assembly that the Rue de Lille was becoming filled with troops, and that the house was being surrounded.

There was not a moment to lose.

M. Benoist-d'Azy said, "Gentlemen, let us go to the Mairie of the tenth arrondissement; there we shall be able to deliberate under the protection of the tenth legion, of which our colleague, General Lauriston, is the colonel."

M. Daru's house had a back entrance by a little door which was at the bottom of the garden. Most of the Representatives went out that way.

M. Daru was about to follow them. Only himself, M. Odilon Barrot, and two or three others remained in the room, when the door opened. A captain entered, and said to M. Daru,—

"Sir, you are my prisoner."

"Where am I to follow you?" asked M. Daru.

"I have orders to watch over you in your own house."

The house, in truth, was militarily occupied, and it was thus that M. Daru was prevented from taking part in the sitting at the Mairie of the tenth arrondissement.

The officer allowed M. Odilon Barrot to go out.

XI

THE HIGH COURT OF JUSTICE

While all this was taking place on the left bank of the river, towards noon a man was noticed walking up and down the great Salles des Pas Perdus of the Palace of Justice. This man, carefully buttoned up in an overcoat, appeared to be attended at a distance by several possible supporters—for certain police enterprises employ assistants whose dubious appearance renders the passers-by uneasy, so much so that they wonder whether they are magistrates or thieves. The man in the buttoned-up overcoat loitered from door to door, from lobby to lobby, exchanging signs of intelligence with the myrmidons who followed him; then came back to the great Hall, stopping on the way the barristers, solicitors, ushers, clerks, and attendants, and repeating to all in a low voice, so as not to be heard by the passers-by, the same question. To this question some answered "Yes," others replied "No." And the man set to work again, prowling about the Palace of Justice with the appearance of a bloodhound seeking the trail.

He was a Commissary of the Arsenal Police.

What was he looking for?

The High Court of Justice.

What was the High Court of Justice doing?

It was hiding.

Why? To sit in Judgment?

Yes and no.

The Commissary of the Arsenal Police had that morning received from the Prefect Maupas the order to search everywhere for the place where the High Court of Justice might be sitting, if perchance it thought it its duty to meet. Confusing the High Court with the Council of State, the Commissary of Police had first gone to the Quai d'Orsay. Having found nothing, not even the Council of State, he had come away empty-handed, at all events had turned his steps towards the Palace of Justice, thinking that as he had to search for justice he would perhaps find it there.

Not finding it, he went away.

The High Court, however, had nevertheless met together.

Where, and how? We shall see.

At the period whose annals we are now chronicling, before the present reconstruction of the old buildings of Paris, when the Palace of Justice was reached by the Cour de Harlay, a staircase the reverse of majestic led thither by turning out into a long corridor called the Gallerie Mercière. Towards the middle of this corridor there were two doors; one on the right, which led to the Court of Appeal, the other on the left, which led to the Court of Cassation. The folding-doors to the left opened upon an old gallery called St. Louis, recently restored, and which serves at the present time for a Salle des Pas Perdus to the barristers of the Court of Cassation. A wooden statue of St. Louis stood opposite the entrance door. An entrance contrived in a niche to the right of this statue led into a winding lobby ending in a sort of blind passage, which apparently was closed by two double doors. On the door to the right might be read "First President's Room"; on the door to the left, "Council Chamber." Between these two doors, for the convenience of the barristers going from the Hall to the Civil Chamber, which formerly was the Great Chamber of Parliament, had been formed a narrow and dark passage, in which, as one of them remarked, "every crime could be committed with impunity."

Leaving on one side the First President's Room and opening the door which bore the inscription "Council Chamber," a large room was crossed, furnished with a huge horse-shoe table, surrounded by green chairs. At the end of this room, which in 1793 had served as a deliberating hall for the juries of the Revolutionary Tribunal, there was a door placed in the wainscoting, which led into a little lobby where were two doors, on the right the door of the room appertaining to the President of the Criminal Chamber, on the left the door of the Refreshment Room. "Sentenced to death!—Now let us go and dine!" These two ideas, Death and Dinner, have jostled against each other for centuries. A third door closed the extremity of this lobby. This door was, so to speak, the last of the Palace of Justice, the farthest off, the least known, the most hidden; it opened into what was called the Library of the Court of Cassation, a large square room lighted by two windows overlooking the great inner yard of the Concièrgerie, furnished with a few leather chairs, a large table covered with green cloth, and with law books lining the walls from the floor to the ceiling.

This room, as may be seen, is the most secluded and the best hidden of any in the Palace.

It was here,—in this room, that there arrived successively on the 2d December, towards eleven o'clock in the morning, numerous men dressed in black, without robes, without badges of office, affrighted, bewildered, shaking their heads, and whispering together. These trembling men were the High Court of Justice.

The High Court of Justice, according to the terms of the Constitution, was composed of seven magistrates; a President, four Judges, and two Assistants, chosen by the Court of Cassation from among its own members and renewed every year.

In December, 1851, these seven judges were named Hardouin, Pataille, Moreau, Delapalme, Cauchy, Grandet, and Quesnault, the two last-named being Assistants.

These men, almost unknown, had nevertheless some antecedents. M. Cauchy, a few years previously President of the Chamber of the Royal Court of Paris, an amiable man and easily frightened, was the brother of the mathematician, member of the Institute, to whom we owe the computation of waves of sound, and of the ex-Registrar Archivist of the Chamber of Peers. M. Delapalme had been Advocate-General, and had taken a prominent part in the Press trials under the Restoration; M. Pataille had been Deputy of the Centre under the Monarchy of July; M. Moreau (de la Seine) was noteworthy, inasmuch he had been nicknamed "de la Seine" to distinguish him from M. Moreau (de la Meurthe), who on his side was noteworthy, inasmuch as he had been nicknamed "de la Meurthe" to distinguish him from M. Moreau (de la Seine). The first Assistant, M. Grandet, had been President of the Chamber at Paris. I have read this panegyric of him: "He is known to possess no individuality or opinion of his own whatsoever." The second Assistant, M. Quesnault, a Liberal, a Deputy, a Public Functionary, Advocate-General, a Conservative, learned, obedient, had attained by making a stepping-stone of each of these attributes, to the Criminal Chamber of the Court of Cassation, where he was known as one of the most severe members. 1848 had shocked his notion of Right, he had resigned after the 24th of February; he did not resign after the 2d December.

M. Hardouin, who presided over the High Court, was an ex-President of Assizes, a religious man, a rigid Jansenist, noted amongst his colleagues as a "scrupulous magistrate," living in Port Royal, a diligent reader of Nicolle, belonging to the race of the old Parliamentarians of the Marais, who used to go to the Palais de Justice mounted on a mule;

the mule had now gone out of fashion, and whoever visited President Hardouin would have found no more obstinacy in his stable than in his conscience.

On the morning of the 2d December, at nine o'clock, two men mounted the stairs of M. Hardouin's house, No. 10, Rue de Condé, and met together at his door. One was M. Pataille; the other, one of the most prominent members of the bar of the Court of Cassation, was the ex-Constituent Martin (of Strasbourg). M. Pataille had just placed himself at M. Hardouin's disposal.

Martin's first thought, while reading the placards of the *coup d'état*, had been for the High Court. M. Hardouin ushered M. Pataille into a room adjoining his study, and received Martin (of Strasbourg) as a man to whom he did not wish to speak before witnesses. Being formally requested by Martin (of Strasbourg) to convene the High Court, he begged that he would leave him alone, declared that the High Court would "do its duty," but that first he must "confer with his colleagues," concluding with this expression, "It shall be done today or tomorrow." "Today or tomorrow!" exclaimed Martin (of Strasbourg); "Mr. President, the safety of the Republic, the safety of the country, perhaps, depends on what the High Court will or will not do. Your responsibility is great; bear that in mind. The High Court of Justice does not do its duty today or tomorrow; it does it at once, at the moment, without losing a minute, without an instant's hesitation."

Martin (of Strasbourg) was right, Justice always belongs to Today.

Martin (of Strasbourg) added, "If you want a man for active work, I am at your service." M. Hardouin declined the offer; declared that he would not lose a moment, and begged Martin (of Strasbourg) to leave him to "confer" with his colleague, M. Pataille.

In fact, he called together the High Court for eleven o'clock, and it was settled that the meeting should take place in the Hall of the Library.

The Judges were punctual. At a quarter-past eleven they were all assembled. M. Pataille arrived the last.

They sat at the end of the great green table. They were alone in the Library.

There was no ceremonial. President Hardouin thus opened the debate: "Gentlemen, there is no need to explain the situation, we all know what it is."

Article 68 of the Constitution was imperative. It was necessary that the High Court should meet *under penalty of high treason*. They gained time, they swore themselves in, they appointed as Recorder of the High Court M. Bernard, Recorder of the Court of Cassation, and they sent to fetch him, and while waiting requested the librarian, M. Denevers, to hold his pen in readiness. They settled the time and place for an evening meeting. They talked of the conduct of the Constituent Martin (of Strasbourg), with which they were offended, regarding it almost as a nudge of the elbow given by Politics to Justice. They spoke a little of Socialism, of the Mountain, and of the Red Republic, and a little also of the judgment which they had to pronounce. They chatted, they told stories, they found fault, they speculated, they spun out the time.

What were they waiting for?

We have related what the Commissary of police was doing for his part in his department.

And, in reference to this design, when the accomplices of the *coup d'état* considered that the people in order to summon the High Court to do its duty, could invade the Palace of Justice, and that they would never look for it where it was assembled, they felt that this room had been excellently chosen. When, however, they considered that the police would also doubtless come to expel the High Court, and that perhaps they would not succeed in finding it, each one regretted to himself the choice of the room. They wished to hide the High Court, they had succeeded too well. It was grievous to think that perhaps when the police and the armed force should arrive, matters would have gone too far, and the High Court would be too deeply compromised.

They had appointed a Recorder, now they must organize a Court. A second step, more serious than the first.

The judges delayed, hoping that fortune would end by deciding on one side or the other, either for the Assembly or for the President, either against the *coup d'état* or for it, and that there might thus be a vanquished party, so that the High Court could then with all safety lay its hands upon somebody.

They lengthily argued the question, whether they should immediately decree the accusation of the President, or whether they should draw up a simple order of inquiry. The latter course was adopted.

They drew up a judgment, not the honest and outspoken judgment which was placarded by the efforts of the Representatives of the Left and published, in which are found these words of bad taste, *Crime* and *High Treason*; this judgment, a weapon of war, has never existed otherwise than as a projectile. Wisdom in a judge sometimes consists in drawing up a judgment which is not one, one of those judgments which has no binding force, in which everything is conditional; in which no one is incriminated, and nothing, is called by its right name. There are species of intermediate courses which allow of waiting and seeing; in delicate crises men who are in earnest must not inconsiderately mingle with possible events that bluntness which is called Justice. The High Court took advantage of this, it drew up a prudent judgment; this judgment is not known; it is published here for the first time. Here it is. It is a masterpiece of equivocal style:—

EXTRACT FROM THE REGISTRY OF THE
HIGH COURT OF JUSTICE.
The High Court of Justice.

"According to Article 68 of the Constitution, considering that printed placards beginning with these words, 'The President of the Republic' and ending with the signatures, 'Louis Napoléon Bonaparte' and 'De Morny, Minister of the Interior,' the said placards ordaining amongst other measures the dissolution of the National Assembly, have been posted today on the walls of Paris, that this fact of the dissolution of the National Assembly by the President of the Republic would be of the nature to constitute the case provided for by Article 68 of the Constitution, and renders, in the terms of the aforesaid article, the meeting of the High Court indispensable.

"It is declared that the High Court of Justice is organized, that it appoints[1] . . . to fulfil with it the functions of the Public Ministry; that M. Bernard, the Recorder of the Court of Cassation, should fulfil the duties of Recorder, and in order to proceed further, according to the terms of the aforesaid Article 68 of the Constitution, the Court will adjourn until tomorrow, the 3d of December, at noon.

"Drawn up and discussed in the Council Chamber, where were sitting MM. Hardouin, president, Pataille, Moreau, Delapalme, and Cauchy, judges, December 2, 1851."

---

1. This line was left blank. It was filled in later on with the name of M. Renouard, Councillor of the Court of Cassation.

The two Assistants, MM. Grandet and Quesnault, offered to sign the decree, but the President ruled that it would be more correct only to accept the signatures of the titular judges, the Assistants not being qualified when the Court was complete.

In the meantime it was one o'clock, the news began to spread through the palace that a decree of deposition against Louis Bonaparte had been drawn up by a part of the Assembly; one of the judges who had gone out during the debate, brought back this rumor to his colleagues. This coincided with an outburst of energy. The President observed that it would be to the purpose to appoint a Procureur-General.

There was a difficulty. Whom should they appoint? In all preceding trials they had always chosen for a Procureur-General at the High Court the Procureur-General at the Court of Appeal of Paris. Why should they introduce an innovation? They determined upon this Procureur-General of the Court of Appeal. This Procureur-General was at the time M. de Royer, who had been keeper of the Seals for M. Bonaparte. Thence a new difficulty and a long debate.

Would M. de Royer consent? M. Hardouin undertook to go and make the offer to him. He had only to cross the Mercière Gallery.

M. de Royer was in his study. The proposal greatly embarrassed him. He remained speechless from the shock. To accept was serious, to refuse was still more serious.

There was risk of treason. On the 2d December, an hour after noon, the *coup d'état* was still a crime. M. de Royer, not knowing whether the high treason would succeed, ventured to stigmatize the deed as such in private, and cast down his eyes with a noble shame before this violation of the laws which, three months later, numerous purple robes, including his own, endorsed with their oaths. But his indignation did not go to the extent of supporting the indictment. An indictment speaks aloud. M. de Royer as yet only murmured. He was perplexed.

M. Hardouin understood this state of conscience. Persistence would have been unreasonable. He withdrew.

He returned to the room where his colleagues were awaiting him.

In the meantime the Commissary of the Arsenal Police had come back.

He had ended by succeeding in "unearthing"—such was his expression—the High Court. He penetrated as far as the Council Chamber of the Civil Chamber; at that moment he had still no other escort than the few police agents of the morning. A boy was passing by.

The Commissary asked him the whereabouts of the High Court. "The High Court?" answered the boy; "what is that?" Nevertheless the boy told the Librarian, who came up. A few words were exchanged between M. Denevers and the Commissary.

"What are you asking for?"

"The High Court."

"Who are you?"

"I want the high Court."

"It is in session."

"Where is it sitting?"

"Here."

And the Librarian pointed to the door.

"Very well," said the Commissary.

He did not add another word, and returned into the Mercière Gallery.

We have just said that he was only accompanied at that time by a few police agents.

The High Court was, in truth, in session. The President was relating to the judges his visit to the Procureur General. Suddenly a tumultuous sound of footsteps is heard in the lobby which leads from the Council Chamber to the room where they were deliberating. The door opens abruptly. Bayonets appear, and in the midst of the bayonets a man in a buttoned-up overcoat, with a tricolored sash upon his coat.

The magistrates stare, stupefied.

"Gentlemen," said the man, "dissolve your meeting immediately."

President Hardouin rises.

"What does this mean? Who are you? Are you aware to whom you are speaking?"

"I am aware. You are the High Court, and I am the Commissary of the Police."

"Well, then?"

"Be off."

There were there thirty-five municipal guards, commanded by a lieutenant, and with a drum at their head.

"But—" said the President.

The Commissary interrupted him with these words, which are literally given,—

"Mr. President, I am not going to enter upon an oratorical combat with you. I have my orders, and I transmit them to you. Obey."

"Whom?"

"The Prefect of Police."

The President asked this strange question, which implied the acceptance of an order,—

"Have you a warrant?"

The Commissary answered,—

"Yes."

And he handed a paper to the President.

The judges turned pale.

The President unfolded the paper; M. Cauchy put his head over M. Hardouin's shoulder. The President read but,—

"You are ordered to dissolve the High Court, and, in case of refusal, to arrest MM. Béranger, Rocher, De Boissieux, Pataille, and Hello."

And, turning towards the judges, the President added,—

"Signed, Maupas."

Then, addressing himself to the Commissary, he resumed,—

"There is some mistake, these are not our names. MM. Béranger, Rocher, and De Boissieux have served their time and are no longer judges of the High Court; as for M. Hello, he is dead."

The High Court, in reality, was temporary and renewable; the *coup d'état* overthrew the Constitution, but did not understand it. The warrant signed "Maupas" was applicable to the preceding High Court. The *coup d'état* had been misled by an old list. Such is the heedlessness of assassins.

"Mr. Commissary of Police," continued the President, "you see that these names are not ours."

"That does not matter to me," replied the Commissary. "Whether this warrant does or does not apply to you, disperse, or I shall arrest all of you."

And he added,—

"At once."

The judges were silenced; one of them picked up from the table a loose sheet of paper, which was the judgment they had drawn up, and put the paper in his pocket.

Then they went away.

The Commissary pointed to the door where the bayonets were, and said,—

"That way."

They went out by the lobby between two ranks of soldiers. The detachment of Republican Guards escorted them as far as the St. Louis Gallery.

There they set them free; their heads bowed down.

It was about three o'clock.

While these events were taking place in the Library, close by, in the former great Chamber of the Parliament, the Court of Cassation was sitting in judgment as usual, without noticing what was happening so near at hand. It would appear, then, that the police exhaled no odor.

Let us at once have done with this High Court.

In the evening at half-past seven the seven judges met together at the house of one of their number, he who had taken away the decree; they framed an official report, drew up a protest, and recognizing the necessity of filling in the line left blank in their decree, on the proposition of M. Quesnault, appointed as Procureur-General M. Renouard, their colleague at the Court of Cessation. M. Renouard, who was immediately informed, consented.

They met together for the last time on the next day, the 3d, at eleven o'clock in the morning, an hour before the time mentioned in the judgment which we have read above,—again in the Library of the Court of Cassation. M. Renouard was present. An official minute was given to him, recording his appointment, as well as certain details with which he asked to be supplied. The judgment which had been drawn up was taken by M. Quesnault to the Recorder's Office, and immediately entered upon the Register of the Secret Deliberations of the Court of Cassation, the High Court not having a Special Register, and having decided, from its creation, to use the Register of the Court of Cassation. After the decree they also transcribed the two documents described as follows on the Register:—

I. An official report recording the interference of the police during the discussion upon the preceding decree.

II. A minute of the appointment of M. Renouard to the office of Procureur-General.

In addition seven copies of these different documents drawn up by the hands of the judges themselves, and signed by them all, were put in a place of safety, as also, it is said, a note-book, in which were written five other secret decisions relating to the *coup d'état*.

Does this page of the Register of the Court of Cassation exist at the present time? Is it true, as has been stated, that the prefect Maupas sent for the Register and tore out the leaf containing the decree? We have not been able to clear up this point. The Register now is shown to no one, and those employed at the Recorder's Office are dumb.

Such are the facts, let us summarize them. If this Court so called "High," had been of a character to conceive such an idea as that of doing its duty—when it had once met together the mere organization of itself was a matter of a few minutes—it would have proceeded resolutely and rapidly, it would have appointed as Procureur-General some energetic man belonging to the Court of Cassation, either from the body of magistrates, such as Freslon, or from the bar, like Martin (of Strasbourg). By virtue of Article 68, and without waiting the initiative of the Assembly, it would have drawn up a judgment stigmatizing the crime, it would have launched an order of arrest against the President and his accomplices and have ordered the removal of the person of Louis Bonaparte to jail. As for the Procureur-General he would have issued a warrant of arrest. All this could have been done by half-past eleven, and at that time no attempt had been made to dissolve the High Court. These preliminary proceedings concluded, the High Court, by going out through a nailed-up door leading into the Salle des Pas Perdus, could have descended into the street, and there have proclaimed its judgment to the people. At this time it would have met with no hindrance. Finally, and this in any case, it should have sat robed on the Judges' Bench, with all magisterial state, and when the police agent and his soldiers appeared should have ordered the soldiers, who perhaps would have obeyed them, to arrest the agent, and if the soldiers had disobeyed, should have allowed themselves to be formally dragged to prison, so that the people could see, under their own eyes, out in the open street, the filthy hoof of the *coup d'état* trampling upon the robe of Justice.

Instead of this, what steps did the High Court take? We have just seen.

"Be off with you!"

"We are going."

We can imagine, after a very different fashion, the dialogue between Mathieu Molé and Vidocq.

XII

THE MAIRIE OF THE TENTH ARRONDISSEMENT

The Representatives, having come out from M. Daru, rejoined each other and assembled in the street. There they consulted briefly, from group to group. There were a large number of them. In less than an hour, by sending notices to the houses on the left bank of the Seine alone, on account of the extreme urgency, more than three hundred members could be called together. But where should they meet? At Lemardelay's? The Rue Richelieu was guarded. At the Salle Martel? It was a long way off. They relied upon the Tenth Legion, of which General Lauriston was colonel. They showed a preference for the Mairie of the Tenth Arrondissement. Besides, the distance was short, and there was no need to cross any bridges.

They formed themselves into column, and set forth.

M. Daru, as we have said, lived in the Rue de Lille, close by the Assembly. The section of the Rue de Lille lying between his house and the Palais Bourbon was occupied by infantry. The last detachment barred his door, but it only barred it on the right, not on the left. The Representatives, on quitting M. Daru, bent their steps on the side of the Rue des Saints-Pères, and left the soldiers behind them. At that moment the soldiers had only been instructed to prevent their meeting in the Palace of the Assembly; they could quietly form themselves into a column in the street, and set forth. If they had turned to the right instead of to the left, they would have been opposed. But there were no orders for the other alternative; they passed through a gap in the instructions.

An hour afterwards this threw St. Arnaud into a fit of fury.

On their way fresh Representatives came up and swelled the column. As the members of the Right lived for the most part in the Faubourg St. Germain, the column was composed almost entirely of men belonging to the majority.

At the corner of the Quai d'Orsay they met a group of members of the Left, who had reunited after their exit from the Palace of the Assembly, and who were consulting together. There were the Representatives Esquiros, Marc Dufraisse, Victor Hennequin, Colfavru, and Chamiot.

Those who were marching at the head of the column left their places, went up to the group, and said, "Come with us."

"Where are you going?" asked Marc Dufraisse.

To the Mairie of the Tenth Arrondissement."

"What do you intend to do there?"

"To decree the deposition of Louis Bonaparte."

"And afterwards?"

"Afterwards we shall go in a body to the Palace of the Assembly; we will force our way in spite of all resistance, and from the top of the steps we will read out the decree of deposition to the soldiers."

"Very good, we will join you," said Mare Dufraisse.

The five members of the Left marched at some distance from the column. Several of their friends who were mingled with the members of the Right rejoined them; and we may here mention a fact without giving it more importance than it possesses, namely, that the two fractions of the Assembly represented in this unpremeditated gathering marched towards the Mairie without being mingled together; one on each side of the street. It chanced that the men of the majority kept on the right side of the street, and the men of the minority on the left.

No one had a scarf of office. No outward token caused them to be recognized. The passers-by stared at them with surprise, and did not understand what was the meaning of this procession of silent men through the solitary streets of the Faubourg St. Germain. One district of Paris was as yet unaware of the *coup d'état*.

Strategically speaking, from a defensive point of view, the Mairie of the tenth Arrondissement was badly chosen. Situated in a narrow street in that short section of the Rue de Grenelle-St.-Germain which lies between the Rue des Saints-Pères and the Rue du Sépulcre, close by the cross-roads of the Croix-Rouge, where the troops could arrive from so many different points, the Mairie of the Tenth Arrondissement, confined, commanded, and blockaded on every side, was a pitiful citadel for the assailed National Representation. It is true that they no longer had the choice of a citadel, anymore than later on they had the choice of a general.

Their arrival at the Mairie might have seemed a good omen. The great gate which leads into a square courtyard was shut; it opened. The post of the National Guards, composed of some twenty men, took up their arms and rendered military honors to the Assembly. The Representatives entered, a Deputy Mayor received them with respect on the threshold of the Mairie. "The Palace of the Assembly is closed by the troops," said the Representatives, "we have come to deliberate here." The Deputy Mayor led them to the first story, and admitted them to the Great Municipal Hall. The National Guard cried, "Long live the National Assembly!"

The Representatives having entered, the door was shut. A crowd began to gather in the street and shouted "Long live the Assembly!" A certain number of strangers to the Assembly entered the Mairie at the same time as the Representatives. Overcrowding was feared, and two sentries were placed at a little side-door, which was left open, with orders only to allow members of the Assembly who might come afterwards to enter. M. Howyn Tranchère stationed himself at this door, and undertook to identify them.

On their arrival at the Mairie, the Representatives numbered somewhat under three hundred. They exceeded this number later on. It was about eleven o'clock in the morning. All did not go up at once into the hall where the meeting was to take place. Several, those of the Left in particular, remained in the courtyard, mingling with the National Guards and citizens.

They talked of what they were going to do.

This was the first difficulty.

The Father of the meeting was M. de Kératry.

Was he going to preside?

The Representatives who were assembled in the Great Hall were in his favor.

The Representatives remaining in the courtyard hesitated.

Marc Dufraisse went up to MM. Jules de Lasteyrie and Léon de Maleville, who had stayed behind with the Representatives of the Left, and said to them, "What are they thinking of upstairs? To make Kératry President? The name of Kératry would frighten the people as thoroughly as mine would frighten the middle classes."

A member of the Right, M. de Keranflech, came up, and intending to support the objection, added, "And then, think of Kératry's age. It is madness to pit a man of eighty against this hour of danger."

But Esquiros exclaimed,—

"That is a bad reason! Eighty years! They constitute a force."

"Yes; where they are well borne," said Colfavru. "Kératry bears them badly."

"Nothing is greater," resumed Esquiros, "than great octogenarians."

"It is glorious," added Chamiot, "to be presided over by Nestor."

"No, by Gerontes,"[1] said Victor Hennequin.

These words put an end to the debate. Kératry was thrown out. MM. Léon de Maleville and Jules de Lasteyrie, two men respected by all parties, undertook to make the members of the Right listen to reason. It was decided that the "bureau"[2] should preside. Five members of the "bureau" were present; two Vice-Presidents, MM. Benoist d'Azy and Vitet, and three Secretaries, MM. Griumult, Chapot, and Moulin. Of the two other Vice-Presidents, one, General Bedrau, was at Mazas; the other, M. Daru, was under guard in his own house. Of the three other Secretaries, two, MM. Peapin and Lacaze, men of the Elysée, were absentees; the other, M. Yvan, a member of the Left, was at the meeting of the Left, in the Rue Blanche, which was taking place almost at the same moment.

In the meantime an usher appeared on the steps of the Mairie, and cried out, as on the most peaceful days of the Assembly, "Representatives, to the sitting!"

This usher, who belonged to the Assembly, and who had followed it, shared its fortunes throughout this day, the sequestration on the Quai d'Orsay included.

At the summons of the usher all the Representatives in the courtyard, and amongst whom was one of the Vice-Presidents, M. Vitei, went upstairs to the Hall, and the sitting was opened.

This sitting was the last which the Assembly held under regular conditions. The Left, which, as we have seen, had on its side boldly recaptured the Legislative power, and had added to it that which circumstances required—as was the duty of Revolutionists; the Left, without a "bureau," without an usher, and without secretaries, held sittings in which the accurate and passionless record of shorthand was wanting, but which live in our memories and which History will gather up.

Two shorthand writers of the Assembly, MM. Grosselet and Lagache, were present at the sitting at the Mairie of the Tenth Arrondissement. They have been able to record it. The censorship of

---

1. The Gerontes, or Gerontia, were the Elders of Sparta, who constituted the Senate.

2. The "bureau" of the Assembly consists of the President, for the time being of the Assembly, assisted by six secretaries, whose duties mainly lie in deciding in what sense the Deputies have voted. The "bureau" of the Assembly should not be confounded with the fifteen "bureaux" of the Deputies, which answer to our Select Committees of the House of Commons, and are presided over by self-chosen Presidents.

the victorious *coup d'état* has mutilated their report and has published through its historians this mangled version as the true version. One lie more. That does not matter. This shorthand recital belongs to the brief of the 2d December, it is one of the leading documents in the trial which the future will institute. In the notes of this book will be found this document complete. The passages in inverted commas are those which the censorship of M. Bonaparte has suppressed. This suppression is a proof of their significance and importance.

Shorthand reproduces everything except life. Stenography is an ear. It hears and sees not. It is therefore necessary to fill in here the inevitable blanks of the shorthand account.

In order to obtain a complete idea of this sitting of the Tenth Arrondissement, we must picture the great Hall of the Mairie, a sort of parallelogram, lighted on the right by four or five windows overlooking the courtyard; on the left, along the wall, furnished with several rows of benches which had been hastily brought thither, on which were piled up the three hundred Representatives, assembled together by chance. No one was sitting down, those in front were standing, those behind were mounted on the benches. Here and there were a few small tables. In the centre people walked to and fro. At the bottom, at the end opposite the door, was a long table furnished with benches, which occupied the whole width of the wall, behind which sat the "bureau." "Sitting" is merely the conventional term. The "bureau" did not "sit"; like the rest of the Assembly it was on its feet. The secretaries, M.M. Chapot, Moulin, and Grimault wrote standing. At certain moments the two Vice-Presidents mounted on the benches so as to be better seen from all points of the room. The table was covered by an old green tablecloth, stained with ink, three or four inkstands had been brought in, and a quire of paper was scattered about. There the decrees were written as soon as they were drawn up. They multiplied the copies, some Representatives became secretaries on the spur of the moment, and helped the official secretaries.

This great hall was on a level with the landing. It was situated, as we have said, on the first floor; it was reached by a very narrow staircase.

We must recollect that nearly the whole of the members present were members of the Right.

The first moment was a serious one. Berryer came out to advantage. Berryer, like all those extemporizers without style, will only be remembered as a name, and a much disputed name, Berryer having been rather a special pleader than an orator who believed what he said. On that day Berryer was to the point, logical and earnest. They began by this cry, "What shall we do?" "Draw up a declaration," said M. de Falloux. "A protest," said M. de Flavigny. "A decree," said Berryer.

In truth a declaration was empty air, a protest was noise, a decree was action. They cried out, "What decree?" "Deposition," said Berryer. Deposition was the extreme limit of the energy of the Right. Beyond deposition, there was outlawry; deposition was practicable for the Right, outlawry was only possible for the Left. In fact it was the Left who outlawed Louis Bonaparte. They did it at their first meeting in the Rue Blanche. We shall see this later on. At deposition, Legality came to an end; at outlawry, the Revolution began. The recurrence of Revolutions are the logical consequences of *coups d'état*. The deposition having been voted, a man who later on turned traitor, Quentin Bauchart, exclaimed, "Let us all sign it." All signed it. Odilon Barrot came in and signed it. Antony Thouret came in and signed it. Suddenly M. Piscatory announced that the Mayor was refusing to allow Representatives who had arrived to enter the Hall. "Order him to do so by decree," said Berryer. And the decree was voted. Thanks to this decree, MM. Favreau and Monet entered; they came from the Legislative Palace; they related the cowardice of Dupin. M. Dahirel, one of the leaders of the Right, was exasperated, and said, "We have received bayonet thrusts." Voices were raised, "Let us summon the Tenth Legion. Let the call to arms be beaten. Lauriston hesitates. Let us order him to protect the Assembly." "Let us order him by decree," said Berryer. This decree was drawn up, which, however, did not prevent Lauriston from refusing. Another decree, again proposed by Berryer, pronounced anyone who had outraged the Parliamentary inviolability to be a traitor, and ordered the immediate release of those Representatives who had been wrongfully made prisoners. All this was voted at once without debate, in a sort of great unanimous confusion, and in the midst of a storm of fierce conversations. From time to time Berryer imposed silence. Then the angry outcries broke forth again. "The *coup d'état* will not dare to come here." "We are masters here." "We are at home." "It would be impossible to attack us here." "These wretches will not dare to do so." If the uproar had been less violent, the Representatives might have heard through the open windows close at hand, the sound of soldiers loading their guns.

A regiment of Chasseurs of Vincennes had just entered silently into the garden of the Mairie, and, while waiting for orders, were loading their guns.

Little by little the sitting, at first disorderly and tumultuous, had assumed an ordinary aspect. The uproar had relapsed into a murmur. The voice of the usher, crying "Silence, gentlemen," had succeeded in overcoming the hubbub. Every moment fresh Representatives came in, and hastened to sign the decree of deposition at the "bureau." As there was a great crowd round the "bureau" waiting to sign, a dozen loose sheets of paper to which the Representatives affixed their signatures were circulated in the great Hall and the two adjoining rooms.

The first to sign the decree of deposition was M. Dufaure, the last was M. Betting de Lancastel. Of the two Presidents, one, M. Benoist d'Azy, was addressing the Assembly; the other, M. Vitet, pale, but calm and resolute, distributed instructions and orders. M. Benoist d'Azy maintained a decorous countenance, but a certain hesitation in his speech revealed an inner agitation. Divisions, even in the Right, had not disappeared at this critical moment. A Legitimist member was overheard saying in a low voice, while speaking of one of the Vice-Presidents, "This great Vitet looks like a whited sepulchre." Vitet was an Orleanist.

Given this adventurer with whom they had to deal, this Louis Bonaparte, capable of everything, the hour and the man being wrapt in mystery, some Legitimist personages of a candid mind were seriously but comically frightened. The Marquis of ——, who acted the fly on the coach-wheel to the Right, went hither and thither, harangued, shouted, declaimed, remonstrated, proclaimed, and trembled. Another, M. A—— N——, perspiring, red-faced, out of breath, rushed about distractedly. "Where is the guard? How many men are there? Who commands them? The officer! send me the officer! Long live the Republic! National Guard, stand firm! Long live the Republic!" All the Right shouted this cry. "You wish then to kill it," said Esquiros. Some of them were dejected; Bourbousson maintained the silence of a vanquished placeman. Another, the Viscount of ——, a relative of the Duke of Escars, was so alarmed that every moment he adjourned to a corner of the courtyard. In the crowd which filled the courtyard there was a *gamin* of Paris, a child of Athens, who has since become am elegant and charming poet, Albert Glatigny. Albert Glatigny cried out to this frightened Viscount, "Hulloa there! Do you think that *coups d'état* are extinguished in the way Gulliver put out the fire?"

Oh, Laughter, how gloomy you are when attended with Tragedy!

The Orleanists were quieter, and maintained a more becoming attitude. This arose from the fact that they ran greater danger.

Pascal Duprat replaced at the top of the decrees the words, "République Française," which had been forgotten.

From time to time men who were not speaking on the subject of the moment mentioned this strange word, "Dupin," open which there ensued shouts of derision and bursts of laughter. "Utter the name of that coward no more," cried Antony Thouret.

There were motions and counter-motions; it was a continual uproar interrupted by deep and solemn silences. Alarmist phrases circulated from group to group. "We are in a blind alley." "We are caught here as in a rat trap"; and then on each motion voices were raised: "That is it!" "It is right!" "It is settled!" They agreed in a low voice upon a rendezvous at No. 19, Rue de la Chaussée-d'Antin, in case they should be expelled from the Mairie. M. Bixio carried off the decree of deposition to get it printed. Esquiros, Marc Dufraisse, Pascal Duprat, Rigal, Lherbette, Chamiot, Latrade, Colfavru, Antony Thouret, threw in here and there energetic words of advice. M. Dufaure, resolute and indignant, protested with authority. M. Odilon Barrot, motionless in a corner, maintained the silence of stupefied silliness.

MM. Passy and de Tocqueville, in the midst of the groups, described that when they were Ministers they had always entertained an uneasy suspicion of a *coup d'état*, and that they clearly perceived this fixed idea in the brain of Louis Bonaparte. M. de Tocqueville added, "I said to myself every night, 'I lie down to sleep a Minister; what if I should awake a prisoner?'" Some of those men who were termed "men of order," muttered while signing the degree of deposition, "Beware of the Red Republic!" and seemed to entertain an equal fear of failure and of success. M. de Vatimesnil pressed the hands of the men of the Left, and thanked them for their presence. "You make us popular," said he. And Antony Thouret answered him, "I know neither Right nor Left today; I only see the Assembly."

The younger of the two shorthand writers handed their written sheets to the Representatives who had spoken, and, asked them to revise them at once, saying, "We shall not have the time to read them over." Some Representatives went down into the street, and showed the people copies of the decree of deposition, signed by the members of the "bureau." One of the populace took one of these copies, and cried out, "Citizens! the ink is still quite wet! Long live the Republic!"

The Deputy-Mayor stood at the door of the Hall; the staircase was crowded with National Guards and spectators. In the Assembly several had penetrated into the Hall, and amongst them the ex-Constituent Beslay, a man of uncommon courage. It was at first wished to turn them out, but they resisted, crying, "This is our business. You are the Assembly, but we are the People." "They are right," said M. Berryer.

M. de Falloux, accompanied by M. de Kéranflech, came up the Constituent Beslay, and leaned by his side on the stove, saying to him, "Good-day, colleague"; and reminded him that they both had formed part of the Committee of the National Workshops, and that they had together visited the Workmen at the Parc Monceaux. The Right felt themselves falling; they became affectionate towards Republicans. The Republic is called Tomorrow.

Each spoke from his place; this member upon a bench, that member on a chair, a few on the tables. All contradictory opinions burst forth at once. In a corner some ex-leaders of "order" were scared at the possible triumph of the "Reds." In another the men of the Right surrounded the men of the Left, and asked them: "Are not the faubourgs going to rise?"

The narrator has but one duty, to tell his story; he relates everything, the bad as well as the good. Whatever may have taken place, however, and notwithstanding all these details of which it was our duty to speak, apart from the exceptions which we had mentioned, the attitude of the men of the Right who composed the large majority of this meeting was in many respects honorable and worthy. Some of them, as we have just mentioned, even prided themselves upon their resolution and their energy, almost as though they had wished to rival the members of the Left.

We may here remark—for in the course of this narrative we shall more than once see the gaze of some members of the Right turned towards the people, and in this no mistake should be made—that these monarchical men who talked of popular insurrection and who invoked the faubourgs were a minority in the majority,—an imperceptible minority. Antony Thouret proposed to those who were leaders there to go in a body through the working-class neighborhoods with the decree of deposition in their hands. Brought to bay, they refused. They declared that they would only protect themselves by organized powers, not by the people. It is a strange thing to say, but it must be noted, that with their habits of political shortsightedness, the popular armed resistance, even in the name of the Law, seemed sedition to them. The utmost appearance of revolution which they could endure was a regiment of the National Guard, with their drums at their head; they shrank from the barricade; Right in a blouse was no longer Right, Truth armed with a pike was no longer Truth, Law unpaving a street gave them the impression of a Fury. In the main, however, and taking them for what they were, and considering their position as politicians, these members of the Right were well-advised. What would they have done with the people? And what would the people have done with them? How would they have proceeded to set fire to the masses? Imagine Falloux as a tribune, fanning the Faubourg St. Antoine into a flame!

Alas! in the midst of this dense gloom, in these fatal complications of circumstances by which the *coup d'état* profited so odiously and so perfidiously, in that mighty misunderstanding which comprised the whole situation, for kindling the revolutionary spark in the heart of the people, Danton himself would not have sufficed.

The *coup d'état* entered into this meeting impudently, with its convict's cap on its head. It possessed an infamous assurance there, as well as everywhere else. There were in this majority three hundred Representatives of the People. Louis Napoleon sent a sergeant to drive them away. The Assembly, having resisted the sergeant, he sent an officer, the temporary commander of the sixth battalion of the Chasseurs de Vincennes. This officer, young, fair-haired, a scoffer, half laughing, half threatening, pointed with his finger to the stairs filled with bayonets, and defied the Assembly. "Who is this young spark?" asked a member of the Right. A National Guard who was there said, "Throw him out of the window!" "Kick him downstairs!" cried one of the people.

This Assembly, grievous as were its offences against the principles of the Revolution—and with these wrongs Democracy alone had the right to reproach it—this Assembly, I repeat, was the National Assembly, that is to say, the Republic incarnate, the living Universal Suffrage, the Majesty of the Nation, upright and visible. Louis Bonaparte assassinated this Assembly, and moreover insulted it. A slap on the face is worse than a poniard thrust.

The gardens of the neighborhood occupied by the troops were full of broken bottles. They had plied the soldiers with drink. They obeyed the "epaulettes" unconditionally, and according to the expression of eyewitnesses, appeared "dazed-drunk." The Representatives appealed to them, and said to them, "It is a crime!" They answered, "We are not aware of it."

One soldier was heard to say to another, "What have you done with your ten francs of this morning?"

The sergeants hustled the officers. With the exception of the commander, who probably earned his cross of honor, the officers were respectful, the sergeants brutal.

A lieutenant showing signs of flinching, a sergeant cried out to him, "You are not the only one who commands here! Come, therefore, march!"

M. de Vatimesnil asked a soldier, "Will you dare to arrest us—us, the Representatives of the People?"

"Assuredly!" said the soldier.

Several soldiers hearing some Representatives say that they had eaten nothing since the morning, offered them their ration bread. Some Representatives accepted. M. de Tocqueville, who was unwell, and who was noticed to be pale and leaning on the sill of a window, received from a soldier a piece of this bread, which he shared with M. Chambolle.

Two Commissaries of Police appeared in "full dress," in black coats girded with their sash-girdles and their black corded hats. One was an old man, the other a young man. The first was named Lemoine-Tacherat, and not Bacherel, as has been wrongly printed: the second was named Barlet. These names should be noted. The unprecedented assurance of this Barlet was remarked. Nothing was wanting in him,— cynical speech, provoking gesture, sardonic intonation. It was with an inexpressible air of insolence that Barlet, when summoning the meeting to dissolve itself, added, "Rightly or Wrongly." They murmured on the benches of the Assembly, "Who is this scoundrel?" The other, compared to him, seemed moderate and inoffensive. Emile Péan exclaimed, "The old man is simply working in his profession, but the young man is working out his promotion."

Before this Tacherat and this Barlet entered, before the butts of the muskets had been heard ringing on the stones of the staircase, this Assembly had talked of resistance. Of what kind of resistance? We have just stated. The majority could only listen to a regular organized resistance, a military resistance in uniform and in epaulets. Such a resistance was easy to decree, but it was difficult to organize. The Generals on whom the Assembly were accustomed to rely having been arrested, there only remained two possible Generals, Oudinot and Lauriston. General Marquis de Lauriston, ex-peer of France, and at the same time Colonel of the Tenth Legion and Representative of the People, drew a distinction between his duty as Representative and his duty as Colonel. Summoned by some of his friends of the Right to beat to arms and call together the Tenth Legion, he answered, "As Representative of the People I ought to indict the Executive Power, but as Colonel I ought to obey it." It appears that he obstinately shut himself up in this singular reasoning, and that it was impossible to draw him out of it.

"How stupid he is!" said Piscatory.

"How sharp he is!" said Falloux.

The first officer of the National Guard who appeared in uniform, seemed to be recognized by two members of the Right, who said, "It is M. de Perigord!" They made a mistake, it was M. Guilbot, major of the third battalion of the Tenth Legion. He declared that he was ready to march on the first order from his Colonel, General Lauriston. General Lauriston went down into the courtyard, and came up a moment afterwards, saying, "They do not recognize my authority. I have just resigned," Moreover, the name of Lauriston was not familiar to the soldiers. Oudinot was better known in the army. But how?

At the moment when the name of Oudinot was pronounced, a shudder ran through this meeting, almost exclusively composed of members of the Right. In fact at this critical time, at this fatal name of Oudinot, reflections crowded upon each other in every mind.

What was the *coup d'état*?

It was the "Roman expedition at home." Which was undertaken against whom? Against those who had undertaken the "Roman expedition abroad." The National Assembly of France, dissolved by violence, could find only one single General to defend it in its dying hour. And whom? Precisely he, who in the name of the National Assembly of France had dissolved by violence the National Assembly of Rome. What power could Oudinot, the strangler of a Republic, possess to save a Republic? Was it not evident that his own soldiers would answer him, "What do you want with us? That which we have done at Rome we now do at Paris." What a story is this story of treason! The French Legislature had written the first chapter with the blood of the Roman Constituent Assembly: Providence wrote the second chapter with the blood of the French Legislature, Louis Bonaparte holding the pen.

In 1849, Louis Bonaparte had assassinated the sovereignty of the People in the person of its Roman Representatives; in 1851 he assassinated it in the person of its French Representatives. It was logical, and although it was infamous, it was just. The Legislative Assembly bore at the same time the weight of two crimes; it was the accomplice of the first, the victim of the second. All these men of the majority felt this, and were humbled. Or rather it was the same crime, the crime of the Second of July, 1849, ever erect, ever alive, which had only changed its name, which now called itself the Second of December, and which, the offspring of this Assembly, stabbed it to the heart. Nearly all crimes are parricidal. On a certain day they recoil upon those who have committed them, and slay them.

At this moment, so full of anxiety, M. de Falloux must have glanced round for M. de Montalembert. M. de Montalembert was at the Elysée.

When Tamisier rose and pronounced this terrifying word, "The Roman Question?" distracted M. de Dampierre shouted to him, "Silence! You kill us!"

It was not Tamisier who was killing them—it was Oudinot.

M. de Dampierre did not perceive that he cried "Silence!" to history.

And then without even reckoning the fatal remembrance which at such a moment would have crushed a man endowed in the highest degree with great military qualities, General Oudinot, in other respects an excellent officer, and a worthy son of his brave father, possessed none of those striking qualities which in the critical hour of revolution stir the soldier and carry with them the people. At that instant to win back an army of a hundred thousand men, to withdraw the balls from the cannons' mouths, to find beneath the wine poured out to the Praetorians the true soul of the French soldier half drowned and nearly dead, to tear the flag from the *coup d'état* and restore it to the Law, to surround the Assembly with thunders and lightnings, it would have needed one of those men who exist no longer; it would have needed the firm hand, the calm oratory, the cold and searching glance of Desaix, that French Phocion; it would have needed the huge shoulders, the commanding stature, the thundering voice, the abusive, insolent, cynical, gay, and sublime eloquence of Kléber, that military Mirabeau. Desaix, the countenance of a just man, or Kléber, the face of the lion! General Oudinot, little, awkward, embarrassed, with an indecisive and dull gaze, red cheeks, low forehead, with grizzled and lank hair, polite tone of voice, a humble smile, without oratory, without gesture, without power, brave before the enemy, timid before the first comer, having assuredly the bearing of a soldier, but having also the bearing of a priest; he caused the mind to hesitate between the sword and the taper; he had in his eyes a sort of "Amen!"

He had the best intentions in the world, but what could he do? Alone, without prestige, without true glory, without personal authority, and dragging Rome after him! He felt all this himself, and he was as it were paralyzed by it. As soon as they had appointed him he got upon a chair and thanked the Assembly, doubtless with a firm heart, but with hesitating speech. When the little fair-haired officer dared to look him in the face and insult him, he, holding the sword of the people, he, General of the sovereign Assembly, he only knew how to stammer out such wretched phrases as these, "I have just declared to you that we are unable, 'unless compelled and constrained,' to obey the order which prohibits us from remaining assembled together." He spoke of obeying, he who ought to command. They had girded him with his scarf, and it seemed to make him uncomfortable. He inclined his head alternately first to one shoulder and then to the other; he held his hat and cane in his hand, he had a benevolent aspect. A Legitimist member muttered in a low voice to his neighbor, "One might imagine he was a bailiff speechifying at a wedding." And his neighbor, a Legitimist also, replied, "He reminds me of the Duc d'Angoulême."

What a contrast to Tamisier! Tamisier, frank, earnest confident, although a mere Captain of Artillery, had the bearing of a General. Had Tamisier, with his grave and gentle countenance, high intelligence, and dauntless heart, a species of soldier-philosopher, been better known, he could have rendered decisive services. No one can tell what would have happened if Providence had given the soul of Tamisier to Oudinot, or the epaulets of Oudinot to Tamisier.

In this bloody enterprise of December we failed to find a General's uniform becomingly worn. A book might be written on the part which gold lace plays in the destiny of nations.

Tamisier, appointed Chief of the Staff some instants before the invasion of the hall, placed himself at the disposal of the Assembly. He was standing on a table. He spoke with a resonant and hearty voice. The most downcast became reassured by this modest, honest, devoted attitude. Suddenly he drew himself up, and looking all that Royalist majority in the face, exclaimed, "Yes, I accept the charge you offer me. I accept the charge of defending the Republic! Nothing but the Republic! Do you perfectly understand?"

A unanimous shout answered him. "Long live the Republic!"

"Ah!" said Beslay, "the voice comes back to you as on the Fourth of May."

"Long live the Republic! Nothing but the Republic!" repeated the men of the Right, Oudinot louder than the others. All arms were stretched towards Tamisier, every hand pressed his. Oh Danger! irresistible converter! In his last hour the Atheist invokes God, and the Royalist the Republic. They cling to that which they have repudiated.

The official historians of the *coup d'état* have stated that at the beginning of the sitting two Representatives had been sent by the Assembly to the Ministry of the Interior to "negotiate." What is certain is that these two Representatives had no authority. They presented themselves, not on behalf of the Assembly, but in their own name. They offered themselves as intermediaries to procure a peaceable termination of the catastrophe which had begun. With an honesty which bordered on simplicity they summoned Morny to yield himself a prisoner, and to return within the law, declaring that in case of refusal the Assembly would do its duty, and call the people to the defence of the Constitution and of the Republic. Marny answered them with a smile, accompanied by these plain words, "If you appeal to arms, and if I find any Representatives on the barricades, I will have them all shot to the last man."

The meeting in the Tenth Arrondissement yielded to force. President Vitet insisted that they should forcibly arrest him. A police agent who seized him turned pale and trembled. In certain circumstances, to lay violent hands upon a man is to lay them upon Right, and those who dare to do so are made to tremble by outraged Law. The exodus from the Mairie was long and beset with obstructions. Half-an-hour elapsed while the soldiers were forming a line, and while the Commissaries of Police, all the time appearing solely occupied with the care of driving back the crowd in the street, sent for orders to the Ministry of the Interior. During that time some of the Representatives, seated round a table in the great Hall, wrote to their families, to their wives, to their friends. They snatched up the last leaves of paper; the pens failed; M. de Luynes wrote to his wife a letter in pencil. There were no wafers; they were forced to send the letters unsealed; some soldiers offered to post them. M. Chambolle's son, who had accompanied his father thus far, undertook to take the letters addressed to Mesdames de Luynes, de Lasteyrie, and Duvergier de Hauranne. General Forey—the same who had refused a battalion to the President of the Constituent Assembly, Marrast, who had promoted him from a colonel to a general—General Forey, in the centre of the courtyard of the Mairie, his face inflamed, half drunk, coming out, they said, from breakfast at the Elysée, superintended the outrage. A member, whose name we regret we do not know, dipped his boot into the gutter and wiped it along the gold stripe of the regimental trousers of General Forey. Representative Lherbette came up to General Forey, and said to him, "General, you are a coward." Then turning to his colleagues, he exclaimed, "Do you hear? I tell this general that he is a coward." General Forey did not stir. He kept the mud on his uniform and the epithet on his cheek.

The meeting did not call the people to arms. We have just explained that it was not strong enough to do so; nevertheless, at the last moment, a member of the Left, Latrade, made a fresh effort. He took M. Berryer aside, and said to him, "Our official measures of resistance have come to an end; let us not allow ourselves now to be arrested. Let us disperse throughout the streets crying, 'To arms!'" M. Berryer consulted a few seconds on the matter with the Vice-President, M. Benoist d'Azy, who refused.

The Deputy Mayor, hat in hand, reconducted the members of the Assembly as far as the gate of the Mairie. As soon as they appeared in the courtyard ready to go out between two lines of soldiers, the post of National Guards presented arms, acid shouted, "Long live the Assembly! Long live the Representatives of the People!" The National Guards were at once disarmed, almost forcibly, by the Chasseurs de Vincennes.

There was a wine-shop opposite the Mairie. As soon as the great folding gates of the Mairie opened, and the Assembly appeared in the street, led by General Forey on horseback, and having at its head the Vice-President Vitet, grasped by the necktie by a police agent, a few men in white blouses, gathered at the windows of this wine-shop, clapped their hands and shouted, "Well done! down with the 'twenty-five francs!'"[3]

They set forth.

The Chasseurs de Vincennes, who marched in a double line on each side of the prisoners, cast at them looks of hatred. General Oudinot said in a whisper, "These little infantry soldiers are terrible fellows. At the siege of Rome they flung themselves at the assault like madmen. These lads are very devils." The officers avoided the gaze of the Representatives. On leaving the Mairie, M. de Coislin passed

3. An allusion to the twenty-five francs a day officially payable to the members of the Assembly.

by an officer and exclaimed, "What a disgrace for the uniform!" the officer retaliated with angry words, and incensed M. de Coislin. Shortly afterwards, during the march, he came up to M. de Coislin and said to him, "Sir, I have reflected; it is I who am wrong."

They proceeded on the way slowly. At a few steps from the Mairie the precession met M. Chegaray. The Representatives called out to him, "Come!" He answered, while making an expressive gesture with his hands and his shoulders, "Oh! I dare say! As they have not arrested me. . ." and he feigned as though he would pass on. He was ashamed, however, and went with them. His name is found in the list of the roll-call at the barracks.

A little further on M. de Lespérut passed them. They cried out to him. "Lespérut! Lespérut!" "I am with you," answered he. The soldiers pushed him back. He seized the butt-ends of the muskets, and forced his way into the column.

In one of the streets through which they went a window was opened. Suddenly a woman appeared with a child; the child, recognizing its father amongst the prisoners, held out its arms and called to him, the mother wept in the background.

It was at first intended to take the Assembly in a body straight to Mazas, but this was counter-ordered by the Ministry of the Interior. It was feared that this long walk, in broad daylight, through populous and easily aroused streets, might prove dangerous; the D'Orsay barracks were close at hand. They selected these as a temporary prison.

One of the commanders insolently pointed out with his sword the arrested Representatives to the passers-by, and said in a fond voice, "These are the Whites, we have orders to spare them. Now it is the turn of the Red Representatives, let them look out for themselves!"

Wherever the procession passed, the populace shouted from the pavements, at the doors, at the windows, "Long live the National Assembly!" When they perceived a few Representatives of the Left sprinkled in the column they cried, "Vive la République!" "Vive la Constitution!" and "Vive la Loi!" The shops were not shut, and passers-by went to and fro. Some people said, "Wait until the evening; this is not the end of it."

A staff-officer on horseback, in full uniform, met the procession, recognized M. de Vatimesnil, and came up to greet him. In the Rue de Beaune, as they passed the house of the *Démocratic Pacifique* a group shouted, "Down with the Traitor of the Elysée!"

On the Quai d'Orsay, the shouting was redoubled. There was a great crowd there. On either side of the quay a file of soldiers of the Line, elbow to elbow, kept back the spectators. In the middle of the space left vacant, the members of the Assembly slowly advanced between a double file of soldiers, the one stationary, which threatened the people, the other on the march, which threatened tire Representatives.

Serious reflections arise in the presence of all the details of the great crime which this book is designed to relate. Every honest man who sets himself face to face with the *coup d'état* of Louis Bonaparte hears nothing but a tumult of indignant thoughts in his conscience. Whoever reads our work to the end will assuredly not credit us with the intention of extenuating this monstrous deed. Nevertheless, as the deep logic of actions ought always to be italicized by the historian, it is necessary here to call to mind and to repeat, even to satiety, that apart from the members of the Left, of whom a very small number were present, and whom we have mentioned by name, the three hundred Representatives who thus defiled before the eyes of the crowd, constituted the old Royalists and reactionary majority of the Assembly. If it were possible to forget, that—whatever were their errors, whatever were their faults, and, we venture to add, whatever were their illusions—these persons thus treated were the Representatives of the leading civilized nation, were sovereign Legislators, senators of the people, inviolable Deputies, and sacred by the great law of Democracy, and that in the same manner as each man bears in himself something of the mind of God, so each of these nominees of universal suffrage bore something of the soul of France; if it were possible to forget this for a moment, it assuredly would be a spectacle perhaps more laughable than sad, and certainly more philosophical than lamentable to see, on this December morning, after so many laws of repression, after so many exceptional measures, after so many votes of censure and of the state of siege, after so many refusals of amnesty, after so many affronts to equity, to justice, to the human conscience, to the public good faith, to right, after so many favors to the police, after so many smiles bestowed on absolution, the entire Party of Order arrested in a body and taken to prison by the *sergents de ville*!

One day, or rather, one night, the moment having come to save society, the *coup d'état* abruptly seizes the Demagogues, and finds that it holds by the collar, Whom? the Royalists.

They arrived at the barracks, formerly the barracks of the Royal Guard, and on the pediment of which is a carved escutcheon, whereon are still visible the traces of the three *fleurs de lis* effaced in 1830. They halted. The door was opened. "Why!" said M. de Broglie, "here we are."

At that moment a great placard posted on the barrack wall by the side of the door bore in big letters—

"REVISION OF THE CONSTITUTION."

It was the advertisement of a pamphlet, published two or three days previous to the *coup d'état*, without any author's name, demanding the Empire, and was attributed to the President of the Republic.

The Representatives entered and the doors were closed upon them. The shouts ceased; the crowd, which occasionally has its meditative moments, remained for sometime on the quay, dumb, motionless, gazing alternately at the closed gate of the Barracks, and at the silent front of the Palace of the Assembly, dimly visible in the misty December twilight, two hundred paces distant.

The two Commissaries of Police went to report their "success" to M. de Morny. M. de Morny said, "Now the struggle has begun. Excellent! These are the last Representatives who will be made prisoners."

XIII

Louis Bonaparte's Side-Face

The minds of all these men, we repeat, were very differently affected. The extreme Legitimist party, which represents the White of the flag, was not, it must be said, highly exasperated at the *coup d'état*. Upon many faces might be read the saying of M. de Falloux: "I am so satisfied that I have considerable difficulty in affecting to be only resigned." The ingenuous spirits cast down their eyes—that is becoming to purity; more daring spirits raised their heads. They felt an impartial indignation which permitted a little admiration. How cleverly these generals have been ensnared! The Country assassinated,— it is a horrible crime; but they were enraptured at the jugglery blended with the parricide. One of the leaders said, with a sigh of envy and regret, "We do not possess a man of such talent." Another muttered, "It is Order." And he added, "Alas!" Another exclaimed, "It is a frightful crime, but well carried out." Some wavered, attracted on one side by the lawful power which rested in the Assembly, and on the other by the abomination which was in Bonaparte; honest souls poised between duty and infamy. There was a M. Thomines Desmazures who went as far as the door of the Great Hall of the Mairie, halted, looked inside, looked outside, and did not enter. It would be unjust not to record that others amongst the pure Royalists, and above all M. de Vatimesnil, had the sincere intonation and the upright wrath of justice.

Be it as it may, the Legitimist party, taken as a whole, entertained no horror of the *coup d'état*. It feared nothing. In truth, should the Royalists fear Louis Bonaparte? Why?

Indifference does not inspire fear. Louis Bonaparte was indifferent. He only recognized one thing, his object. To break through the road in order to reach it, that was quite plain; the rest might be left alone. There lay the whole of his policy, to crush the Republicans, to disdain the Royalists.

Louis Bonaparte had no passion. He who writes these lines, talking one day about Louis Bonaparte with the ex-king of Westphalia, remarked, "In him the Dutchman tones down the Corsican."—"If there be any Corsican," answered Jérome.

Louis Bonaparte has never been other than a man who has lain wait for fortune, a spy trying to dupe God. He had that livid dreaminess of the gambler who cheats. Cheating admits audacity, but excludes anger. In his prison at Ham he only read one book, "The Prince." He belonged to no family, as he could hesitate between Bonaparte and Verhuell; he had no country, as he could hesitate between France and Holland.

This Napoleon had taken St. Helena in good part. He admired England. Resentment! To what purpose? For him on earth there only existed his interests. He pardoned, because he speculated; he forgot everything, because he calculated upon everything. What did his uncle matter to him? He did not serve him; he made use of him. He rested his shabby enterprise upon Austerlitz. He stuffed the eagle.

Malice is an unproductive outlay. Louis Bonaparte only possessed as much memory as is useful. Hudson Lowe did not prevent him from smiling upon Englishmen; the Marquis of Montchenu did not prevent him from smiling upon the Royalists.

He was a man of earnest politics, of good company, wrapped in his own scheming, not impulsive, doing nothing beyond that which he intended, without abruptness, without hard words, discreet, accurate, learned, talking smoothly of a necessary massacre, a slaughterer, because it served his purpose.

All this, we repeat, without passion, and without anger. Louis Bonaparte was one of those men who had been influenced by the profound iciness of Machiavelli.

It was through being a man of that nature that he succeeded in submerging the name of Napoleon by superadding December upon Brumaire.

XIV

The D'Orsay Barracks

I t was half-past three.

The arrested Representatives entered into the courtyard of the barracks, a huge parallelogram closed in and commanded by high walls. These walls are pierced by three tiers of windows, and posses that dismal appearance which distinguishes barracks, schools, and prisons.

This courtyard is entered by an arched portal which extends through all the breadth of the front of the main building. This archway, under which the guard-house has been made, is close on the side of the quay by large solid folding doors, and on one side of the courtyard by an iron grated gateway. They closed the door and the grated gateway upon the Representatives. They "set them at liberty" in the bolted and guarded courtyard.

"Let them stroll about," said an officer.

The air was cold, the sky was gray. Some soldiers, in their shirt-sleeves and wearing foraging caps, busy with fatigue duty, went hither and thither amongst the prisoners.

First M. Grimault and then M. Antony Thouret instituted a roll-call. The Representatives made a ring around them. Lherbette said laughingly, "This just suits the barracks. We look like sergeant-majors who have come to report." They called over the seven hundred and fifty names of the Representatives. To each name they answered "Absent" or "Present," and the secretary jotted down with a pencil those who were present. When the name of Morny was reached, someone cried out, "At Clichy!" At the name of Persigny, the same voice exclaimed, "At Poissy!" The inventor of these two jokes, which by the way are very poor, has since allied himself to the Second of December, to Morny and Persigny; he has covered his cowardice with the embroidery of a senator.

The roll-call verified the presence of two hundred and twenty Representatives, whose names were as follows:—

Le Duc de Luynes, d'Andigné de la Chasse, Antony Thouret, Arène, Audren de Kerdrel (Ille-et-Vilaine), Audren de Kerdrel (Morbihan), de Balzac, Barchou de Penhoen, Barillon, O. Barrot, Barthélemy Saint-Hilaire, Quentin Bauchard, G. deBeaumont, Béchard, Behaghel, de

Belèvze, Benoist-d'Azy, de Benardy, Berryer, de Berset, Basse, Betting de Lancastel, Blavoyer, Bocher, Boissié, de Botmillan, Bouvatier, le Duc de Broglie, de la Broise, de Bryas, Buffet, Caillet du Tertre, Callet, Camus de la Guibourgère, Canet, de Castillon, de Cazalis, Admiral Cécile, Chambolle, Chamiot, Champannet, Chaper, Chapot, de Charencey, Chasseigne, Chauvin, Chazant, de Chazelles, Chegaray, Comte de Coislin, Colfavru, Colas de la Motte, Coquerel, de Corcelles, Cordier, Corne, Creton, Daguilhon, Pujol, Dahirel, Vicomte Dambray, Marquis de Dampierre, de Brotonne, de Fontaine, de Fontenay, Vicomte de Sèze, Desmars, de la Devansaye, Didier, Dieuleveult, Druet-Desvaux, A. Dubois, Dufaure, Dufougerais, Dufour, Dufournel, Marc Dufraisse, P. Duprat, Duvergier de Hauranne, Étienne, Vicomte de Falloux, de Faultrier, Faure (Rhône), Favreau, Ferre, des Ferrès, Vicomte de Flavigny, de Foblant, Frichon, Gain, Gasselin, Germonière, de Gicquiau, de Goulard, de Gouyon, de Grandville, de Grasset, Grelier-Dufougerais, Grévy, Grillon, Grimault, Gros, Guislier de la Tousche, Harscouët de Saint-Georges, Marquis d'Havrincourt, Hennequin, d'Hespel, Houel, Hovyn-Tranchère, Huot, Joret, Jouannet, de Kéranflech, de Kératry, de Kéridec, de Kermazec, de Kersauron Penendreff, Lèo de Laborde, Laboulie, Lacave, Oscar Lafayette, Lafosse, Lagarde, Lagrenée Laimé, Lainé, Comte Lanjuinais, Larabit, de Larcy, J. de Lasteyrie, Latrade, Laureau, Laurenceau, General Marquis de Lauriston, de Laussat, Lefebvre de Grosriez, Legrand, Legros-Desvaux, Lemaire, Emile Leroux, Lespérut, de l'Espinoy, Lherbette, de Linsaval, de Luppé, Maréchal, Martin de Villers, Maze-Saunay, Mèze, Arnauld de Melun, Anatole de Melun, Merentié, Michaud, Mispoulet, Monet, Duc de Montebello, de Montigny, Moulin, Murat-Sistrière, Alfred Nettement, d'Olivier, General Oudinot, Duc de Reggio, Paillat, Duparc, Passy, Emile Péan, Pécoul, Casimir Perier, Pidoux, Pigeon, de Piogé, Piscatory, Proa, Prudhomme, Querhoent, Randoing, Raudot, Raulin, de Ravinel, de Rémusat, Renaud, Rezal, Comte de Rességuier, Henri de Riancey, Rigal, de la Rochette, Rodat, de Roquefeuille des Rotours de Chaulieu, Rouget-Lafosse, Rouillé, Roux-Carbonel, Saint-Beuve, de Saint-Germain, General Comte de Saint-Priest, Salmon (Meuse), Marquis Sauvaire-Barthélemy, de Serré, Comte de Sesmaisons, Simonot, de Staplande, de Surville, Marquis de Talhouet, Talon, Tamisier, Thuriot de la Rosière, de Tinguy, Comte de Tocqueville, de la Tourette, Comte de Tréveneue, Mortimer-Ternaux, de Vatimesnil, Baron de Vandoeuvre, Vernhette (Hérault), Vernhette (Aveyron), Vézin, Vitet, Comte de Vogué.

After this list of names may be read as follows in the shorthand report:—

"The roll-call having been completed, General Oudinot asked the Representatives who were scattered about in the courtyard to come round him, and made the following announcement to them,—

"'The Captain-Adjutant-Major, who has remained here to command the barracks, has just received an order to have rooms prepared for us, where we are to withdraw, as we are considered to be in custody. (Hear! hear!) Do you wish me to bring the Adjutant-Major here! (No, no; it is useless.) I will tell him that he had better execute his orders.' (Yes, yes, that is right.)"

The Representatives remained "penned" and "strolling" about in this yard for two long hours. They walked about arm in arm. They walked quickly, so as to warm themselves. The men of the Right said to the men of the Left, "Ah! if you had only voted the proposals of the Questors!" They also exclaimed: "Well, how about the *invisible sentry*!"[1] And they laughed. Then Marc Dufraisse answered, "Deputies of the People! deliberate in peace!" It was then the turn of the Left to laugh. Nevertheless, there was no bitterness. The cordiality of a common misfortune reigned amongst them.

They questioned his ex-ministers about Louis Bonaparte. They asked Admiral Cécile, "Now, really, what does this mean?" The Admiral answered by this definition: "It is a small matter." M. Vézin added, "He wishes History to call him 'Sire.'" "Poor Sire, then," said M. de Camas de la Guibourgère. M. Odilon Barrot exclaimed, "What a fatality, that we should have been condemned to employ this man!"

This said, these heights attained, political philosophy was exhausted, and they ceased talking.

On the right, by the side of the door, there was a canteen elevated a few steps above the courtyard. "Let us promote this canteen to the dignity of a refreshment room," said the ex-ambassador to China, M. de Lagrenée. They entered, some went up to the stove, others asked for a basin of soup. MM. Favreau, Piscatory, Larabit, and Vatimesnil took refuge in a corner. In the opposite corner drunken soldiers chatted with the maids of the barracks. M. de Kératry, bent with his eighty

---

1. Michel de Bourges had thus characterized Louis Bonaparte as the guardian of the Republic against the Monarchical parties.

years, was seated near the stove on an old worm-eaten chair; the chair tottered; the old man shivered.

Towards four o'clock a regiment of Chasseurs de Vincennes arrived in the courtyard with their platters, and began to eat, singing, with loud bursts of merriment. M. de Broglie looked at them and said to M. Piscatory, "It is a strange spectacle to see the porringers of the Janissaries vanished from Constantinople reappearing at Paris!"

Almost at the same moment a staff officer informed the Representatives on behalf of General Forey that the apartments assigned to them were ready, and requested them to follow him. They were taken into the eastern building, which is the wing of the barracks farthest from the Palace of the Council of State; they were conducted to the third floor. They expected chambers and beds. They found long rooms, vast garrets with filthy walls and low ceilings, furnished with wooden tables and benches. These were the "apartments." These garrets, which adjoin each other, all open on the same corridor, a narrow passage, which runs the length of the main building. In one of these rooms they saw, thrown into a corner, side-drums, a big drum, and various instruments of military music. The Representatives scattered themselves about in these rooms. M. de Tocqueville, who was ill, threw his overcoat on the floor in the recess of a window, and lay down. He remained thus stretched upon the ground for several hours.

These rooms were warmed very badly by cast-iron stoves, shaped like hives. A Representative wishing to poke the fire, upset one, and nearly set fire to the wooden flooring.

The last of these rooms looked out on the quay. Antony Thouret opened a window and leaned out. Several Representatives joined him. The soldiers who were bivouacking below on the pavement, caught sight of them and began to shout, "Ah! there they are, those rascals at 'twenty-five francs a day,' who wish to cut down our pay!" In fact, on the preceding evening, the police had spread this calumny through the barracks that a proposition had been placed on the Tribune to lessen the pay of the troops. They had even gone so far as to name the author of this proposition. Antony Thouret attempted to undeceive the soldiers. An officer cried out to him, "It is one of your party who made the proposal. It is Lamennais!"

In about an hour and a half there were ushered into these rooms MM. Vallette, Bixio, and Victor Lefranc, who had come to join their colleagues and constitute themselves prisoners.

Night came. They were hungry. Several had not eaten since the morning. M. Howyn de Tranchère, a man of considerable kindness and devotion, who had acted as porter at the Mairie, acted as forager at the barracks. He collected five francs from each Representative, and they sent and ordered a dinner for two hundred and twenty from the Café d'Orsay, at the corner of the Quay, and the Rue du Bac. They dined badly, but merrily. Cookshop mutton, bad wine, and cheese. There was no bread. They ate as they best could, one standing, another on a chair, one at a table, another astride on his bench, with his plate before him, "as at a ball-room supper," a dandy of the Right said laughingly, Thuriot de la Rosière, son of the regicide Thuriot. M. de Rémusat buried his head in his hands. Emile Péan said to him, "We shall get over it." And Gustave de Beaumont cried out, addressing himself to the Republicans, "And your friends of the Left! Will they preserve their honor? Will there be an insurrection at least?" They passed each other the dishes and plates, the Right showing marked attention to the Left. "Here is the opportunity to bring about a fusion," said a young Legitimist. Troopers and canteen men waited upon them. Two or three tallow candles burnt and smoked on each table. There were few glasses. Right and Left drank from the same. "Equality, fraternity," exclaimed the Marquis Sauvaire-Barthélemy, of the Right. And Victor Hannequin answered him, "But not Liberty."

Colonel Feray, the son-in-law of Marshal Bugeaud, was in command at the barracks; he offered the use of his drawing-room to M. de Broglie and to M. Odilon Barrot, who accepted it. The barrack doors were opened to M. de Kératry, on account of his great age, to M. Dufaure, as his wife had just been confined, and to M. Etienne, on account of the wound which he had received that morning in the Rue de Bourgogne. At the same time there were added to the two hundred and twenty MM. Eugène Sue, Benoist (du Rhône), Fayolle, Chanay, Toupet des Vignes, Radoubt-Lafosse, Arbey, and Teillard-Latérisse, who up to that time had been detained in the new Palace of Foreign Affairs.

Towards eight o'clock in the evening, when dinner was over, the restrictions were a little relaxed, and the intermediate space between the door and the barred gate of the barracks began to be littered with carpet bags and articles of toilet sent by the families of the imprisoned Representatives.

The Representatives were summoned by their names. Each went down in turn, and briskly remounted with his cloak, his coverlet, or his foot-warmer. A few ladies succeeded in making their way to their husbands. M.M. Chambolle was able to press his son's hand through the bars.

Suddenly a voice called out, "Oho! We are going to spend the night here." Mattresses were brought in, which were thrown on the tables, on the floor, anywhere.

Fifty or sixty Representatives found resting-places on them. The greater number remained on their benches. Marc Dufraisse settled himself to pass the night on a footstool, leaning on a table. Happy was the man who had a chair.

Nevertheless, cordiality and gaiety did not cease to prevail. "Make room for the 'Burgraves!'" said smilingly a venerable veteran of the Right. A young Republican Representative rose, and offered him his mattress. They pressed on each offers of overcoats, cloaks, and coverlets.

"Reconciliation," said Chamiot, while offering the half of his mattress to the Duc de Luynes. The Duc de Luynes, who had 80,000 francs a year, smiled, and replied to Chamiot, "You are St. Martin, and I am the beggar."

M. Paillet, the well-known barrister, who belonged to the "Third Estate," used to say, "I passed the night on a Bonapartist straw mattress, wrapped in a burnouse of the Mountain, my feet in a Democratic and Socialist sheepskin, and my head in a Legitimist cotton nightcap." The Representatives, although prisoners in the barracks, could stroll about freely. They were allowed to go down into the courtyard. M. Cordier (of Calvados) came upstairs again, saying, "I have just spoken to the soldiers. They did not know that their generals had been arrested. They appeared surprised and discontented." This incident raised the prisoners' hopes.

Representative Michel Renaud of the Basses-Pyrénées, found several of his compatriots of the Basque country amongst the Chasseurs de Vincennes who occupied the courtyard. Some had voted for him, and reminded him of the fact. They added, "Ah! We would again vote for the 'Red' list." One of them, quite a young man, took him aside, and said to him. "Do you want any money, sir? I have a forty-sous piece in my pocket."

Towards ten o'clock in the evening a great hubbub arose in the courtyard. The doors and the barred gate turned noisily upon their hinges. Something entered which rumbled like thunder. They leaned out of window, and saw at the foot of the steps a sort of big, oblong chest, painted black, yellow, red, and green, on four wheels, drawn by post-horses, and surrounded by men in long overcoats, and with fierce-looking faces, holding torches. In the gloom, and with the help of imagination, this vehicle appeared completely black. A door could be seen, but no other opening. It resembled a great coffin on wheels. "What is that? Is it a hearse?" "No, it is a police-van." "And those people, are they undertakers?" "No, they are jailers." "And for whom has this come?"

"For you, gentlemen!" cried out a voice.

It was the voice of an officer; and the vehicle which had just entered was in truth a police-van.

At the same time a word of command was heard: "First squadron to horse." And five minutes afterwards the Lancers who were to escort the vehicle formed in line in the courtyard.

Then arose in the barracks the buzz of a hive of angry bees. The Representatives ran up and down the stairs, and went to look at the police-van close at hand. Some of them touched it, and could not believe their eyes. M. Piscatory met M. Chambolle, and cried out to him, "I am leaving in it!" M. Berryer met Eugène Sue, and they exchanged these words: "Where are you going?" "To Mount Valérien. And you?" "I do not know."

At half-past ten the roll-call of those who were to leave began. Police agents stationed themselves at a table between two candles in a parlor at the foot of the stairs, and the Representatives were summoned two by two. The Representatives agreed not to answer to their names, and to reply to each name which should be called out, "He is not here." But those "Burgraves" who had accepted the hospitality of Colonel Feray considered such petty resistance unworthy of them, and answered to the calling out of their names. This drew the others after them. Everybody answered. Amongst the Legitimists some serio-comic scenes were enacted. They who alone were not threatened insisted on believing that they were in danger. They would not let one of their orators go. They embraced him, and held him back, almost with tears, crying out, "Do not go away! Do you know where they are taking you? Think of the trenches of Vincennes!"

The Representatives, having been summoned two by two, as we have just said, filed in the parlor before the police agents, and then they were ordered to get into the "robbers' box." The stowage was apparently made at haphazard and promiscuously; nevertheless, later, by the difference of the treatment accorded to the Representatives in the various prisons, it was apparent that this promiscuous loading had perhaps been somewhat prearranged. When the first vehicle was full, a second, of a similar construction drew up. The police agents, pencil and pocket-book in hand, noted down the contents of each vehicle. These men knew the Representatives. When Marc Dufraisse, called in his turn, entered the parlor, he was accompanied by Benoist (du Rhône). "Ah! here is Marc Dufraisse," said the attendant who held the pencil. When asked for his name, Benoist replied "Benoist." "Du Rhône," added the police agent; and he continued, "for there are also Benoist d'Azy and Benoist-Champy."

The loading of each vehicle occupied nearly half an hour. The successive arrivals had raised the number of imprisoned Representatives to two hundred and thirty-two Their embarkation, or, to use the expression of M. de Vatimesnil, their "barrelling up," which began a little after ten in the evening, was not finished until nearly seven o'clock in the morning. When there were no more police-vans available omnibuses were brought in. These various vehicles were portioned off into three detachments, each escorted by Lancers. The first detachment left towards one o'clock in the morning, and was driven to Mont Valérien; the second towards five o'clock, and was driven to Mazas; the third towards half-past six, to Vincennes.

As this business occupied a long time, those who had not yet been called benefited by the mattresses and tried to sleep. Thus, from time to time, silence reigned in the upper rooms. In the midst of one of these pauses M. Bixio sat upright, and raising his voice, cried out, "Gentlemen, what do you think of 'passive obedience'?" An unanimous burst of laughter was the reply. Again, during one of these pauses another voice exclaimed,—

"Romieu will be a senator."

Emile Péan asked,—

"What will become of the Red Spectre?"

"He will enter the priesthood," answered Antony Thouret, "and will turn into the Black Spectre."

Other exclamations which the historians of the Second of December have spread abroad were not uttered. Thus, Marc Dufraisse never made the remark with which the men of Louis Bonaparte have wished to excuse their crimes: "If the President does not shoot all those among us who resist, he does not understand his business."

For the *coup d'état* such a remark might be convenient; but for History it is false.

The interior of the police-vans was lighted while the Representatives were entering. The air-holes of each compartment were not closed. In this manner Marc Dufraisse through the aperture could see M. du Rémusat in the opposite cell to his own. M. du Rémusat had entered the van coupled with M. Duvergier de Hauranne.

"Upon my word, Monsieur Marc Dufraisse," exclaimed Duvergier de Hauranne when they jostled each other in the gangway of the vehicle, "upon my word, if anyone had said to me, 'You will go to Marzas in a police-van,' I should have said, 'It is improbable;' but if they had added, 'You will go with Marc Dufraisse,' I should have said, 'It is impossible!'"

As soon as the vehicle was full, five or six policemen entered and stood in the gangway. The door was shut, the steps were thrown up, and they drove off.

When all the police-vans had been filled, there were still some Representatives left. As we have said, omnibuses were brought into requisition. Into these Representatives were thrust, one upon the other, rudely, without deference for either age or name. Colonel Feray, on horseback, superintended and directed operations. As he mounted the steps of the last vehicle but one, the Duc de Montebello cried out to him, "Today is the anniversary of the battle of Austerlitz, and the son-in-law of Marshal Bugeaud compels the son of Marshal Lannes to enter a convict's van."

When the last omnibus was reached, there were only seventeen places for eighteen Representatives. The most active mounted first. Antony Thouret, who himself alone equalled the whole of the Right, for he had as much mind as Thiers and as much stomach as Murat; Antony Thouret, corpulent and lethargic, was the last. When he appeared on the threshold of the omnibus in all his hugeness, a cry of alarm arose;— Where was he going to sit?

Antony Thouret, noticing Berryer at the bottom of the omnibus, went straight up to him, sat down on his knees, and quietly said to him, "You wanted 'compression,' Monsieur Berryer. Now you have it."

XV

MAZAS

The police-vans, escorted as far as Mazas by Lancers, found another squadron of Lancers ready to receive them at Mazas. The Representatives descended from the vehicle one by one. The officer commanding the Lancers stood by the door, and watched them pass with a dull curiosity.

Mazas, which had taken the place of the prison of La Force, now pulled down, is a lofty reddish building, close to the terminus of the Lyons Railway, and stands on the waste land of the Faubourg St. Antoine. From a distance the building appears as though built of bricks, but on closer examination it is seen to be constructed of flints set in cement. Six large detached buildings, three stories high, all radiating from a rotunda which serves as the common centre, and touching each other at the starting-point, separated by courtyards which grow broader in proportion as the buildings spread out, pierced with a thousand little dormer windows which give light to the cells, surrounded by a high wall, and presenting from a bird's-eye point of view the drape of a fan— such is Mazas. From the rotunda which forms the centre, springs a sort of minaret, which is the alarm-tower. The ground floor is a round room, which serves as the registrar's office. On the first story is a chapel where a single priest says mass for all; and the observatory, where a single attendant keeps watch over all the doors of all the galleries at the same time. Each building is termed a "division." The courtyards are intersected by high walls into a multitude of little oblong walks.

As each Representative descended from the vehicle he was conducted into the rotunda where the registry office was situated. There his name was taken down, and in exchange for his name he was assigned a number. Whether the prisoner be a thief or a legislator, such is always the rule in this prison; the *coup d'état* reduced all to a footing of equality. As soon as a Representative was registered and numbered, he was ordered to "file off." They said to him, "Go upstairs," or "Go on"; and they announced him at the end of the corridor to which he was allotted by calling out, "Receive number So-and-So." The jailer in that particular corridor answered, "Send him on." The prisoner mounted alone, went straight on, and on his arrival found the jailer standing near an open door. The jailer said, "Here it is, sir." The prisoner entered, the jailer shut the door, and they passed on to another.

The *coup d'état* acted in a very different manner towards the various Representatives. Those whom it desired to conciliate, the men of the Bight, were placed in Vincennes; those whom it detested, the men of the Left, were placed in Mazas. Those at Vincennes had the quarters of M. Montpensier, which were expressly reopened for them; an excellent dinner, eaten in company; wax candles, fire, and the smiles and bows of the governor, General Courtigis.

This is how it treated those at Mazas.

A police-van deposited them at the prison. They were transferred from one box to another. At Mazas a clerk registered them, weighed them, measured them, and entered them into the jail book as convicts. Having passed through the office, each of them was conducted along a gallery shrouded in darkness, through a long damp vault to a narrow door which was suddenly opened. This reached, a jailer pushed the Representative in by the shoulders, and the door was shut.

The Representative, thus immured, found himself in a little, long, narrow, dark room. It is this which the prudent language of modern legislation terms a "cell." Here the full daylight of a December noon only produced a dusky twilight. At one end there was a door, with a little grating; at the other, close to the ceiling, at a height of ten or twelve feet, there was a loophole with a fluted glass window. This window dimmed the eye, and prevented it from seeing the blue or gray of the sky, or from distinguishing the cloud from the sun's ray, and invested the wan daylight of winter with an indescribable uncertainty. It was even less than a dim light, it was a turbid light. The inventors of this fluted window succeeded in making the heavens squint.

After a few moments the prisoner began to distinguish objects confusedly, and this is what he found: White-washed walls here and there turned green by various exhalations; in one corner a round hole guarded by iron bars, and exhaling a disgusting smell; in another corner a slab turning upon a hinge like the bracket seat of a *fiacre*, and thus capable of being used as a table; no bed; a straw-bottomed chair; under foot a brick floor. Gloom was the first impression; cold was the second. There, then, the prisoner found himself, alone, chilled, in this semi-darkness, being able to walk up and down the space of eight square feet like a caged wolf, or to remain seated on his chair like an idiot at Bicêtre.

In this situation an ex-Republican of the Eve, who had become a member of the majority, and on occasions sided somewhat with the Bonapartists, M. Emile Leroux, who had, moreover, been thrown into Mazas by mistake, having doubtless been taken for someother Leroux, began to weep with rage. Three, four, five hours thus passed away. In the meanwhile they had not eaten since the morning; some of them, in the excitement caused by the *coup d'état* had not even breakfasted. Hunger came upon them. Were they to be forgotten there? No; a bell rang in the prison, the grating of the door opened, and an arm held out to the prisoner a pewter porringer and a piece of bread.

The prisoner greedily seized the bread and the porringer. The bread was black and sticky; the porringer contained a sort of thick water, warm and reddish. Nothing can be compared to the smell of this "soup." As for the bread, it only smelt of mouldiness.

However great their hunger, most of the prisoners during the first moment threw down their bread on the floor, and emptied the porringer down the hole with the iron bars.

Nevertheless the stomach craved, the hours passed by, they picked up the bread, and ended by eating it. One prisoner went so far as to pick up the porringer and to attempt to wipe out the bottom with his bread, which he afterwards devoured. Subsequently, this prisoner, a Representative set at liberty in exile, described to me this dietary, and said to me, "A hungry stomach has no nose."

Meanwhile there was absolute solitude and profound silence. However, in the course of a few hours, M. Emile Leroux—he himself has told the fact to M. Versigny—heard on the other side of the wall on his right a sort of curious knocking, spaced out and intermittent at irregular intervals. He listened, and almost at the same moment on the other side of the wall to his left a similar rapping responded. M. Emile Leroux, enraptured—what a pleasure it was to hear a noise of some kind!—thought of his colleagues, prisoners like himself, and cried out in a tremendous voice, "Oh, oh! you are there also, you fellows!" He had scarcely uttered this sentence when the door of his cell was opened with a creaking of hinges and bolts; a man—the jailer—appeared in a great rage, and said to him,—

"Hold your tongue!"

The Representative of the People, somewhat bewildered, asked for an explanation.

"Hold your tongue," replied the jailer, "or I will pitch you into a dungeon."

This jailer spoke to the prisoner as the *coup d'état* spoke to the nation.

M. Emile Leroux, with his persistent parliamentary habits, nevertheless attempted to insist.

"What!" said he, "can I not answer the signals which two of my colleagues are making to me?"

"Two of your colleagues, indeed," answered the jailer, "they are two thieves." And he shut the door, shouting with laughter.

They were, in fact, two thieves, between whom M. Emile Leroux was, not crucified, but locked up.

The Mazas prison is so ingeniously built that the least word can be heard from one cell to another. Consequently there is no isolation, notwithstanding the cellular system. Thence this rigorous silence imposed by the perfect and cruel logic of the rules. What do the thieves do? They have invented a telegraphic system of raps, and the rules gain nothing by their stringency. M. Emile Leroux had simply interrupted a conversation which had been begun.

"Don't interfere with our friendly patter," cried out his thief neighbor, who for this exclamation was thrown into the dungeon.

Such was the life of the Representatives at Mazas. Moreover, as they were in secret confinement, not a book, not a sheet of paper, not a pen, not even an hour's exercise in the courtyard was allowed to them.

The thieves also go to Mazas, as we have seen.

But those who know a trade are permitted to work; those who know how to read are supplied with books; those who know how to write are granted a desk and paper; all are permitted the hour's exercise required by the laws of health and authorized by the rules.

The Representatives were allowed nothing whatever. Isolation, close confinement, silence, darkness, cold, "the amount of *ennui* which engenders madness," as Linguet has said when speaking of the Bastille.

To remain seated on a chair all day long, with arms and legs crossed: such was the situation. But the bed! Could they lie down?

No.

There was no bed.

At eight o'clock in the evening the jailer came into the cell, and reached down, and removed something which was rolled up on a plank near the ceiling. This "something" was a hammock.

The hammock having been fixed, hooked up, and spread out, the jailer wished his prisoner "Goodnight."

There was a blanket on the hammock, sometimes a mattress some two inches thick. The prisoner, wrapt in this covering, tried to sleep, and only succeeded in shivering.

But on the morrow he could at least remain lying down all day in his hammock?

Not at all.

At seven o'clock in the morning the jailer came in, wished the Representative "Good-morning," made him get up, and rolled up the hammock on its shelf near the ceiling.

But in this case could not the prisoner take down the authorized hammock, unroll it, hook it up, and lie down again?

Yes, he could. But then there was the dungeon.

This was the routine. The hammock for the night, the chair for the day.

Let us be just, however. Some obtained beds, amongst others MM. Thiers and Roger (du Nord). M. Grévy did not have one.

Mazas is a model prison of progress; it is certain that Mazas is preferable to the *piombi* of Venice, and to the under-water dungeon of the Châtelet. Theoretical philanthropy has built Mazas. Nevertheless, as has been seen, Mazas leaves plenty to be desired. Let us acknowledge that from a certain point of view the temporary solitary confinement of the law-makers at Mazas does not displease us. There was perhaps something of Providence in the *coup d'état*. Providence, in placing the Legislators at Mazas, has performed an act of good education. Eat of your own cooking; it is not a bad thing that those who own prisons should try them.

XVI

THE EPISODE OF THE BOULEVARD ST. MARTIN

When Charamaule and I reached No. 70, Rue Blanche, a steep lonely street, a man in a sort of naval sub-officer's uniform, was walking up and down before the door. The portress, who recognized us, called our attention to him. "Nonsense," said Charamaule, "a man walking about in that manner, and dressed after that fashion, is assuredly not a police spy."

"My dear colleague," said I, "Bedeau has proved that the police are blockheads."

We went upstairs. The drawing-room and a little ante-chamber which led to it were full of Representatives, with whom were mingled a good many persons who did not belong to the Assembly. Some ex-members of the Constituent Assembly were there, amongst others, Bastide and several Democratic journalists. The *Nationale* was represented by Alexander Rey and Léopold Duras, the *Révolution* by Xavier Durrieu, Vasbenter, and Watripon, the *Avénement du Peuple* by H. Coste, nearly all the other editors of the *Avénement* being in prison. About sixty members of the Left were there, and among others Edgar Quinet, Schoelcher, Madier de Montjau, Carnot, Noël Parfait, Pierre Lefranc, Bancel, de Flotte, Bruckner, Chaix, Cassal, Esquiros, Durand-Savoyat, Yvan, Carlos Forel, Etchegoyen, Labrousse, Barthélemy (Eure-et-Loire), Huguenin, Aubrey (du Nord), Malardier, Victor Chauffour, Belin, Renaud, Bac, Versigny, Sain, Joigneaux, Brives, Guilgot, Pelletier, Doutre, Gindrier, Arnauld (de l'Ariége), Raymond (de l'Isère), Brillier, Maigne, Sartin, Raynaud, Léon Vidal, Lafon, Lamargue, Bourzat, and General Rey.

All were standing. They were talking without order. Léopold Duras had just described the investment of the Café Bonvalet. Jules Favre and Baudin, seated at a little table between the two windows, were writing. Baudin had a copy of the Constitution open before him, and was copying Article 68.

When we entered there was silence, and they asked us, "Well, what news?"

Charamaule told them what had just taken place on the Boulevard du Temple, and the advice which he had thought right to give me. They approved his action.

"What is to be done?" was asked on every side. I began to speak.

"Let us go straight to the fact and to the point," said I. "Louis Bonaparte is gaining ground, and we are losing ground, or rather, we should say, he has as yet everything, and we have as yet nothing. Charamaule and I have been obliged to separate ourselves from Colonel Forestier. I doubt if he will succeed. Louis Bonaparte is doing all he can to suppress us, we must no longer keep in the background. We must make our presence felt. We must fan this beginning of the flame of which we have seen the spark on the Boulevard du Temple. A proclamation must be made, no matter by whom it is printed, or how it is placarded, but it is absolutely necessary, and that immediately. Something brief, rapid, and energetic. No set phrases. Ten lines—an appeal to arms! We are the Law, and there are occasions when the Law should utter a war-cry. The Law, outlawing the traitor, is a great and terrible thing. Let us do it."

They interrupted me with "Yes, that is right, a proclamation!"

"Dictate! dictate!"

"Dictate," said Baudin to me, "I will write."

I dictated:—

"To the People.
    "Louis Napoléon Bonaparte is a traitor.
    "He has violated the Constitution.
    "He is forsworn.
    "He is an outlaw—"

They cried out to me on every side,—

"That is right! Outlaw him."

"Go on."

I resumed the dictation. Baudin wrote,—

"The Republican Representatives refer the People and the Army
    to Article 68—"

They interrupted me: "Quote it in full."

"No," said I, "it would be too long. Something is needed which can be placarded on a card, stuck with a wafer, and which can be read in a minute. I will quote Article 110. It is short and contains the appeal to arms."

I resumed,—

"The Republican Representatives refer the People and the Army to Article 68 and to Article 110, which runs thus—'The Constituent Assembly confides the existing Constitution and the Laws which it consecrates to the keeping and the patriotism of all Frenchmen.'

"The People henceforward and forever in possession of universal suffrages and who need no Prince for its restitution, will know how to chastise the rebel.

"Let the People do its duty. The Republican Representatives are marching at its head.

"Vive la République! To Arms!"

They applauded.

"Let us all sign," said Pelletier.

"Let us try to find a printing-office without delay," said Schoelcher, "and let the proclamation be posted up immediately."

"Before nightfall—the days are short," added Joigneaux.

"Immediately, immediately, several copies!" called out the Representatives.

Baudin, silent and rapid, had already made a second copy of the proclamation.

A young man, editor of the provincial Republican journal, came out of the crowd, and declared that, if they would give him a copy at once, before two hours should elapse the Proclamation should be posted at all the street corners in Paris.

I asked him,—

"What is your name?"

He answered me,—

"Millière."

Millière. It is in this manner that this name made its first appearance in the gloomy days of our History. I can still see that pale young man, that eye at the same time piercing and half closed, that gentle and forbidding profile. Assassination and the Pantheon awaited him. He was too obscure to enter into the Temple, he was sufficiently deserving to die on its threshold. Baudin showed him the copy which he had just made.

Millière went up to him.

"You do not know me," said he; "my name is Millière; but I know you, you are Baudin."

Baudin held out his hand to him.

I was present at the handshaking between these two spectres.

Xavier Durrieu, who was editor of the *Révolution* made the same offer as Millière.

A dozen Representatives took their pens and sat down, some around a table, others with a sheet of paper on their knees, and called out to me,—

"Dictate the Proclamation to us."

I had dictated to Baudin, "Louis Napoléon Bonaparte is a traitor." Jules Favre requested the erasure of the word Napoléon, that name of glory fatally powerful with the People and with the Army, and that there should be written, "Louis Bonaparte is a traitor."

"You are right," said I to him.

A discussion followed. Some wished to strike out the word "Prince." But the Assembly was impatient. "Quick! quick!" they cried out. "We are in December, the days are short," repeated Joigneaux.

Twelve copies were made at the same time in a few minutes. Schoelcher, Rey, Xavier Durrieu, and Millière each took one, and set out in search of a printing office.

As they went out a man whom I did not know, but who was greeted by several Representatives, entered and said, "Citizens, this house is marked. Troops are on the way to surround you. You have not a second to lose."

Numerous voices were raised,—

"Very well! Let them arrest us!"

"What does it matter to us?"

"Let them complete their crime."

"Colleagues," said I, "let us not allow ourselves to be arrested. After the struggle, as God pleases; but before the combat,—No! It is from us that the people are awaiting the initiative. If we are taken, all is at an end. Our duty is to bring on the battle, our right is to cross swords with the *coup d'état*. It must not be allowed to capture us, it must seek us and not find us. We must deceive the arm which it stretches out against us, we must remain concealed from Bonaparte, we must harass him, weary him, astonish him, exhaust him, disappear and reappear unceasingly, change our hiding-place, and always fight him, be always before him, and never beneath his hand. Let us not leave the field. We have not numbers, let us have daring."

They approved of this. "It is right," said they, "but where shall we go?"

Labrousse said,—

"Our former colleague of the Constituent Assembly, Beslay, offers us his house."

"Where does he live?"

"No. 33, Rue de la Cérisaie, in the Marais."

"Very well," answered I, "let us separate. We will meet again in two hours at Beslay's, No. 33, Rue de la Cérisaie."

All left; one after another, and in different directions. I begged Charamaule to go to my house and wait for me there, and I walked out with Noël Parfait and Lafon.

We reached the then still uninhabited district which skirts the ramparts. As we came to the corner of the Rue Pigalle, we saw at a hundred paces from us, in the deserted streets which cross it, soldiers gliding all along the houses, bending their steps towards the Rue Blanche.

At three o'clock the members of the Left rejoined each other in the Rue de la Cérisaie. But the alarm had been given, and the inhabitants of these lonely streets stationed themselves at the windows to see the Representatives pass. The place of meeting, situated and hemmed in at the bottom of a back yard, was badly chosen in the event of being surrounded: all these disadvantages were at once perceived, and the meeting only lasted a few seconds. It was presided over by Joly; Xavier Durrieu and Jules Gouache, who were editors of the *Révolution*, also took part, as well as several Italian exiles, amongst others Colonel Carini and Montanelli, ex-Minister of the Grand Duke of Tuscany. I liked Montanelli, a gentle and dauntless spirit.

Madier de Montjau brought news from the outskirts. Colonel Forestier, without losing and without taking away hope, told them of the obstacles which he had encountered in his attempts to call together the 6th Legion. He pressed me to sign his appointment as Colonel, as well as Michel de Bourges; but Michel de Bourges was absent, and besides, neither Michel de Bourges nor I had yet at drat time the authority from the Left. Nevertheless, under this reservation I signed his appointment. The perplexities were becoming more and more numerous. The Proclamation was not yet printed, and the evening was closing in. Schoelcher explained the difficulties: all the printing offices closed and guarded; an order placarded that whoever should print an appeal to arms world be immediately shot; the workmen terrified; no money. A hat was sent round, and each threw into it what money he had about him. They collected in this manner a few hundred francs.

Xavier Durrieu, whose fiery courage never flagged for a single moment, reiterated that he would undertake the printing, and promised that by eight o'clock that evening there should be 40,000 copies of the Proclamation. Time pressed. They separated, after fixing as a rendezvous the premises of the Society of Cabinet-makers in the Rue de Charonne, at eight o'clock in the evening, so as to allow time for the situation to reveal itself. As we went out and crossed the Rue Beautreillis I saw Pierre Leroux coming up to me. He had taken no part in our meetings. He said to me,—

"I believe this struggle to be useless. Although my point of view is different from yours, I am your friend. Beware. There is yet time to stop. You are entering into the catacombs. The catacombs are Death."

"They are also Life," answered I.

All the same, I thought with joy that my two sons were in prison, and that this gloomy duty of street fighting was imposed upon me alone.

There yet remained five hours until the time fixed for the rendezvous. I wished to go home, and once more embrace my wife and daughter before precipitating myself into that abyss of the "unknown" which was there, yawning and gloomy, and which several of us were about to enter, never to return.

Arnauld (de l'Ariége) gave me his arm. The two Italian exiles, Carini aril Montanelli, accompanied me.

Montanelli took my hands and said to me, "Right will conquer. You will conquer. Oh! that this time France may not be selfish as in 1848, and that she may deliver Italy." I answered him, "She will deliver Europe."

Those were our illusions at that moment, but this, however, does not prevent them from being our hopes today. Faith is thus constituted; shadows demonstrate to it the light.

There is a cabstand before the front gate of St. Paul. We went there. The Rue St. Antoine was alive with that indescribable uneasy swarming which precedes those strange battles of ideas against deeds which are called Revolutions. I seemed to catch, in this great working-class district, a glimpse of a gleam of light which, alas, died out speedily. The cabstand before St. Paul was deserted. The drivers had foreseen the possibility of barricades, and had fled.

Three miles separated Arnauld and myself from our houses. It was impossible to walk there through the middle of Paris, without being recognized at each step. Two passers-by extricated us from our difficulty. One of them said to the other, "The omnibuses are still running on the Boulevards."

We profited by this information, and went to look for a Bastille omnibus. All four of us got in.

I entertained at heart, I repeat, wrongly or rightly, a bitter reproach for the opportunity lost during the morning. I said to myself that on critical days such moments come, but do not return. There are two theories of Revolution: to arouse the people, or to let them come of themselves. The first theory was mine, but, through force of discipline, I had obeyed the second. I reproached myself with this. I said to myself, "The People offered themselves, and we did not accept them. It is for us now not to offer ourselves, but to do more, to give ourselves."

Meanwhile the omnibus had started. It was full. I had taken my place at the bottom on the left; Arnauld (de l'Ariége) sat next to me, Carini opposite, Montanelli next to Arnauld. We did not speak; Arnauld and myself silently exchanged that pressure of hands which is a means of exchanging thoughts.

As the omnibus proceeded towards the centre of Paris the crowd became denser on the Boulevard. As the omnibus entered into the cutting of the Porte St. Martin a regiment of heavy cavalry arrived in the opposite direction. In a few seconds this regiment passed by the side of us. They were cuirassiers. They filed by at a sharp trot and with drawn swords. The people leaned over from the height of the pavements to see them pass. Not a single cry. On the one side the people dejected, on the other the soldiers triumphant. All this stirred me.

Suddenly the regiment halted. I do not know what obstruction momentarily impeded its advance in this narrow cutting of the Boulevard in which we were hemmed in. By its halt it stopped the omnibus. There were the soldiers. We had them under our eyes, before us, at two paces distance, their horses touching the horses of our vehicle, these Frenchmen who had become Mamelukes, these citizen soldiers of the Great Republic transformed into supporters of the degraded Empire. From the place where I sat I almost touched them; I could no longer restrain myself.

I lowered the window of the omnibus. I put out my head, and, looking fixedly at the dense line of soldiers which faced me, I called out, "Down with Louis Bonaparte. Those who serve traitors are traitors!"

VICTOR HUGO

Those nearest to me turned their heads towards me and looked at me with a tipsy air; the others did not stir, and remained at "shoulder arms," the peaks of their helmets over their eyes, their eyes fixed upon the ears of their horses.

In great affairs there is the immobility of statues; in petty mean affairs there is the immobility of puppets.

At the shout which I raised Arnauld turned sharply round. He also had lowered his window, and he was leaning half out of the omnibus, with his arms extended towards the soldiers, and he shouted, "Down with the traitors!"

To see him thus with his dauntless gesture, his handsome head, pale and calm, his fervent expression, his beard and his long chestnut hair, one seemed to behold the radiant and fulminating face of an angry Christ.

The example was contagious and electrical.

"Down with the traitors!" shouted Carini and Montanelli.

"Down with the Dictator! Down with the traitors!" repeated a gallant young man with whom we were not acquainted, and who was sitting next to Carini.

With the exception of this young man, the whole omnibus seemed seized with terror!

"Hold your tongues!" exclaimed these poor frightened people; "you will cause us all to be massacred." One, still more terrified, lowered the window, and began to shout to the soldiers, "Long live Prince Napoléon! Long live the Emperor!"

There were five of us, and we overpowered this cry by our persistent protest, "Down with Louis Bonaparte! Down with the traitors!"

The soldiers listened in gloomy silence. A corporal turned with a threatening air towards us, and shook his sword. The crowd looked on in bewilderment.

What passed within me at that moment? I cannot tell! I was in a whirlwind. I had at the same time yielded to a calculation, finding the opportunity good, and to a burst of rage, finding the encounter insolent.

A woman cried out to us from the pavement, "You will get yourselves cut to pieces." I vaguely imagined that some collision was about to ensue, and that, either from the crowd or from the Army, the spark would fly out. I hoped for a sword-cut from the soldiers or a shout of anger from the people. In short I had obeyed rather an instinct than an idea.

But nothing came of it, neither the sword-cut nor the shout of anger. The soldiers did not bestir themselves and the people maintained silence. Was it too late? Was it too soon?

The mysterious man of the Elysée had not foreseen the event of an insult to his name being thrown in the very face of the soldiers. The soldiers had no orders. They received them that evening. This was seen on the morrow.

In another moment the regiment broke into a gallop, and the omnibus resumed its journey. As the cuirassiers filed past us Arnauld (de l'Ariége), still leaning out of the vehicle, continued to shout in their ears, for as I have just said, their horses touched us, "Down with the Dictator! Down with the traitors!"

We alighted in the Rue Lafitte. Carini, Montanelli, and Arnauld left me, and I went on alone towards the Rue de la Tour d'Auvergne. Night was coming on. As I turned the corner of the street a man passed close by me. By the light of a street lamp I recognized a workman at a neighboring tannery, and he said to me in a low tone, and quickly, "Do not return home. The police surround your house."

I went back again towards the Boulevard, through the streets laid out, but not then built, which make a Y under my windows behind my house. Not being able to embrace my wife and daughter, I thought over what I could do during the moments which remained to me. A remembrance came into my mind.

XVII

The Rebound of the 24th June, 1848, On the 2d December, 1851

On Sunday, 26th June, 1848, that four days' combat, that gigantic combat so formidable and so heroic on both sides, still continued, but the insurrection had been overcome nearly everywhere, and was restricted to the Faubourg St. Antoine. Four men who had been amongst the most dauntless defenders of the barricades of the Rue Pont-aux-Choux, of the Rue St. Claude, and of the Rue St. Louis in the Marais, escaped after the barricades had been taken, and found safe refuge in a house, No. 12, Rue St. Anastase. They were concealed in an attic. The National Guards and the Mobile Guards were hunting for them, in order to shoot them. I was told of this. I was one of the sixty Representatives sent by the Constituent Assembly into the middle of the conflict, charged with the task of everywhere preceding the attacking column, of carrying, even at the peril of their lives, words of peace to the barricades, to prevent the shedding of blood, and to stop the civil war. I went into the Rue St. Anastase, and I saved the lives of those four men.

Amongst those men there was a poor workman of the Rue de Charonne, whose wife was being confined at that very moment, and who was weeping. One could understand, when hearing his sobs and seeing his rags, how he had cleared with a single bound these three steps—poverty, despair, rebellion. Their chief was a young man, pale and fair, with high cheek bones, intelligent brow, and an earnest and resolute countenance. As soon as I set him free, and told him my name, he also wept. He said to me, "When I think that an hour ago I knew that you were facing us, and that I wished that the barrel of my gun had eyes to see and kill you!" He added, "In the times in which we live we do not know what may happen. If ever you need me, for whatever purpose, come." His name was Auguste, and he was a wine-seller in the Rue de la Roquette.

Since that time I had only seen him once, on the 26th August, 1819, on the day when I held the corner of Balzac's pall. The funeral possession was going to Père la Chaise. Auguste's shop was on the way. All the streets through which the procession passed were crowded. Auguste was at his door with his young wife and two or three workmen. As I passed he greeted me.

It was this remembrance which came back to my mind as I descended the lonely streets behind my house; in the presence of the 2d of December I thought of him. I thought that he might give me information about the Faubourg St. Antoine, and help us in rousing the people. This young man had at once given me the impression of a soldier and a leader. I remembered the words which he had spoken to me, and I considered it might be useful to see him. I began by going to find in the Rue St. Anastase the courageous woman who had hidden Auguste and his three companions, to whom she had several times since rendered assistance. I begged her to accompany me. She consented.

On the way I dined upon a cake of chocolate which Charamaule had given me.

The aspects of the boulevards, in coming down the Italiens towards the Marais, had impressed rue. The shops were open everywhere as usual. There was little military display. In the wealthy quarters there was much agitation and concentration of troops; but on advancing towards the working-class neighborhoods solitude reigned paramount. Before the Café Turc a regiment was drawn up. A band of young men in blouses passed before the regiment singing the "Marseillaise." I answered them by crying out "To Arms!" The regiment did not stir. The light shone upon the playbills on an adjacent wall; the theatres were open. I looked at the trees as I passed. They were playing *Hernani* at the Theatre des Italiens, with a new tenor named Guasco.

The Place de la Bastille was frequented, as usual, by goers and comers, the most peaceable folk in the world. A few workmen grouped round the July Column, and, chatting in a low voice, were scarcely noticeable. Through the windows of a wine shop could be seen two men who were disputing for and against the *coup d'état*. He who favored it wore a blouse, he who attacked it wore a cloth coat. A few steps further on a juggler had placed between four candles his X-shaped table, and was displaying his conjuring tricks in the midst of a crowd, who were evidently thinking only of the juggler. On looking towards the gloomy loneliness of the Quai Mazas several harnessed artillery batteries were dimly visible in the darkness. Some lighted torches here and there showed up the black outline of the cannons.

I had some trouble in finding Auguste's door in the Rue de la Roquette. Nearly all the shops were shut, thus making the street very dark. At length, through a glass shop-front I noticed a light which gleamed on a pewter counter. Beyond the counter, through a partition also of glass and ornamented with white curtains, another light, and the shadows of two or three men at table could be vaguely distinguished. This was the place.

I entered. The door on opening rang a bell. At the sound, the door of the glazed partition which separated the shop from the parlor opened, and Auguste appeared.

He knew me at once, and came up to me.

"Ah, Sir," said he, "it is you!"

"Do you know what is going on?" I asked him.

"Yes, sir."

This "Yes, sir," uttered with calmness, and even with a certain embarrassment, told me all. Where I expected an indignant outcry I found this peaceable answer. It seemed to me that I was speaking to the Faubourg St. Antoine itself. I understood that all was at an end in this district, and that we had nothing to expect from it. The people, this wonderful people, had resigned themselves. Nevertheless, I made an effort.

"Louis Bonaparte betrays the Republic," said I, without noticing that I raised my voice.

He touched my arm, and pointing with his finger to the shadows which were pictured on the glazed partition of the parlor, "Take care, sir; do not talk so loudly."

"What!" I exclaimed, "you have come to this—you dare not speak, you dare not utter the name of 'Bonaparte' aloud; you barely mumble a few words in a whisper here, in this street, in the Faubourg St. Antoine, where, from all the doors, from all the windows, from all the pavements, from all the very stones, ought to be heard the cry, 'To arms.'"

Auguste demonstrated to me what I already saw too clearly, and what Girard had shadowed forth in the morning—the moral situation of the Faubourg—that the people were "dazed"—that it seemed to all of them that universal suffrage was restored; that the downfall of the law of the 31st of May was a good thing.

Here I interrupted him.

"But this law of the 31st of May, it was Louis Bonaparte who instigated it, it was Rouher who made it, it was Baroche who proposed it, and the Bonapartists who voted it. You are dazzled by a thief who has taken your purse, and who restores it to you!"

"Not I," said Auguste, "but the others."

And he continued, "To tell the whole truth, people did not care much for the Constitution, they liked the Republic, but the Republic was maintained too much by force for their taste. In all this they could only see one thing clearly, the cannons ready to slaughter them—they remembered June, 1848—there were some poor people who had suffered greatly—Cavaignac had done much evil—women clung to the men's blouses to prevent them from going to the barricades— nevertheless, with all this, when seeing men like ourselves at their head, they would perhaps fight, but this hindered them, they did not know for what." He concluded by saying, "The upper part of the Faubourg is doing nothing, the lower end will do better. Round about here they will fight. The Rue de la Roquette is good, the Rue de Charonne is good; but on the side of Père la Chaise they ask, 'What good will that do us?' They only recognize the forty sous of their day's work. They will not bestir themselves; do not reckon upon the masons." He added, with a smile, "Here we do not say 'cold as a stone,' but 'cold as a mason'"—and he resumed, "As for me, if I am alive, it is to you that I owe my life. Dispose of me. I will lay down my life, and will do what you wish."

While he was speaking I saw the white curtain of the glazed partition behind him move a little. His young wife, uneasy, was peeping through at us.

"Ah! my God," said I to him, "what we want is not the life of one man but the efforts of all."

He was silent. I continued,—

"Listen to me, Auguste, you who are good and intelligent. So, then, the Faubourgs of Paris—which are heroes even when they err—the Faubourgs of Paris, for a misunderstanding, for a question of salary wrongly construed, for a bad definition of socialism, rose in June, 1848, against the Assembly elected by themselves, against universal suffrage, against their own vote; and yet they will not rise in December, 1851, for Right, for the Law, for the People, for Liberty, for the Republic. You say that there is perplexity, and that you do not understand; but, on the contrary, it was in June that all was obscure, and it is today that everything is clear!"

While I was saying these last words the door of the parlor was softly opened, and someone came in. It was a young man, fair as Auguste, in an overcoat, and wearing a workman's cap. I started. Auguste turned round and said to me, "You can trust him."

The young man took off his cap, came close up to me, carefully turning his back on the glazed partition, and said to me in a low voice, "I know you well. I was on the Boulevard du Temple today. We asked you what we were to do; you said, 'We must take up arms.' Well, here they are!"

He thrust his hands into the pockets of his overcoat and drew out two pistols.

Almost at the same moment the bell of the street door sounded. He hurriedly put his pistols back into his pockets. A man in a blouse came in, a workman of some fifty years. This man, without looking at anyone, without saying anything, threw down a piece of money on the counter. Auguste took a small glass and filled it with brandy, the man drank it off, put down the glass upon the counter and went away.

When the door was shut: "You see," said Auguste to me, "they drink, they eat, they sleep, they think of nothing. Such are they all!"

The other interrupted him impetuously: "One man is not the People!"

And turning towards me,—

"Citizen Victor Hugo, they will march forward. If all do not march, some will march. To tell the truth, it is perhaps not here that a beginning should be made, it is on the other side of the water."

And suddenly checking himself,—"After all, you probably do not know my name."

He took a little pocket-book from his pocket, tore out a piece of paper, wrote on it his name, and gave it to me. I regret having forgotten that name. He was a working engineer. In order not to compromise him, I burnt this paper with many others on the Saturday morning, when I was on the point of being arrested.

"It is true, sir," said Auguste, "you must not judge badly of the Faubourg. As my friend has said, it will perhaps not be the first to begin; but if there is a rising it will rise."

I exclaimed, "And who would you have erect if the Faubourg St. Antoine be prostrate! Who will be alive if the people be dead!"

The engineer went to the street door, made certain that it was well shut, then came back, and said,—

"There are many men ready and willing. It is the leaders who are wanting. Listen, Citizen Victor Hugo, I can say this to you, and," he added, lowering his voice, "I hope for a movement tonight."

"Where?"

"On the Faubourg St. Marceau."

"At what time?"

"At one o'clock."

"How do you know it?"

"Because I shall be there."

He continued: "Now, Citizen Victor Hugo, if a movement takes place tonight in the Faubourg St. Marceau, will you head it? Do you consent?"

"Yes."

"Have you your scarf of office?"

I half drew it out of my pocket. His eyes glistened with joy.

"Excellent," said he. "The Citizen has his pistols, the Representative his scarf. All are armed."

I questioned him. "Are you sure of your movement for tonight?"

He answered me, "We have prepared it, and we reckon to be there."

"In that case," said I, "as soon as the first barricade is constructed I will be behind it. Come and fetch me."

"Where?"

"Wherever I may be."

He assured me that if the movement should take place during the night he would know it at half-past ten that evening at the latest, and that I should be informed of it before eleven o'clock. We settled that in whatever place I might be at that hour I would send word to Auguste, who undertook to let him know.

The young woman continued to peep out at us. The conversation was growing prolonged, and might seem singular to the people in the parlor. "I am going," said I to Auguste.

I had opened the door, he took my hand, pressed it as a woman might have done, and said to me in a deeply-moved tone, "You are going: will you come back?"

"I do not know."

"It is true," said he. "No one knows what is going to happen. Well, you are perhaps going to be hunted and sought for as I have been. It will perhaps be your turn to be shot, and mine to save you. You know the mouse may sometimes prove useful to the lion. Monsieur Victor Hugo, if you need a refuge, this house is yours. Come here. You will find a bed where you can sleep, and a man who will lay down his life for you."

I thanked him by a hearty shake of the hand, and I left. Eight o'clock struck. I hastened towards the Rue de Charonne.

XVIII

THE REPRESENTATIVES HUNTED DOWN

At the corner of the Rue de Faubourg St. Antoine before the shop of the grocer Pepin, on the same spot where the immense barricade of June, 1848, was erected as high as the second story, the decrees of the morning had been placarded. Some men were inspecting them, although it was pitch dark, and they could not read them, and an old woman said, "The 'Twenty-five francs' are crushed—so much the better!"

A few steps further I heard my name pronounced. I turned round. It was Jules Favre, Bourzat, Lafon, Madier de Montjau, and Michel de Bourges, who were passing by. I took leave of the brave and devoted woman who had insisted upon accompanying me. A *fiacre* was passing. I put her in it, and then rejoined the five Representatives. They had come from the Rue de Charonne. They had found the premises of the Society of Cabinet Makers closed. "There was no one there," said Madier de Montjau. "These worthy people are beginning to get together a little capital, they do not wish to compromise it, they are afraid of us. They say, '*coups d'état* are nothing to us, we shall leave them alone!'"

"That does not surprise me," answered I, "a society is shopkeeper."

"Where are we going?" asked Jules Favre.

Lafon lived two steps from there, at No. 2, Quai Jemmapes. He offered us the use of his rooms. We accepted, and took the necessary measures to inform the members of the Left that we had gone there.

A few minutes afterwards we were installed in Lafon's rooms, on the fourth floor of an old and lofty house. This house had seen the taking of the Bastille.

This house was entered by a side-door opening from the Quai Jemmapes upon a narrow courtyard a few steps lower than the Quai itself. Bourzat remained at this door to warn us in case of any accident, and to point out the house to those Representatives who might come up.

In a few moments a large number of us had assembled, and we again met—all those of the morning, with a few added. Lafon gave up his drawing-room to us, the windows of which overlooked the back yard. We organized a sort of "bureau," and we took our places, Jules Favre,

Carnot, Michel, and myself, at a large table, lighted by two candles, and placed before the fire. The Representatives and the other people present sat around on chairs and sofas. A group stood before the door.

Michel de Bourges, on entering, exclaimed, "We have come to seek out the people of the Faubourg St. Antoine. Here we are. Here we must remain."

These words were applauded.

They set forth the situation—the torpor of the Faubourgs, no one at the Society of Cabinet Makers, the doors closed nearly everywhere. I told them what I had seen and heard in the Rue de la Roquette, the remarks of the wine-seller, Auguste, on the indifference of the people, the hopes of the engineer, and the possibility of a movement during the night in the Faubourg St. Marceau. It was settled that on the first notice that might be given I should go there.

Nevertheless nothing was yet known of what had taken place during the day. It was announced that M. Havin, Lieutenant-Colonel of the 5th Legion of the National Guard, had ordered the officers of his Legion to attend a meeting.

Some Democratic writers came in, amongst whom were Alexander Rey and Xavier Durrieu, with Kesler, Villiers, and Amable Lemaître of the *Révolution*; one of these writers was Millière.

Millière had a large bleeding wound above his eye-brow; that same morning on leaving us, as he was carrying away one of the copies of the Proclamation which I had dictated, a man had thrown himself upon him to snatch it from him. The police had evidently already been informed of the Proclamation, and lay in wait for it; Millière had a hand-to-hand struggle with the police agent, and had overthrown him, not without bearing away this gash. However, the Proclamation was not yet printed. It was nearly nine o'clock in the evening and nothing had come. Xavier Durrieu asserted that before another hour elapsed they should have the promised forty thousand copies. It was hoped to cover the walls of Paris with them during the night. Each of those present was to serve as a bill-poster.

There were amongst us—an inevitable circumstance in the stormy confusion of the first moments—a good many men whom we did not know. One of these men brought in ten or twelve copies of the appeal to arms. He asked me to sign them with my own hand, in order, he said, that he might be able to show my signature to the people—"Or to the police," whispered Baudin to me smiling. We were not in a position to take such precautions as these. I gave this man all the signatures that he wanted.

Madier de Montjau began to speak. It was of consequence to organize the action of the Left, to impress the unity of impulse upon the movement which was being prepared; to create a centre for it, to give a pivot to the insurrection, to the Left a direction, and to the People a support. He proposed the immediate formation of a committee representing the entire Left in all its shades, and charged with organizing and directing the insurrection.

All the Representatives cheered this eloquent and courageous man. Seven members were proposed. They named at once Carnot, De Flotte, Jules Favre, Madier de Montjau, Michel de Bourges, and myself; and thus was unanimously formed this Committee of Insurrection, which at my request was called a Committee of Resistance; for it was Louis Bonaparte who was tire insurgent. For ourselves, the were the Republic. It was desired that one workman-Representative should be admitted into the committee. Faure (du Rhône) was nominated. But Faure, we learned later on, had been arrested that morning. The committee then was, it fact, composed of six members.

The committee organized itself during the sitting. A Committee of Permanency was formed from amongst it, and invested with the authority of decreeing "urgency" in the name of all the Left, of concentrating all news, information, directions, instructions, resources, orders. This Committee of Permanency was composed of four members, who were Carnot, Michel de Bourges, Jules Favre, and myself. De Flotte and Madier de Montjau were specially delegated, De Flotte for the left bank of the river and the district of the schools, Madier for the Boulevards and the outskirts.

These preliminary operations being terminated, Lafon took aside Michel de Bourges and myself, and told us that the ex-Constituent Proudhon had inquired for one of us two, that he had remained downstairs nearly a quarter of an hour, and that he had gone away, saying that he would wait for us in the Place de la Bastille.

Proudhon, who was at that time undergoing a term of three years' imprisonment at St. Pélagie for an offence against Louis Bonaparte, was granted leave of absence from tine to time. Chance willed it that one of these liberty days had fallen on the 2d of December.

This is an incident which one cannot help noting. On the 2d of December Proudhon was a prisoner by virtue of a lawful sentence, and at the same moment at which they illegally imprisoned the inviolable Representatives, Proudhon, whom they could have legitimately detained, was allowed to go out. Proudhon had profited by his liberty to come and find us.

I knew Proudhon from having seen him at the Concièrgerie, where my two sons were shut up, and my two illustrious friends, Auguste Vacquérie and Paul Meurice, and those gallant writers, Louis Jourdan, Erdan, and Suchet. I could not help thinking that on that day they would assuredly not have given leave of absence to these men.

Meanwhile Xavier Durrieu whispered to me, "I have just left Proudhon. He wishes to see you. He is waiting for you down below, close by, at the entrance to the Place. You will find him leaning on the parapet of the canal."

"I am going," said I.

I went downstairs.

I found in truth, at the spot mentioned, Proudhon, thoughtful, leaning with his two elbows on the parapet. He wore that broad-brimmed hat in which I had often seen him striding alone up and down the courtyard of the Concièrgerie.

I went up to him.

"You wish to speak to me."

"Yes," and he shook me by the hand.

The corner where we were standing was lonely. On the left there was the Place de la Bastille, dark and gloomy; one could see nothing there, but one could feel a crowd; regiments were there in battle array; they did not bivouac, they were ready to march; the muffled sound of breathing could be heard; the square was full of that glistening shower of pale sparks which bayonets give forth at night time. Above this abyss of shadows rose up black and stark the Column of July.

Proudhon resumed,—

"Listen. I come to give you a friendly warning. You are entertaining illusions. The People are ensnared in this affair. They will not stir. Bonaparte will carry them with him. This rubbish, the restitution of universal suffrage, entraps the simpletons. Bonaparte passes for a Socialist. He has said, 'I will be the Emperor of the Rabble.' It is a piece of insolence. But insolence has a chance of success when it has this at its service."

And Proudhon pointed with his finger to the sinister gleam of the bayonets. He continued,—

"Bonaparte has an object in view. The Republic has made the People. He wishes to restore the Populace. He will succeed and you will fail. He has on his side force, cannons, the mistake of the people, and the folly of the Assembly. The few of the Left to which you belong will not succeed in overthrowing the *coup d'état*. You are honest, and he has this advantage over you—that he is a rogue. You have scruples, and he has this advantage over you—that he has none. Believe me. Resist no longer. The situation is without resources. We must wait; but at this moment fighting would be madness. What do you hope for?"

"Nothing," said I.

"And what are you going to do?"

"Everything."

By the tone of my voice he understood that further persistence was useless.

"Goodbye," he said.

We parted. He disappeared in the darkness. I have never seen him since.

I went up again to Lafon's rooms.

In the meantime the copies of the appeal to arms did not come to hand. The Representatives, becoming uneasy, went up and downstairs. Some of them went out on the Quai Jemmapes, to wait there and gain information about them. In the room there was a sound of confused talking the members of the Committee, Madier de Montjau, Jules Favre, and Carnot, withdrew, and sent word to me by Charamaule that they were going to No. 10, Rue des Moulins, to the house of the ex-Constituent Landrin, in the division of the 5th Legion, to deliberate more at their ease, and they begged me to join them. But I thought I should do better to remain. I had placed myself at the disposal of the probable movement of the Faubourg St. Marceau. I awaited the notice of it through Auguste. It was most important that I should not go too far away; besides, it was possible that if I went away, the Representatives of the Left, no longing seeing a member of the committee amongst them, would disperse without taking any resolution, and I saw in this more than one disadvantage.

Time passed, no Proclamations. We learned the next day that the packages had been seized by the police. Cournet, an ex-Republican naval officer who was present, began to speak. We shall see presently what sort of a man Cournet was, and of what an energetic and determined nature he was composed. He represented to us that as we had been there nearly two hours the police would certainly end by being informed of our whereabouts, that the members of the Left had an imperative duty—to keep themselves at all costs at the head of the People, that the necessity itself of their situation imposed upon them the precaution of frequently changing their place of retreat, and he ended by offering us, for our deliberation, his house and his workshops, No. 82, Rue Popincourt, at the bottom of a blind alley, and also in the neighborhood of the Faubourg St. Antoine.

This offer was accepted. I sent to inform Auguste of our change of abode, and of Cournet's address. Lafon remained on the Quai Jemmapes in order to forward on the Proclamations as soon as they arrived, and we set out at once.

Charamaule undertook to send to the Rue des Moulins to tell the other members of the committee that we would wait for them at No. 82, Rue Popincourt.

We walked, as in the morning, in little separate groups. The Quai Jemmapes skirts the left bank of the St. Martin Canal; we went up it. We only met a few solitary workmen, who looked back when we had passed, and stopped behind us with an air of astonishment. The night was dark. A few drops of rain were falling.

A little beyond the Rue de Chemin Vert we turned to the right and reached the Rue Popincourt. There all was deserted, extinguished, closed, and silent, as in the Faubourg St. Antoine. This street is of great length. We walked for a long time; we passed by the barracks. Cournet was no longer with us; he had remained behind to inform some of his friends, and we were told to take defensive measures in case his house was attacked. We looked for No. 82. The darkness was such that we could not distinguish the numbers on the houses. At length, at the end of the street, on the right, we saw a light; it was a grocer's shop, the only one open throughout the street. One of us entered, and asked the grocer, who was sitting behind his counter, to show us M. Cournet's house. "Opposite," said the grocer, pointing to an old and low carriage entrance which could be seen on the other side of the street, almost facing his shop.

We knocked at this door. It was opened. Baudin entered first, tapped at the window of the porter's lodge, and asked "Monsieur Cournet?"— An old woman's voice answered, "Here."

The portress was in bed; all in the house sleeping. We went in.

Having entered, and the gate being shut behind us, we found

ourselves in a little square courtyard which formed the centre of a sort of a two-storied ruin; the silence of a convent prevailed, not a light was to be seen at the windows; near a shed was seen a low entrance to a narrow, dark, and winding staircase. "We have made some mistake," said Charamaule; "it is impossible that it can be here."

Meanwhile the portress, hearing all these trampling steps beneath her doorway, had become wide awake, had lighted her lamp, and we could see her in her lodge, her face pressed against the window, gazing with alarm at sixty dark phantoms, motionless, and standing in her courtyard.

Esquiros addressed her: "Is this really M. Cournet's house?" said he.

"M. Cornet, without doubt," answered the good woman.

All was explained. We had asked for Cournet, the grocer had understood Cornet, the portress had understood Cornet. It chanced that M. Cornet lived there.

We shall see by and by what an extraordinary service chance had rendered us.

We went out, to the great relief of the poor portress, and we resumed our search. Xavier Durrieu succeeded in ascertaining our whereabouts, and extricated us from our difficulty.

A few moments afterwards we turned to the left, and we entered into a blind alley of considerable length and dimly lighted by an old oil lamp—one of those with which Paris was formerly lighted—then again to the left, and we entered through a narrow passage into a large courtyard encumbered with sheds and building materials. This time we had reached Cournet's.

XIX

One Foot in the Tomb

Cournet was waiting for us. He received us on the ground floor, in a parlor where there was a fire, a table, and some chairs; but the room was so small that a quarter of us filled it to overflowing, and the others remained in the courtyard. "It is impossible to deliberate here," said Bancel. "I have a larger room on the first floor," answered Cournet, "but it is a building in course of construction, which is not yet furnished, and where there is no fire."—"What does it matter?" they answered him. "Let us go up to the first floor."

We went up to the first floor by a steep and narrow wooden staircase, and we took possession of two rooms with very low ceilings, but of which one was sufficiently large. The walls were whitewashed, and a few straw-covered stools formed the whole of its furniture.

They called out to me, "Preside."

I sat down on one of the stools in the corner of the first room, with the fire place on my right and on my left the door opening upon the staircase. Baudin said to me, "I have a pencil and paper. I will act as secretary to you." He sat down on a stool next to me.

The Representatives and those present, amongst whom were several men in blouses, remained standing, forming in front of Baudin and myself a sort of square, backed by the two walls of the room opposite to us. This crowd extended as far as the staircase. A lighted candle was placed on the chimney-piece.

A common spirit animated this meeting. The faces were pale, but in every eye could be seen the same firm resolution. In all these shadows glistened the same flame. Several simultaneously asked permission to speak. I requested them to give their names to Baudin, who wrote them down, and then passed me the list.

The first speaker was a workman. He began by apologizing for mingling with the Representatives, he a stranger to the Assembly. The Representatives interrupted him. "No, no," they said, "the People and Representatives are all one! Speak—!" He declared that if he spoke it was in order to clear from all suspicion the honor of his brethren, the workmen of Paris; that he had heard some Representatives express doubt about them. He asserted that this was unjust, that the workmen realized the whole crime of M. Bonaparte and the whole duty of the People, that they would not be deaf to the appeal of the Republican Representatives, and that this would be clearly shown. He said all this, simply, with a sort of proud shyness and of honest bluntness. He kept his word. I found him the next day fighting on the Rambuteau barricade.

Mathieu (de la Drôme) came in as the workman concluded. "I bring news," he exclaimed. A profound silence ensued.

As I have already said, we vaguely knew since the morning that the Right were to have assembled, and that a certain number of our friends had probably taken part in the meeting, and that was all. Mathieu (de la Drôme) brought us the events of the day, the details of the arrests at their own houses carried out without any obstacle, of the meeting which had taken place at M. Daru's house and its rough treatment in the Rue de Bourgogne, of the Representatives expelled from the Hall of the Assembly, of the meanness of President Dupin, of the melting away of the High Court, of the total inaction of the Council of State, of the sad sitting held at the Mairie of the Tenth Arrondissement, of the Oudinot, *fiasco*, of the decree of the deposition of the President, and of the two hundred and twenty forcibly arrested and taken to the Quai d'Orsay. He concluded in a manly style: "The duty of the Left was increasing hourly. The morrow would probably prove decisive." He implored the meeting to take this into consideration.

A workman added a fact. He had happened in the morning to be in the Rue de Grenelle during the passage of the arrested members of the Assembly; he was there at the moment when one of the commanders of the Chasseurs de Vincennes had uttered these words, "Now it is the turn of those gentlemen—the Red Representatives. Let them look out for themselves!"

One of the editors of the *Révolution*, Hennett de Kesler, who afterwards became an intrepid exile, completed the information of Mathieu (de la Drôme). He recounted the action taken by two members of the Assembly with regard to the so-called Minister of the Interior, Morny, and the answer of the said Morny: "If I find any of the Representatives behind the barricades, I will have them shot to the last man," and that other saying of the same witty vagabond respecting the members taken to the Quai d'Orsay, "These are the last Representatives who will be made prisoners." He told us that a placard was at that very moment being printed which declared that "Anyone who should be found at a secret meeting would be immediately shot." The placard, in truth, appeared the next morning.

Baudin rose up. "The *coup d'état* redoubles its rage," exclaimed he. "Citizens, let us redouble our energy!"

Suddenly a man in a blouse entered. He was out of breath. He had run hard. He told us that he had just seen, and he repeated, had seen with "his own eyes," in the Rue Popincourt, a regiment marching in silence, and wending its way towards the blind alley of No. 82, that we were surrounded, and that we were about to be attacked. He begged us to disperse immediately.

"Citizen Representatives," called out Cournet, "I have placed scouts in the blind alley who will fall back and warn us if the regiment penetrates thither. The door is narrow and will be barricaded in the twinkling of an eye. We are here, with you, fifty armed and resolute men, and at the first shot we shall be two hundred. We are provided with ammunition. You can deliberate calmly."

And as he concluded he raised his right arm, and from his sleeve fell a large poniard, which he had concealed, and with the other hand he rattled in his pocket the butts of a pair of pistols.

"Very well," said I, "let us continue."

Three of the youngest and most eloquent orators of the Left, Bancel, Arnauld (de l'Ariége) and Victor Chauffour delivered their opinions in succession. All three were imbued with this notion, that our appeal to arms not having yet been placarded, the different incidents of the Boulevarde du Temple and of the Café Bonvalet having brought about no results, none of our decrees, owing to the repressive measures of Bonaparte, having yet succeeded in appearing, while the events at the Mairie of the Tenth Arrondissement began to be spread abroad through Paris, it seemed as though the Right had commenced active resistance before the Left. A generous rivalry for the public safety spurred them on. It was delightful to them to know that a regiment ready to attack was close by, within a few steps, and that perhaps in a few moments their blood would flow.

Moreover, advice abounded, and with advice, uncertainty. Some illusions were still entertained. A workman, leaning close to me against the fireplace, said in a low voice to one of his comrades that the People must not be reckoned upon, and that if we fought "We should perpetrate a madness."

The incidents and events of the day had in some degree modified my opinion as to the course to be followed in this grave crisis. The silence of the crowd at the moment when Arnauld (de l'Ariége) and I had apostrophized the troops, had destroyed the impression which a few hours before the enthusiasm of the people on the Boulevard du Temple had left with me. The hesitation of Auguste had impressed me, the Society of Cabinet Makers appeared to shun us, the torpor of the Faubourg St. Antoine was manifest, the inertness of the Faubourg St. Marceau was not less so. I ought to have received notice from the engineer before eleven o'clock, and eleven o'clock was past. Our hopes died away one after another. Nevertheless, all the more reason, in my opinion, to astonish and awaken Paris by an extraordinary spectacle, by a daring act of life and collective power on the part of the Representatives of the Left, by the daring of an immense devotion.

It will be seen later on what a combination of accidental circumstances prevented this idea from being realized as I then purposed. The Representatives have done their whole duty. Providence perhaps has not done all on its side. Be it as it may, supposing that we were not at once carried off by some nocturnal and immediate combat, and that at the hour at which I was speaking we had still a "tomorrow," I felt the necessity of fixing every eye upon the course which should be adopted on the day which was about to follow.—I spoke.

I began by completely unveiling the situation. I painted the picture in four words: the Constitution thrown into the gutter; the Assembly driven to prison with the butt-end of a musket, the Council of State dispersed; the High Court expelled by a galley-sergeant, a manifest beginning of victory for Louis Bonaparte, Paris ensnared in the army as though in a net; bewilderment everywhere, all authority overthrown; all compacts annulled; two things only remained standing, the *coup d'état* and ourselves.

"Ourselves! and who are we?"

"We are," said I, "we are Truth and Justice! We are the supreme and sovereign power, the People incarnate—Right!"

I continued,—

"Louis Bonaparte at every minute which elapses advances a step further in his crime. For him nothing is inviolable, nothing is sacred; this morning he violated the Palace of the Representatives of the Nation, a few hours later he laid violent hands on their persons; tomorrow, perhaps in a few moments, he will shed their blood. Well then! he marches upon us, let us march upon him. The danger grows greater, let us grow greater with the danger."

A movement of assent passed through the Assembly. I continued,—

"I repeat and insist. Let us show no mercy to this wretched Bonaparte for any of the enormities which his outrage contains. As he has drawn the wine—I should say the blood—he must drink it up. We are not individuals, we are the Nation. Each of us walks forth clothed with the Sovereignty of the people. He cannot strike our persons without rending that. Let us compel his volleys to pierce our sashes as well as our breasts. This man is on a road where logic grasps him and leads him to parricide. What he is killing in this moment is the country! Well, then! when the ball of Executive Power pierces the sash of Legislative Power, it is visible parricide! It is this that must be understood!"

"We are quite ready!" they cried out. "What measures would you advise us to adopt?"

"No half measures," answered I; "a deed of grandeur! Tomorrow—if we leave here this night—let us all meet in the Faubourg St. Antoine."

They interposed, "Why the Faubourg St. Antoine?"

"Yes," resumed I, "the Faubourg St. Antoine! I cannot believe that the heart of the People has ceased to beat there. Let us all meet tomorrow in the Faubourg St. Antoine. Opposite the Lenoir Market there is a hall which was used by a club in 1848."

They cried out to me, "The Salle Roysin."

"That is it," said I, "The Salle Roysin. We who remain free number a hundred and twenty Republican Representatives. Let us install ourselves in this hall. Let us install ourselves in the fulness and majesty of the Legislative Power. Henceforward we are the Assembly, the whole of the Assembly! Let us sit there, deliberate there, in our official sashes, in the midst of the People. Let us summon the Faubourg St. Antoine to its duty, let us shelter there the National Representation, let us shelter there the popular sovereignty. Let us intrust the People to the keeping of the People. Let us adjure them to protect themselves. If necessary, let us order them!"

A voice interrupted me: "You cannot give orders to the People!"

"Yes!" I cried, "When it is a question of public safety, of the universal safety, when it is a question of the future of every European nationality, when it is a question of defending the Republic, Liberty, Civilization, the Revolution, we have the right—we, the Representatives of the entire nation—to give, in the name of the French people, orders to the people of Paris! Let us, therefore, meet tomorrow at this Salle Roysin; but at what time? Not too early in the morning. In broad day. It is necessary that the shops should be open, that people should be coming and going, that the population should be moving about, that there should be plenty of people in the streets, that they should see us, that they should recognize us, that the grandeur of our example should strike every eye and stir every heart. Let us all be there between nine and ten o'clock in the morning. If we cannot obtain the Salle Roysin we will take the first church at hand, a stable, a shed, some enclosure where we can deliberate; at need, as Michel de Bourges has said, we will hold our sittings in a square bounded by four barricades. But provisionally I suggest the Salle Roysin. Do not forget that in such a crisis there must be no vacuum before the nation. That alarms it. There must be a government somewhere, and it must be known. The rebellion at the Elysée, the Government at the Faubourg St. Antoine; the Left the Government, the Faubourg St. Antoine the citadel; such are the ideas which from tomorrow we must impress upon the mind of Paris. To the Salle Roysin, then! Thence in the midst of the dauntless throng of workmen of that great district of Paris, enclosed in the Faubourg as in a fortress, being both Legislators and Generals, multiplying and inventing means of defence and of attack, launching Proclamations and unearthing the pavements, employing the women in writing out placards while the men are fighting, we will issue a warrant against Louis Bonaparte, we will issue warrants against his accomplices, we will declare the military chiefs traitors, we will outlaw in a body all the crime and all the criminals, we will summon the citizens to arms, we will recall the army to duty, we will rise up before Louis Bonaparte, terrible as the living Republic, we will fight on the one hand with the power of the Law, and on the other with the power of the People, we will overwhelm this miserable rebel, and will rise up above his head both as a great Lawful Power and a great Revolutionary Power!"

While speaking I became intoxicated with my own ideas. My enthusiasm communicated itself to the meeting. They cheered me. I saw that I was becoming somewhat too hopeful, that I allowed myself to be carried away, and that I carried them away, that I presented to them success as possible, as even easy, at a moment when it was important that no one should entertain an illusion. The truth was gloomy, and it was my duty to tell it. I let silence be re-established, and I signed with my hand that I had a last word to say. I then resumed, lowering my voice,—

"Listen, calculate carefully what you are doing. On one side a hundred thousand men, seventeen harnessed batteries, six thousand cannon-mouths in the forts, magazines, arsenals, ammunition sufficient to carry out a Russian campaign; on the other a hundred and twenty Representatives, a thousand or twelve hundred patriots, six hundred muskets, two cartridges per man, not a drum to beat to arms, not a bell to sound the tocsin, not a printing office to print a Proclamation; barely here and there a lithographic press, and a cellar where a hand-bill can be hurriedly and furtively printed with the brush; the penalty of death against anyone who unearths a paving stone, penalty of death against anyone who would enlist in our ranks, penalty of death against anyone who is found in a secret meeting, penalty of death against anyone who shall post up an appeal to arms; if you are taken during the combat, death; if you are taken after the combat, transportation or exile; on the one side an army and a Crime; on the other a handful of men and Right. Such is this struggle. Do you accept it?"

A unanimous shout answered me, "Yes! yes!"

This shout did not come from the mouths, it came from the souls. Baudin, still seated next to me, pressed my hand in silence.

It was settled therefore at once that they should meet again on the next day, Wednesday, between nine and ten in the morning, at the Salle Roysin, that they should arrive singly or by little separate groups, and that they should let those who were absent know of this rendezvous. This done, there remained nothing more but to separate. It was about midnight.

One of Cournet's scouts entered. "Citizen Representatives," he said, "the regiment is no longer there. The street is free."

The regiment, which had probably come from the Popincourt barracks close at hand, had occupied the street opposite the blind alley for more than half an hour, and then had returned to the barracks. Had they judged the attack inopportune or dangerous at night in that narrow blind alley, and in the centre of this formidable Popincourt district, where the insurrection had so long held its own in June, 1848? It appeared certain that the soldiers had searched several houses in the neighborhood. According to details which we learned subsequently, we were followed after leaving No. 2, Quai Jemmapes, by an agent of police, who saw us enter the house where a M. Cornet was lodging, and who at once proceeded to the Prefecture to denounce our place of refuge to his chiefs. The regiment sent to arrest us surrounded the house, ransacked it from attic to cellar, found nothing, and went away.

This quasi-synonym of Cornet and Cournet lead misled the bloodhounds of the *coup d'état*. Chance, we see, had interposed usefully in our affairs.

I was talking at the door with Baudin, and we were making some last arrangements, when a young man with a chestnut beard, dressed like a man of fashion, and possessing all the manners of one, and whom I had noticed while speaking, came up to me.

"Monsieur Victor Hugo," said he, "where are you going to sleep?"

Up to that moment I had not thought of this.

It was far from prudent to go home.

"In truth," I answered, "I have not the least idea."

"Will you come to my house?"

"I shall be very happy."

He told me his mane. It was M. de la R——. He knew my brother Abel's wife and family, the Montferriers, relations of the Chambacères, and he lived in the Rue Caumartin. He had been a Prefect under the Provisional Government. There was a carriage in waiting. We got in, and as Baudin told me that he would pass the night at Cournet's, I gave him the address of M. do la R——, so that he could send for me if any notice of the movement came from the Faubourg St. Marceau or elsewhere. But I hoped for nothing more that night, and I was right.

About a quarter of an hour after the separation of the Representatives, and after we had left the Rue Popincourt, Jules Favre, Madier de Montajau, de Flotte, and Carnot, to whom we had sent word to the Rue des Moulins, arrived at Cournet's, accompanied by Schoelcher, by Charamaule, by Aubry (du Nord), and by Bastide. Some Representatives were still remaining at Cournet's. Several, like Baudin, were going to pass the night there. They told our colleagues what had been settled respecting my proposition, and of the rendezvous at the Salle Roysin; only it appears that there was some doubt regarding the hour agreed upon, and that Baudin in particular did not exactly remember it, and that our colleagues believed that the rendezvous, which had been fixed for nine o'clock in the morning, was fixed for eight.

This alteration in the hour, due to the treachery of memory for which no one can be blamed, prevented the realization of the plan which I had conceived of an Assembly holding its sittings in the Faubourg, and giving battle to Louis Bonaparte, but gave us as a compensation the heroic exploits of the Ste. Marguerite barricade.

XX

The Burial of a Great Anniversary

S uch was the first day. Let us look at it steadfastly. It deserves it. It is the anniversary of Austerlitz; the Nephew commemorates the Uncle. Austerlitz is the most brilliant battle of history; the Nephew set himself this problem—how to commit a baseness equal to this magnificence. He succeeded.

This first day, which will be followed by others, is already complete. Everything is there. It is the most terrible attempt at a thrust backwards that has ever been essayed. Never has such a crumbling of civilization been seen. All that formed the edifice is now in ruin; the soil is strewn with the fragments. In one night the inviolability of the Law, the Right of the Citizen, the Dignity of the Judge, and the Honor of the Soldier have disappeared. Terrible substitutions have taken place; there was the oath, there is perjury; there was the flag, there is a rag; there was the Army, there is a band of brigands; there was Justice, there is treason; there was a code of laws, there is the sabre; there was a Government, there is a crew of swindlers; there was France, there is a den of thieves. This called itself Society Saved.

It is the rescue of the traveller by the highwayman.

France was passing by, Bonaparte cried, "Stand and deliver!"

The hypocrisy which has preceded the Crime, equals in deformity the impudence which has followed it. The nation was trustful and calm. There was a sudden and cynical shock. History has recorded nothing equal to the Second of December. Here there was no glory, nothing but meanness. No deceptive picture. He could have declared himself honest; He declares himself infamous; nothing more simple. This day, almost unintelligible in its success, has proved that Politics possess their obscene side. Louis Bonaparte has shown himself unmasked.

Yesterday President of the Republic, today a scavenger. He has sworn, he still swears: but the tone has changed. The oath has become an imprecation. Yesterday he called himself a maiden, today he becomes a brazen woman, and laughs at his dupes. Picture to yourself Joan of Arc confessing herself to be Messalina. Such is the Second of December.

Women are mixed up in this treason. It is an outrage which savors both of the boudoir and of the galleys. There wafts across the fetidness of blood an undefined scent of patchouli. The accomplices of this act of brigandage are most agreeable men—Romieu, Morny. Getting into debt leads one to commit crimes.

Europe was astounded. It was a thunder bolt from a thief. It must be acknowledged that thunder can fall into bad hands, Palmerston, that traitor, approved of it. Old Metternich, a dreamer in his villa at Rennweg, shook his head. As to Soult, the man of Austerlitz after Napoleon, he did what he ought to do, on the very day of the Crime he died, Alas! and Austerlitz also.

THE SECOND DAY
THE STRUGGLE

I

They Come to Arrest Me

In order to reach the Rue Caumartin from the Rue Popincourt, all Paris has to be crossed. We found a great apparent calm everywhere. It was one o'clock in the morning when we reached M. de la R——'s house. The *fiacre* stopped near a grated door, which M. de la R—— opened with a latch-key; on the right, under the archway, a staircase ascended to the first floor of a solitary detached building which M. de la R—— inhabited, and into which he led me.

We entered a little drawing-room very richly furnished, lighted with a night-lamp, and separated from the bedroom by a tapestry curtain two-thirds drown. M. de la R—— went into the bedroom, and a few minutes afterwards came back again, accompanied by a charming woman, pale and fair, in a dressing-gown, her hair down, handsome, fresh, bewildered, gentle nevertheless, and looking at me with that alarm which in a young face confers an additional grace. Madame de la R—— had just been awakened by her husband. She remained a moment on the threshold of her chamber, smiling, half asleep, greatly astonished, somewhat frightened, looking by turns at her husband and at me, never having dreamed perhaps what civil war really meant, and seeing it enter abruptly into her rooms in the middle of the night under this disquieting form of an unknown person who asks for a refuge.

I made Madame de la R—— a thousand apologies, which she received with perfect kindness, and the charming woman profited by the incident to go and caress a pretty little girl of two years old who was sleeping at the end of the room in her cot, and the child whom she kissed caused her to forgive the refugee who had awakened her.

While chatting M. de la R—— lighted a capital fire in the grate, and his wife, with a pillow and cushions, a hooded cloak belonging to him, and a pelisse belonging to herself, improvised opposite the fire a bed on a sofa, somewhat short, and which we lengthened by means of an arm-chair.

During the deliberation in the Rue Popincourt, at which I had just presided, Baudin had lent me his pencil to jot down some names. I still had this pencil with me. I made use of it to write a letter to my wife, which Madame de la R—— undertook to convey herself to Madame Victor Hugo the next day. While emptying my pockets I found a box for the "Italiens," which I offered to Madame de la R——. On that evening (Tuesday, December 2d) they were to play *Hernani*.

I looked at that cot, these two handsome, happy young people, and at myself, my disordered hair and clothes, my boots covered with mud, gloomy thoughts in my mind, and I felt like an owl in a nest of nightingales.

A few moments afterwards M. and Madame de la R—— had disappeared into their bedroom, and the half-opened curtain was closed. I stretched myself, fully dressed as I was, upon the sofa, and this gentle nest disturbed by me subsided into its graceful silence.

One can sleep on the eve of a battle between two armies, but on the eve of a battle between citizens there can be no sleep. I counted each hour as it sounded from a neighboring church; throughout the night there passed down the street, which was beneath the windows of the room where I was lying, carriages which were fleeing from Paris. They succeeded each other rapidly and hurriedly, one might have imagined it was the exit from a ball. Not being able to sleep, I got up. I had slightly parted the muslin curtains of a window, and I tried to look outside; the darkness was complete. No stars, clouds were flying by with the turbulent violence of a winter night. A melancholy wind howled. This wind of clouds resembled the wind of events.

I watched the sleeping baby. I waited for dawn. It came. M. de la R—— had explained at my request in what manner I could go out without disturbing anyone. I kissed the child's forehead, and left the room. I went downstairs, closing the doors behind me as gently as I could, so not to wake Madame de la R——. I opened the iron door and went out into the street. It was deserted, the shops were still shut, and a milkwoman, with her donkey by her side, was quietly arranging her cans on the pavement.

I have not seen M. de la R—— again. I learned since that he wrote to me in my exile, and that his letter was intercepted. He has, I believe, quitted France. May this touching page convey to him my kind remembrances.

The Rue Caumartin leads into the Rue St. Lazare. I went towards it. It was broad daylight. At every moment I was overtaken and passed by *fiacres* laden with trunks and packages, which were hastening towards the Havre railway station. Passers-by began to appear. Some baggage trains were mounting the Rue St. Lazare at the same time as myself. Opposite No. 42, formerly inhabited by Mdlle. Mars, I saw a new bill posted on the wall. I went up to it, I recognized the type of the National Printing Office, and I read,

COMPOSITION OF THE NEW MINISTRY.

"*Interior*	—M. de Morny.
"*War*	—The General of Division St. Arnaud.
"*Foreign Affairs*	—M. de Turgot.
"*Justice*	—M. Rouher.
"*Finance*	—M. Fould.
"*Marine*	—M. Ducos.
"*Public Works*	—M. Magne.
"*Public Instruction*	—M.H. Fortuol.
"*Commerce*	—M. Lefebre-Duruflé."

I tore down the bill, and threw it into the gutter! The soldiers of the party who were leading the wagons watched me do it, and went their way.

In the Rue St. Georges, near a side-door, there was another bill. It was the "Appeal to the People." Some persons were reading it. I tore it down, notwithstanding the resistance of the porter, who appeared to me to be entrusted with the duty of protecting it.

As I passed by the Place Bréda some *fiacres* had already arrived there. I took one. I was near home, the temptation was too great, I went there. On seeing me cross the courtyard the porter looked at me with a stupefied air. I rang the bell. My servant, Isidore, opened the door, and exclaimed with a great cry, "Ah! it is you, sir! They came during the night to arrest you." I went into my wife's room. She was in bed, but not asleep, and she told me what had happened.

She had gone to bed at eleven o'clock. Towards half-past twelve, during that species of drowsiness which resembles sleeplessness, she heard men's voices. It seemed to her that Isidore was speaking to someone in the antechamber. At first she did not take any notice, and tried to go to sleep again, but the noise of voices continued. She sat up, and rang the bell.

Isidore came in. She asked him,

"Is anyone there?"

"Yes, madame."

"Who is it?"

"A man who wishes to speak to master."

"Your master is out."

"That is what I have told him, madame."

"Well, is not the gentleman going?"

"No, madame, he says that he urgently needs to speak to Monsieur Victor Hugo, and that he will wait for him."

Isidore had stopped on the threshold of the bedroom. While he spoke a fat, fresh-looking man in an overcoat, under which could be seen a black coat, appeared at the door behind him.

Madame Victor Hugo noticed this man, who was silently listening.

"Is it you, sir, who wish to speak to Monsieur Victor Hugo?"

"Yes, madame."

"But what is it about? Is it regarding politics?"

The man did not answer.

"As to politics," continued my wife, "what is happening?"

"I believe, madame, that all is at an end."

"In what sense?"

"In the sense of the President."

My wife looked fixedly at the man, and said to him,—

"You have come to arrest my husband, sir."

"It is true, madame," answered the man, opening his overcoat, which revealed the sash of a Commissary of Police.

He added after a pause, "I am a Commissary of Police, and I am the bearer of a warrant to arrest M. Victor Hugo. I must institute a search and look through the house."

"What is your name, sir?" asked Madame Victor Hugo.

"My name is Hivert."

"You know the terms of the Constitution?"

"Yes, madam."

"You know that the Representatives of the People are inviolable!"

"Yes, madame."

"Very well, sir," she said coldly, "you know that you are committing a crime. Days like this have a tomorrow; proceed."

The Sieur Hivert attempted a few words of explanation, or we should rather say justification; he muttered the word "conscience," he stammered the word "honor." Madame Victor Hugo, who had been calm until then, could not help interrupting him with some abruptness.

"Do your business, sir, and do not argue; you know that every official who lays a hand on a Representative of the People commits an act of treason. You know that in presence of the Representatives the President is only an official like the others, the chief charged with carrying out their orders. You dare to come to arrest a Representative in his own home like a criminal! There is in truth a criminal here who ought to be arrested—yourself!"

The Sieur Hivert looked sheepish and left the room, and through the half-open door my wife could see, behind the well-fed, well-clothed, and bald Commissary, seven or eight poor raw-boned devils, wearing dirty coats which reached to their feet, and shocking old hats jammed down over their eyes—wolves led by a dog. They examined the room, opened here and there a few cupboards, and went away—with a sorrowful air—as Isidore said to me.

The Commissary Hivert, above all, hung his head; he raised it, however, for one moment. Isidore, indignant at seeing these men thus hunt for his master in every corner, ventured to defy them. He opened a drawer and said, "Look and see if he is not in here!" The Commissary of Police darted a furious glance at him: "Lackey, take care!" The lackey was himself.

These men having gone, it was noticed that several of my papers were missing. Fragments of manuscripts had been stolen, amongst others one dated July, 1848, and directed against the military dictatorship of Cavaignac, and in which there were verses written respecting the Censorship, the councils of war, and the suppression of the newspapers, and in particular respecting the imprisonment of a great journalist—Emile de Girardin:—

> ". . . O honte, un lansquenet
> Gauche, et parodiant César dont il hérite,
> Gouverne les esprits du fond de sa guérite!"

These manuscripts are lost.

The police might come back at any moment, in fact they did come back a few minutes after I had left. I kissed my wife; I would not wake my daughter, who had just fallen asleep, and I went downstairs again. Some affrighted neighbors were waiting for me in the courtyard. I cried out to them laughingly, "Not caught yet!"

A quarter of an hour afterwards I reached No. 10, Rue des Moulins. It was not then eight o'clock in the morning, and thinking that my colleagues of the Committee of Insurrection had passed the night there, I thought it might be useful to go and fetch them, so that we might proceed all together to the Salle Roysin.

I found only Madame Landrin in the Rue des Moulins. It was thought that the house was denounced and watched, and my colleagues had changed their quarters to No. 7, Rue Villedo, the house of the ex-Constituent Leblond, legal adviser to the Workmen's Association. Jules Favre had passed the night there. Madame Landrin was breakfasting. She offered me a place by her side, but time pressed. I carried off a morsel of bread, and left.

At No. 7, Rue Villedo, the maid-servant who opened the door to me ushered me into a room where were Carnot, Michel de Bourges, Jules Favre, and the master of the house, our former colleague, Constituent Leblond.

"I have a carriage downstairs," I said to them; "the rendezvous is at the Salle Roysin in the Faubourg St. Antoine; let us go."

This, however, was not their opinion. According to them the attempts made on the previous evening in the Faubourg St. Antoine had revealed this portion of the situation; they sufficed; it was useless to persist; it was obvious that the working-class districts would not rise; we must turn to the side of the tradesmen's districts, renounce our attempt to rouse the extremities of the city, and agitate the centre. We were the Committee of Resistance, the soul of the insurrection; if we were to go to the Faubourg St. Antoine, which was occupied by a considerable force, we should give ourselves up to Louis Bonaparte. They reminded me of what I myself had said on the subject the previous evening in the Rue Blanche. We must immediately organize the insurrection against the *coup d'état* and organize it in practicable districts, that is to say, in the old labyrinths of the streets St. Denis and St. Martin; we must draw up proclamations, prepare decrees, create some method of publicity; they were waiting for important communications from Workmen's Associations and Secret Societies. The great blow which I wished to strike by our solemn meeting at the Salle Roysin would prove a failure; they thought it their duty to remain where they were; and the Committee being few in number, and the work to be done being enormous, they begged me not to leave them.

They were men of great hearts and great courage who spoke to me; they were evidently right; but for myself I could not fail to go to the rendezvous which I myself had fixed. All the reasons which they had given me were good, nevertheless I could have opposed some doubts, but the discussion would have taken too much time, and the hour drew nigh. I did not make any objections, and I went out of the room, making some excuse. My hat was in the antechamber, my *fiacre* was waiting for me, and I drove off to the Faubourg St. Antoine.

The centre of Paris seemed to have retained its everyday appearance. People came and went, bought and sold, chatted and laughed as usual. In the Rue Montorgueil I heard a street organ. Only on nearing the Faubourg St. Antoine the phenomenon which I had already noticed on the previous evening became more and more apparent; solitude reigned, and a certain dreary peacefulness.

We reached the Place de la Bastille.

My driver stopped.

"Go on," I said to him.

II

From the Bastille to the Rue De Cotte

The Place de la Bastille was at the same time empty and filled. Three regiments in battle array were there; not one passer-by.

Four harnessed batteries were drawn up at the foot of the column. Here and there knots of officers talked together in a low voice,—sinister men.

One of these groups, the principal, attracted my attention. That one was silent, there was no talking. There were several men on horseback; one in front of the others, in a general's uniform, with a hat surmounted with black feathers, behind this man were two colonels, and behind the colonels a party of *aides-de-camp* and staff officers. This lace-trimmed company remained immovable, and as though pointing like a dog between the column and the entrance to the Faubourg. At a short distance from this group, spread out, and occupying the whole of the square, were the regiments drawn up and the cannon in their batteries.

"My driver again stopped.

"Go on," I said; "drive into the Faubourg."

"But they will prevent us, sir."

"We shall see."

The truth was that they did not prevent us.

The driver continued on his way, but hesitatingly, and at a walking pace. The appearance of a *fiacre* in the square had caused some surprise, and the inhabitants began to come out of their houses. Several came up to my carriage.

We passed by a group of men with huge epaulets. These men, whose tactics we understood later on, did not even appear to see us.

The emotion which I had felt on the previous day before a regiment of cuirassiers again seized me. To see before me the assassins of the country, at a few steps, standing upright, in the insolence of a peaceful triumph, was beyond my strength: I could not contain myself. I drew out my sash. I held it in my hand, and putting my arm and head out of the window of the *fiacre*, and shaking the sash, I shouted,—

"Soldiers! Look at this sash. It is the symbol of Law, it is the National Assembly visible. Where there this sash is there is Right. Well, then, this is what Right commands you. You are being deceived. Go back to your duty. It is a Representative of the People who is speaking to you, and he who represents the People represents the army. Soldiers, before becoming soldiers you have been peasants, you have been workmen, you have been and you are still citizens. Citizens, listen to me when I speak to you. The Law alone has the right to command you. Well, today the law is violated. By whom? By you. Louis Bonaparte draws you into a crime. Soldiers, you who are Honor, listen to me, for I am Duty. Soldiers, Louis Bonaparte assassinates the Republic. Defend it. Louis Bonaparte is a bandit; all his accomplices will follow him to the galleys. They are there already. He who is worthy of the galleys is in the galleys. To merit fetters is to wear them. Look at that man who is at your head, and who dares to command you. You take him for a general, he is a convict."

The soldiers seemed petrified.

Someone who was there (I thank his generous, devoted spirit) touched my arm, and whispered in my ear, "You will get yourself shot."

But I did not heed, and I listened to nothing. I continued, still waving my sash,—"You, who are there, dressed up like a general, it is you to whom I speak, sir. You know who I am, I am a Representative of the People, and I know who you are. I have told you you are a criminal. Now, do you wish to know my name? This is it."

And I called out my name to him.

And I added,—

"Now tell me yours."

He did not answer.

I continued,—

"Very well, I do not want to know your name as a general, I shall know your number as a galley slave."

The man in the general's uniform hung his head, the others were silent. I could read all their looks, however, although they did not raise their eyes. I saw them cast down, and I felt that they were furious. I had an overwhelming contempt for them, and I passed on.

What was the name of this general? I did not know then, and I do not know now.

One of the apologies for the *coup d'état* in relating this incident, and characterizing it as "an insensate and culpable provocation," states that "the moderation shown by the military leaders on this occasion did honor to General ——:" We leave to the author of this panegyric the responsibility of that name and of this eulogium.

I entered the Rue de Faubourg St. Antoine.

My driver, who now knew my name, hesitated no longer, and whipped up his horse. These Paris coachmen are a brave and intelligent race.

As I passed the first shops of the main street nine o'clock sounded from the Church St. Paul.

"Good," I said to myself, "I am in time."

The Faubourg presented an extraordinary aspect. The entrance was guarded, but not closed, by two companies of infantry. Two other companies were drawn up in echelons farther on, at short distances, occupying the street, but leaving a free passage. The shops, which were open at the end of the Faubourg, were half closed a hundred yards farther up. The inhabitants, amongst whom I noticed numerous workmen in blouses, were talking together at their doors, and watching the proceedings. I noticed at each step the placards of the *coup d'état* untouched.

Beyond the fountain which stands at the corner of the Rue de Charonne the shops were closed. Two lines of soldiers extended on either side of the street of the Faubourg on the kerb of the pavement; the soldiers were stationed at every five paces, with the butts of their muskets resting on their hips, their chests drawn in, their right hand on the trigger, ready to bring to the present, keeping silence in the attitude of expectation. From that point a piece of cannon was stationed at the mouth of each of the side streets which open out of the main road of the Faubourg. Occasionally there was a mortar. To obtain a clear idea of this military arrangement one must imagine two rosaries, extending along the two sides of the Faubourg St. Antoine, of which the soldiers should form the links and the cannon the beads.

Meanwhile my driver became uneasy. He turned round to me and said, "It looks as though we should find barricades out there, sir; shall we turn back?"

"Keep on," I replied.

He continued to drive straight on.

Suddenly it became impossible to do so. A company of infantry ranged three deep occupied the whole of the street from one pavement to the other. On the right there was a small street. I said to the driver,—

"Take that turning."

He turned to the right and then to the left. We turned into a labyrinth of streets.

Suddenly I heard a shot.

The driver asked me,—

"Which way are we to go, sir?"

"In the direction in which you hear the shots."

We were in a narrow street; on my left I saw the inscription above a door, "Grand Lavoir," and on my right a square with a central building, which looked like a market. The square and the street were deserted. I asked the driver,—

"What street are we in?"

"In the Rue de Cotte."

"Where is the Café Roysin?"

"Straight before us."

"Drive there."

He drove on, but slowly. There was another explosion, this time close by us, the end of the street became filled with smoke; at the moment we were passing No. 22, which has a side-door above which I read, "Petit Lavoir."

Suddenly a voice called out to the driver, "Stop!"

The driver pulled up, and the window of the *fiacre* being down, a hand was stretched towards mine. I recognized Alexander Rey.

This daring man was pale.

"Go no further," said he; "all is at an end."

"What do you mean, all at an end?"

"Yes, they must have anticipated the time appointed; the barricade is taken: I have just come from it. It is a few steps from here straight before us."

And he added,—

"Baudin is killed."

The smoke rolled away from the end of the street.

"Look," said Alexander Rey to me.

I saw, a hundred steps before us, at the junction of the Rue de Cotte and the Rue Ste. Marguerite, a low barricade which the soldiers were pulling down. A corpse was being borne away.

It was Baudin.

III

THE ST. ANTOINE BARRICADE

This is what had happened.

During that same night, and as early as four o'clock in the morning, De Flotte was in the Faubourg St. Antoine. He was anxious, in case any movement took place before daylight, that a Representative of the People should be present, and he was one of those who, when the glorious insurrection of Right should burst forth, wished to unearth the paving-stones for the first barricade.

But nothing was stirring. De Flotte, alone in the midst of this deserted and sleeping Faubourg, wandered from street to street throughout the night.

Day breaks late in December. Before the first streaks of dawn De Flotte was at the rendezvous opposite the Lenoir Market.

This spot was only weakly guarded. The only troops in the neighborhood were the post itself of the Lenoir Market, and another post at a short distance which occupied the guard-house at the corner of the Faubourg and the Rue de Montreuil, close to the old Tree of Liberty planted in 1793 by Santerre. Neither of these posts were commanded by officers.

De Flotte reconnoitred the position. He walked sometime up and down the pavement, and then seeing no one coming as yet, and fearing to excite attention, he went away, and returned to the side-streets of the Faubourg.

For his part Aubry (du Nord) got up at five o'clock. Having gone home in the middle of the night, on his return from the Rue Popincourt, he had only taken three hours' rest. His porter told him that some suspicious persons had inquired for him during the evening of the 2d, and that they had been to the house opposite, No. 12 of the same street, Rue Racine, to arrest Huguenin. This determined Aubry to leave his house before daylight.

He walked to the Faubourg St. Antoine. As he reached the place of rendezvous he met Cournet and the others from the Rue Popincourt. They were almost immediately joined by Malardier.

It was dawn. The Faubourg was solitary. They walked along wrapt in thought and speaking in a low voice. Suddenly an impetuous and singular procession passed them.

They looked round. It was a detachment of Lancers which surrounded something which in the dim light they recognized to be a police-van. The vehicle rolled noiselessly along the macadamized road.

They were debating what this could mean, when a second and similar group appeared, then a third, and then a fourth. Ten police vans passed in this manner, following each other very closely, and almost touching.

"Those are our colleagues!" exclaimed Aubry (du Nord).

In truth the last batch of the Representatives, prisoners of the Quai d'Orsay, the batch destined for Vincennes, was passing through the Faubourg. It was about seven o'clock in the morning. Some shops were being opened and were lighted inside, and a few passers-by came out of the houses.

Three carriages defiled one after the other, closed, guarded, dreary, dumb; no voice came out, no cry, no whisper. They were carrying off in the midst of swords, of sabres, and of lances, with the rapidity and fury of the whirlwind, something which kept silence; and that something which they were carrying off, and which maintained this sinister silence, was the broken Tribune, the Sovereignty of the Assemblies, the supreme initiative whence all civilization is derived; it was the word which contains the future of the world, it was the speech of France!

A last carriage arrived, which by some chance had been delayed. It was about two or three hundred yards behind the principal convoy, and was only escorted by three Lancers. It was not a police-van, it was an omnibus, the only one in the convoy. Behind the conductor, who was a police agent, there could distinctly be seen the Representatives heaped up in the interior. It seemed easy to rescue them.

Cournet appealed to the passers-by; "Citizens," he cried, "these are your Representatives, who are being carried off! You have just seen them pass in the vans of convicts! Bonaparte arrests them contrary to every law. Let us rescue them! To arms!"

A knot formed of men in blouses and of workmen going to work. A shout came from the knot, "Long live the Republic!" and some men rushed towards the vehicle. The carriage and the Lancers broke into a gallop.

"To arms!" repeated Cournet.

"To arms!" repeated the men of the people.

There was a moment of impulse. Who knows what might have happened? It would have been a singular accident if the first barricade against the *coup d'état* had been made with this omnibus, which, after having aided in the crime, would this have aided in the punishment. But at the moment when the people threw themselves on the vehicle they saw several of the Representative-prisoners which it contained sign to them with both hands to refrain. "Eh!" said a workman, "they do not wish it!"

A second repeated, "They do not wish for liberty!"

Another added, "They did not wish us to have it, they do not wish it for themselves."

All was said, and the omnibus was allowed to pass on. A moment afterwards the rear-guard of the escort came up and passed by at a sharp trots and the group which surrounded Aubry (du Nord), Malardier, and Cournet dispersed.

The Café Roysin had just opened. It may be remembered that the large hall of this *café* had served for the meeting of a famous club in 1848. It was there, it may also be remembered, that the rendezvous had been settled.

The Café Roysin is entered by a passage opening out upon the street, a lobby of some yards in length is next crossed, and then comes a large hall, with high windows, and looking-glasses on the walls, containing in the centre several billiard-tables, some small marble-topped tables, chairs, and velvet-covered benches. It was this hall, badly arranged, however, for a meeting where we could have deliberated, which had been the hall of the Roysin Club. Cournet, Aubry, and Malardier installed themselves there. On entering they did not disguise who they were; they were welcomed, and shown an exit through the garden in case of necessity.

De Flotte had just joined them.

Eight o'clock was striking when the Representatives began to arrive. Bruckner, Maigne, and Brillier first, and then successively Charamaule, Cassal, Dulac, Bourzat, Madier de Montjau, and Baudin. Bourzat, on account of the mud, as was his custom, wore wooden shoes. Whoever thought Bourzat a peasant would be mistaken. He rather resembled a Benedictine monk. Bourzat, with his southern imagination, his quick intelligence, keen, lettered, refined, possesses an encyclopedia in his head, and wooden shoes on his feet. Why not? He is Mind and People. The ex-Constituent Bastide came in with Madier de Montjau. Baudin shook the hands of all with warmth, but he did not speak. He was pensive. "What is the matter with you, Baudin?" asked Aubry (du Nord). "Are you mournful?" "I?" said Baudin, raising his head, "I have never been more happy."

Did he feel himself already chosen? When we are so near death, all radiant with glory, which smiles upon us through the gloom, perhaps we are conscious of it.

A certain number of men, strangers to the Assembly, all as determined as the Representatives themselves, accompanied them and surrounded them.

Cournet was the leader. Amongst them there were workmen, but no blouses. In order not to alarm the middle classes the workmen had been requested, notably those employed by Derosne and Cail, to come in coats.

Baudin had with him a copy of the Proclamation which I had dictated to him on the previous day. Cournet unfolded it and read it. "Let us at once post it up in the Faubourg," said he. "The People must know that Louis Bonaparte is outlawed." A lithographic workman who was there offered to print it without delay. All the Representatives present signed it, and they added my name to their signatures. Aubry (du Nord) headed it with these words, "National Assembly." The workman carried off the Proclamation, and kept his word. Some hours afterwards Aubry (du Nord), and later on a friend of Cournet's named Gay, met him in the Faubourg du Temple paste-pot in hand, posting the Proclamation at every street corner, even next to the Maupas placard, which threatened the penalty of death to anyone who should be found posting an appeal to arms. Groups read the two bills at the same time. We may mention an incident which ought to be noted, a sergeant of the line, in uniform, in red trousers, accompanied him and protected him. He was doubtless a soldier who had lately left the service.

The time fixed on the preceding evening for the general rendezvous was from nine to ten in the morning. This hour had been chosen so that there should be time to give notice to all the members of the Left; it was expedient to wait until the Representatives should arrive, so that the group should the more resemble an Assembly, and that its manifestation should have more authority on the Faubourg.

Several of the Representatives who had already arrived had no sash of office. Some were made hastily in a neighboring house with strips of red, white, and blue calico, and were brought to them. Baudin and De Flotte were amongst those who girded on these improvised sashes.

Meanwhile it was not yet nine o'clock, when impatience already began to be manifested around them.[1]

Many shared this glorious impatience.

Baudin wished to wait.

"Do not anticipate the hour," said he; "let us allow our colleagues time to arrive."

But they murmured round Baudin, "No, begin, give the signal, go outside. The Faubourg only waits to see your sashes to rise. You are few in number, but they know that your friends will rejoin you. That is sufficient. Begin."

The result proved that this undue haste could only produce a failure. Meanwhile they considered that the first example which the Representatives of the People ought to set was personal courage. The spark must not be allowed to die out. To march the first, to march at the head, such was their duty. The semblance of any hesitation would have been in truth more disastrous than any degree of rashness.

Schoelcher is of an heroic nature, he has the grand impatience of danger.

"Let us go," he cried; "our friends will join us, let us go outside."

They had no arms.

"Let us disarm the post which is over there," said Schoelcher.

They left the Salle Roysin in order, two by two, arm in arm. Fifteen or twenty men of the people escorted them. They went before them, crying, "Long live the Republic! To arms!"

Some children preceded and followed them, shouting, "Long live the Mountain!"

The entrances of the closed shops were half opened. A few men appeared at the doors, a few women showed themselves at the windows.

---

1. "There was also a misunderstanding respecting the appointed time. Some made a mistake, and thought it was nine o'clock. The first arrivals impatiently awaited their colleagues. They were, as we have said, some twelve or fifteen in number at half-past eight. 'Time is being lost,' exclaimed one of them who had hardly entered; 'let us gird on our sashes; let us show the Representatives to the People, let us join it in raising barricades.' We shall perhaps save the country, at all events we shall save the honor of our party. 'Come, let us to the barricades!' This advice was immediately and unanimously acclaimed: one alone, Citizen Baudin, interposed the forcible objection, 'we are not sufficiently numerous to adopt such a resolution.' But he spiritedly joined in the general enthusiasm, and with a calm conscience, after having reserved the principle, he was not the last to gird on his sash."—SCHOELCHER, *Histoire des Crimes du 2d Decembre*, pp. 130–131.

Knots of workmen going to their work watched them pass. They cried, "Long live our Representatives! Long live the Republic!"

Sympathy was everywhere, but insurrection nowhere. The procession gathered few adherents on the way.

A man who was leading a saddled horse joined them. They did not know this man, nor whence this horse came. It seemed as if the man offered his services to anyone who wished to fly. Representative Dulac ordered this man to be off.

In this manner they reached the guard-house of the Rue de Montrenil. At their approach the sentry gave the alarm, and the soldiers came out of the guard-house in disorder.

Schoelcher, calm, impassive, in ruffles and a white tie, clothed, as usual, in black, buttoned to the neck in his tight frock coat, with the intrepid and brotherly air of a Quaker, walked straight up to them.

"Comrades," he said to them, "we are the Representatives of the People, and come in the name of the people to demand your arms for the defence of the Constitution and of the Laws!"

The post allowed itself to be disarmed. The sergeant alone made any show of resistance, but they said to him, "You are alone," and he yielded. The Representatives distributed the guns and the cartridges to the resolute band which surrounded them.

Some soldiers exclaimed, "Why do you take away our muskets! We would fight for you and with you!"

The Representatives consulted whether they should accept this offer. Schoelcher was inclined to do so. But one of them remarked that some Mobile Guards had made the same overtures to the insurgents of June, and had turned against the Insurrection the arms which the Insurrection had left them.

The muskets therefore were not restored.

The disarming having been accomplished, the muskets were counted; there were fifteen of them.

"We are a hundred and fifty," said Cournet, "we have not enough muskets."

"Well, then," said Schoelcher, "where is there a post?"

"At the Lenoir Market."

"Let us disarm it."

With Schoelcher at their head and escorted by fifteen armed men the Representatives proceeded to the Lenoir Market. The post of the Lenoir Market allowed themselves to be disarmed even more willingly than the post in the Rue de Montreuil. The soldiers turned themselves round so that the cartridges might be taken from their pouches.

The muskets were immediately loaded.

"Now," exclaimed De Flotte, "we have thirty guns, let us look for a street corner, and raise a barricade."

There were at that time about two hundred combatants.

They went up the Rue de Montreuil.

After some fifty steps Schoelcher said, "Where are we going? We are turning our backs on the Bastille. We are turning our backs upon the conflict."

They returned towards the Faubourg.

They shouted, "To arms!" They Where answered by "Long live our Representatives!" But only a few young men joined them. It was evident that the breeze of insurrection was not blowing.

"Never mind," said De Flotte, "let us begin the battle. Let us achieve the glory of being the first killed."

As they reached the point where the Streets Ste. Marguerite and de Cotte open out and divide the Faubourg, a peasant's cart laden with dung entered the Rue Ste. Marguerite.

"Here," exclaimed De Flotte.

They stopped the dung-cart, and overturned it in the middle of the Faubourg St. Antoine.

A milkwoman came up.

They overturned the milk-cart.

A baker was passing in his bread-cart. He saw what was being done, attempted to escape, and urged his horse to a gallop. Two or three street Arabs—those children of Paris brave as lions and agile as cats—sped after the baker, ran past his horse, which was still galloping, stopped it, and brought back the cart to the barricade which had been begun.

They overturned the bread-cart.

An omnibus came up on the road from the Bastille.

"Very well!" said the conductor, "I see what is going on."

He descended with a good grace, and told his passengers to get down, while the coachman unharnessed his horses and went away shaking his cloak.

They overturned the omnibus.

The four vehicles placed end to end barely barred the street of the Faubourg, which in this part is very wide. While putting them in line the men of the barricade said,—

"Let us not injure the carts more than we can help."

This formed an indifferent barricade, very low, too short, and which left the pavements free on either side.

At this moment a staff officer passed by followed by an orderly, saw the barricade, and fled at a gallop.

Schoelcher calmly inspected the overturned vehicles. When he reached the peasant's cart, which made a higher heap than the others, he said, "that is the only good one."

The barricade grew larger. They threw a few empty baskets upon it, which made it thicker and larger without strengthening it.

They were still working when a child came up to them shouting, "The soldiers!"

In truth two companies arrived from the Bastille, at the double, through the Faubourg, told off in squads at short distances apart, and barring the whole of the street.

The doors and the windows were hastily closed.

During this time, at a corner of the barricade, Bastide, impassive, was gravely telling a story to Madier de Montjau. "Madier," said he, "nearly two hundred years ago the Prince de Condé, ready to give battle in this very Faubourg St. Antoine, where we now are, asked an officer who was accompanying him, 'Have you ever seen a battle lost?'—'No, sire.' 'Well, then, you will see one now.'—Madier, I tell you today,—you will speedily see a barricade taken."

In the meanwhile those who were armed had assumed their places for the conflict behind the barricade.

The critical moment drew nigh.

"Citizens," cried Schoelcher, "do not fire a shot. When the Army and the Faubourgs fight, the blood of the People is shed on both sides. Let us speak to the soldiers first."

He mounted on one of the baskets which heightened the barricade. The other Representatives arranged themselves near him on the omnibus. Malardier and Dulac were on his right. Dulac said to him, "You scarcely know me, Citizen Schoelcher, but I love you. Let me have the charge of remaining by your side. I only belong to the second rank in the Assembly, but I want to be in the first rank of the battle."

At this moment some men in blouses, those whom the Second of December had enlisted, appeared at the corner of the Rue Ste. Marguerite, close to the barricade, and shouted, "Down with the 'Twenty-five francs!'"

Baudin who had already selected his post for the combat, and who was standing on the barricade, looked fixedly at these men, and said to them,—

"You shall see how one can die for 'twenty-five francs!'"

There was a noise in the street. Some few doors which had remained half opened were closed. The two attacking columns had arrived in sight of the barricade. Further on could be seen confusedly other lines of bayonets. They were those which had barred my passage.

Schoelcher, raising his arm with authority, signed to the captain, who commanded the first squad, to halt.

The captain made a negative sign with his sword. The whole of the Second of December was in these two gestures. The Law said, "Halt!" The Sabre answered, "No!"

The two companies continued to advance, but slowly, and keeping at the same distance from each other.

Schoelcher came down from the barricade into the street. De Flotte, Dulac, Malardier, Brillier, Maigne, and Bruckner followed him.

Then was seen a grand spectacle.

Seven Representatives of the People, armed only with their sashes, that is to say, majestically clothed with Law and Right, advanced in the street beyond the barricade, and marched straight to the soldiers, who awaited them with their guns pointed at them.

The other Representatives who had remained at the barricade made their last preparations for resistance. The combatants maintained an intrepid bearing. The Naval Lieutenant Cournet towered above them all with his tall stature. Baudin, still standing on the overturned omnibus, leaned half over the barricade.

On seeing the Representatives approach, the soldiers and their officers were for the moment bewildered. Meanwhile the captain signed to the Representatives to stop.

They stopped, and Schoelcher said in an impressive voice,—

"Soldiers! we are the Representatives of the Sovereign People, we are your Representatives, we are the Elect of Universal Suffrage. In the name of the Constitution, in the name of Universal Suffrage, in the name of the Republic, we, who are the National Assembly, we, who are the Law, order you to join us, we summon you to obey. We ourselves are your leaders. The Army belongs to the People, and the Representatives of the People are the Chiefs of the Army. Soldiers! Louis Bonaparte violates the Constitution, we have outlawed him. Obey us."

The officer who was in command, a captain named Petit, did not allow him to finish.

"Gentlemen," he said, "I have my orders. I belong to the People. I am a Republican as you are, but I am only an instrument."

"You know the Constitution?" said Schoelcher.

"I only know my instructions."

"There is an instruction above all other instructions," continued Schoelcher, "obligatory upon the Soldier as upon the Citizen—the Law."

He turned again towards the soldiers to harangue them, but the captain cried out to him,—

"Not another word! You shall not go on! If you add one word, I shall give the order to fire."

"What does that matter to us?" said Schoelcher.

At this moment an officer arrived on horseback. It was the major of the regiment. He whispered for a moment to the captain.

"Gentlemen! Representatives!" continued the captain, waving his sword, "withdraw, or I shall fire."

"Fire!" shouted De Flotte.

The Representatives—strange and heroic copy of Fontenoy—took off their hats, and faced the muskets.

Schoelcher alone kept his hat on his head, and waited with his arms crossed.

"Fix bayonets," said the captain. And turning towards the squads, "Charge!"

"Vive la République!" cried out the Representatives.

The bayonets were lowered, the companies moved forward, the soldiers came on at the double upon the motionless Representatives.

It was a terrible and superb moment.

The seven Representatives saw the bayonets at their breasts without a word, without a gesture, without one step backwards. But the hesitation which was not in their soul was in the heart of the soldiers.

The soldiers felt distinctly that this was a double stain upon their uniform—the outrage upon the Representatives of the People—which was treason, and the slaughter of unarmed men, which was cowardice. Now treason and cowardice are two epaulets to which a general sometimes becomes reconciled, the soldier—never.

When the bayonets were so close to the Representatives that they touched their breasts, they turned aside of their own accord, and the soldier's by an unanimous movement passed between the Representatives without doing them any harm. Schoelcher alone had his coat pierced in two places, and in his opinion this was awkwardness instead of intention. One of the soldiers who faced him wished to push him away from the captain, and touched him with his bayonet. The point encountered the book of the addresses of the Representatives, which Schoelcher had in his pocket, and only pierced his clothing.

A soldier said to De Flotte, "Citizen, we do not wish to hurt you."

Nevertheless a soldier came up to Bruckner and pointed his gun at him.

"Well," said Bruckner, "fire."

The soldier, touched, lowered his arm, and shook Bruckner's hand.

It was singular that, notwithstanding the order given by the officers, the two companies successively came up to the Representatives, charged with the bayonet, and turned aside. Instructions may order, but instinct prevails; instructions may be crime, but instinct is honor. Major P——said afterwards, "They had told us that we should have to deal with brigands, we had to deal with heroes."

Meanwhile those on the barricade were growing uneasy, and seeing their colleagues surrounded, and wishing to succor them, they fired a musket shot. This unfortunate shot killed a soldier between De Flotte and Schoelcher.

The officer who commanded the second attacking squad passed close to Schoelcher as the poor soldier fell. Schoelcher pointed out the fallen man to the officer, and said to him, "Lieutenant, look!"

The officer answered by a gesture of despair,—

"What would you have us do?"

The two companies replied to the shot by a general volley, and rushed to the assault of the barricade, leaving behind them the seven Representatives astounded at being still alive.

The barricade replied by a volley, but it could not hold out. It was carried.

Baudin was killed.

He had remained standing in his position on the omnibus. Three balls reached him. One struck him in the right eye and penetrated into the brain. He fell. He never regained consciousness. Half-an-hour afterwards he was dead. His body was taken to the Ste. Marguerite Hospital.

Bourzat, who was close to Baudin, with Aubry (du Nord), had his coat pierced by a ball.

We must again remark a curious incident,—the soldiers made no prisoner on this barricade. Those who defended it dispersed through the streets of the Faubourg, or took refuge in the neighboring houses. Representative Maigne, pushed by some affrighted women behind a door, was shut in with one of the soldiers who had just taken the barricade. A moment afterwards the soldier and the Representative went out together. The Representatives could freely leave this first field of battle.

At this solemn moment of the struggle a last glimmer of Justice and of Right still flickered, and military honesty recoiled with a sort of dread anxiety before the outrage upon which they were entering. There is the intoxication of good, and there is an intoxication of evil: this intoxication later on drowned the conscience of the Army.

The French Army is not made to commit crimes. When the struggle became prolonged, and ferocious orders of the day had to be executed, the soldiers must have been maddened. They obeyed not coldly, which would have been monstrous, but with anger, and this History will invoke as their excuse; and with many, perhaps, despair was at the root of their anger.

The fallen soldier had remained on the ground. It was Schoelcher who raised him. A few women, weeping, but brave, came out of a house. Some soldiers came up. They carried him, Schoelcher holding his head, first to a fruiterer's shop, then to the Ste. Marguerite Hospital, where they had already taken Baudin.

He was a conscript. The ball had entered his side. Through his gray overcoat buttoned to the collar, could be seen a hole stained with blood. His head had sunk on his shoulder, his pale countenance, encircled by the chinstrap of his shako, had no longer any expression, the blood oozed out of his mouth. He seemed barely eighteen years old. Already a soldier and still a boy. He was dead.

This poor soldier was the first victim of the *coup d'état*. Baudin was the second.

Before being a Republican Baudin had been a tutor. He came from that intelligent and brave race of schoolmasters ever persecuted, who have fallen from the Guizot Law into the Falloux Law, and from the Falloux Law into the Dupanloup Law. The crime of the schoolmaster is to hold a book open; that suffices, the Church condemns him. There is now, in France, in each village, a lighted torch—the schoolmaster—and a mouth which blows upon it—the curé. The schoolmasters of France, who knew how to die of hunger for Truth and for Science, were worthy that one of their race should be killed for Liberty.

The first time that I saw Baudin was at the Assembly on January 13, 1850. I wished to speak against the Law of Instruction. I had not put my name down; Baudin's name stood second. He offered me his turn. I accepted, and I was able to speak two days afterwards, on the 15th.

Baudin was one of the targets of Sieur Dupin, for calls to order and official annoyances. He shared this honor with the Representatives Miot and Valentin.

Baudin ascended the Tribune several times. His mode of speaking, outwardly hesitating, was energetic in the main. He sat on the crest of the Mountain. He had a firm spirit and timid manners. Thence there was in his constitution an indescribable embarrassment, mingled with decision. He was a man of middle height. His face ruddy and full, his broad chest, his wide shoulders announced the robust man, the laborer-schoolmaster, the peasant-thinker. In this he resembled Bourzat. Baudin leaned his head on his shoulder, listened with intelligence, and spoke with a gentle and grave voice. He had the melancholy air and the bitter smile of the doomed.

On the evening of the Second of December I had asked him, "How old are you?" He had answered me, "Not quite thirty-three years."

"And you?" said he.

"Forty-nine."

And he replied,—

"Today we are of the same age."

He thought in truth of that tomorrow which awaited us, and in which was hidden that "perhaps" which is the great leveller.

The first shots had been fired, a Representative had fallen, and the people did not rise! What bandage had they on their eyes, what weight had they on their hearts? Alas! the gloom which Louis Bonaparte had known how to cast over his crime, far from lifting, grew denser. For the first time in the sixty years, that the Providential era of Revolutions had been open, Paris, the city of intelligence, seemed not to understand!

On leaving the barricade of the Rue Ste. Marguerite, De Flotte went to the Faubourg St. Marceau, Madier de Montjau went to Belleville, Charamaule and Maigne proceeded to the Boulevards. Schoelcher, Dulac, Malardier, and Brillier again went up the Faubourg St. Antoine by the side streets which the soldiers had not yet occupied. They shouted, "Vive la République!" They harangued the people on the doorsteps: "Is it the Empire that you want?" exclaimed Schoelcher. They even went as far as to sing the "Marseillaise." People took off their hats as they passed and shouted "Long live the Representatives!" But that was all.

They were thirsty and weary. In the Rue de Reuilly a man came out of a door with a bottle in his hand, and offered them drink.

Sartin joined them on the way. In the Rue de Charonne they entered the meeting-place of the Association of Cabinet Makers, hoping to find there the committee of the association in session. There was no one there. But nothing discouraged them.

As they reached the Place de la Bastille, Dulac said to Schoelcher, "I will ask permission to leave you for an hour or two, for this reason: I am alone in Paris with my little daughter, who is seven years old. For the past week she has had scarlet fever. Yesterday, when the *coup d'état* burst forth, she was at death's door. I have no one but this child in the world. I left her this morning to come with you, and she said to me, 'Papa, where are you going?' As I am not killed, I will go and see if she is not dead."

Two hours afterwards the child was still living, and we were holding a permanent sitting at No. 15, Rue Richelieu, Jules Favre, Carnot, Michel de Bourges, and myself, when Dulac entered, and said to us, "I have come to place myself at your disposal."

IV

The Workmen's Societies Ask Us for the Order to Fight

In presence of the fact of the barricade of the Faubourg St. Antoine so heroically constructed by the Representatives, so sadly neglected by the populace, the last illusions, even mine, should have been dispersed. Baudin killed, the Faubourg cold. Such things spoke aloud. It was a supreme, manifest, absolute demonstration of that fact, the inaction of the people, to which I could not resign myself—a deplorable inaction, if they understood, a self-treason, if they did not understand, a fatal neutrality in every case, a calamity of which all the responsibility, we repeat, recoiled not upon the people but upon those who in June, 1848, after having promised them amnesty, had refused it, and who had unhinged the great soul of the people of Paris by breaking faith with them. What the Constituent Assembly had sown the Legislative Assembly harvested. We, innocent of the fault, had to submit to the consequence.

The spark which we had seen flash for an instant through the crowd— Michel de Bourges from the height of Bonvalet's balcony, myself from the Boulevard du Temple—this spark seemed extinguished. Maigne firstly, then Brillier, then Bruckner, later on Charmaule, Madier de Montjau, Bastide, and Dulac came to report to us what had passed at the barricade of St. Antoine, the motives which had decided the Representatives present not to await the hour appointed for the rendezvous, and Baudin's death. The report which I made myself of what I had seen, and which Cassal and Alexander Rey completed by adding new circumstances, enabled us to ascertain the situation. The Committee could no longer hesitate: I myself renounced the hopes which I had based upon a grand manifestation, upon a powerful reply to the *coup d'état*, upon a sort of pitched battle waged by the guardians of the Republic against the banditti of the Elysée. The Faubourgs failed us; we possessed the lever—Right, but the mass to be raised, the People, we did not possess. There was nothing more to hope for, as those two great orators, Michel de Bourges and Jules Favre, with their keen political perception, had declared from the first, save a slow long struggle, avoiding decisive engagements, changing quarters, keeping Paris on the alert, saying to each, It is not at an end; leaving time for the departments to prepare their resistance, wearying the troops out, and in which struggle the Parisian people, who do not long smell powder with impunity, would perhaps ultimately take fire. Barricades raised everywhere, barely defended, re-made immediately, disappearing and multiplying themselves at the same time, such was the strategy indicated by the situation. The Committee adopted it, and sent orders in every direction to this effect. At that moment we were sitting at No. 15, Rue Richelieu, at the house of our colleague Grévy, who had been arrested in the Tenth Arrondissement on the preceding day, who was at Mazas. His brother had offered us his house for our deliberations. The Representatives, our natural emissaries, flocked around us, and scattered themselves throughout Paris, with our instructions to organize resistance at every point. They were the arms and the Committee was the soul. A certain number of ex-Constituents, intrepid men, Garnier-Pagès, Marie, Martin (de Strasbourg), Senart, formerly President of the Constituent Assembly, Bastide, Laissac, Landrin, had joined the Representatives on the preceding day. They established, therefore, in all the districts where it was possible Committees of Permanence in connection with us, the Central Committee, and composed either of Representatives or of faithful citizens. For our watchword we chose "Baudin."

Towards noon the centre of Paris began to grow agitated.

Our appeal to arms was first seen placarded on the Place de la Bourse and the Rue Montmartre. Groups pressed round to read it, and battled with the police, who endeavored to tear down the bills. Other lithographic placards contained in two parallel columns the decree of deposition drawn up by the Right at the Mairie of the Tenth Arrondissement, and the decree of outlawry voted by the Left. There were distributed, printed on gray paper in large type, the judgment of the High Court of Justice, declaring Louis Bonaparte attainted with the Crime of High Treason, and signed "Hardouin" (President), "Delapalme," "Moreau" (of the Seine), "Cauchy," "Bataille" (Judges). This last name was thus mis-spelt by mistake, it should read "Pataille."

At that moment people generally believed, and we ourselves believed, in this judgment, which, as we have seen, was not the genuine judgment.

At the same time they posted in the populous quarters, at the corner of every street, two Proclamations. The first ran thus:—

To the People.

"Article III.[1]

"The Constitution is confided to the keeping and to the patriotism of French citizens. Louis Napoleon is outlawed.

"The State of Siege is abolished.

"Universal suffrage is re-established.

"Long Live the Republic.

"To Arms!

"For the United Mountain.

The Delegate, Victor Hugo

The second ran thus:—

Inhabitants of Paris.

"The National Guards and the People of the Departments are marching on Paris to aid you in seizing the Traitor, Louis Napoléon Bonaparte.

For the Representatives of the People,
Victor Hugo, President
Schoelcher, Secretary

This last placard, printed on little squares of paper, was distributed abroad, says an historian of the *coup d'état*, by thousands of copies.

For their part the criminals installed in the Government offices replied by threats: the great white placards, that is to say, the official bills, were largely multiplied. On one could be read:—

---

1. A typographical error—it should read "Article LXVIII." On the subject of this placard the author of this book received the following letter. It does honor to those who wrote it:—

Citizen Victor Hugo,

We know that you have made an appeal to arms. We have not been able to obtain it. We replace it by these bills which we sign with your name. You will not disown us. When France is in danger your name belongs to all; your name is a Public Power.

Felix Bony
Dabat

"Decree as follows:—

"Article I. All meetings are rigorously prohibited. They will be immediately dispersed by force.

"Article II. All seditious shouts, all reading in public, all posting of political documents not emanating from a regularly constituted authority, are equally prohibited.

"Article III. The agents of the Public Police will enforce the execution of the present decree.

"Given at the Prefecture of Police, December 3, 1851.

"De Maupas, Prefect of Police.

Seen and approved,
De Morny, Minister of the Interior

On another could be read,—

The Minister of War,

"By virtue of the Law on the State of Siege,

"Decrees:—

"Every person taken constructing or defending a barricade, or carrying arms, Will Be Shot.

"General of Division,

Minister of war,
De Saint-Arnaud

We reproduce this Proclamation exactly, even to the punctuation. The words "Will be shot" were in capital letters in the placards signed "De Saint-Arnaud."

The Boulevards were thronged with an excited crowd. The agitation increasing in the centre reached three Arrondissements, the 6th, 7th, and the 12th. The district of the schools began to disorderly. The Students of Law and of Medicine cheered De Flotte on the Place de Panthéon. Madier de Montjau, ardent and eloquent, went through and aroused Belleville. The troops, growing more numerous every moment, took possession of all the strategical points of Paris.

At one o'clock, a young man was brought to us by the legal adviser of the Workmen's Societies, the ex-Constituent Leblond, at whose house the Committee had deliberated that morning. We were sitting in permanence, Carnot, Jules Favre, Michel de Bourges, and myself. This young man, who had an earnest mode of speaking and an intelligent countenance, was named King. He had been sent to us by the Committee of the Workmen's Society, from whom he was delegated. "The Workmen's Societies," he said to us, "place themselves at the disposal of the Committee of Legal Insurrection appointed by the Left. They can throw into the struggle five or six thousand resolute men. They will manufacture powder; as for guns, they will be found." The Workmen's Society requested from us an order to fight signed by us. Jules Favre took a pen and wrote,—"The undersigned Representatives authorize Citizen King and his friends to defend with them, and with arms in their hands, Universal Suffrage, the Republic, the Laws." He dated it, and we all four signed it. "That is enough," said the delegate to us, "you will hear of us."

Two hours afterwards it was reported to us that the conflict had begun. They were fighting in the Rue Aumaire.

V

BAUDIN'S CORPSE

With regard to the Faubourg St. Antoine, we had, as I said, lost nearly all hope, but the men of the *coup d'état* had not lost all uneasiness. Since the attempts at rising and the barricades of the morning a rigorous supervision had been organized. Anyone who entered the Faubourg ran the risk of being examined, followed, and upon the slightest suspicion, arrested. The supervision was nevertheless sometimes at fault. About two o'clock a short man, with an earnest and attentive air, crossed the Faubourg. A *sergent de ville* and a police agent in plain clothes barred his passage. "Who are you?" "You seem a passenger." "Where are you going?" "Over there, close by, to Bartholomé's, the overseer of the sugar manufactory.—" They search him. He himself opened his pocket-book; the police agents turned out the pockets of his waistcoat and unbuttoned his shirt over his breast; finally the *sergent de ville* said gruffly, "Yet I seem to have seen you here before this morning. Be off!" It was the Representative Gindrier. If they had not stopped at the pockets of his waistcoat—and if they had searched his great-coat, they would have found his sash there—Gindrier would have been shot.

Not to allow themselves to be arrested, to keep their freedom for the combat—such was the watchword of the members of the Left. That is why we had our sashes upon us, but not outwardly visible.

Gindrier had had no food that day; he thought he would go home, and returned to the new district of the Havre Railway Station, where he resided. In the Rue de Calais, which is a lonely street running from Rue Blanche to the Rue de Clichy, a *fiacre* passed him. Gindrier heard his name called out. He turned round and saw two persons in a *fiacre*, relations of Baudin, and a man whom he did not know. One of the relations of Baudin, Madame L——, said to him, "Baudin is wounded!" She added, "They have taken him to the St. Antoine Hospital. We are going to fetch him. Come with us." Gindrier got into the *fiacre*. The stranger, however, was an emissary of the Commissary of Police of the Rue Ste. Marguerite St. Antoine. He had been charged by the commissary of Police to go to Baudin's house, No, 88, Rue de Clichy, to inform the family. Having only found the women at home he had confined himself to telling them that Representative Baudin was wounded. He offered to accompany them, and went with them in the *fiacre*. They had uttered the name of Gindrier before him. This might have been imprudent. They spoke to him; he declared that he would not betray the Representative, and it was settled that before the Commissary of Police Gindrier should assume to be a relation, and be called Baudin.

The poor women still hoped. Perhaps the wound was serious, but Baudin was young, and had a good constitution. "They will save him," said they. Gindrier was silent. At the office of the Commissary of Police the truth was revealed.—"How is he?" asked Madame L—— on entering. "Why?" said the Commissary, "he is dead." "What do you mean? Dead!" "Yes; killed on the spot."

This was a painful moment. The despair of these two women who had been so abruptly struck to the heart burst forth in sobs. "Ah, infamous Bonaparte!" cried Madame L——. "He has killed Baudin. Well, then, I will kill him. I will be the Charlotte Corday of this Marat."

Gindrier claimed the body of Baudin. The Commissary of Police only consented to restore it to the family on exacting a promise that they would bury it at once, and without any ostentation, and that they would not exhibit it to the people. "You understand," he said, "that the sight of a Representative killed and bleeding might raise Paris." The *coup d'état* made corpses, but did not wish that they should be utilized.

On these conditions the Commissary of Police gave Gindrier two men and a safe conduct to fetch the body of Baudin from the hospital where he had been carried.

Meanwhile Baudin's brother, a young man of four-and-twenty, a medical student, came up. This young man has since been arrested and imprisoned. His crime is his brother. Let us continue. They proceeded to the hospital. At the sight of the safe conduct the director ushered Gindrier and young Baudin into the parlor. There were three pallets there covered with white sheets, under which could be traced the motionless forms of three human bodies. The one which occupied the centre bed was Baudin. On his right lay the young soldier killed a minute before him by the side of Schoelcher, and on the left an old woman who had been struck down by a spent ball in the Rue de Cotte, and whom the executioners of the *coup d'état* had gathered up later on; in the first moment one cannot find out all one's riches.

The three corpses were naked under their winding sheets.

They had left to Baudin alone his shirt and his flannel vest. They had found on him seven francs, his gold watch and chain, his Representative's medal, and a gold pencil-case which he had used in the Rue de Popincourt, after having passed me the other pencil, which I still preserve. Gindrier and young Baudin, bare-headed, approached the centre bed. They raised the shroud, and Baudin's dead face became visible. He was calm, and seemed asleep. No feature appeared contracted. A livid tint began to mottle his face.

They drew up an official report. It is customary. It is not sufficient to kill people. An official report must also be drawn up. Young Baudin had to sign it, upon which, on the demand of the Commissary of Police, they "made over" to him the body of his brother. During these signatures, Gindrier in the courtyard of the hospital, attempted if not to console, at least to calm the two despairing women.

Suddenly a man who had entered the courtyard, and who had attentively watched him for some moments, came abruptly up to him,—

"What are you doing there?"

"What is that to you?" said Gindrier.

"You have come to fetch Baudin's body?"

"Yes."

"Is this your carriage?"

"Yes."

"Get in at once, and pull down the blinds."

"What do you mean?"

"You are the Representative Gindrier. I know you. You were this morning on the barricade. If any other than myself should see you, you are lost."

Gindrier followed his advice and got into the *fiacre*. While getting in he asked the man:

"Do you belong to the Police?"

The man did not answer. A moment after he came and said in a low voice, near the door of the *fiacre* in which Gindrier was enclosed,—

"Yes, I eat the bread, but I do not do the work."

The two men sent by the Commissary of Police took Baudin on his wooden bed and carried him to the *fiacre*. They placed him at the bottom of the *fiacre* with his face covered, and enveloped from head to foot in a shroud. A workman who was there lent his cloak, which was thrown over the corpse in order not to attract the notice of passers-by. Madame L—— took her place by the side of the body, Gindrier opposite, young Baudin next to Gindrier. A *fiacre* followed, in which were the other relative of Baudin and a medical student named Dutèche. They set off. During the journey the head of the corpse, shaken by the carriage, rolled from shoulder to shoulder; the blood began to flow from the wound and appeared in large red patches through the white sheet. Gindrier with his arms stretched out and his hand placed on its breast, prevented it from falling forwards; Madame L—— held it up by the side.

They had told the coachman to drive slowly; the journey lasted more than an hour.

When they reached No. 88, Rue de Clichy, the bringing out of the body attracted a curious crowd before the door. The neighbors flocked thither. Baudin's brother, assisted by Gindrier and Dutèche, carried up the corpse to the fourth floor, where Baudin resided. It was a new house, and he had only lived there a few months.

They carried him into his room, which was in order, and just as he had left it on the morning of the 2d. The bed, on which he had not slept the preceding night, had not been disturbed. A book which he had been reading had remained on the table, open at the page where he had left off. They unrolled the shroud, and Gindrier cut off his shirt and his flannel vest with a pair of scissors. They washed the body. The ball had entered through the corner of the arch of the right eye, and had gone out at the back of the head. The wound of the eye had not bled. A sort of swelling had formed there; the blood had flowed copiously through the hole at the back of the head. They put clean linen on him, and clean sheets on the bed, and laid him down with his head on the pillow, and his face uncovered. The women were weeping in the next room.

Gindrier had already rendered the same service to the ex-Constituent James Demontry. In 1850 James Demontry died in exile at Cologne. Gindrier started for Cologne, went to the cemetery, and had James Demontry exhumed. He had the heart extracted, embalmed it, and enclosed it in a silver vase, which he took to Paris. The party of the Mountain delegated him, with Chollet and Joigneux, to convey this heart to Dijon, Demontry's native place, and to give him a solemn funeral. This funeral was prohibited by an order of Louis Bonaparte, then President of the Republic. The burial of brave and faithful men was unpleasing to Louis Bonaparte—not so their death.

When Baudin had been laid out on the bed, the women came in, and all this family, seated round the corpse, wept. Gindrier, whom other duties called elsewhere, went downstairs with Dutèche. A crowd had formed before the door.

A man in a blouse, with his hat on his head, mounted on a kerbstone, was speechifying and glorifying the *coup d'état*. Universal Suffrage re-established, the Law of the 31st May abolished, the "Twenty-five francs" suppressed; Louis Bonaparte has done well, etc.—Gindrier, standing on the threshold of the door, raised his voice: "Citizens! above lies Baudin, a Representative of the People, killed while defending the People; Baudin the Representative of you all, mark that well! You are before his house; he is there bleeding on his bed, and here is a man who dares in this place to applaud his assassin! Citizens! shall I tell you the name of this man? He is called the Police! Shame and infamy to traitors and to cowards! Respect to the corpse of him who has died for you!"

And pushing aside the crowd, Gindrier took the man who had been speaking by the collar, and knocking his hat on to the ground with the back of his hand, he cried, "Hats off!"

VI

The Decrees of the Representatives Who Remained Free

The text of the judgment which was believed to have been dawn up by the High Court of Justice had been brought to us by the ex-Constituent Martin (of Strasbourg), a lawyer at the Court of Cassation. At the same time we learned what was happening in the Rue Aumaire. The battle was beginning, it was important to sustain it, and to feed it; it was important ever to place the legal resistance by the side of the armed resistance. The members who had met together on the preceding day at the Mairie of the Tenth Arrondissement had decreed the deposition of Louis Bonaparte; but this decree, drawn up by a meeting almost exclusively composed of the unpopular members of the majority, might have no effect on the masses; it was necessary that the Left should take it up, should adopt it, should imprint upon it a more energetic and more revolutionary accent, and also take possession of the judgment of the High Court, which was believed to be genuine, to lend assistance to this judgment, and put it into execution.

In our appeal to arms we had outlawed Louis Bonaparte. The decree of deposition taken up and counter-signed by us added weight to this outlawry, and completed the revolutionary act by the legal act.

The Committee of Resistance called together the Republican Representatives.

The apartments of M. Grévy, where we had been sitting, being too small, we appointed for our meeting-place No. 10. Rue des Moulins, although warned that the police had already made a raid upon this house. But we had no choice; in time of Revolution prudence is impossible, and it is speedily seen that it is useless. Confidence, always confidence; such is the law of those grand actions which at times determine great events. The perpetual improvisation of means, of policy, of expedients, of resources, nothing step by step, everything on the impulse of the moment, the ground never sounded, all risks taken as a whole, the good with the bad, everything chanced on all sides at the same time, the hour, the place, the opportunity, friends, family, liberty, fortune, life,—such is the revolutionary conflict.

Towards three o'clock about sixty Representatives were meeting at No. 10, Rue des Moulins, in the large drawing-room, out of which opened a little room where the Committee of Resistance was in session.

It was a gloomy December day, and darkness seemed already to have almost set in. The publisher Hetzel, who might also be called the poet Hetzel, is of a noble mind and of great courage. He has, as is known, shown unusual political qualities as Secretary-General of the Ministry of Foreign Affairs under Bastide; he came to offer himself to us, as the brave and patriotic Hingray had already done in the morning. Hetzel knew that we needed a printing-office above everything; we had not the faculty of speech, and Louis Bonaparte spoke alone. Hetzel had found a printer who had said to him, "*Force me, put a pistol to my throat, and I will print whatever you wish.*" It was only a question, therefore, of getting a few friends together, of seizing this printing-office by main force, of barricading it, and, if necessary, of sustaining a siege, while our Proclamations and our decrees were being printed. Hetzel offered this to us. One incident of his arrival at our meeting-place deserves to be noted. As he drew near the doorway he saw in the twilight of this dreary December day a man standing motionless at a short distance, and who seemed to be lying in wait. He went up to this man, and recognized M. Yon, the former Commissary of Police of the Assembly.

"What are you doing there?" said Hetzel abruptly. "Are you there to arrest us? In that case, here is what I have got for you," and he took out two pistols from his pocket.

M. Yon answered smiling,—

"I am in truth watching, not against you, but for you; I am guarding you."

M. Yon, aware of our meeting at Landrin's house and fearing that we should be arrested, was, of his own accord, acting as police for us.

Hetzel had already revealed his scheme to Representative Labrousse, who was to accompany him and give him the moral support of the Assembly in his perilous expedition. A first rendezvous which had been agreed upon between them at the Café Cardinal having failed, Labrousse had left with the owner of the *café* for Hetzel a note couched in these terms:—

"Madame Elizabeth awaits M. Hetzel at No. 10, Rue des Moulins."

In accordance with this note Hetzel had come.

We accepted Hetzel's offer, and it was agreed that at nightfall Representative Versigny, who performed the duties of Secretary to the

Committee, should take him our decrees, our Proclamation, such items of news as may have reached us, and all that we should judge proper to publish. It was settled that Hetzel should await Versigny on the pavement at the end of the Rue de Richelieu which runs alongside the Café Cardinal.

Meanwhile Jules Favre, Michel de Bourges and myself had drawn up a final decree, which was to combine the deposition voted by the Right with the outlawry voted by us. We came back into the large room to read it to the assembled Representatives, and for them to sign it.

At this moment the door opened, and Emile de Girardin appeared. We had not seen him since the previous evening.

Emile de Girardin—after dispersing from around him that mist which envelopes every combatant in party warfare, and which at a distance changes or obscures the appearance of a man—Emile de Girardin is an extraordinary thinker, an accurate writer, energetic, logical, skilful, hearty; a journalist in whom, as in all great journalists, can be seen the statesman. We owe to Emile de Girardin this great work of progress, the cheap Press. Emile de Girardin has this great gift, a clearheaded stubbornness. Emile de Girardin is a public watchman; his journal is his sentry-box; he waits, he watches, he spies out, he enlightens, he lies in wait, he cries "Who goes there?" at the slightest alarm, he fires volleys with his pen. He is ready for every form of combat, a sentinel today, a General tomorrow. Like all earnest minds he understands, he sees, he recognizes, he handles, so to speak, the great and magnificent identity embraced under these three words, "Revolution, Progress, Liberty"; he wishes for the Revolution, but above all through Progress; he wishes for progress, but solely through Liberty. One can, and according to our opinion sometimes rightly, differ from him as to the road to be taken, as to the attitude to be assumed, and the position to be maintained, but no one can deny his courage, which he has proved in every form, nor reject his object, which is the moral and physical amelioration of the lot of all. Emile de Girardin is more Democratic than Republican, more Socialist than Democratic; on the day when these three ideas, Democracy, Republicanism, Socialism, that is to say, the principle, the form, and the application, are balanced in his mind the oscillations which still exist in him will cease. He has already Power, he will have Stability.

In the course of this sitting, as we shall see, I did not always agree with Emile de Girardin. All the more reason that I should record here how greatly I appreciate the mind formed of light and of courage. Emile de Girardin, whatever his failings may be, is one of those men who do honor to the Press of today; he unites in the highest degree the dexterity of the combatant with the serenity of the thinker.

I went up to him, and I asked him,—

"Have you any workmen of the *Presse* still remaining?"

He answered me,—

"Our presses are under seal, and guarded by the *Gendarmerie Mobile*, but I have five or six willing workmen, they can produce a few placards with the brush."

"Well then," said I, "print our decrees and our Proclamation." "I will print anything," answered he, "as long as it is not an appeal to arms."

He added, addressing himself to me, "I know your Proclamation. It is a war-cry, I cannot print that."

They remonstrated at this. He then declared that he for his part made Proclamations, but in a different sense from ours. That according to him Louis Bonaparte should not be combated by force of arms, but by creating a vacuum. By an armed conflict he would be the conqueror, by a vacuum he would be conquered. He urged us to aid him in isolating the "deposed of the Second December." "Let us bring about a vacuum around him!" cried Emile de Girardin, "let us proclaim an universal strike. Let the merchant cease to sell, let the consumer cease from buying, let the workman cease from working, let the butcher cease from killing, let the baker cease from baking, let everything keep holiday, even to the National Printing Office, so that Louis Bonaparte may not find a compositor to compose the *Moniteur*, not a pressman to machine it, not a bill-sticker to placard it! Isolation, solitude, a void space round this man! Let the nation withdraw from him. Every power from which the nation withdraws falls like a tree from which the roots are divided. Louis Bonaparte abandoned by all in his crime will vanish away. By simply folding our arms as we stand around him he will fall. On the other hand, fire on him and you will consolidate him. The army is intoxicated, the people are dazed and do not interfere, the middle classes are afraid of the President, of the people, of you, of everyone! No victory is possible. You will go straight before you, like brave men, you risk your heads, very good; you will carry with you two or three thousand daring men, whose blood mingled with yours, already flows. It is heroic, I grant you. It is not politic. As for me, I will not print an appeal to arms, and I reject the combat. Let us organize an universal strike."

This point of view was haughty and superb, but unfortunately I felt it to be unattainable. Two aspects of the truth seized Girardin, the logical side and the practical side. Here, in my opinion, the practical side was wanting.

Michel de Bourges answered him. Michel de Bourges with his sound logic and quick reasoning put his finger on what was for us the immediate question; the crime of Louis Bonaparte, the necessity to rise up erect before this crime. It was rather a conversation than a debate, but Michel de Bourges and Jules Favre, who spoke next, raised it to the highest eloquence. Jules Favre, worthy to understand the powerful mind of Girardin would willingly have adopted this idea, if it had seemed practicable, of the universal strike, of the void around the man; he found it great, but impossible. A nation does not pull up short. Even when struck to the heart, it still moves on. Social movement, which is the animal life of society, survives all political movement. Whatever Emile de Girardin might hope, there would always be a butcher who would kill, a baker who would bake, men must eat! "To make universal labor fold its arms is a chimera!" said Jules Favre, "a dream! The People fight for three days, for four days, for a week; society will not wait indefinitely." As to the situation, it was doubtless terrible, it was doubtless tragical, and blood flowed, but who had brought about this situation? Louis Bonaparte. For ourselves we would accept it, such as it was, and nothing more.

Emile de Girardin, steadfast, logical, absolute in his idea, persisted. Some might be shaken. Arguments, which were so abundant in this vigorous and inexhaustible mind, crowded upon him. As for me, I saw Duty before me like a torch.

I interrupted him. I cried out, "It is too late to deliberate what we are to do. We have not got to do it. It is done. The gauntlet of the *coup d'état* is thrown down, the Left takes it up. The matter is as simple as this. The outrage of the Second December is an infamous, insolent, unprecedented defiance to Democracy, to Civilization, to Liberty, to the People, to France. I repeat that we have taken up this gauntlet, we are the Law, but the living Law which at need can arm itself and fight. A gun in our hands is a protest. I do not know whether we shall conquer, but it is our duty to protest. To protest first in Parliament; when Parliament is closed, to protest in the street; when the street is closed, to protest in exile; when exile is fulfilled, to protest in the tomb. Such is our part, our office, our mission. The authority of the Representatives is elastic; the People bestow it, events extend it."

While we were deliberating, our colleague, Napoleon Bonaparte, son of the ex-King of Westphalia, came in. He listened. He spoke. He energetically blamed, in a tone of sincere and generous indignation, his cousin's crime, but he declared that in his opinion a written protest would suffice. A protest of the Representatives, a protest of the Council of State, a protest of the Magistracy, a protest of the Press, that this protest would be unanimous and would enlighten France, but that no other form of resistance would obtain unanimity. That as for himself, having always considered the Constitution worthless, having contended against it from the first in the Constituent Assembly, he would not defend it at the last, that he assuredly would not give one drop of blood for it. That the Constitution was dead, but that the Republic was living, and that we must save, not the Constitution, a corpse, but the Republic, the principle!

Remonstrances burst forth. Bancel, young, glowing, eloquent, impetuous, overflowing with self-confidence, cried out that we ought not to look at the shortcomings of the Constitution, but at the enormity of the crime which had been committed, the flagrant treason, the violated oath; he declared that we might have voted against the Constitution in the Constituent Assembly, and yet defend it today in the presence of an usurper; that this was logical, and that many amongst us were in this position. He cited me as an example. Victor Hugo, said he, is a proof of this. He concluded thus: "You have been present at the construction of a vessel, you have considered it badly built, you have given advice which has not been listened to. Nevertheless, you have been obliged to embark on board this vessel, your children and your brothers are there with you, your mother is on board. A pirate ranges up, axe in one hand, to scuttle the vessel, a torch in the other to fire it. The crew are resolved to defend themselves and run to arms. Would you say to this crew, 'For my part I consider this vessel badly built, and I will let it be destroyed'?"

"In such a case," added Edgar Quinet, "whoever is not on the side of the vessel is on the side of the pirates."

They shouted on all sides, "The decree! Read the decree!"

I was standing leaning against the fire place. Napoleon Bonaparte came up to me, and whispered in my ear,—

"You are undertaking," said he, "a battle which is lost beforehand."

I answered him, "I do not look at success, I look at duty."

He replied, "You are a politician, consequently you ought to look forward to success. I repeat, before you go any further, that the battle is lost beforehand."

I resumed, "If we enter upon the conflict the battle is lost. You say so, I believe it; but if we do not enter upon it, honor is lost. I would rather lose the battle than honor."

He remained silent for a moment, then he took my hand.

"Be it so," continued he, "but listen to me. You run, you yourself personally, great dancer. Of all the men in the Assembly you are the one whom the President hates the most. You have from the height of the Tribune nicknamed him, 'Napoleon the Little.' You understand that will never be forgotten. Besides, it was you who dictated the appeal to arms, and that is known. If you are taken, you are lost. You will be shot on the spot, or at least transported. Have you a safe place where you can sleep tonight?"

I had not as yet thought of this. "In truth, no," answered I.

He continued, "Well, then, come to my house. There is perhaps only one house in Paris where you would be in safety. That is mine. They will not come to look for you there. Come, day or night, at what hour you please, I will await you, and I will open the door to you myself. I live at No. 5, Rue d'Alger."

I thanked him. It was a noble and cordial offer. I was touched by it. I did not make use of it, but I have not forgotten it.

They cried out anew, "Read the decree! Sit down! sit down!"

There was a round table before the fire place; a lamp, pens, blotting-books, and paper were brought there; the members of the Committee sat down at this table, the Representatives took their places around them on sofas, on arm-chairs, and on all the chairs which could be found in the adjoining rooms. Some looked about for Napoleon Bonaparte. He had withdrawn.

A member requested that in the first place the meeting should declare itself to be the National Assembly, and constitute itself by immediately appointing a President and Secretaries. I remarked that there was no need to declare ourselves the Assembly, that we were the Assembly by right as well as in fact, and the whole Assembly, our absent colleagues being detained by force; that the National Assembly, although mutilated by the *coup d'état*, ought to preserve its entity and remain constituted afterwards in the same manner as before; that to appoint another President and another staff of Secretaries would be to give Louis Bonaparte an advantage over us, and to acknowledge in some manner the Dissolution; that we ought to do nothing of the sort; that our decrees should be published, not with the signature of a President, whoever he might be, but with the signature of all the members of the Left who had not been arrested, that they would thus carry with them full authority over the People, and full effect. They relinquished the idea of appointing a President. Noël Parfait proposed that our decrees and our resolutions should be drawn up, not with the formula: "The National Assembly decrees," etc.; but with the formula: "The Representatives of the People remaining at liberty decree," etc. In this manner we should preserve all the authority attached to the office of the Representatives of the People without associating the arrested Representatives with the responsibility of our actions. This formula had the additional advantage of separating us from the Right. The people knew that the only Representatives remaining free were the members of the Left. They adopted Noël Parfait's advice.

I read aloud the decree of deposition. It was couched in these words:—

DECLARATION.

"The Representatives of the people remaining at liberty, by virtue of Article 68 of the Constitution, which runs as follows:—

"'Article 68.—Every measure by which the President of the Republic dissolves the Assembly, prorogues it, or obstructs the exercise of its authority, is a crime of High Treason.

"'By this action alone the President is deposed from his office; the citizens are bound to refuse him obedience; the executive power passes by right to the National Assembly; the judges of the High Court of Justice should meet together immediately under penalty of treason, and convoke the juries in a place which they shall appoint to proceed to the judgment of the President and his accomplices.'

"Decree:—

"ARTICLE I.—Louis Bonaparte is deposed from his office of President of the Republic.

"ARTICLE II.—All citizens and public officials are bound to refuse him obedience under penalty of complicity.

"ARTICLE III.—The judgment drawn up on December 2d by the High Court of Justice, and which declares Louis Bonaparte attainted with the Crime of High Treason, shall be published and executed. Consequently the civil and military authorities are summoned under penalty of Treason to lend their active assistance to the execution of the said judgment.

"Given at Paris, in permanent session, December 3d, 1851."

The decree having been read, and voted unanimously, we signed it, and the Representatives crowded round the table to add their signatures to ours. Sain remarked that this signing took time, that in addition we numbered barely more than sixty, a large number of the members of the Left being at work in the streets in insurrection. He asked if the Committee, who had full powers from the whole of the Left, had any objection to attach to the decree the names of all the Republican Representatives remaining at liberty, the absent as well as those present. We answered that the decree signed by all would assuredly better answer its purpose. Besides, it was the counsel which I had already given. Bancel had in his pocket on old number of the *Moniteur* containing the result of a division.

They cut out a list of the names of the members of the Left, the names of those who were arrested were erased, and the list was added to the decree.[1]

The name of Emile de Girardin upon this list caught my eye. He was still present.

"Do you sign this decree?" I asked him.

"Unhesitatingly."

"In that case will you consent to print it?"

"Immediately."

He continued,—

"Having no longer any presses, as I have told you, I can only print it as a handbill, and with the brush. It takes a long time, but by eight o'clock this evening you shall have five hundred copies."

"And," continued I, "you persist in refusing to print the appeal to arms?"

"I do persist."

A second copy was made of the decree, which Emile de Girardin took away with him. The deliberation was resumed. At each moment Representatives came in and brought items of news: Amiens in insurrection—Rheims and Rouen in motion, and marching on Paris—

---

1. This list, which belongs to History, having served as the base of the proscription list, will be found complete in the sequel to this book to be published hereafter.

General Canrobert resisting the *coup d'état*—General Castellane hesitating—the Minister of the United States demanding his passports. We placed little faith in these rumors, and facts proved that we were right.

Meanwhile Jules Favre had drawn up the following decree, which he proposed, and which was immediately adopted:—

DECREE.

FRENCH REPUBLIC

"Liberty,—Equality,—Fraternity.

"The undersigned Representatives remaining at liberty, assembled in Permanent Session,—

"Considering the arrest of the majority of our colleagues, and the urgency of the moment:

"Considering that for the accomplishment of his crime Louis Bonaparte has not contented himself with multiplying the most formidable means of destruction against the lives and property of the citizens of Paris, that he has trampled under foot every law, that he has annihilated all the guarantees of civilized nations:

"Considering that these criminal madnesses only serve to augment the violent denunciation of every conscience and to hasten the hour of national vengeance, but that it is important to proclaim the Right:

"Decree:

"ARTICLE I.—The State of Siege is raised in all Departments where it has been established, the ordinary laws resume their authority.

"ARTICLE II.—It is enjoined upon all military leaders under penalty of Treason immediately to lay down the extraordinary powers which have been conferred upon them.

"ARTICLE III.—Officials and agents of the public force are charged under penalty of treason to put this present decree into execution.

"Given in Permanent Session, 3d December, 1851."

Madier de Montjau and De Flotte entered. They came from outside. They had been in all the districts where the conflict was proceeding, they had seen with their own eyes the hesitation of a part of the population in the presence of these words, "The Law of the 31st May is abolished, Universal Suffrage is re-established." The placards of Louis Bonaparte were manifestly working mischief. It was necessary to oppose effort to effort, and to neglect nothing which could open the eyes of the people. I dictated the following Proclamation:—

PROCLAMATION.

"People! you are being deceived.

"Louis Bonaparte says that he has re-established you in your rights, and that he restores to you Universal Suffrage.

"Louis Bonaparte has lied.

"Read his placards. He grants you—what infamous mockery!—the right of conferring on him, on him *alone*, the Constituent power; that is to say, the Supreme power, which belongs to you. He grants you the right to appoint him Dictator *for ten years*. In other words, he grants you the right of abdicating and of crowning him. A right which even you do not possess, O People! for one generation cannot dispose of the sovereignty of the generation which shall follow it.

"Yes, he grants to you, Sovereign, the right of giving yourself a master, and that master himself.

"Hypocrisy and treason!

"People! we unmask the hypocrite. It is for you to punish the traitor!

"The Committee of Resistance:

"Jules Favre, De Flotte, Carnot, Madier de Montjau, Mathieu (de la Drôme), Michel de Bourges, Victor Hugo."

Baudin had fallen heroically. It was necessary to let the People know of his death, and to honor his memory. The decree below was voted on the proposition of Michel de Bourges:—

DECREE.

"The Representatives of the People remaining at liberty considering that the Representative Baudin has died on the barricade of the Faubourg St. Antoine for the Republic and for the laws, and that he has deserved well of his country, decree:

"That the honors of the Panthéon are adjudged to Representative Baudin.

"Given in Permanent Session, 3d December, 1851."

After honor to the dead and the needs of the conflict it was necessary in my opinion to enunciate immediately and dictatorially some great popular benefit. I proposed the abolition of the *octroi* duties and of the duty on liquors. This objection was raised, "No caresses to the people! After victory, we will see. In the meantime let them fight! If they do not fight, if they do not rise, if they do not understand that it is for them, for their rights that we the Representatives, that we risk our heads at this moment—if they leave us alone at the breach, in the presence of the *coup d'état*—it is because they are not worthy of Liberty!"

Bancel remarked that the abolition of the *octroi* duties and the duty on liquors were not caresses to the People, but succor to the poor, a great economical and reparatory measure, a satisfaction to the public demand—a satisfaction which the Right had always obstinately refused, and that the Left, master of the situation, ought hasten to accord. They voted, with the reservation that it should not be published until after victory, the two decrees in one; in this form:—

DECREE.

"The Representatives remaining at liberty decree:

"The *Octroi* Duties are abolished throughout the extent of the territory of the Republic.

"Given in permanent Session, 3d December, 1851."

Versigny, with a copy of the Proclamations and of the Decree, left in search of Hetzel. Labrousse also left with the same object. They settled to meet at eight o'clock in the evening at the house of the former member of the Provisional Government Marie, Rue Neuve des Petits Champs.

As the members of the Committee and the Representatives withdrew I was told that someone had asked to speak to me. I went into a sort of little room attached to the large meeting-room, and I found there a man in a blouse, with an intelligent and sympathetic air. This man had a roll of paper in his hand.

"Citizen Victor Hugo," said he to me, "you have no printing office. Here are the means which will enable you to dispense with one."

He unfolded on the mantel-piece the roll which he had in his hand. It was a species of blotting-book made of very thin blue paper, and which seemed to be slightly oiled. Between each leaf of blue paper there was a sheet of white paper. He took out of his pocket a sort of blunt bodkin, saying, "The first thing to hand will serve your purpose, a nail or a match," and he traced with his bodkin on the first leaf of the book the word "Republic." Then turning over the leaves, he said, "Look at this."

The word "Republic" was reproduced upon the fifteen or twenty white leaves which the book contained.

He added, "This paper is usually used to trace the designs of manufactured fabrics. I thought that it might be useful at a moment like this. I have at home a hundred books like this on which I can make a hundred copies of what you want—a Proclamation, for instance—in the same space of time that it takes to write four or five. Write something, whatever you may think useful at the present moment, and tomorrow morning five hundred copies shall be posted throughout Paris."

I had none of the documents with me which we had just drawn up. Versigny had gone away with the copies. I took a sheet of paper, and, leaning on the corner of the chimney-piece, I wrote the following Proclamation:—

To The Army.

"Soldiers!

"A man has just broken the Constitution. He tears up the oath which he has sworn to the people; he suppresses the law, stifles Right, stains Paris with blood, chokes France, betrays the Republic!

"Soldiers, this man involves you in his crime.

"There are two things holy; the flag which represents military honor and the law which represents the National Right. Soldiers, the greatest of outrages is the flag raised against the Law! Follow no longer the wretched man who misleads you. Of such a crime French soldiers should be the avengers, not the accomplices.

"This man says he is named Bonaparte. He lies, for Bonaparte is a word which means glory. This man says that he is named Napoléon. He lies, for Napoléon is a word which means genius.

As for him, he is obscure and insignificant. Give this wretch up to the law. Soldiers, he is a false Napoléon. A true Napoléon would once more give you a Marengo; he will once more give you a Transnonain.

"Look towards the true function of the French army; to protect the country, to propagate the Revolution, to free the people, to sustain the nationalities, to emancipate the Continent, to break chains everywhere, to protect Right everywhere, this is your part amongst the armies of Europe. You are worthy of great battle-fields.

"Soldiers, the French Army is the advanced guard of humanity.

"Become yourselves again, reflect; acknowledge your faults; rise up! Think of your Generals arrested, taken by the collar by galley sergeants and thrown handcuffed into robbers' cells! The malefactor, who is at the Elysée, thinks that the Army of France is a band of mercenaries; that if they are paid and intoxicated they will obey. He sets you an infamous task, he causes you to strangle, in this nineteenth century, and in Paris itself, Liberty, Progress, and Civilization. He makes you—you, the children of France—destroy all that France has so gloriously and laboriously built up during the three centuries of light and in sixty years of Revolution! Soldiers! you are the 'Grand Army!' respect the 'Grand Nation!'

"We, citizens; we, Representatives of the People and of yourselves; we, your friends, your brothers; we, who are Law and Right; we, who rise up before you, holding out our arms to you, and whom you strike blindly with your swords—do you know what drives us to despair? It is not to see our blood which flows; it is to see your honor which vanishes.

"Soldiers! one step more in the outrage, one day more with Louis Bonaparte, and you are lost before universal conscience. The men who command you are outlaws. They are not generals— they are criminals. The garb of the galley slave awaits them; see it already on their shoulders. Soldiers! there is yet time—Stop! Come back to the country! Come back to the Republic! If you continue, do you know what History will say of you? It will say, They have trampled under the feet of their horses and crushed beneath the wheels of their cannon all the laws of their country; they, French soldiers, they have dishonored the anniversary of Austerlitz, and by their fault, by their crime, the name of Napoléon sprinkles as much shame today upon France as in other times it has showered glory!

"French soldiers! cease to render assistance to crime!"

My colleagues of the Committee having left, I could not consult them—time pressed—I signed:

"For the Representatives of the People remaining at liberty, the Representative member of the Committee of Resistance,

VICTOR HUGO

The man in the blouse took away the Proclamation saying, "You will see it again tomorrow morning." He kept his word. I found it the nest day placarded in the Rue Rambuteau, at the corner of the Rue de l'Homme-Armé and the Chapelle-Saint-Denis. To those who were not in the secret of the process it seemed to be written by hand in blue ink.

I thought of going home. When I reached the Rue de la Tour d'Auvergne, opposite my door, it happened curiously and by some chance to be half open. I pushed it, and entered. I crossed the courtyard, and went upstairs without meeting anyone.

My wife and my daughter were in the drawing-room round the fire with Madame Paul Meurice. I entered noiselessly; they were conversing in a low tone. They were talking of Pierre Dupont, the popular song-writer, who had come to me to ask for arms. Isidore, who had been a soldier, had some pistols by him, and had lent three to Pierre Dupont for the conflict.

Suddenly these ladies turned their heads and saw me close to them. My daughter screamed. "Oh, go away," cried my wife, throwing her arms round my neck, "you are lost if you remain here a moment. You will be arrested here!" Madame Paul Meurice added, "They are looking for you. The police were here a quarter of an hour ago." I could not succeed in reassuring them. They gave me a packet of letters offering me places of refuge for the night, some of them signed with names unknown to me. After some moments, seeing them more and more frightened, I went away. My wife said to me, "What you are doing, you are doing for justice. Go, continue!" I embraced my wife and my daughter; five months have elapsed at the time when I am writing these lines. When I went into exile they remained near my son Victor in prison; I have not seen them since that day.

I left as I had entered. In the porter's lodge there were only two or three little children seated round a lamp, laughing and looking at pictures in a book.

VII

The Archbishop

On this gloomy and tragical day an idea struck one of the people. He was a workman belonging to the honest but almost imperceptible minority of Catholic Democrats. The double exaltation of his mind, revolutionary on one side, mystical on the other, caused him to be somewhat distrusted by the people, even by his comrades and his friends. Sufficiently devout to be called a Jesuit by the Socialists, sufficiently Republican to be called a Red by the Reactionists, he formed an exception in the workshops of the Faubourg. Now, what is needed in these supreme crises to seize and govern the masses are men of exceptional genius, not men of exceptional opinion. There is no revolutionary originality. In order to be something, in the time of regeneration and in the days of social combat, one must bathe fully in those powerful homogeneous mediums which are called parties. Great currents of men follow great currents of ideas, and the true revolutionary leader is he who knows how best to drive the former in accordance with the latter.

Now the Gospel is in accordance with the Revolution, but Catholicism is not. This is due to the fact that in the main the Papacy is not in accordance with the Gospel. One can easily understand a Christian Republican, one cannot understand a Catholic Democrat. It is a combination of two opposites. It is a mind in which the negative bars the way to the affirmative. It is a neuter.

Now in time revolution, whoever is neuter of is impotent. Nevertheless, during the first hours of resistance against the *coup d'état* the democratic Catholic workman, whose noble effort we are here relating, threw himself so resolutely into the cause of Justice and of Truth, that in a few moments he transformed distrust into confidence, and was hailed by the people. He showed such gallantry at the rising of the barricade of the Rue Aumaire that with an unanimous voice they appointed him their leader. At the moment of the attack he defended it as he had built it, with ardor. That was a sad but glorious battle-field; most of his companions were killed, and he escaped only by a miracle.

However, he succeeded in returning home, saying to himself bitterly, "All is lost."

It seemed evident to him that the great masses of the people would not rise. Thenceforward it appeared impossible to conquer the *coup d'état* by a revolution; it could be only combated by legality. What had been the risk at the beginning became the hope at the end, for he believed the end to be fatal, and at hand. In his opinion it was necessary, as the people were defaulters, to try now to arouse the middle classes. Let one legion of National Guards go out in arms, and the Elysée was lost. For this a decisive blow must be struck—the heart of the middle classes must be reached—the "bourgeois" must be inspired by a grand spectacle which should not be a terrifying spectacle.

It was then that this thought came to this workman, "Write to the Archbishop of Paris."

The workman took a pen, and from his humble garret he wrote to the Archbishop of Paris an enthusiastic and earnest letter in which he, a man of the people and a believer, said this to his Bishop; we give the substance of his letter:—

"This is a solemn hour, Civil War sets by the ears the Army and People, blood is being shed. When blood flows the Bishop goes forth. M. Sibour should follow in the path of M. Affre. The example is great, the opportunity is still greater.

"Let the Archbishop of Paris, followed by all his clergy, the Pontifical cross before him, his mitre on his head, go forth in procession through the streets. Let him summon to him the National Assembly and the High Court, the Legislators in their sashes, the Judges in their scarlet robes; let him summon to him the citizens, let him summon to him the soldiers, let him go straight to the Elysée. Let him raise his hand in the name of Justice against the man who is violating the laws, and in the name of Jesus against the man who is shedding blood. Simply with his raised hand he will crush the *coup d'état*.

"And he will place his statue by the side of M. Affre, and it will be said that twice two Archbishops of Paris have trampled Civil War beneath their feet."

"The Church is holy, but the Country is sacred. There are times when the Church should succor the Country."

The letter being finished, he signed it with his workman's signature.

But now a difficulty arose; how should it be conveyed to its destination?

Take it himself!

But would he, a mere workman in a blouse, be allowed to penetrate to the Archbishop!

And then, in order to reach the Archiepiscopal Palace, he would have to cross those very quarters in insurrection, and where, perhaps, the resistance was still active. He would have to pass through streets obstructed by troops, he would be arrested and searched; his hands smelt of powder, he would be shot; and the letter would not reach its destination.

What was to be done?

At the moment when he had almost despaired of a solution, the name of Arnauld de l'Ariége came to his mind.

Arnauld de l'Ariége was a Representative after his own heart. Arnauld de l'Ariége was a noble character. He was a Catholic Democrat like the workman. At the Assembly he raised aloft, but he bore nearly alone, that banner so little followed which aspires to ally the Democracy with the Church. Arnauld de l'Ariége, young, handsome, eloquent, enthusiastic, gentle, and firm, combined the attributes of the Tribune with the faith of the knight. His open nature, without wishing to detach itself from Rome, worshipped Liberty. He had two principles, but he had not two faces. On the whole the democratic spirit preponderated in him. He said to me one day, "I give my hand to Victor Hugo. I do not give it to Montalembert."

The workman knew him. He had often written to him, and had sometimes seen him.

Arnauld de l'Ariége lived in a district which had remained almost free.

The workman went there without delay.

Like the rest of us, as has been seen, Arnauld de l'Ariége had taken part in the conflict. Like most of the Representatives of the Left, he had not returned home since the morning of the 2d. Nevertheless, on the second day, he thought of his young wife whom he had left without knowing if he should see her again, of his baby of six months old which she was suckling, and which he had not kissed for so many hours, of that beloved hearth, of which at certain moments one feels an absolute need to obtain a fleeting glimpse, he could no longer resist; arrest, Mazas, the cell, the hulks, the firing party, all vanished, the idea of danger was obliterated, he went home.

It was precisely at that moment that the workman arrived there.

Arnauld de l'Ariége received him, read his letter, and approved of it.

Arnauld de l'Ariége knew the Archbishop of Paris personally.

M. Sibour, a Republican priest appointed Archbishop of Paris by General Cavaignac, was the true chief of the Church dreamed of by the liberal Catholicism of Arnauld de l'Ariége. On behalf of the Archbishop, Arnauld de l'Ariége represented in the Assembly that Catholicism which M. de Montalembert perverted. The democratic Representative and the Republic Archbishop had at times frequent conferences, in which acted as intermediatory the Abbé Maret, an intelligent priest, a friend of the people and of progress, Vicar-General of Paris, who has since been Bishop *in partibus* of Surat. Some days previously Arnauld had seen the Archbishop, and had received his complaints of the encroachment of the Clerical party upon the episcopal authority, and he even proposed shortly to interpellate the Ministry on this subject and to take the question into the Tribune.

Arnauld added to the workman's letter a letter of introduction, signed by himself, and enclosed the two letters in the same envelope.

But here the same question arose.

How was the letter to be delivered?

Arnauld, for still weightier reasons than those of the workman, could not take it himself.

And time pressed!

His wife saw his difficulty and quietly said,—

"I will take charge of it."

Madame Arnauld de l'Ariége, handsome and quite young, married scarcely two years, was the daughter of the Republican ex-Constituent Guichard, worthy daughter of such a father, and worthy wife of such a husband.

They were fighting in Paris; it was necessary to face the dangers of the streets, to pass among musket-balls, to risk her life.

Arnauld de l'Ariége hesitated.

"What do you want to do?" he asked.

"I will take this letter."

"You yourself?"

"I myself."

"But there is danger."

She raised her eyes, and answered,—

"Did I make that objection to you when you left me the day before yesterday?"

He kissed her with tears in his eyes, and answered, "Go."

But the police of the *coup d'état* were suspicious, many women were searched while going through the streets; this letter might be found on Madame Arnauld. Where could this letter be hidden?

"I will take my baby with me," said Madame Arnauld.

She undid the linen of her little girl, hid the letter there, and refastened the swaddling band.

When this was finished the father kissed his child on the forehead, and the mother exclaimed laughingly,—

"Oh, the little Red! She is only six months' old, and she is already a conspirator!"

Madame Arnauld reached the Archbishop's Palace with some difficulty. Her carriage was obliged to take a long round. Nevertheless she arrived there. She asked for the Archbishop. A woman with a child in her arms could not be a very terrible visitor, and she was allowed to enter.

But she lost herself in courtyards and staircases. She was seeking her way somewhat discouraged, when she met the Abbé Maret. She knew him. She addressed him. She told him the object of her expedition. The Abbé Maret read the workman's letter, and was seized with enthusiasm: "This may save all," said he.

He added, "Follow me, madam, I will introduce you."

The Archbishop of Paris was in the room which adjoins his study. The Abbé Maret ushered Madame Arnauldé into the study, informed the Archbishop, and a moment later the Archbishop entered. Besides the Abbé Maret, the Abbé Deguerry, the Curé of the Madeleine, was with him.

Madame Arnauld handed to M. Sibour the two letters of her husband and the workman. The Archbishop read them, and remained thoughtful.

"What answer am I to take back to my husband?" asked Madame Arnauld.

"Madame," replied the Archbishop, "it is too late. This should have been done before the struggle began. Now, it would be only to risk the shedding of more blood than perhaps has yet been spilled."

The Abbé Deguerry was silent. The Abbé Maret tried respectfully to turn the mind of his Bishop towards the grand effort unsoiled by the workman. He spoke eloquently. He laid great stress open this argument, that the appearance of the Archbishop would bring about a manifestation of the National Guard, and that a manifestation of the National Guard would compel the Elysée to draw back.

"No," said the Archbishop, "you hope for the impossible. The Elysée will not draw back now. You believe that I should stop the bloodshed— not at all; I should cause it to flow, and that in torrents. The National Guard has no longer any influence. If the legions appeared, the Elysée could crush the legions by the regiments. And then, what is an Archbishop in the presence of the Man of the *coup d'état*? Where is the oath? Where is the sworn faith? Where is the Respect for Right? A man does not turn back when he has made three steps in such a crime. No! No! Do not hope. This man will do all. He has struck the Law in the hand of the Representatives. He will strike God in mine."

And he dismissed Madame Arnauld with the look of a man overwhelmed with sorrow.

Let us do the duty of the Historian. Six weeks afterwards, in the Church of Notre Dame, someone was singing the *Te Deum* in honor of the treason of December—thus making God a partner in a crime.

This man was the Archbishop Sibour.

VIII

MOUNT VALÉRIEN

Of the two hundred and thirty Representatives prisoners at the barracks of the Quai d'Orsay fifty-three had been sent to Mount Valérien. They loaded them in four police vans. Some few remained who were packed in an omnibus. MM. Benoist d'Azy, Falloux, Piscatory, Vatimesail, were locked in the wheeled cells, as also Eugène Sue and Esquiros. The worthy M. Gustave de Beaumont, a great upholder of the cellular system, rode in a cell vehicle. It is not an undesirable thing, as we have said, that the legislator should taste of the law.

The Commandant of Mount Valérien appeared under the archway of the fort to receive the Representative prisoners.

He at first made some show of registering them in the jailer's book. General Oudinot, under whom he had served, rebuked him severely,—

"Do you know me?"

"Yes, General."

"Well then, let that suffice. Ask no more."

"Yes," said Tamisier. "Ask more and salute. We are more than the Army; we are France."

The commandant understood. From that moment he was hat in hand before the generals, and bowed low before the Representatives.

They led them to the barracks of the fort and shut them up promiscuously in a dormitory, to which they added fresh beds, and which the soldiers had just quitted. They spent their first night there. The beds touched each other. The sheets were dirty.

Next morning, owing to a few words which had been heard outside, the rumor spread amongst them that the fifty-three were to be sorted, and that the Republicans were to be placed by themselves. Shortly afterwards the rumor was confirmed. Madame de Luynes gained admission to her husband, and brought some items of news. It was asserted, amongst other things, that the Keeper of the Seals of the *coup d'état*, the man who signed himself Eugène Rouher, "Minister of Justice," had said, "Let them set the men of the Right at liberty, and send the men of the Left to the dungeon. If the populace stirs they will answer for everything. As a guarantee for the submission of the Faubourgs we shall have the head of the Reds."

We do not believe that M. Rouher uttered these words, in which there is so much audacity. At that moment M. Rouher did not possess any. Appointed Minister on the 2d December, he temporized, he exhibited a vague prudery, he did not venture to install himself in the Place Vendôme. Was all that was being done quite correct? In certain minds the doubt of success changes into scruples of conscience. To violate every law, to perjure oneself, to strangle Right, to assassinate the country, are all these proceedings wholly honest? While the deed is not accomplished they hesitate. When the deed has succeeded they throw themselves upon it. Where there is victory there is no longer treason; nothing serves like success to cleanse and render acceptable that unknown thing which is called crime. During the first moments M. Rocher reserved himself. Later on he has been one of the most violent advisers of Louis Bonaparte. It is all very simple. His fear beforehand explains his subsequent zeal.

The truth is, that these threatening words had been spoken not by Rouher, but by Persigny.

M. de Luynes imparted to his colleagues what was in preparation, and warned them that they would be asked for their names in order that the white sheep might be separated from the scarlet goats. A murmur which seemed to be unanimous arose. These generous manifestations did honor to the Representatives of the Right.

"No! no! Let us name no one, let us not allow ourselves to be sorted," exclaimed M. Gustave de Beaumont.

M. de Vatimesnil added, "We have come in here all together, we ought to go out all together."

Nevertheless a few moments afterwards Antony Thouret was informed that a list of names was being secretly prepared, and that the Royalist Representatives were invited to sign it. They attributed, doubtless wrongly, this unworthy resolution to the honorable M. de Falloux.

Antony Thouret spoke somewhat warmly in the centre of the group, which were muttering together in the dormitory.

"Gentlemen," said he, "a list of names is being prepared. This would be an unworthy action. Yesterday at the Mairie of the Tenth Arrondissement you said to us, 'There is no longer Left or Right; we are the Assembly.' You believed in the victory of the People, and you sheltered yourself behind us Republicans. Today you believe in the victory of the *coup d'état*, and you would again become Royalists, to deliver us up, us Democrats! Truly excellent. Very well! Pray do so."

A universal shout arose.

"No! No! No more Right or Left! All are the Assembly. The same lot for all!"

The list which had been begun was seized and burnt.

"By decision of the Chamber," said M. de Vatimesnil, smiling. A Legitimist Representative added,—

"Of the Chamber? No, let us say of the Chambered."

A few moments afterwards the Commissary of the fort appeared, and in polite phrases, which, however, savored somewhat of authority, invited each of the Representatives of the People to declare his name in order that each might be allotted to his ultimate destination.

A shout of indignation answered him.

"No one! No one will give his name," said General Oudinot.

Gustave de Beaumont added,—

"We all bear the same name: Representatives of the People."

The Commissary saluted them and went away.

After two hours he came back. He was accompanied this time by the Chief of the Ushers of the Assembly, a man named Duponceau, a species of arrogant fellow with a red face and white hair, who on grand days strutted at the foot of the Tribune with a silvered collar, a chain over his stomach, and a sword between his legs.

The Commissary said to Duponceau,—"Do your duty."

What the Commissary meant, and what Duponceau understood by this word *duty*, was that the Usher should denounce the Legislators. Like the lackey who betrays his masters.

It was done in this manner.

This Duponceau dared to look in the faces of the Representatives by turn, and he named them one after the other to a policeman, who took notes of them.

The Sieur Duponceau was sharply castigated while holding this review.

"M. Duponceau," said M. Vatimesnil to him, "I always thought you an idiot, but I believed you to be an honest man."

The severest rebuke was administered by Antony Thouret. He looked Sieur Duponceau in the face, and said to him, "You deserve to be named Dupin."

The Usher in truth was worthy of being the President, and the President was worthy of being the Usher.

The flock having been counted, the classification having been made, there were found to be thirteen goats: ten Representatives of the Left; Eugène Sue, Esquires, Antony Thouret, Pascal Duprat, Chanay, Fayolle, Paulin Durrien, Benoit, Tamisier, Tailard Latérisse, and three members of the Right, who since the preceding day had suddenly become Red in the eyes of the *coups d'état*; Oudinot, Piscatory, and Thuriot de la Rosière.

They confined these separately, and they set at liberty one by one the forty who remained.

IX

The Lightning Begins to Flash
Among the People

The evening wore a threatening aspect.

Groups were formed on the Boulevards. As night advanced they grew larger and became mobs, which speedily mingled together, and only formed one crowd. An enormous crowd, reinforced and agitated by tributary currents from the side-streets, jostling one against another, surging, stormy, and whence ascended an ominous hum. This hubbub resolved itself into one word, into one name which issued simultaneously from every mouth, and which expressed the whole of the situation: "Soulouque!"[1] Throughout that long line from the Madeleine to the Bastille, the roadway nearly everywhere, except (was this on purpose?) at the Porte St. Denis and the Porte St. Martin, was occupied by the soldiers—infantry and cavalry, ranged in battle-order, the artillery batteries being harnessed; on the pavements on each side of this motionless and gloomy mass, bristling with cannon, swords, and bayonets, flowed a torrent of angry people. On all sides public indignation prevailed. Such was the aspect of the Boulevards. At the Bastille there was a dead calm.

At the Porte St. Martin the crowd, hemmed together and uneasy, spoke in low tones. Groups of workmen talked in whispers. The Society of the 10th December made some efforts there. Men in white blouses, a sort of uniform which the police assumed during those days, said, "Let us leave them alone; let the 'Twenty-five francs' settle it amongst themselves! They deserted us in June, 1848; today let them get out of the difficulty alone! It does not concern us!" Other blouses, blue blouses, answered them, "We know what we have to do. This is only the beginning, wait and see."

Others told how the barricades of the Rue Aumaire were being rebuilt, how a large number of persons had already been killed there,

---

1. A popular nickname for Louis Bonaparte. Faustin Soulouque was the negro Emperor of Hayti, who, when President of the Republic, had carried out a somewhat similar *coup d'état* in 1848, being subsequently elected Emperor. He treated the Republicans with great cruelty, putting most of them to death.

how they fired without any summons, how the soldiers were drunk, how at various points in the district there were ambulances already crowded with killed and wounded. All this was said seriously, without loud speaking, without gesture, in a confidential tone. From time to time the crowd were silent and listened, and distant firing was heard.

The groups said, "Now they are beginning to tear down the curtain."

We were holding Permanent Session at Marie's house in the Rue Croix des Petits Champs. Promises of co-operation poured in upon us from every side. Several of our colleagues, who had not been able to find us on the previous day, had joined us, amongst others Emmanuel Arago, gallant son of an illustrious father; Farconnet and Roussel (de l'Yonne), and some Parisian celebrities, amongst whom was the young and already well-known defender of the *Avénement du Peuple*, M. Desmarets.

Two eloquent men, Jules Favre and Alexander Rey, seated at a large table near the window of the small room, were drawing up a Proclamation to the National Guard. In the large room Sain, seated in an arm-chair, his feet on the dog-irons, drying his wet boots before a huge fire, said, with that calm and courageous smile which he wore in the Tribune, "Things are looking badly for us, but well for the Republic. Martial law is proclaimed; it will be carried out with ferocity, above all against us. We are laid in wait for, followed, tracked, there is little probability that we shall escape. Today, tomorrow, perhaps in ten minutes, there will be a 'miniature massacre' of Representatives. We shall be taken here or elsewhere, shot down on the spot or killed with bayonet thrusts. They will parade our corpses, and we must hope that that will at length raise the people and overthrow Bonaparte. We are dead, but Bonaparte is lost."

At eight o'clock, as Emile de Girardin had promised, we received from the printing office of the *Presse* five hundred copies of the decree of deposition and of outlawry endorsing the judgment of the High Court, and with all our signatures attached. It was a placard twice as large as one's hand, and printed on paper used for proofs. Noël Parfait brought us the five hundred copies, still damp, between his waistcoat and his shirt. Thirty Representatives divided the bills amongst them, and we sent them on the Boulevards to distribute the Decree to the People.

The effect of this Decree falling in the midst of the crowd was marvellous. Some *cafés* had remained open, people eagerly snatched the bills, they pressed round the lighted shop windows, they crowded under the street lamps. Some mounted on kerbstones or on tables, and read aloud the Decree.—"That is it! Bravo!" cried the people. "The signatures!" "The signatures!" they shouted. The signatures were read out, and at each popular name the crowd applauded. Charamaule, merry and indignant, wandered through the groups, distributing copies of the Decree; his great stature, his loud and bold words, the packet of handbills which he raised, and waved above his head, caused all hands to be stretched out towards him. "Shout 'Down with Soulouque!'" said he, "and you shall have some." All this in the presence of the soldiers. Even a sergeant of the line, noticing Charamaule, stretched out his hand for one of the bills which Charamaule was distributing. "Sergeant," said Charamaule to him, "cry, 'Down with Soulouque!'" The sergeant hesitated for a moment, and answered "No." "Well, then," replied Charamaule, "Shout, 'Long live Soulouque.'" This time the sergeant did not hesitate, he raised his sword, and, amid bursts of laughter and of applause, he resolutely shouted, "Long live Soulouque!"

The reading of the Decree added a gloomy warmth to the popular anger. They set to work on all sides to tear down the placards of the *coup d'état*. At the door of the Café des Variétés a young man cried out to the officers, "You are drunk!" Some workmen on the Boulevard Bonne-Nouvelle shook their fists at the soldiers and said, "Fire, then, you cowards, on unarmed men! If we had guns you would throw the butts of your muskets in the air." Charges of cavalry began to be made in front of the Café Cardinal.

As there were no troops on the Boulevard St. Martin and the Boulevard du Temple, the crowd was more compact pact there than elsewhere. All the shops were shut there; the street lamps alone gave any light. Against the gloss of the unlighted windows heads might be dimly seen peering out. Darkness produced silence; this multitude, as we have already said, was hushed. There was only heard a confused whispering. Suddenly a light, a noise, an uproar burst forth from the entrance of the Rue St. Martin. Every eye was turned in that direction; a profound upheaving agitated the crowd; they rushed forward, they pressed against the railings of the high pavements which border the cutting between the theatres of the Porte St. Martin and the Ambigu. A moving mass was seen, and an approaching light. Voices were singing. This formidable chorus was recognized,

"Aux armes, Citoyens; formez vos bataillons!"

　　　　　　　　　　　　　　　　　　　VICTOR HUGO

Lighted torches were coming, it was the "Marseillaise," that other torch of Revolution and of warfare which was blazing.

The crowd made way for the mob which carried the torches, and which were singing. The mob reached the St. Martin cutting, and entered it. It was then seen what this mournful procession meant. The mob was composed of two distinct groups. The first carried on its shoulders a plank, on which could be seen stretched an old man with a white beard, stark, the mouth open, the eyes fixed, and with a hole in his forehead. The swinging movement of the bearers shook the corpse, and the dead head rose and fell in a threatening and pathetic manner. One of the men who carried him, pale, and wounded in the breast, placed his hand to his wound, leant against the feet of the old man, and at times himself appeared ready to fall. The other group bore a second litter, on which a young man was stretched, his countenance pale and his eyes closed, his shirt stained, open over his breast, displaying his wounds. While bearing the two litters the groups sang. They sang the "Marseillaise," and at each chorus they stopped and raised their torches, crying, "To arms!" Some young men waved drawn swords. The torches shed a lurid light on the pallid foreheads of the corpses and on the livid faces of the crowd. A shudder ran through the people. It appeared as though they again saw the terrible vision of February, 1848.

This gloomy procession came from the Rue Aumaire. About eight o'clock some thirty workmen gathered together from the neighborhood of the markets, the same who on the next day raised the barricade of the Guérin-Boisseau, reached the Rue Aumaire by the Rue de Petit Lion, the Rue Neuve-Bourg-l'Abbé, and the Carré St. Martin. They came to fight, but here the combat was at an end. The infantry had withdrawn after having pulled down the barricades. Two corpses, an old man of seventy and a young man of five-and-twenty, lay at the corner of the street on the ground, with uncovered faces, their bodies in a pool of blood, their heads on the pavement where they had fallen. Both were dressed in overcoats, and seemed to belong to the middle class. The old man had his hat by his side; he was a venerable figure with a white beard, white hair, and a calm expression. A ball had pierced his skull.

The young man's breast was pierced with buck-shot. One was the father, the other the son. The son, seeing his father fall, had said, "I also will die." Both were lying side by side.

Opposite the gateway of the Conservatoire des Arts et Metiers there was a house in course of building. They fetched two planks from it, they laid the corpses on the planks, the crowd raised them upon their shoulders, they brought torches, and they began their march. In the Rue St. Denis a man in a white blouse barred the way. "Where are you going?" said he to them. "You will bring about disasters! You are helping the 'Twenty-five francs!'" "Down with the police! Down with the white blouse!" shouted the crowd. The man slunk away.

The mob swelled on its road; the crowd opened out and repeated the "Marseillaise" in chorus, but with the exception of a few swords no one was armed. On the boulevard the emotion was intense. Women clasped their hands in pity. Workmen were heard to exclaim, "And to think that we have no arms!"

The procession, after having for sometime followed the Boulevards, re-entered the streets, followed by a deeply-affected and angry multitude. In this manner it reached the Rue de Gravilliers. Then a squad of twenty *sergents de ville* suddenly emerging from a narrow street rushed with drawn swords upon the men who were carrying the litters, and overturned the corpses into the mud. A regiment of Chasseurs came up at the double, and put an end to the conflict with bayonet thrusts. A hundred and two citizen prisoners were conducted to the Prefecture. The two corpses received several sword-cuts in the confusion, and were killed a second time. The brigadier Revial, who commanded the squad of the *sergents de ville*, received the Cross of Honor for this deed of arms.

At Marie's we were on the point of being surrounded. We decided to leave the Rue Croix des Petits Champs.

At the Elysée they commenced to tremble. The ex-Commandant Fleury, one of the aides-de-camp of the Presidency, was summoned into the little room where M. Bonaparte had remained throughout the day. M. Bonaparte conferred a few moments alone with M. Fleury, then the aide-de-camp came out of the room, mounted his horse, and galloped off in the direction of Mazas.

After this the men of the *coup d'état* met together in M. Bonaparte's room, and held council. Matters were visibly going badly; it was probable that the battle would end by assuming formidable proportions. Up to that time they had desired this, now they did not feel sure that they did not fear it. They pushed forward towards it, but they mistrusted it. There were alarming symptoms in the steadfastness of the resistance, and others not less serious in the cowardice of adherents. Not one of the new Ministers appointed during the morning had taken possession of his Ministry—a significant timidity on the part of people ordinarily so prompt to throw themselves upon such things. M. Roulier, in particular, had disappeared, no one knew where—a sign of tempest. Putting Louis Bonaparte on one side, the *coup d'état* continued to rest solely upon three names, Morny, St. Arnaud, and Maupas. St. Arnaud answered for Magnan. Morny laughed and said in a whisper, "But does Magnan answer for St. Arnaud?" These men adopted energetic measures, they sent for new regiments; an order to the garrisons to march upon Paris was despatched in the one direction as far as Cherbourg, and on the other as far as Maubeuge. These criminals, in the main deeply uneasy, sought to deceive each other. They assumed a cheerful countenance; all spoke of victory; each in the background arranged for flight; in secret, and saying nothing, in order not to give the alarm to his compromised colleagues, so as, in case of failure, to leave the people some men to devour. For this little school of Machiavellian apes the hopes of a successful escape lie in the abandonment of their friends. During their flight they throw their accomplices behind them.

X

What Fleury Went to Do at Mazas

During the same night towards four o'clock the approaches of the Northern Railway Station were silently invested by two regiments; one of Chasseurs de Vincennes, the other of *Gendarmerie Mobile*. Numerous squads of *sergents de ville* installed themselves in the terminus. The station-master was ordered to prepare a special train and to have an engine ready. A certain number of stokers and engineers for night service were retained. No explanation however was vouchsafed to anyone, and absolute secrecy was maintained. A little before six o'clock a movement was apparent in the troops. Some *sergents de ville* came running up, and a few minutes afterwards a squadron of Lancers emerged at a sharp trot from the Rue du Nord. In the centre of the squadron and between the two lines of horse-soldiers could be seen two police-vans drawn by post-horses, behind each vehicle came a little open barouche, in which there sat one man. At the head of the Lancers galloped the aide-de-camp Fleury.

The procession entered the courtyard, then the railway station, and the gates and doors were reclosed.

The two men in the barouches made themselves known to the Special Commissary of the station, to whom the aide-de-camp Fleury spoke privately. This mysterious convoy excited the curiosity of the railway officials; they questioned the policemen, but these knew nothing. All that they could tell was that these police-vans contained eight places, that in each van there were four prisoners, each occupying a cell, and that the four other cells were filled by four *sergents de ville* placed between the prisoners so as to prevent any communication between the cells.

After various consultations between the aide-de-camp of the Elysée and the men of the Prefect Maupas, the two police-vans were placed on railway trucks, each having behind it the open barouche like a wheeled sentry-box, where a police agent acted as sentinel. The engine was ready, the trucks were attached to the tender, and the train started. It was still pitch dark.

For a long time the train sped on in the most profound silence. Meanwhile it was freezing, in the second of the two police-vans, the

VICTOR HUGO

sergents de ville, cramped and chilled, opened their cells, and in order to warm and stretch themselves walked up and down the narrow gangway which runs from end to end of the police-vans. Day had broken, the four *sergents de ville* inhaled the outside air and gazed at the passing country through a species of port-hole which borders each side of the ceiling of the passage. Suddenly a loud voice issued from one of the cells which had remained closed, and cried out, "Hey! there! it is very cold, cannot I relight my cigar here?"

Another voice immediately issued from a second cell, and said, "What! it is you? Good-morning, Lamoricière!"

"Good-morning, Cavaignac!" replied the first voice.

General Cavaignac and General Lamoricière had just recognized each other.

A third voice was raised from a third cell. "Ah! you are there, gentlemen. Good-morning and a pleasant journey."

He who spoke then was General Changarnier.

"Generals?" cried out a fourth voice. "I am one of you!"

The three generals recognized M. Baze. A burst of laughter came from the four cells simultaneously.

This police-van in truth contained, and was carrying away from Paris, the Questor Baze, and the Generals Lamoricière, Cavaignac, and Changarnier. In the other vehicle, which was placed foremost on the trucks, there were Colonel Charras, Generals Bedeau and Le Flô, and Count Roger (du Nord).

At midnight these eight Representative prisoners were sleeping in their cells at Mazas, when they heard a sudden knocking at their doors, and a voice cried out to them, "Dress, they are coming to fetch you." "Is it to shoot us?" cried Charras from the other side of the door. They did not answer him. It is worth remarking that this idea came simultaneously to all. And in truth, if we can believe what has since transpired through the quarrels of accomplices, it appears that in the event of a sudden attack being made by us upon Mazas to deliver them, a fusillade had been resolved upon, and that St. Arnaud had in his pocket the written order, signed "Louis Bonaparte."

The prisoners got up. Already on the preceding night a similar notice had been given to them. They had passed the night on their feet, and at six o'clock in the morning the jailer said to them, "You can go to bed." The hours passed by; they ended by thinking it would be the same as the preceding night, and many of them, hearing five o'clock strike from the clock tower inside the prison, were going to get back into bed, when the doors of their cells were opened. All the eight were taken downstairs one by one into the clerk's office in the Rotunda, and were then ushered into the police-van without having met or seen each other during the passage. A man dressed in black, with an impertinent bearing, seated at a table with pen in hand, stopped them on their way, and asked their names. "I am no more disposed to tell you my name than I am curious to learn yours," answered General Lamoricière, and he passed outside.

The aide-de-camp Fleury, concealing his uniform under his hooded cloak, stationed himself in the clerk's office. He was charged, to use his own words, to "embark" them, and to go and report their "embarkation" at the Elysée. The aide-de-camp Fleury had passed nearly the whole of his military career in Africa in General Lamoricière's division; and it was General Lamoricière who in 1848, then being Minister of War, had promoted him to the rank of major. While passing through the clerk's office, General Lamoricière looked fixedly at him.

When they entered the police-vans the generals were smoking cigars. They took them from them. General Lamoricière had kept his. A voice from outside cried three separate times, "Stop his smoking!" A *sergent de ville* who was standing by the door of the cell hesitated for sometime, but however ended by saying to the general, "Throw away your cigar."

Thence later on ensued the exclamation which caused General Cavaignac to recognize General Lamoricière. The vehicles having been loaded they set off.

They did not know either with whom they were or where they were going. Each observed for himself in his box the turnings of the streets, and tried to speculate. Some believed that they were being taken to the Northern Railway Station; others thought to the Havre Railway Station. They heard the trot of the escort on the paving-stones.

On the railway the discomfort of the cells greatly increased. General Lamoricière, encumbered with a parcel and a cloak, was still more jammed in than the others. He could not move, the cold seized him, and he ended by the exclamation which put all four of them in communication with each other.

On hearing the names of the prisoners their keepers, who up to that time had been rough, became respectful. "I say there," said General Changarnier, "open our cells, and let us walk up and down the passage like yourselves." "General," said a *sergent de ville*, "we are forbidden to do so. The Commissary of Police is behind the carriage in a barouche, whence he sees everything that is taking place here." Nevertheless, a few moments afterwards, the keepers, under pretext of cold, pulled up the ground-glass window which closed the vehicle on the side of the Commissary, and having thus "blocked the police," as one of them remarked, they opened the cells of the prisoners.

It was with great delight that the four Representatives met again and shook hands. Each of these three generals at this demonstrative moment maintained the character of his temperament. Lamoricière, impetuous and witty, throwing himself with all his military energy upon "the Bonaparte"; Cavaignac, calm and cold; Changarnier, silent and looking out through the port-hole at the landscape. The *sergents de ville* ventured to put in a word here and there. One of them related to the prisoners that the ex-Prefect Carlier had spent the night of the First and Second at the Prefecture of Police. "As for me," said he, "I left the Prefecture at midnight, but I saw him up to that hour, and I can affirm that at midnight he was there still."

They reached Creil, and then Noyon. At Noyon they gave them some breakfast, without letting them get out, a hurried morsel and a glass of wine. The Commissaries of Police did not open their lips to them. Then the carriages were reclosed, and they felt they were being taken off the trucks and being replaced on the wheels. Post horses arrived, and the vehicles set out, but slowly; they were now escorted by a company of infantry *Gendarmerie Mobile*.

When they left Noyon they had been ten hours in the police-van. Meanwhile the infantry halted. They asked permission to get out for a moment "We consent," said one of the Commissaries of the Police, "but only for a minute, and on condition that you will give your word of honor not to escape." "We will give our word of honor," replied the prisoners. "Gentlemen," continued the Commissary, "give it to me only for one minute, the time to drink a glass of water." "No," said General Lamoricière, "but the time to do the contrary," and he added, "To Louis Bonaparte's health." They allowed them to get out, one by one, and they were, able to inhale for a moment the fresh air in the open country by the side of the road.

Then the convoy resumed its march.

As the day waned they saw through their port-hole a mass of high walls, somewhat overtopped by a great round tower. A moment afterwards the carriages entered beneath a low archway, and then stopped in the centre of a long courtyard, steeply embanked, surrounded by high walls, and commanded by two buildings, of which one had the appearance of a barrack, and the other, with bars at all the windows, had the appearance of a prison. The doors of the carriages were opened. An officer who wore a captain's epaulets was standing by the steps. General Changarnier came down first. "Where are we?" said he. The officer answered, "You are at Ham."

This officer was the Commandant of the Fort. He had been appointed to this post by General Cavaignac.

The journey from Noyon to Ham had lasted three hours and a half. They had spent thirteen hours in the police van, of which ten were on the railway.

They led them separately into the prison, each to the room that was allotted to him. However, General Lamoricière having been taken by mistake into Cavaignac's room, the two generals could again exchange a shake of the hand. General Lamoricière wished to write to his wife; the only letter which the Commissaries of Police consented to take charge of was a note containing this line: "I am well."

The principal building of the prison of Ham is composed of a story above the ground floor. The ground floor is traversed by a dark and low archway, which leads from the principal courtyard into a back yard, and contains three rooms separated by a passage; the first floor contains five rooms. One of the three rooms on the ground floor is only a little ante-room, almost uninhabitable; there they lodged M. Baze. In the remaining lower chambers they installed General Lamoricière and General Changarnier. The five other prisoners were distributed in the five rooms of the first floor.

The room allotted to General Lamoricière had been occupied in the time of the captivity of the Ministers of Charles X. by the ex-Minister of Marine, M. d'Haussez. It was a low, damp room, long uninhabited, and which had served as a chapel, adjoining the dreary archway which led from one courtyard to the other, floored with great planks slimy and mouldy, to which the foot adhered, papered with a gray paper which had turned green, and which hung in rags, exuding saltpetre from the floor to the ceiling, lighted by two barred windows looking on to the courtyard, which had always to be left open on account of the smoky chimney. At the bottom of the room was the bed, and between the windows a table and two straw-bottomed chairs. The damp ran down the walls. When General Lamoricière left this room he carried away rheumatism with him; M. de Haussez went out crippled.

When the eight prisoners had entered their rooms, the doors were shut upon them; they heard the bolts shot from outside, and they were told: "You are in close confinement."

General Cavaignac occupied on the first floor the former room of M. Louis Bonaparte, the best in the prison. The first thing which struck the eye of the General was an inscription traced on the well, and stating the day when Louis Bonaparte had entered this fortress, and the day when he had left it, as is well known, disguised as a mason, and with a plank on his shoulder. Moreover, the choice of this building was an attention on the part of M. Louis Bonaparte, who having in 1848 taken the place of General Cavaignac in power; wished that in 1851 General Cavaignac should take his place in prison.

"Turn and turn about!" Morny had said, smiling.

The prisoners were guarded by the 48th of the Line, who formed the garrison at Ham. The old Bastilles are quite impartial. They obey those who make *coups d'état* until the day when they clutch them. What do these words matter to them, Equity, Truth, Conscience, which moreover in certain circles do not move men anymore than stones? They are the cold and gloomy servants of the just and of the unjust. They take whatever is given them. All is good to them. Are they guilty? Good! Are they innocent? Excellent! This man is the organizer of an ambush. To prison! This man is the victim of an ambush! Enter him in the prison register! In the same room. To the dungeon with all the vanquished!

These hideous Bastilles resemble that old human justice which possessed precisely as much conscience as they have, which condemned Socrates and Jesus, and which also takes and leaves, seizes and releases, absolves and condemns, liberates and incarcerates, opens and shuts, at the will of whatever hand manipulates the bolt from outside.

XI

The End of the Second Day

We left Marie's house just in time. The regiment charged to track us and to arrest us was approaching. We heard the measured steps of soldiers in the gloom. The streets were dark. We dispersed. I will not speak of a refuge which was refused to us.

Less than ten minutes after our departure M. Marie's house was invested. A swarm of guns and swords poured in, and overran it from cellar to attic. "Everywhere! everywhere!" cried the chiefs. The soldiers sought us with considerable energy. Without taking the trouble to lean down and look, they ransacked under the beds with bayonet thrusts. Sometimes they had difficulty in withdrawing the bayonets which they had driven into the wall. Unfortunately for this zeal, we were not there.

This zeal came frown higher sources. The poor soldiers obeyed. "Kill the Representatives," such were their instructions. It was at that moment when Morny sent this despatch to Maupas: "If you take Victor Hugo, do what you like with him." These were their politest phrases. Later on the *coup d'état* in its decree of banishment, called us "those individuals," which caused Schoelcher to say these haughty words: "These people do not even know how to exile politely."

Dr. Véron who publishes in his "Mémoires" the Morny-Maupas despatch, adds: "M. du Maupas sent to look for Victor Hugo at the house of his brother-in-law, M. Victor Foucher, Councillor to the Court of Cassation. He did not find him."

An old friend, a man of heart and of talent, M. Henry d'E——, had offered me a refuge in rooms which he occupied in the Rue Richelieu; these rooms adjoining the Théâtre Français, were on the first floor of a house which, like M. Grévy's residence, had an exit into the Rue Fontaine Molière.

I went there. M. Henry d'E—— being from home, his porter was awaiting me, and handed me the key.

A candle lighted the room which I entered. There was a table near the fire, a blotting-book, and some paper. It was past midnight, and I was somewhat tired; but before going to bed, foreseeing that if I should survive this adventure I should write its history, I resolved immediately to note down some details of the state of affairs in Paris at the end of this day, the second of the *coup d'état*. I wrote this page, which I reproduce here, because it is a life-like portrayal—a sort of direct photograph:—

"Louis Bonaparte has invented something which he calls a 'Consultative Committee,' and which he commissions to draw up the postscript of his crimes.

"Léon Foucher refuses to be in it; Montalember hesitates; Baroche accepts.

"Falloux despises Dupin.

"The first shots were fired at the Record Office. In the Markets in the Rue Rambuteau, in the Rue Beaubourg I heard firing.

"Fleury, the aide-de-camp, ventured to pass down the Rue Montmartre. A musket ball pierced his képi. He galloped quickly off. At one o'clock the regiments were summoned to vote on the *coup d'état*. All gave their adhesion. The students of law and medicine assembled together at the Ecole de Droit to protest. The Municipal Guards dispersed them. There were a great many arrests. This evening, patrols are everywhere. Sometimes an entire regiment forms a patrol.

"Representative Hespel, who is six feet high, was not able to find a cell long enough for him at Mazas, and he has been obliged to remain in the porter's lodge, where he is carefully watched.

"Mesdames Odilon Barrot and de Tocqueville do not know where their husbands are. They go from Mazas to Mont Valérien. The jailers are dumb. It is the 19th Light Infantry which attacked the barricade when Baudin was killed. Fifty men of the *Gendarmerie Mobile* have carried at the double the barricade of the Oratoire in the Rue St. Honoré. Moreover, the conflict reveals itself. They sound the tocsin at the Chapelle Bréa. One barricade overturned sets twenty barricades on their feet. There is the barricade of the Schools in the Rue St. André des Arts, the barricade of the Rue du Temple, the barricade of the Carrefour Phélippeaux defended by twenty young men who have all been killed; they are reconstructing it; the barricade of the Rue de Bretagne, which at this moment Courtigis is bombarding. There is the barricade of the Invalides, the barricade of the Barrière des Martyres, the barricade of the Chapelle St. Denis. The councils of war are sitting in permanence, and order all prisoners to be shot. The 30th of the Line have shot a woman. Oil upon fire.

"The colonel of the 49th of the Line has resigned. Louis Bonaparte has appointed in his place Lieutenant Colonel Négrier. M. Brun,

Officer of the Police of the Assembly, was arrested at the same time as the Questors.

"It is said that fifty members of the majority have signed a protest at M. Odilon Barrot's house.

"This evening there is an increasing uneasiness at the Elysée. Incendiarism is feared. Two battalions of engineer-sappers have reinforced the Fire Brigade. Maupas has placed guards over the gasometers.

"Here are the military talons by which Paris has been grasped:— Bivouacs at all the strategical points. At the Pont Neuf and the Quai aux Fleurs, the Municipal Guards; at the Place de la Bastille twelve pieces of cannon, three mortars, lighted matches; at the corner of the Faubourg the six-storied houses are occupied by soldiers from top to bottom; the Marulaz brigade at the Hôtel de Ville; the Sauboul brigade at the Panthéon; the Courtigis brigade at the Faubourg St. Antoine; the Renaud division at the Faubourg St. Marceau. At the Legislative Palace the Chasseurs de Vincennes, and a battalion of the 15th Light Infantry; in the Champs Elysées infantry and cavalry; in the Avenue Marigny artillery. Inside the circus is an entire regiment; it has bivouacked there all night. A squadron of the Municipal Guard is bivouacking in the Place Dauphine. A bivouac in the Council of State. A bivouac in the courtyard of the Tuileries. In addition, the garrisons of St. Germain and of Courbevoie. Two colonels killed, Loubeau, of the 75th, and Quilio. On all sides hospital attendants are passing, bearing litters. Ambulances are everywhere; in the Bazar de l'Industry (Boulevard Poissionière); in the Salle St. Jean at the Hôtel de Ville; in the Rue du Petit Carreau. In this gloomy battle nine brigades are engaged. All have a battery of artillery; a squadron of cavalry maintains the communications between the brigades; forty thousand men are taking part in the struggle; with a reserve of sixty thousand men; a hundred thousand soldiers upon Paris. Such is the Army of the Crime. The Reibell brigade, the first and second Lancers, protect the Elysée. The Ministers are all sleeping at the Ministry of the Interior, close by Morny. Morny watches, Magnan commands. Tomorrow will be a terrible day."

This page written, I went to bed, and fell asleep.

THE THIRD DAY
THE MASSACRE

I

Those Who Sleep and He Who Does Not Sleep

During this night of the 3d and 4th of December, while we who were overcome with fatigue and betrothed to calamity slept an honest slumber, not an eye was closed at the Elysée. An infamous sleeplessness reigned there. Towards two o'clock in the morning the Comte Roguet, after Morny the most intimate of the confidants of the Elysée, an ex-peer of France and a lieutenant-general, came out of Louis Bonaparte's private room; Roguet was accompanied by Saint-Arnaud. Saint-Arnaud, it may be remembered, was at that time Minister of War.

Two colonels were waiting in the little ante-room.

Saint-Arnaud was a general who had been a supernumerary at the Ambigu Theatre. He had made his first appearance as a comedian in the suburbs. A tragedian later on. He may be described as follows:—tall, bony, thin, angular, with gray moustaches, lank air, a mean countenance. He was a cut-throat, and badly educated. Morny laughed at him for his pronunciation of the "Sovereign People." "He pronounces the word no better than he understands the thing," said he. The Elysée, which prides itself upon its refinement, only half-accepted Saint-Arnaud. His bloody side had caused his vulgar side to be condoned. Saint-Arnaud was brave, violent, and yet timid; he had the audacity of a gold-laced veteran and the awkwardness of a man who had formerly been "down upon his luck." We saw him one day in the tribune, pale, stammering, but daring. He had a long bony face, and a distrust-inspiring jaw. His theatrical name was Florivan. He was a strolling player transformed into a trooper. He died Marshal of France. An ill-omened figure.

The two colonels who awaited Saint-Arnaud in the anteroom were two business-like men, both leaders of those decisive regiments which at critical times carry the other regiments with them, according to their instructions, into glory, as at Austerlitz, or into crime, as on the Eighteenth Brumaire. These two officers belonged to what Morny called "the cream of indebted and free-living colonels." We will not mention their names here; one is dead, the other is still living; he will recognize himself. Besides, we have caught a glimpse of them in the first pages of this book.

One, a man of thirty-eight, was cunning, dauntless, ungrateful, three qualifications for success. The Duc d'Aumale had saved his life in the Aurés. He was then a young captain. A ball had pierced his body; he fell into a thicket; the Kabyles rushed up to cut off and carry away his head, when the Duc d'Aumale arriving with two officers, a soldier, and a bugler, charged the Kabyles and saved this captain. Having saved him, he loved him. One was grateful, the other was not. The one who was grateful was the deliverer. The Duc d'Aumale was pleased with this young captain for having given him an opportunity for a deed of gallantry. He made him a major; in 1849 this major became lieutenant-colonel, and commanded a storming column at the siege of Rome; he then came back to Africa, where Fleury bought him over at the same time as Saint-Arnaud. Louis Bonaparte made him colonel in July, 1851, and reckoned upon him. In November this colonel of Louis Bonaparte wrote to the Duc d'Aumale, "Nothing need be apprehended from this miserable adventurer." In December he commanded one of the massacring regiments. Later on, in the Dobrudscha, an ill-used horse turned upon him and bit off his cheek, so that there was only room on his face for one slap.

The other man was growing gray, and was about forty-eight. He also was a man of pleasure and of murder. Despicable as a citizen; brave as a soldier. He was one of the first who had sprung into the breach at Constantine. Plenty of bravery and plenty of baseness. No chivalry but that of the green cloth. Louis Bonaparte had made him colonel in 1851. His debts had been twice paid by two Princes; the first time by the Duc d'Orléans, the second time by the Duc de Némours.

Such were these colonels.

Saint-Arnaud spoke to them for sometime in a low tone.

II

The Proceedings of the Committee

As soon as it was daylight we had assembled in the house of our imprisoned colleague, M. Grévy. We had been installed in his private room. Michel de Bourges and myself were seated near the fireplace; Jules Favre and Carnot were writing, the one at a table near the window, the other at a high desk. The Left had invested us with discretionary powers. It became more and more impossible at every moment to meet together again in session. We drew up in its name and remitted to Hingray, so that he might print it immediately, the following decree, compiled on the spur of the moment by Jules Favre:—

FRENCH REPUBLIC.
Liberty, Equality, Fraternity

"The undersigned Representatives of the People who still remain at liberty, having met together in an Extraordinary Permanent Session, considering the arrest of the majority of their colleagues, considering the urgency of the moment;

"Seeing that the crime of Louis Napoleon Bonaparte in violently abolishing the operations of the Public Powers has reinstated the Nation in the direct exercise of its sovereignty, and that all which fetters that sovereignty at the present time should be annulled;

"Seeing that all the prosecutions commenced, all the sentences pronounced, by what right soever, on account of political crimes or offences are quashed by the imprescriptible right of the People;

DECREE:

"ARTICLE I. All prosecutions which have begun, and all sentences which have been pronounced, for political crimes or offences are annulled as regards all their civil or criminal effects.

"ARTICLE II. Consequently, all directors of jails or of houses of detention are enjoined immediately to set at liberty all persons detained in prison for the reasons above indicated.

"ARTICLE III. All magistrates' officers and officers of the judiciary police are similarly enjoined, under penalty of treason, to annul all the prosecutions which have been begun for the same causes.

"ARTICLE IV. The police functionaries and agents are charged with the execution of the present decree.

"Given at Paris, in Permanent Session, on the 4th December, 1851."

Jules Favre, as he passed me the decree for my signature, said to me, smiling, "Let us set your sons and your friends at liberty." "Yes," said I, "four combatants the more on the barricades." The Representative Duputz, a few hours later, received from our hands a duplicate of the decree, with the charge to take it himself to the Concièrgerie as soon as the surprise which we premeditated upon the Prefecture of Police and the Hôtel de Ville should have succeeded. Unhappily this surprise failed.

Landrin came in. His duties in Paris in 1848 had enabled him to know the whole body of the political and municipal police. He warned us that he had seen suspicious figures roving about the neighborhood. We were in the Rue Richelieu, almost opposite the Théâtre Français, one of the points where passers-by are most numerous, and in consequence one of the points most carefully watched. The goings and comings of the Representatives who were communicating with the Committee, and who came in and out unceasingly, would be inevitably noticed, and would bring about a visit from the Police. The porters and the neighbors already manifested an evil-boding surprise. We ran, so Landrin declared and assured us, the greatest danger. "You will be taken and shot," said he to us.

He entreated us to go elsewhere. M. Grévy's brother, consulted by us, stated that he could not answer for the people of his house.

But what was to be done? Hunted now for two days, we had exhausted the goodwill of nearly everybody, one refuge had been refused on the preceding evening, and at this moment no house was offered to us. Since the night of the 2d we had changed our refuge seventeen times, at times going from one extremity of Paris to the other. We began to experience some weariness. Besides, as I have already said, the house where we were had this signal advantage—a back outlet upon the Rue Fontaine-Molière. We decided to remain. Only we thought we ought to take precautionary measures.

Every species of devotion burst forth from the ranks of the Left around us. A noteworthy member of the Assembly—a man of rare mind and of rare courage—Durand-Savoyat—who from the preceding evening until the last day constituted himself our doorkeeper, and even more than this, our usher and our attendant, himself had placed a bell on our table, and had said to us, "When you want me, ring, and I will come in." Wherever we went, there was he. He remained in the ante-chamber, calm, impassive, silent, with his grave and noble countenance, his buttoned frock coat, and his broad-brimmed hat, which gave him the appearance of an Anglican clergyman. He himself opened the entrance door, scanned the faces of those who came, and kept away the importunate and the useless. Besides, he was always cheerful, and ready to say unceasingly, "Things are looking well." We were lost, yet he smiled. Optimism in Despair.

We called him in. Landrin set forth to him his misgivings. We begged Durand-Savoyat in future to allow no one to remain in the apartments, not even the Representatives of the People, to take note of all news and information, and to allow no one to penetrate to us but men who were indispensable, in short, as far as possible, to send away everyone in order that the goings and comings might cease. Durand-Savoyat nodded his head, and went back into the ante-chamber, saying, "It shall be done." He confined himself of his own accord to these two formulas; for us, "Things are looking well," for himself, "It shall be done." "It shall be done," a noble manner in which to speak of duty.

Landrin and Durand-Savoyat having left, Michel de Bourges began to speak.

"The artifice of Louis Bonaparte, imitator of his uncle in this as in everything," said Michel de Bourges, "had been to throw out in advance an appeal to the People, a vote to be taken, a plebiscitum, in short, to create a Government in appearance at the very moment when he overturned one. In great crises, where everything totters and seems ready to fall, a People has need to lay hold of something. Failing any other support, it will take the sovereignty of Louis Bonaparte. Well, it was necessary that a support should be offered to the people, by us, in the form of its own sovereignty. The Assembly," continued Michel de Bourges, "was, as a fact, dead. The Left, the popular stump of this hated

Assembly, might suffice for the situation for a few days. No more. It was necessary that it should be reinvigorated by the national sovereignty. It was therefore important that we also should appeal to universal suffrage, should oppose vote to vote, should raise erect the Sovereign People before the usurping Prince, and should immediately convoke a new Assembly." Michel de Bourges proposed a decree.

Michel de Bourges was right. Behind the victory of Louis Bonaparte could be seen something hateful, but something which was familiar— the Empire; behind the victory of the Left there was obscurity. We must bring in daylight behind us. That which causes the greatest uneasiness to people's imagination is the dictatorship of the Unknown. To convoke a new Assembly as soon as possible, to restore France at once into the hands of France, this was to reassure people's minds during the combat, and to rally them afterwards; this was the true policy.

For sometime, while listening to Michel de Bourges and Jules Favre, who supported him, we fancied we heard, in the next room, a murmur which resembled the sound of voices. Jules Favre had several times exclaimed, "Is anyone there?"

"It is not possible," was the answer. "We have instructed Durand-Savoyat to allow no one to remain there." And the discussion continued. Nevertheless the sound of voices insensibly increased, and ultimately grew so distinct that it became necessary to see what it meant. Carnot half opened the door. The room and the ante-chamber adjoining the room where we were deliberating were filled with Representatives, who were peaceably conversing.

Surprised, we called in Durand-Savoyat.

"Did you not understand us?" asked Michel de Bourges.

"Yes, certainly," answered Durand-Savoyat.

"This house is perhaps marked," resumed Carnot; "we are in danger of being taken."

"And killed upon the spot," added Jules Favre, smiling with his calm smile.

"Exactly so," answered Durand-Savoyat, with a look still quieter than Jules Favre's smile. "The door of this inner room is shrouded in the darkness, and is little noticeable. I have detained all the Representatives who have come in, and have placed them in the larger room and in the ante-chamber, whichever they have wished. A species of crowd has thus been formed. If the police and the troops arrive, I shall say to them, 'Here we are.' They will take us. They will not perceive the door of the inner room, and they will not reach you. We shall pay for you. If there is anyone to be killed, they will content themselves with us."

And without imagining that he had just uttered the words of a hero, Durand-Savoyat went back to the antechamber.

We resumed our deliberation on the subject of a decree. We were unanimously agreed upon the advantage of an immediate convocation of a New Assembly. But for what date? Louis Bonaparte had appointed the 20th of December for his Plebiscitum; we chose the 21st. Then, what should we call this Assembly? Michel de Bourges strongly advocated the title of "National Convention," Jules Favre that its name should be "Constituent Assembly," Carnot proposed the title of "Sovereign Assembly," which, awakening no remembrances, would leave the field free to all hopes. The name of "Sovereign Assembly" was adopted.

The decree, the preamble of which Carnot insisted upon writing from my dictation, was drawn up in these terms. It is one of those which has been printed and placarded.

Decree.

"The crime of Louis Bonaparte imposes great duties upon the Representatives of the People remaining at liberty.

"Brute force seeks to render the fulfilment of these duties impossible.

"Hunted, wandering from refuge to refuge, assassinated in the streets, the Republican Representatives deliberate and act, notwithstanding the infamous police of the *coup d'état*.

"The outrage of Louis Napoleon, in overturning all the Public Powers, has only left one authority standing,—the supreme authority,—the authority of the people: Universal Suffrage.

"It is the duty of the Sovereign People to recapture and reconstitute all the social forces which today are dispersed.

"Consequently, the Representatives of the People decree:—

"Article I.—The People are convoked on the 21st December, 1851, for the election of a Sovereign Assembly.

"Article II.—The election will take place by Universal Suffrage, according to the formalities determined by the decree of the Provisional Government of March 5, 1848.

"Given at Paris, in Permanent Session, December 4, 1851."

As I finished signing this decree, Durand-Savoyat entered and whispered to me that a woman had asked for me, and was waiting in the ante-chamber. I went out to her. It was Madame Charassin. Her husband had disappeared. The Representative Charassin, a political economist, an agriculturist, a man of science, was at the same time a man of great courage. We had seen him on the preceding evening at the most perilous points. Had he been arrested? Madame Charassin came to ask me if we knew where he was. I was ignorant. She went to Mazas to make inquiries for him there. A colonel who simultaneously commanded in the army and in the police, received her, and said, "I can only permit you to see your husband on one condition." "What is that?" "You will talk to him about nothing." "What do you mean Nothing?" "No news, no politics." "Very well." "Give me your word of honor." And she had answered him, "How is it that you wish me to give you my word of honor, since I should decline to receive yours?"

I have since seen Charassin in exile.

Madame Charassin had just left me when Théodore Bac arrived. He brought us the protest of the Council of State.

Here it is:—

PROTEST OF THE COUNCIL OF STATE.

"The undersigned members of the Council of State, elected by the Constituent and Legislative Assemblies, having assembled together, notwithstanding the decree of the 2d of December, at their usual place, and having found it surrounded by an armed force, which prohibited their access thereto, protest against the decree which has pronounced the dissolution of the Council of State, and declare that they only ceased their functions when hindered by force.

"Paris, this 3d December, 1851.

"Signed: BETHMONT, VIVIEN, BUREAU DE PUZY, ED. CHARTON, CUVIER, DE RENNEVILLE, HORACE SAY, BOULATIGNIER, GAUTIER DE RUMILLY, DE JOUVENCEL, DUNOYER, CARTERET, DE FRESNE, BOUCHENAY-LEFER, RIVET, BOUDET, CORMENIN, PONS DE L'HERAULT."

Let us relate the adventure of the Council of State.

Louis Bonaparte had driven away the Assembly by the Army, and the High Court of Justice by the Police; he expelled the Council of State by the porter.

On the morning of the 2d of December, at the very hour at which the Representatives of the Right had gone from M. Daru's to the Mairie of the Tenth Arrondissement, the Councillors of State betook themselves to the Hotel on the Quai d'Orsay. They went in one by one.

The quay was thronged with soldiers. A regiment was bivouacking there with their arms piled.

The Councillors of State soon numbered about thirty. They set to work to deliberate. A draft protest was drawn up. At the moment when it was about to be signed the porter came in, pale and stammering. He declared that he was executing his orders, and he enjoined them to withdraw.

Upon this several Councillors of State declared that, indignant as they were, they could not place their signatures beside the Republican signatures.

A means of obeying the porter.

M. Bethmont, one of the Presidents of the Council of State, offered the use of his house. He lived in the Rue Saint-Romain. The Republican members repaired there, and without discussion signed the protocol which has been given above.

Some members who lived in the more distant quarters had not been able to come to the meeting. The youngest Councillor of State, a man of firm heart and of noble mind, M. Edouard Charton, undertook to take the protest to his absent colleagues.

He did this, not without serious risk, on foot, not having been able to obtain a carriage, and he was arrested by the soldiery and threatened with being searched, which would have been highly dangerous. Nevertheless he succeeded in reaching some of the Councillors of State. Many signed, Pons de l'Hérault resolutely, Cormenin with a sort of fever, Boudet after some hesitation. M. Boudet trembled, his family were alarmed, they heard through the open window the discharge of artillery. Charton, brave and calm, said to him, "Your friends, Vivien, Rivet, and Stourm have signed." Boullet signed.

Many refused, one alleging his great age, another the *res angusta domi*, a third "the fear of doing the work of the Reds." "Say 'fear,' in short," replied Charton.

On the following day, December 3d, MM. Vivien and Bethmont took the protest to Boulay de la Meurthe, Vice-President of the Republic, and President of the Council of State, who received them in his dressing-gown, and exclaimed to them, "Be off! Ruin yourselves, if you like, but without me."

On the morning of the 4th, M. de Cormenin erased his signature, giving this unprecedented but authentic excuse: "The word *ex-*Councillor of State does not look well in a book; I am afraid of injuring my publisher."

Yet another characteristic detail. M. Béhic, on the morning of the 2d, had arrived while they were drawing up the protest. He had half opened the door. Near the door was standing M. Gautier de Rumilly, one of the most justly respected members of the Council of State. M. Béhic had asked M. Gautier de Rumilly, "What are they doing? It is a crime. What are we doing?" M. Gautier de Rumilly had answered, "A protest." Upon, this word M. Béhic had reclosed the door, and had disappeared. He reappeared later on under the Empire—a Minister.

III

INSIDE THE ELYSÉE

During the morning Dr. Yvan met Dr. Conneau. They were acquainted. They talked together. Yvan belonged to the Left. Conneau belonged to the Elysée. Yvan knew through Conneau the details of what had taken place during the night at the Elysée, which he transmitted to us.

One of these details was the following:—

An inexorable decree had been compiled, and was about to be placarded. This decree enjoined upon all submission to the *coup d'état*. Saint-Arnaud, who, as Minister of War, should sign the decree, had drawn it up. He had reached the last paragraph, which ran thus: "Whoever shall be detected constructing a barricade, posting a placard of the ex-Representatives, or reading it, shall be. . ." here Saint-Arnaud had paused; Morny had shrugged his shoulders, had snatched the pen from his hand, and written "*shot!*"

Other matters had been decided, but these were not recorded.

Various pieces of information came in in addition to these.

A National Guard, named Boillay de Dole, had formed one of the Guard at the Elysée, on the night of the 3d and 4th. The windows of Louis Bonaparte's private room, which was on the ground floor, were lighted up throughout the night. In the adjoining room there was a Council of War. From the sentry-box where he was stationed Boillay saw defined on the windows black profiles and gesticulating shadows, which were Magnan, Saint-Arnaud, Persigny, Fleury,—the spectres of the crime.

Korte, the General of the Cuirassiers, had been summoned, as also Carrelet, who commanded the division which did the hardest work on the following day, the 4th. From midnight to three o'clock in the morning Generals and Colonels "did nothing but come and go." Even mere captains had come there. Towards four o'clock some carriages arrived "with women." Treason and debauchery went hand in hand. The boudoir in the palace answered to the brothel in the barracks.

The courtyard was filled with lancers, who held the horses of the generals who were deliberating.

Two of the women who came that night belong in a certain measure to History. There are always feminine shadows of this sort in the background. These women influenced the unhappy generals. Both belonged to the best circles. The one was the Marquise of ——, she who became enamored of her husband after having deceived him. She discovered that her lover was not worth her husband. Such a thing does happen. She was the daughter of the most whimsical Marshal of France, and of that pretty Countess of —— to whom M. de Chateaubriand, after a night of love, composed this quatrain, which may now be published—all the personages being dead.

The Dawn peeps in at the window, she paints the sky with red;
And over our loving embraces her rosy rays are shed:
She looks on the slumbering world, love, with eyes that seem divine.
But can she show on her lips, love, a smile as sweet as thine?[1]

The smile of the daughter was as sweet as that of the mother, and more fatal. The other was Madame K——, a Russian, fair, tall, blonde, lighthearted, involved in the hidden paths of diplomacy, possessing and displaying a casket full of love letters from Count Molé somewhat of a spy, absolutely charming and terrifying.

The precautions which had been taken in case of accident were visible even from outside. Since the preceding evening there had been seen from the windows of the neighboring houses two post-chaises in the courtyard of the Elysée, horsed, ready to start, the postilions in their saddles.

In the stables of the Elysée in the Rue Montaigne there were other carriages horsed, and horses saddled and bridled.

Louis Bonaparte had not slept. During the night he had given mysterious orders; thence when morning came there was on this pale face a sort of appalling serenity.

The Crime grown calm was a disquieting symptom.

---

1. The above is a free rendering of the original, which is as follows:—

Des rayons du matin l'horizon se colore,
Le jour vient éclairer notre tendre entretien,
Mais est-il un sourire aux lèvres de l'aurore.
Aussi doux que le tien?

During the morning he had almost laughed. Morny had come into his private room. Louis Bonaparte, having been feverish, had called in Conneau, who joined in the conversation. People are believed to be trustworthy, nevertheless they listen.

Morny brought the police reports. Twelve workmen of the National Printing Office had, during the night of the Second, refused to print the decrees and the proclamations. They had been immediately arrested. Colonel Forestier was arrested. They had transferred him to the Fort of Bicêtre, together with Crocé Spinelli, Genillier, Hippolyte Magen, a talented and courageous writer, Goudounèche, a schoolmaster, and Polino. This last name had struck Louis Bonaparte. "Who is this Polino?" Morny had answered, "An ex-officer of the Shah of Persia's service." And he had added, "A mixture of Don Quixote and Sancho Panza." These prisoners had been placed in Number Six Casemate. Further questions on the part of Louis Bonaparte, "What are these casemates?" And Morny had answered, "Cellars without air or daylight, twenty-four mètres long, eight wide, five high, dripping walls, damp pavements." Louis Bonaparte had asked, "Do they give them a truss of straw?" And Morny had said, "Not yet, we shall see by and by." He had added, "Those who are to be transported are at Bicêtre, those who are to be shot are at Ivry."

Louis Bonaparte had inquired, "What precautions had been taken?" Morny gave him full particulars; that guards had been placed in all the steeples; that all printing-presses had been placed under seal; that all the drums of the National Guard had been locked up; that there was therefore no fear either of a proclamation emanating from a printing-office, or of a call to arms issuing from a Mairie, or of the tocsin ringing from a steeple.

Louis Bonaparte had asked whether all the batteries contained their full complements, as each battery should be composed of four pieces and two mortars. He had expressly ordered that only pieces of eight, and mortars of sixteen centimètres in diameter should be employed.

"In truth," Morny, who was in the secret, had said, "all this apparatus will have work to do."

Then Morny had spoken of Mazas, that there were 600 men of the Republican Guards in the courtyard, all picked men, and who when attacked would defend themselves to the bitter end; that the soldiers received the arrested Representatives with shouts of laughter, and that they had gone so far as to stare Thiers in the face; that the officers kept the soldiers at a distance, but with discretion and with a "species of respect"; that three prisoners were kept in solitary confinement, Greppo, Nadaud, and a member of the Socialist Committee, Arsène Meunier. This last named occupied No. 32 of the Sixth Division. Adjoining, in No. 30, there was a Representative of the Right, who sobbed and cried unceasingly. This made Arsène Meunier laugh, and this made Louis Bonaparte laugh.

Another detail. When the *fiacre* bringing M. Baze was entering the courtyard of Mazas, it had struck against the gate, and the lamp of the *fiacre* had fallen to the ground and been broken to pieces. The coachman, dismayed at the damage, bewailed it. "Who will pay for this?" exclaimed he. One of the police agents, who was in the carriage with the arrested Questor, had said to the driver, "Don't be uneasy, speak to the Brigadier. In matters such as this, *where there is a breakage*, it is the Government which pays."

And Bonaparte had smiled, and muttered under his moustache, "That is only fair."

Another anecdote from Morny also amused him. This was Cavaignac's anger on entering his cell at Mazas. There is an aperture at the door of each cell, called the "spy-hole," through which the prisoners are played the spy upon unknown to themselves. The jailers had watched Cavaignac. He had begun by pacing up and down with folded arms, and then the space being too confined, he had seated himself on the stool in his cell. These stools are narrow pieces of plank upon three converging legs, which pierce the seat in the centre, and project beyond the plank, so that one is uncomfortably seated. Cavaignac had stood up, and with a violent kick had sent the stool to the other end of the cell. Then, furious and swearing, he had broken with a blow of his fist the little table of five inches by twelve, which, with the stool, formed the sole furniture of the dungeon.

This kick and fisticuff amused Louis Bonaparte.

"And Maupas is as frightened as ever," said Morny. This made Bonaparte laugh still further.

Morny having given in his report, went away. Louis Bonaparte entered an adjoining room; a woman awaited him there. It appears that she came to entreat mercy for someone. Dr. Conneau heard these expressive words: "Madam, I wink at your loves; do you wink at my hatreds."

IV

BONAPARTE'S FAMILIAR SPIRITS

M. Mérimée was vile by nature, he must not be blamed for it. With regard to M. de Morny it is otherwise, he was more worthy; there was something of the brigand in him.

M. de Morny was courageous. Brigandage has its sentiments of honor.

M. Mérimée has wrongly given himself out as one of the confederates of the *coup d'état*. He had, however, nothing to boast of in this.

The truth is that M. Mérimée was in no way a confidant. Louis Bonaparte made no useless confidences.

Let us add that it is little probable, notwithstanding some slight evidence to the contrary, that M. Mérimée, at the date of the 2d December, had any direct relations with Louis Bonaparte. This ensued later on. At first Mérimée only knew Morny.

Morny and Mérimée were both intimate at the Elysée, but on a different footing. Morny can be believed, but not Mérimée. Morny was in the great secrets, Mérimée in the small ones. Commissions of gallantry formed his vocation.

The familiars of the Elysée were of two kinds, the trustworthy confederates and the courtiers.

The first of the trustworthy confederates was Morny; the first—or the last—of the courtiers was Mérimée.

This is what made the fortune of M. Mérimée.

Crimes are only glorious during the first moment; they fade quickly. This kind of success lacks permanency; it is necessary promptly to supplement it with something else.

At the Elysée a literary ornament was wanted. A little savor of the Academy is not out of place in a brigand's cavern. M. Mérimée was available. It was his destiny to sign himself "the Empress's Jester." Madame de Montijo presented him to Louis Bonaparte, who accepted him, and who completed his Court with this insipid but plausible writer.

This Court was a heterogeneous collection; a dinner-wagon of basenesses, a menagerie of reptiles, a herbal of poisons.

Besides the trustworthy confederates who were for use, and the courtiers who were for ornament, there were the auxiliaries.

Certain circumstances called for reinforcements; sometimes these were women, *the Flying Squadron.*

Sometimes men: Saint-Arnaud, Espinasse, Saint-George, Maupas.

Sometimes neither men nor women: the Marquis de C.

The whole troop was noteworthy.

Let us say a few words of it.

There was Vieillard the preceptor, an atheist with a tinge of Catholicism, a good billiard player.

Vieillard was an anecdotist. He recounted smilingly the following:—Towards the close of 1807 Queen Hortense, who of her own accord lived in Paris, wrote to the King Louis that she could not exist any longer without seeing him, that she could not do without him, and that she was about to come to the Hague. The King said, "She is with child." He sent for his minister Van Maanen, showed him the Queen's letter, and added, "She is coming. Very good. Our two chambers communicate by a door; the Queen will find it walled up." Louis took his royal mantle in earnest, for he exclaimed, "A King's mantle shall never serve as coverlet to a harlot." The minister Van Maanen, terrified, sent word of this to the Emperor. The Emperor fell into a rage, not against Hortense, but against Louis. Nevertheless Louis held firm; the door was not walled up, but his Majesty was; and when the Queen came he turned his back upon her. This did not prevent Napoleon III from being born.

A suitable number of salvoes of cannon saluted this birth.

Such was the story which, in the summer of 1840, in the house called La Terrasse, before witnesses, among whom was Ferdinand B——, Marquis de la L——, a companion during boyhood of the author of this book, was told by M. Vieillard, an ironical Bonapartist, an arrant sceptic.

Besides Vieillard there was Vaudrey, whom Louis Bonaparte made a General at the same time as Espinasse. In case of need a Colonel of Conspiracies can become a General of Ambuscades.

There was Fialin,[1] the corporal who became a Duke.

There was Fleury, who was destined to the glory of travelling by the side of the Czar on his buttocks.

There was Lacrosse, a Liberal turned Clerical, one of those Conservatives who push order as far as the embalming, and preservation as far as the mummy: later on a senator.

---

1. Better known afterwards as Persigny.

There was Larabit, a friend of Lacrosse, as much a domestic and not less a senator.

There was Canon Coquereau, the "Abbé of La Belle-Poule." The answer is known which he made to a princess who asked him, "What is the Elysée?" It appears that one can say to a princess what one cannot say to a woman.

There was Hippolyte Fortoul, of the climbing genus, of the worth of a Gustave Planche or of some Philarête Chasles, an ill-tempered writer who had become Minister of the Marine, which caused Béranger to say, "This Fortoul knows all the spars, including the 'greased pole.'"

There were some Auvergants there. Two. They hated each other. One had nicknamed the other "the melancholy tinker."

There was Sainte-Beuve, a distinguished but inferior man, having a pardonable fondness for ugliness. A great critic like Cousin is a great philosopher.

There was Troplong, who had had Dupin for Procurator, and whom Dupin had had for President. Dupin, Troplong; the two side faces of the mask placed upon the brow of the law.

There was Abbatucci; a conscience which let everything pass by. Today a street.

There was the Abbé M——, later on Bishop of Nancy, who emphasized with a smile the oaths of Louis Bonaparte.

There were the frequenters of a famous box at the Opera, Montg— and Sept——, placing at the service of an unscrupulous prince the deep side of frivolous men.

There was Romieu—the outline of a drunkard behind a Red spectre.

There was Malitourne—not a bad friend, coarse and sincere.

There was Cuch——, whose name caused hesitation amongst the ushers at the saloon doors.

There was Suin—a man able to furnish excellent counsel for bail actions.

There was Dr. Veron—who had on his cheek what the other men of the Elysée had in their hearts.

There was Mocquart—once a handsome member of the Dutch Court. Mocquart possessed romantic recollections. He might by age, and perhaps otherwise, have been the father of Louis Bonaparte. He was a lawyer. He had shown himself quick-witted about 1829, at the same time as Romieu. Later on he had published something, I no longer remember what, which was pompous and in quarto size, and which he sent to me. It was he who in May, 1847, had come with Prince de la Moskowa to bring me King Jérome's petition to the Chamber of Peers. This petition requested the readmittance of the banished Bonaparte family into France. I supported it; a good action, and a fault which I would again commit.

There was Billault, a semblance of an orator, rambling with facility, and making mistakes with authority, a reputed statesman. What constitutes the statesman is a certain superior mediocrity.

There was Lavalette, completing Morny and Walewski.

There was Bacciochi.

And yet others.

It was at the inspiration of these intimate associates that during his Presidency Louis Bonaparte, a species of Dutch Machiavelli, went hither and thither, to the Chamber and elsewhere, to Tours, to Ham, to Dijon, snuffling, with a sleepy air, speeches full of treason.

The Elysée, wretched as it was, holds a place in the age. The Elysée, has engendered catastrophes and ridicule.

One cannot pass it over in silence.

The Elysée was the disquieting and dark corner of Paris. In this bad spot, the denizens were little and formidable. They formed a family circle—of dwarfs. They had their maxim: to enjoy themselves. They lived on public death. There they inhaled shame, and they throve on that which kills others. It was there that was reared up with art, purpose, industry, and goodwill, the decadence of France. There worked the bought, fed, and obliging public men;—read prostituted. Even literature was compounded there as we have shown; Vieillard was a classic of 1830, Morny created Choufleury, Louis Bonaparte was a candidate for the Academy. Strange place. Rambouillet's hotel mingled itself with the house of Bancal. The Elysée has been the laboratory, the counting-house, the confessional, the alcove, the den of the reign. The Elysée assumed to govern everything, even the morals—above all the morals. It spread the paint on the bosom of women at the same time as the color on the faces of the men. It set the fashion for toilette and for music. It invented the crinoline and the operetta. At the Elysée a certain ugliness was considered as elegance; that which makes the countenance noble was there scoffed at, as was that which makes the soul great; the phrase, "human face divine" was ridiculed at the Elysée, and it was there that for twenty years every baseness was brought into fashion—effrontery included.

History, whatever may be its pride, is condemned to know that the Elysée existed. The grotesque side does not prevent the tragic side. There is at the Elysée a room which has seen the second abdication, the abdication after Waterloo. It is at the Elysée that Napoleon the First ended and that Napoleon the Third began. It is at the Elysée that Dupin appeared to the two Napoleons; in 1815 to depose the Great, in 1851 to worship the Little. At this last epoch this place was perfectly villainous. There no longer remained one virtue there. At the Court of Tiberius there was still Thraseas, but round Louis Bonaparte there was nobody. If one sought Conscience, one found Baroche; if one sought Religion, one found Montalembert.

V

A Wavering Ally

During this terribly historical morning of the 4th of December, a day the master was closely observed by his satellites, Louis Bonaparte had shut himself up, but in doing so he betrayed himself. A man who shuts himself up meditates, and for such men to meditate is to premeditate. What could be the premeditation of Louis Bonaparte? What was working in his mind. Questions which all asked themselves, two persons excepted,—Morny, the man of thought; Saint-Arnaud, the man of action.

Louis Bonaparte claimed, justly, a knowledge of men. He prided himself upon it, and from a certain point of view he was right. Others have the power of divination; he had the faculty of scent. It is brute-like, but trustworthy.

He had assuredly not been mistaken in Maupas. To pick the lock of the Law he needed a skeleton key. He took Maupas. Nor could any burglar's implement have answered better in the lock of the Constitution than Maupas. Neither was he mistaken in Q.B. He saw at once that this serious man had in him the necessary composite qualities of a rascal. And in fact, Q.B., after having voted and signed the Deposition at the Mairie of the Tenth Arrondissement, became one of the three reporters of the Joint Commissions; and his share in the abominable total recorded by history amounts to *sixteen hundred and thirty four victims*.

Louis Bonaparte, however, at times judged amiss, especially respecting Peauger. Peauger, though chosen by him, remained an honest man. Louis Bonaparte, mistrusting the workmen of the National Printing-Office, and not without reason, for twelve, as has been seen, were refractory, had improvised a branch establishment in case of emergency, a sort of State Sub-Printing-Office, as it were, situated in the Rue de Luxembourg, with steam and hand presses, and eight workmen. He had given the management of it to Peauger. When the hour of the Crime arrived, and with it the necessity of printing the nefarious placards, he sounded Peauger, and found him rebellious. He then turned to Saint Georges, a more subservient lackey.

He was less mistaken, but still he was mistaken, in his appreciation of X.

On the 2d of December, X, an ally thought necessary by Morny, became a source of anxiety to Louis Bonaparte.

X was forty-four years of age, loved women, craved promotion, and, therefore, was not over-scrupulous. He began his career in Africa under Colonel Combes in the forty-seventh of the line. He showed great bravery at Constantine; at Zaatcha he extricated Herbillon, and the siege, badly begun by Herbillon, had been brought to a successful termination by him. X, who was a little short man, his head sunk in his shoulders, was intrepid, and admirably understood the handling of a brigade. Bugeaud, Lamoricière, Cavaignac, and Changarnier were his four stepping-stones to advancement. At Paris, in 1851, he met Lamoricière, who received him coldly, and Changarnier, who treated him better. He left Satory indignant, exclaiming, "*We must finish with this Louis Bonaparte. He is corrupting the army. These drunken soldiers make one sick at heart. I shall return to Africa.*" In October Changarnier's influence decreased, and X's enthusiasm abated. X then frequented the Elysée, but without giving his adherence. He promised his support to General Bedeau, who counted upon him. At daybreak on the 2d of December someone came to waken X. It was Edgar Ney. X was a prop for the *coup d'état*, but would he consent? Edgar Ney explained the affair to him, and left him only after seeing him leave the barracks of the Rue Verte at the head of the first regiment. X took up his position at the Place de la Madeleine. As he arrived there La Rochejaquelein, thrust back from the Chamber by its invaders, crossed the Place. La Rochejaquelein, not yet a Bonapartist, was furious. He perceived X, his old schoolfellow at the Ecole Militaire in 1830, with whom he was on intimate terms. He went up to him, exclaiming, "This is an infamous act. What are you doing?" "*I am waiting,*" answered X. La Rochejaquelein left him; X dismounted, and went to see a relation, a Councillor of State, M.R., who lived in the Rue de Suresne. He asked his advice. M.R., an honest man, did not hesitate. He answered, "I am going to the Council of State to do my duty. It is a Crime." X shook his head, and said, "*We must wait and see.*"

This *I am waiting*, and *We must see*, preoccupied Louis Bonaparte. Morny said, "*Let us make use of the flying squadron.*"

VI

Denis Dussoubs

Gaston Dussoubs was one of the bravest members of the Left. He was a Representative of the Haute-Vienne. At the time of his first appearance in the Assembly he wore, as formerly did Théophile Gautier, a red waistcoat, and the shudder which Gautier's waistcoat caused among the men of letters in 1830, Gaston Dussoubs' waistcoat caused among the Royalists of 1851. M. Parisis, Bishop of Langres, who would have had no objection to a red hat, was terrified by Gaston Dussoubs' red waistcoat. Another source of horror to the Right was that Dussoubs had, it was said, passed three years at Belle Isle as a political prisoner, a penalty incurred by the "Limoges Affair." Universal Suffrage had, it would seem, taken him thence to place him in the Assembly. To go from the prison to the Senate is certainly not very surprising in our changeful times, although it is sometimes followed by a return from the Senate to the prison. But the Right was mistaken, the culprit of Limoges was, not Gaston Dussoubs, but his brother Denis.

In fine, Gaston Dussoubs inspired fear. He was witty, courageous, and gentle.

In the summer of 1851 I went to dine everyday at the Concièrgerie with my two sons and my two imprisoned friends. These great hearts and great minds, Vacquerie, Meurice, Charles, and François Victor, attracted men of like quality. The livid half-light that crept in through latticed and barred windows disclosed a family circle at which there often assembled eloquent orators, among others Crémieux, and powerful and charming writers, including Peyrat.

One day Michel de Bourges brought to us Gaston Dussoubs.

Gaston Dussoubs lived in the Faubourg St. Germain, near the Assembly.

On the 2d of December we did not see him at our meetings. He was ill, "nailed down" as he wrote me, by rheumatism of the joints, and compelled to keep his bed.

He had a brother younger than himself, whom we have just mentioned, Denis Dussoubs. On the morning of the 4th his brother went to see him.

Gaston Dussoubs knew of the *coup d'état*, and was exasperated at being obliged to remain in bed. He exclaimed, "I am dishonored. There will be barricades, and my sash will not be there!"

"Yes," said his brother. "It will be there!"

"How?"

"Lend it to me."

"Take it."

Denis took Gaston's sash, and went away.

We shall see Denis Dussoubs later on.

VII

ITEMS AND INTERVIEWS

Lamoricière on the same morning found means to convey to me by Madame de Courbonne[1] the following information.

"—— Fortress of Ham.—The Commandant's name is Baudot. His appointment, made by Cavaignac in 1848, was countersigned by Charras. Both are today his prisoners. The Commissary of Police, sent by Morny to the village of Ham to watch the movements of the jailer and the prisoners, is Dufaure de Pouillac."[2]

I thought when I received this communication that the Commandant Baudot, "the jailer," had connived at its rapid transmission.

A sign of the instability of the central power.

Lamoricière, by the same means, put me in possession of some details concerning his arrest and that of his fellow-generals.

These details complete those which I have already given.

The arrests of the Generals were affected at the same time at their respective homes under nearly similar circumstances. Everywhere houses surrounded, doors opened by artifice or burst open by force, porters deceived, sometimes garotted, men in disguise, men provided with ropes, men armed with axes, surprises in bed, nocturnal violence. A plan of action which resembled, as I have said, an invasion of brigands.

General Lamoricière, according to his own expression, was a sound sleeper. Notwithstanding the noise at his door, he did not awake. His servant, a devoted old soldier, spoke in a loud voice, and called out to arouse the General. He even offered resistance to the police. A police agent wounded him in the knee with a sword thrust.[3] The General was awakened, seized, and carried away.

While passing in a carriage along the Quai Malaquais, Lamoricière noticed troops marching by with their knapsacks on their backs. He leaned quickly forward out of the window. The Commissary of Police thought he was about to address the soldiers. He seized the General

---

1. No. 16, Rue d'Anjou, Saint Honoré.
2. The author still has in his possession the note written by Lamoricière.
3. Later on, the wound having got worse, he was obliged to have his leg taken off.

by the arm, and said to him, "General, if you say a word I shall put this on you." And with the other hand he showed him in the dim light something which proved to be a gag.

All the Generals arrested were taken to Mazas. There they were locked up and forgotten. At eight in the evening General Changarnier had eaten nothing.

These arrests were not pleasant tasks for the Commissaries of Police. They were made to drink down their shame in large draughts. Cavaignac, Leflô, Changarnier, Bedeau, and Lamoricière did not spare them anymore than Charras did. As he was leaving, General Cavaignac took some money with him. Before putting it in his pocket, he turned towards Colin, the Commissary of Police who had arrested him, and said, "Will this money be safe on me?"

The Commissary exclaimed, "Oh, General, what are you thinking of?"

"What assurance have I that you are not thieves?" answered Cavaignac. At the same time, nearly the same moment, Charras said to Courteille, the Commissary of Police, "Who can tell me that you are not pick-pockets?"

A few days afterwards these pitiful wretches all received the Cross of the Legion of Honor.

This cross given by the last Bonaparte to policemen after the 2d of December is the same as that affixed by the first Napoleon to the eagles of the Grand Army after Austerlitz.

I communicated these details to the Committee. Other reports came in. A few concerned the Press. Since the morning of the 4th the Press was treated with soldierlike brutality. Serrière, the courageous printer, came to tell us what had happened at the *Presse*. Serrière published the *Presse* and the *Avénement du Peuple*, the latter a new name for the *Evénement*, which had been judicially suppressed. On the 2d, at seven o'clock in the morning, the printing-office had been occupied by twenty-eight soldiers of the Republican Guard, commanded by a Lieutenant named Pape (since decorated for this achievement). This man had given Serrière an order prohibiting the printing of any article signed "Nusse." A Commissary of Police accompanied Lieutenant Pape. This Commissary had notified Serrière of a "decree of the President of the Republic," suppressing the *Avénement du Peuple*, and had placed sentinels over the presses. The workmen had resisted, and one of them said to the soldiers, "*We shall print it in spite of you.*" Then forty additional

Municipal Guards arrived, with two quarter-masters, four corporals, and a detachment of the line, with drums at their head, commanded by a captain. Girardin came up indignant, and protested with so much energy that a quarter-master said to him, "*I should like a Colonel of your stamp.*" Girardin's courage communicated itself to the workmen, and by dint of skill and daring, under the very eyes of the gendarmes, they succeeded in printing Girardin's proclamations with the hand-press, and ours with the brush. They carried them away wet, in small packages, under their waistcoats.

Luckily the soldiers were drunk. The gendarmes made them drink, and the workmen, profiting by their revels, printed. The Municipal Guards laughed, swore and jested, drank champagne and coffee, and said, "*We fill the places of the Representatives, we have twenty-five francs a day.*" All the printing-houses in Paris were occupied in the same manner by the soldiery. The *coup d'état* reigned everywhere. The Crime even ill-treated the Press which supported it. At the office of the *Moniteur Parisien*, the police agents threatened to fire on anyone who should open a door. M. Delamare, director of the *Patrie*, had forty Municipal Guards on his hands, and trembled lest they should break his presses. He said to one of them, "*Why, I am on your side.*" The gendarme replied, "*What is that to me?*"

At three o'clock on the morning of the 4th all the printing-offices were evacuated by the soldiers. The Captain said to Serrière, "We have orders to concentrate in our own quarters." And Serrière, in announcing this fact, added, "Something is in preparation."

I had had since the previous night several conversations with Georges Biscarrat, an honest and brave man, of whom I shall have occasion to speak hereafter. I had given him rendezvous at No. 19, Rue Richelieu. Many persons came and went during this morning of the 4th from No. 15, where we deliberated, to No. 19, where I slept.

As I left this honest and courageous man in the street I saw M. Mérimée, his exact opposite, coming towards me.

"Oh!" said M. Mérimée, "I was looking for you."

I answered him,—

"I hope you will not find me."

He held out his hand to me, and I turned my back on him.

I have not seen him since. I believe he is dead.

In speaking one day in 1847 with Mérimée about Morny, we had the following conversation:—Mérimée said, "M. de Morny has a great future before him." And he asked me, "Do you know him?"

I answered,—

"Ah! he has a fine future before him! Yes, I know M. de Morny. He is a clever man. He goes a great deal into society, and conducts commercial operations. He started the Vieille Montagne affair, the zinc-mines, and the coal-mines of Liège. I have the honor of his acquaintance. He is a sharper."

There was this difference between Mérimée and myself: I despised Morny, and he esteemed him.

Morny reciprocated his feeling. It was natural.

I waited until Mérimée had passed the corner of the street. As soon as he disappeared I went into No. 15.

There, they had received news of Canrobert. On the 2d he went to see Madame Leflô, that noble woman, who was most indignant at what had happened. There was to be a ball next day given by Saint-Arnaud at the Ministry of War. General and Madame Leflô were invited, and had made an appointment there with General Canrobert. But the ball did not form a part of Madame Leflô's conversation with him. "General," said she, "all your comrades are arrested; is it possible that you give your support to such an act?" "What I intend giving," replied Canrobert, "is my resignation and," he added, "you may tell General Leflô so." He was pale, and walked up and down, apparently much agitated. "Your resignation, General?" "Yes, Madame." "Is it positive?" "Yes, Madame, if there is no riot." "General Canrobert," exclaimed Madame Leflô, "that *if* tells me your intentions."

Canrobert, however, had not yet taken his decision. Indeed, indecision was one of his chief characteristics. Pelissier, who was cross-grained and gruff, used to say, "Judge men by their names, indeed! I am christened *Amable*, Randon *César*, and Canrobert *Certain*."

VIII

THE SITUATION

Although the fighting tactics of the Committee were, for the reasons which I have already given, not to concentrate all their means of resistance into one hour, or in one particular place, but to spread them over as many points and as many days as possible, each of us knew instinctively, as also the criminals of the Elysée on their side, that the day would be decisive.

The moment drew near when the *coup d'état* would storm us from every side, and when we should have to sustain the onslaught of an entire army. Would the people, that great revolutionary populace of the faubourgs of Paris, abandon their Representatives? Would they abandon themselves? Or, awakened and enlightened, would they at length arise? A question more and more vital, and which we repeated to ourselves with anxiety.

The National Guard had shown no sign of earnestness. The eloquent proclamation, written at Marie's by Jules Favre and Alexander Rey, and addressed in our name to the National Legions, had not been printed. Hetzel's scheme had failed. Versigny and Lebrousse had not been able to rejoin him; the place appointed for their meeting, the corner of the boulevard and the Rue de Richelieu, having been continually scoured by charges of cavalry. The courageous effort of Colonel Grassier to win over the Sixth Legion, the more timid attempt of Lieutenant Colonel Howyne upon the Fifth, had failed. Nevertheless indignation began to manifest itself in Paris. The preceding evening had been significant.

Hingray came to us during the morning, bringing under his cloak a bundle of copies of the Decree of Deposition, which had been reprinted. In order to bring them to us he had twice run the risk of being arrested and shot. We immediately caused these copies to be distributed and placarded. This placarding was resolutely carried out; at several points our placards were posted by the side of the placards of the *coup d'état*, which pronounced the penalty of death against anyone who should placard the decrees emanating from the Representatives. Hingray told us that our proclamations and our decrees had been lithographed and distributed by hand in thousands. It Was urgently necessary that we should continue our publications. A printer, who had formerly been a publisher of several democratic journals, M. Boulé, had offered me his services on the preceding evening. In June, 1848, I had protected his printing-office, then being devastated by the National Guards. I wrote to him: I enclosed our judgments and our decrees in the letter, and the Representative Montaigu undertook to take them to him. M. Boulé excused himself; his printing-presses had been seized by the police at midnight.

Through the precautions which we had taken, and thanks to the patriotic assistance of several young medical and chemical students, powder had been manufactured in several quarters. At one point alone, the Rue Jacob, a hundred kilogrammes had been turned out during the night. As, however, this manufacture was principally carried out on the left bank of the river, and as the fighting took place on the right bank, it was necessary to transport this powder across the bridges. They managed this In the best manner they could. Towards nine o'clock we were warned that the police, having been informed of this, had organized a system of inspection, and that all persons crossing the river were searched, particularly on the Pont Neuf.

A certain strategical plan became manifest. The ten central bridges mere militarily guarded.

People were arrested in the street on account of their personal appearance. A sergent-de-ville, at the corner of he Pont-au-Change, exclaimed, loud enough for the passers-by to hear, "We shall lay hold of all those who have not their beards properly trimmed, or who do not appear to have slept."

Notwithstanding all this we had a little powder; the disarming of the National Guard at various points had produced about eight hundred muskets, our proclamations and our decrees were being placarded, our voice was reaching the people, a certain confidence was springing up.

"The wave is rising! the wave is rising!" exclaimed Edgar Quinet, who had come to shake my hand.

We were informed that the schools were rising in insurrection during the day, and that they offered us a refuge in the midst of them.

Jules Favre exclaimed joyfully,—

"Tomorrow we shall date our decrees from the Pantheon."

Signs of good omen grew more numerous. An old hotbed of insurrection, the Rue Saint-André-des-Arts, was becoming agitated. The association called La Presse du Travail gave signs of life. Some brave workmen, at the house of one of their colleagues, Nétré No. 13, Rue du Jardinet, had organized a little printing-press in a garret, a few steps from the barracks of the Gendarmerie Mobile. They had spent the night first in compiling, and then in printing "A Manifesto to Working Men," which called the people to arms. They were five skilful and determined men; they had procured paper, they had perfectly new type; some of them moistened the paper, while the others composed; towards two o'clock in the morning they began to print. It was essential that they should not be heard by the neighbors; they had succeeded in muffling the hollow blows of the ink-rollers, alternating with the rapid sound of the printing blankets. In a few hours fifteen hundred copies were pulled, and at daybreak they were placarded at the corners of the streets. The leader of these intrepid workmen, A. Desmoulins, who belonged to that sturdy race of men who are both cultured and who can fight, had been greatly disheartened on the preceding day; he now had become hopeful.

On the preceding day he wrote:—"Where are the Representatives? The communications are cut. The quays and the boulevards can no longer be crossed. It has become impossible to reunite the popular Assembly. The people need direction. De Flotte in one district, Victor Hugo in another, Schoelcher in a third, are actively urging on the combat, and expose their lives a score of times, but none feel themselves supported by any organized body: and moreover the attempt of the Royalists in the Tenth Arrondissement has roused apprehension. People dread lest they should see them reappear when all is accomplished."

Now, this man so intelligent and so courageous recovered confidence, and he wrote,—

"Decidedly, Louis Napoleon is afraid. The police reports are alarming for him. The resistance of the Republican Representatives is bearing fruit. Paris is arming. Certain regiments appear ready to turn back. The Gendarmerie itself is not to be depended upon, and this morning an entire regiment refused to march. Disorder is beginning to show itself in the services. Two batteries fired upon each other for a long time without recognition. One would say that the *coup d'état* is about to fail."

The symptoms, as may be seen, were growing more reassuring.

Had Maupas become unequal to the task? Had they resorted to a more skilful man? An incident seemed to point to this. On the preceding evening a tall man had been seen, between five and seven o'clock, walking up and down before the café of the Place Saint-Michel;

he had been joined by two of the Commissaries of the Police who had effected the arrests of the 2d of December, and had talked to them for a long time. This man was Carlier. Was he about to supplant Maupas?

The Representative Labrousse, seated at a table of the café, had witnessed this conspirators' parley.

Each of the two Commissaries was followed by that species of police agent which is called "the Commissary's dog."

At the same time strange warnings reached the Committee; the following letter[1] was brought to our knowledge.

3d December

MY DEAR BOCAGE,
"Today at six o'clock, 25,000 francs has been offered to anyone who arrests or kills Hugo.

"You know where he is. He must not go out under any pretext whatever.

Yours ever,
AL. DUMAS

At the back was written, "Bocage, 18, Rue Cassette." It was necessary that the minutest details should be considered. In the different places of combat a diversity of passwords prevailed, which might cause danger. For the password on the day before we had given the name of "Baudin." In imitation of this the names of other Representatives had been adopted as passwords on barricades. In the Rue Rambuteau the password was "Eugène Sue and Michel de Bourges"; in the Rue Beaubourg, "Victor Hugo"; at the Saint Denis chapel, "Esquiros and De Flotte." We thought it necessary to put a stop to this confusion, and to suppress the proper names, which are always easy to guess. The password settled upon was, "What is Joseph doing?"

At every moment items of news and information came to us from all sides, that barricades were everywhere being raised, and that firing was beginning in the central streets. Michel de Bourges exclaimed, "Construct a square of four barricades, and we will go and deliberate in the centre."

---

1. The original of this note is in the hands of the author of this book. It was handed to us by M. Avenel on the part of M. Bocage.

We received news from Mont Valérien. Two prisoners the more. Rigal and Belle had just been committed. Both of the Left. Dr. Rigal was the Representative of Gaillac, and Belle of Lavaur. Rigal was ill; they had arrested him in bed. In prison he lay upon a pallet, and could not dress himself. His colleague Belle acted as his *valet de chambre*.

Towards nine o'clock an ex-Captain of the 8th Legion of the National Guard of 1848, named Jourdan, came to place himself at our service. He was a bold man, one of those who had carried out, on the morning of the 24th February, the rash surprise of the Hôtel de Ville. We charged him to repeat this surprise, and to extend it to the Prefecture of Police. He knew how to set about the work. He told us that he had only a few men, but that during the day he would cause certain houses of strategical importance on the Quai des Cèvres, on the Quai Lepelletier, and in the Rue de la Cité, to be silently occupied, and that if it should chance that the leaders of the *coup d'état*, owing to the combat in the centre of Paris growing more serious, should be forced to withdraw the troops from the Hôtel de Ville and the Prefecture, an attack would be immediately commenced on these two points. Captain Jourdan, we may at once mention, did what he had promised us; unfortunately, as we learnt that evening, he began perhaps a little too soon. As he had foreseen, a moment arrived when the square of the Hôtel de Ville was almost devoid of troops, General Herbillon having been forced to leave it with his cavalry to take the barricades of the centre in the rear. The attack of the Republicans burst forth instantly. Musket shots were fired from the windows on the Quai Lepelletier; but the left of the column was still on the Pont d'Arcole, a line of riflemen had been placed by a major named Larochette before the Hôtel de Ville, the 44th retraced its steps, and the attempt failed.

Bastide arrived, with Chauffour and Laissac.

"Good news," said he to us, "all is going on well." His grave, honest, and dispassionate countenance shone with a sort of patriotic serenity. He came from the barricades, and was about to return thither. He had received two balls in his cloak. I took him aside, and said to him, "Are you going back?" "Yes." "Take me with you." "No," answered he, "you are necessary here. Today you are the general, I am the soldier." I insisted in vain. He persisted in refusing, repeating continually. "The Committee is our centre, it should not disperse itself. It is your duty to remain here. Besides," added he, "Make your mind easy. You run here more risk than we do. If you are taken you will be shot." "Well, then," said I, "the moment may come when our duty will be to join in the combat." "Without doubt." I resumed, "You who are on the barricades will be better judges than we shall of that moment. Give me your word of honor that you will treat me as you would wish me to treat you, and that you will come and fetch us." "I give it you," he answered, and he pressed my two hands in his own.

Later on, however, a few moments after Bastide had left, great as was my confidence in the loyal word of this courageous and generous man, I could no longer restrain myself, and I profited by an interval of two hours of which I could dispose, to go and see with my own eyes what was taking place, and in what manner the resistance was behaving.

I took a carriage in the square of the Palais Royal. I explained to the driver who I was, and that I was about to visit and encourage the barricades; that I should go sometimes on foot, sometimes in the carriage, and that I trusted myself to him. I told him my name.

The first comer is almost always an honest man. This true-hearted coachman answered me, "I know where the barricades are. I will drive you wherever it is necessary. I will wait for you wherever it is necessary. I will drive you there and bring you back; and if you have no money, do not pay me, I am proud of such an action."

And we started.

IX

THE PORTE SAINT MARTIN

I mportant deeds had been already achieved during the morning.
"It is taking root," Bastide had said.

The difficulty is not to spread the flames but to light the fire.

It was evident that Paris began to grow ill-tempered. Paris does not get angry at will. She must be in the humor for it. A volcano possesses nerves. The anger was coming slowly, but it was coming. On the horizon might be seen the first glimmering of the eruption.

For the Elysée, as for us, the critical moment was drawing nigh. From the preceding evening they were nursing their resources. The *coup d'état* and the Republic were at length about to close with each other. The Committee had in vain attempted to drag the wheel; some irresistible impulse carried away the last defenders of liberty and hurried them on to action. The decisive battle was about to be fought.

In Paris, when certain hours have sounded, when there appears an immediate necessity for a progressive movement to be carried out, or a right to be vindicated, the insurrections rapidly spread throughout the whole city. But they always begin at some particular point. Paris, in its vast historical task, comprises two revolutionary classes, the "middle-class" and the "people." And to these two combatants correspond two places of combat; the Porte Saint Martin when the middle-class are revolting, the Bastille when the people are revolting. The eye of the politician should always be fixed on these two points. There, famous in contemporary history, are two spots where a small portion of the hot cinders of Revolution seem ever to smoulder.

When a wind blows from above, these burning cinders are dispersed, and fill the city with sparks.

This time, as we have already explained, the formidable Faubourg Antoine slumbered, and, as has been seen, nothing had been able to awaken it. An entire park of artillery was encamped with lighted matches around the July Column, that enormous deaf-and-dumb memento of the Bastille. This lofty revolutionary pillar, this silent witness of the great deeds of the past, seemed to have forgotten all. Sad to say, the paving stones which had seen the 14th of July did not rise under the cannon-wheels of the 2d of December. It was therefore not the Bastille which began, it was the Porte Saint Martin.

From eight o'clock in the morning the Rue Saint Denis and the Rue Saint Martin were in an uproar throughout their length; throngs of indignant passers-by went up and down those thoroughfares. They tore down the placards of the *coup d'état*; they posted up our Proclamations; groups at the corners of all the adjacent streets commented upon the decree of outlawry drawn up by the members of the Left remaining at liberty; they snatched the copies from each other. Men mounted on the kerbstones read aloud the names of the 120 signatories, and, still more than on the day before, each significant or celebrated name was hailed with applause. The crowd increased every moment—and the anger. The entire Rue Saint Denis presented the strange aspect of a street with all the doors and windows closed, and all the inhabitants in the open air. Look at the houses, there is death; look at the street, it is the tempest.

Some fifty determined men suddenly emerged from a side alley, and began to run through the streets, saying, "To arms! Long live the Representatives of the Left! Long live the Constitution!" The disarming of the National Guards began. It was carried out more easily than on the preceding evening. In less than an hour more than 150 muskets had been obtained.

In the meanwhile the street became covered with barricades.

X

My Visit to the Barricades

My coachman deposited me at the corner of Saint Eustache, and said to me, "Here you are in the hornets' nest."

He added, "I will wait for you in the Rue de la Vrillière, near the Place des Victoires. Take your time."

I began walking from barricade to barricade.

In the first I met De Flotte, who offered to serve me as a guide. There is not a more determined man than De Flotte. I accepted his offer; he took me everywhere where my presence could be of use.

On the way he gave me an account of the steps taken by him to print our proclamations; Boulé's printing-office having failed him, he had applied to a lithographic press, at No. 30, Rue Bergère, and at the peril of their lives two brave men had printed 500 copies of our decrees. These two true-hearted workmen were named, the one Rubens, the other Achille Poincellot.

While walking I made jottings in pencil (with Baudin's pencil, which I had with me); I registered facts at random; I reproduce this page here. These living facts are useful for History; the *coup d'état* is there, as though freshly bleeding.

"Morning of the 4th. It looks as if the combat was suspended. Will it burst forth again? Barricades visited by me: one at the corner of Saint Eustache. One at the Oyster Market. One in the Rue Mauconseil. One in the Rue Tiquetonne. One in the Rue Mandar (Rocher de Cancale). One barring the Rue du Cadran and the Rue Montorgueil. Four closing the Petit-Carreau. The beginning of one between the Rue des Deux Portes and the Rue Saint Sauveur, barring the Rue Saint Denis. One, the largest, barring the Rue Saint Denis, at the top of the Rue Guérin-Boisseau. One barring the Rue Grenetat. One farther on in the Rue Grenetat, barring the Rue Bourg-Labbé (in the centre an overturned flour wagon; a good barricade). In the Rue Saint Denis one barring the Rue de Petit-Lion-Saint-Sauveur. One barring the Rue du Grand Hurleur, with its four corners barricaded. This barricade has already been attacked this morning. A combatant, Massonnet, a comb-maker of 154, Rue Saint Denis, received a ball in his overcoat; Dupapet, called 'the man with the long beard,' was the last to stay on the summit of the barricade. He was heard to cry out to the officers commanding the attack, 'You are traitors!' He is believed to have been shot. The troops retired—strange to say without demolishing the barricade. A barricade is being constructed in the Rue du Renard. Some National Guards in uniform watch its construction, but do not work on it. One of them said to me, 'We are not against you, you are on the side of Right.' They add that there are twelve or fifteen barricades in the Rue Rambuteau. This morning at daybreak the cannon had fired 'steadily,' as one of them remarks, in the Rue Bourbon-Villeneuve. I visit a powder manufactory improvised by Leguevel at a chemist's opposite the Rue Guérin-Boisseau.

"They are constructing the barricades amicably, without angering anyone. They do what they can not to annoy the neighborhood. The combatants of the Bourg-Labbé barricades are ankle-deep in mud on account of the rain. It is a perfect sewer. They hesitate to ask for a truss of straw. They lie down in the water or on the pavement.

"I saw there a young man who was ill, and who had just got up from his bed with the fever still on him. He said to me, 'I am going to my death' (he did so).

"In the Rue Bourbon-Villeneuve they had not even asked a mattress of the 'shopkeepers,' although, the barricade being bombarded, they needed them to deaden the effect of the balls.

"The soldiers make bad barricades, because they make them too well. A barricade should be tottering; when well built it is worth nothing; the paving-stones should want equilibrium, 'so that they may roll down on the troopers,' said a street-boy to me, 'and break their paws.' Sprains form a part of barricade warfare.

"Jeanty Sarre is the chief of a complete group of barricades. He presented his first lieutenant to me, Charpentier, a man of thirty-six, lettered and scientific. Charpentier busies himself with experiments with the object of substituting gas for coal and wood in the firing of china, and he asks permission to read a tragedy to me 'one of these days.' I said to him, 'We shall make one.'

"Jeanty Sarre is grumbling at Charpentier; the ammunition is failing. Jeanty Sarre, having at his house in the Rue Saint Honoré a pound of fowling-powder and twenty army cartridges, sent Charpentier to get them. Charpentier went there, and brought back the fowling-powder and the cartridges, but distributed them to the combatants on the barricades whom he met on the way. 'They were as though famished,' said he. Charpentier had never in his life touched a fire-arm. Jeanty Sarre showed him how to load a gun.

"They take their meals at a wine-seller's at the corner, and they warm themselves there. It is very cold. The wine-seller says, 'Those who are hungry, go and eat.' A combatant asked him, 'Who pays?' 'Death,' was the answer. And in truth some hours afterwards he had received seventeen bayonet thrusts.

"They have not broken the gas-pipes—always for the sake of not doing unnecessary damage. They confine themselves to requisitioning the gasmen's keys, and the lamplighters' winches in order to open the pipes. In this manner they control the lighting or extinguishing.

"This group of barricades is strong, and will play an important part. I had hoped at one moment that they would attack it while I was there. The bugle had approached, and then had gone away again. Jeanty Sarre tells me 'it will be for this evening.'

"His intention is to extinguish the gas in the Rue du Petit-Carreau and all the adjoining streets, and to leave only one jet lighted in the Rue du Cadran. He has placed sentinels as far as the corner of the Rue Saint Denis; at that point there is an open side, without barricades, but little accessible to the troops, on account of the narrowness of the streets, which they can only enter one by one. Thence little danger exists, an advantage of narrow streets; the troops are worth nothing unless massed together. The soldier does not like isolated action; in war the feeling of elbow to elbow constitutes half the bravery. Jeanty Sarre has a reactionary uncle with whom he is not on good terms, and who lives close by at No. 1, Rue du Petit-Carreau.—'What a fright we shall give him presently!' said Jeanty Sarre to me, laughing. This morning Jeanty Sarre has inspected the Montorgueil barricade. There was only one man on it, who was drunk, and who put the barrel of his gun against his breast, saying, 'No thoroughfare.' Jeanty Sarre disarmed him.

"I go to the Rue Pagevin. There at the corner of the Place des Victoires there is a well-constructed barricade. In the adjoining barricade in the Rue Jean Jacques Rousseau, the troops this morning made no prisoners. The soldiers had killed everyone. There are corpses as far as the Place des Victoires. The Pagevin barricade held its own. There are fifty men there, well armed. I enter. 'Is all going on well?' 'Yes.' 'Courage.' I press all these brave hands; they make a report to me. They had seen a

VICTOR HUGO

Municipal Guard smash in the head of a dying man with the butt end of his musket. A pretty young girl, wishing to go home, took refuge in the barricade. There, terrified, she remained for an hour. When all danger was over, the chef of the barricade caused her to be reconducted home by the eldest of his men.

"As I was about to leave the barricade Pagevin, they brought me a prisoner, a police spy, they said.

"He expected to be shot. I had him set at liberty."

Bancel was in this barricade of the Rue Pagevin. We shook hands.

He asked me,—

"Shall we conquer?"

"Yes," I answered.

We then could hardly entertain a doubt.

De Flotte and Bancel wished to accompany me, fearing that I should be arrested by the regiment guarding the Bank.

The weather was misty and cold, almost dark. This obscurity concealed and helped us. The fog was on our side.

As we reached the corner of the Rue de la Vrillière, a group on horseback passed by.

It consisted of a few others, preceded by a man who seemed a soldier, but who was not in uniform. He wore a cloak with a hood.

De Flotte nudged me with his elbow, and whispered,—

"Do you know Fialin?"

I answered,—

"No."

"Have you seen him?

"No."

"Do you wish to see him?"

"No."

"Look at him."

I looked at him.

This man in truth was passing before us. It was he who preceded the group of officers. He came out of the Bank. Had he been there to effect a new forced loan? The people who were at the doors looked at him with curiosity, and without anger. His entire bearing was insolent. He turned from time to time to say a word to one of his followers. This little cavalcade "pawed the ground" in the mist and in the mud. Fialin had the arrogant air of a man who caracoles before a crime. He gazed at the passers-by with a haughty look. His horse was very handsome, and, poor beast, seemed very proud. Fialin was smiling. He had in his hand the whip that his face deserved.

He passed by. I never saw the man except on this occasion.

De Flotte and Bancel did not leave me until they had seen me get into my vehicle. My true-hearted coachman was waiting for me in the Rue de la Vrillière. He brought me back to No 15, Rue Richelieu.

XI

The Barricade of the Rue Meslay

The first barricade of the Rue Saint Martin was erected at the junction of the Rue Meslay. A large cart was overturned, placed across the street, and the roadway was unpaved; some flag-stones of the footway were also torn up. This barricade, the advanced work of defence of the whole revolted street, could only form a temporary obstacle. No portion of the piled-up stones was higher than a man. In a good third of the barricade the stones did not reach above the knee. "It will at all events be good enough to get killed in," said a little street Arab who was rolling numerous flag-stones to the barricade. A hundred combatants took up their position behind it. Towards nine o'clock the movements of the troops gave warning of the attack. The head of the column of the Marulaz Brigade occupied the corner of the street on the side of the boulevard. A piece of artillery, raking the whole of the street, was placed in position before the Porte Saint Martin. For sometime both sides gazed on each other in that moody silence which precedes an encounter; the troops regarding the barricade bristling with guns, the barricade regarding the gaping cannon. After a while the order for a general attack was given. The firing commenced. The first shot passed above the barricade, and struck a woman who was passing some twenty paces in the rear, full in the breast. She fell, ripped open. The fire became brisk without doing much injury to the barricade. The cannon was too near; the bullets flew too high.

The combatants, who had not yet lost a man, received each bullet with a cry of "Long live the Republic!" but without firing. They possessed few cartridges, and they husbanded them. Suddenly the 49th regiment advanced in close column order.

The barricade fired.

The smoke filled the street; when it cleared away, there could be seen a dozen men on the ground, and the soldiers falling back in disorder by the side of the houses. The leader of the barricade shouted, "They are falling back. Cease firing! Let us not waste a ball."

The street remained for sometime deserted. The cannon recommenced fining. A shot came in every two minutes, but always badly aimed. A man with a fowling-piece came up to the leader of the barricade, and said to him, "Let us dismount that cannon. Let us kill the gunners."

"Why!" said the chief, smiling, "they are doing us no harm, let us do none to them."

Nevertheless the sound of the bugle could be distinctly heard on the other side of the block of houses which concealed the troops echelloned on the Square of Saint Martin, and it was manifest that a second attack was being prepared.

This attack would naturally be furious, desperate, and stubborn.

It was also evident that, if this barricade were carried, the entire street would be scoured. The other barricades were still weaker than the first, and more feebly defended. The "middle class" had given their guns, and had re-entered their houses. They lent their street, that was all.

It was therefore necessary to hold the advanced barricade as long as possible. But what was to be done, and how was the resistance to be maintained? They had scarcely two shots per man left.

An unexpected source of supply arrived.

A young man, I can name him, for he is dead—Pierre Tissié,[1] who was a workman, and who also was a poet, had worked during a portion of the morning at the barricades, and at the moment when the firing began he went away, stating as his reason that they would not give him a gun. In the barricade they had said, "There is one who is afraid."

Pierre Tissié was not afraid, as we shall see later on.

He left the barricade.

Pierre Tissié had only his knife with him, a Catalan knife; he opened it at all hazards, he held it in his hand, and went on straight before him.

As he came out of the Rue Saint Sauveur, he saw at the corner of a little lonely street, in which all the windows were closed, a soldier of the line standing sentry, posted there doubtlessly by the main guard at a little distance.

This soldier was at the halt with his gun to his shoulder ready to fire.

He heard the step of Pierre Tissié, and cried out,—

"Who goes there?"

"Death!" answered Pierre Tissié.

The soldier fired, and missed Pierre Tissié, who sprang on him, and struck him down with a blow of his knife.

---

1. It must not be forgotten that this has been written in exile, and that to name a hero was to condemn him to exile.

The soldier fell, and blood spurted out of his mouth.

"I did not know I should speak so truly," muttered Pierre Tissié.

And he added, "Now for the ambulance!"

He took the soldier on his back, picked up the gun which had fallen to the ground, and came back to the barricade. "I bring you a wounded man," said he.

"A dead man," they exclaimed.

In truth the soldier had just expired.

"Infamous Bonaparte!" said Tissié. "Poor red breeches! All the same, I have got a gun."

They emptied the soldier's pouch and knapsack. They divided the cartridges. There were 150 of them. There were also two gold pieces of ten francs, two days' pay since the 2d of December. These were thrown on the ground, no one would take them.

They distributed the cartridges with shouts of "Long live the Republic!"

Meanwhile the attacking party had placed a mortar in position by the side of the cannon.

The distribution of the cartridges was hardly ended when the infantry appeared, and charged upon the barricade with the bayonet. This second assault, as had been foreseen, was violent and desperate. It was repulsed. Twice the soldiers returned to the charge, and twice they fell back, leaving the street strewn with dead. In the interval between the assaults, a shell had pierced and dismantled the barricade, and the cannon began to fire grape-shot.

The situation was hopeless; the cartridges were exhausted. Some began to throw down their guns and go away. The only means of escape was by the Rue Saint Sauveur, and to reach the corner of the Rue Saint Sauveur it was necessary to get over the lower part of the barricade, which left nearly the whole of the fugitives unprotected. There was a perfect rain of musketry and grape-shot. Three or four were killed there, one, like Baudin, by a ball in his eye. The leader of the barricade suddenly noticed that he was alone with Pierre Tissié, and a boy of fourteen years old, the same who had rolled so many stones for the barricade. A third attack was pending, and the soldiers began to advance by the side of the houses.

"Let us go," said the leader of the barricade.

"I shall remain," said Pierre Tissié.

"And I also," said the boy.

And the boy added,—

"I have neither father nor mother. As well this as anything else."

The leader fired his last shot, and retired like the others over the lower part of the barricade. A volley knocked off his hat. He stooped down and picked it up again. The soldiers were not more than twenty-five paces distant.

He shouted to the two who remained,—

"Come along!"

"No," said Pierre Tissié.

"No," said the boy.

A few moments afterwards the soldiers scaled the barricade already half in ruins.

Pierre Tissié and the boy were killed with bayonet thrusts.

Some twenty muskets were abandoned in this barricade.

XII

THE BARRICADE OF THE MAIRIE OF THE FIFTH ARRONDISSEMENT

National Guards in uniform filled the courtyard of the Mairie of the Fifth Arrondissement. Others came in every moment. An ex-drummer of the Garde Mobile had taken a drum from a lower room at the side of the guard-room, and had beaten the call to arms in the surrounding streets. Towards nine o'clock a group of fourteen or fifteen young men, most of whom were in white blouses, entered the Mairie, shouting, "Long live the Republic!" They were armed with guns. The National Guard received them with shouts of "Down with Louis Bonaparte!" They fraternized in the courtyard. Suddenly there was a movement. It was caused by the arrival of the Representatives Doutre and Pelletier.

"What is to be done?" shouted the crowd.

"Barricades," said Pelletier.

They unharnessed the horses, which the carter led away, and they turned the cart round without upsetting it across the wide roadway of the faubourg. The barricade was completed in a moment. A truck came up. They took it and stood it against the wheels of the cart, just as a screen is placed before a fireplace.

The remainder was made up of casks and paving-stones. Thanks to the flour-cart the barricade was lofty, and reached to the first story of the houses. It intersected the faubourg at the corner of the little Rue Saint Jean. A narrow entrance had been contrived at the barricade at the corner of the street.

"One barricade is not sufficient," said Doutre, "we must place the Mairie between two barriers, so as to be able to defend both sides at the same time."

They constructed a second barricade, facing the summit of the faubourg. This one was low and weakly built, being composed only of planks and of paving-stones. There was about a hundred paces distance between the two barricades.

There were three hundred men in this space. Only one hundred had guns. The majority had only one cartridge.

The firing began about ten o'clock. Two companies of the line appeared and fired several volleys. The attack was only a feint. The barricade replied, and made the mistake of foolishly exhausting its ammunition. The troops retired. Then the attack began in earnest. Some Chasseurs de Vincennes emerged from the corner of the boulevard.

Following out the African mode of warfare, they glided along the side of the walls, and then, with a run, they threw themselves upon the barricade.

No more ammunition in the barricade. No quarter to be expected.

Those who had no more powder or balls threw down their guns. Some wished to reoccupy their position in the Mairie, but it was impossible for them to maintain any defence there, the Mairie being open and commanded from every side; they scaled the walls and scattered themselves about in the neighboring houses; others escaped by the narrow passage of the boulevard which led into the Rue Saint Jean; most of the combatants reached the opposite side of the boulevard, while those who had a cartridge left fired a last volley upon the troops from the height of the paving-stones. Then they awaited their death. All were killed.

One of those who succeeded in slipping into the Rue Saint Jean, where moreover they ran the gauntlet of a volley from their assailants, was M.H. Coste, Editor of the *Evénement* and of the *Avénement du Peuple*.

M. Coste had been a captain in the Garde Mobile. At a bend in the street, which placed him out of reach of the balls, M. Conte noticed in front of him the drummer of the Garde Mobile, who, like him, had escaped by the Rue Saint Jean, and who was profiting by the loneliness of the street to get rid of his drum.

"Keep your drum," cried he to him.

"For what purpose?"

"To beat the call to arms."

"Where?"

"At Batignolles."

"I will keep it," said the drummer.

These two men came out from the jaws of death, and at once consented to re-enter them.

But how should they cross all Paris with this drum? The first patrol which met them would shoot them. A porter of an adjoining house, who noticed their predicament, gave them a packing-cloth. They enveloped the drum in it, and reached Batignolles by the lonely streets which skirt the walls.

VIII

The Barricade of the Rue Thévenot

Georges Biscarrat was the man who had given the signal for the looting in the Rue de l'Echelle.

I had known Georges Biscarrat ever since June, 1848. He had taken part in that disastrous insurrection. I had had an opportunity of being useful to him. He had been captured, and was kneeling before the firing-party; I interfered, and I saved his life, together with that of some others, M., D., D., B., and that brave-hearted architect Rolland, who when an exile, later on, so ably restored the Brussels Palace of Justice.

This took place on the 24th June, 1848, in the underground floor of No. 93, Boulevard Beaumarchais, a house then in course of construction.

Georges Biscarrat became attached to me. It appeared that he was the nephew of one of the oldest and best friends of my childhood, Félix Biscarrat, who died in 1828. Georges Biscarrat came to see me from time to time, and on occasions he asked my advice or gave me information.

Wishing to preserve him from evil influences, I had given him, and he had accepted, this guiding maxim, "No insurrection except for Duty and for Right."

What was this hooting in the Rue de l'Echelle? Let us relate the incident.

On the 2d of December, Bonaparte had made an attempt to go out. He had ventured to go and look at Paris. Paris does not like being looked at by certain eyes; it considers it an insult, and it resents an insult more than a wound. It submits to assassination, but not to the leering gaze of the assassin. It took offence at Louis Bonaparte.

At nine o'clock in the morning, at the moment when the Courbevoie garrison was descending upon Paris, the placards of the *coup d'état* being still fresh upon the walls, Louis Bonaparte had left the Elysée, had crossed the Place de la Concorde, the Garden of the Tuileries, and the railed courtyard of the Carrousel, and had been seen to go out, by the gate of the Rue de l'Echelle. A crowd assembled at once.

Louis Bonaparte was in a general's uniform; his uncle, the ex-King Jérôme, accompanied him, together with Flahaut, who kept in the near. Jérôme wore the full uniform of a Marshal of France, with a hat with a white feather; Louis Bonaparte's horse was a head before Jérôme's horse. Louis Bonaparte was gloomy, Jérôme attentive, Flahaut beaming. Flahaut had his hat on one side. There was a strong escort of Lancers. Edgar Ney followed. Bonaparte intended to go as far as the Hôtel de Ville. Georges Biscarrat was there. The street was unpaved, the road was being macadamized; he mounted on a heap of stones, and shouted, "Down with the Dictator! Down with the Praetorians!" The soldiers looked at him with bewilderment, and the crowd with astonishment. Georges Biscarrat (he told me so himself) felt that this cry was too erudite, and that it would not be understood, so he shouted, "Down with Bonaparte! Down with the Lancers!"

The effect of this shout was electrical. "Down with Bonaparte! Down with the Lancers!" cried the people, and the whole street became stormy and turbulent. "Down with Bonaparte!" The outcry resembled the beginning of an execution; Bonaparte made a sudden movement to the right, turned back, and re-entered the courtyard of the Louvre.

Georges Biscarrat felt it necessary to complete his shout by a barricade.

He said to the bookseller, Benoist Mouilhe, who had just opened his shop, "Shouting is good, action is better." He returned to his house in the Rue du Vert Bois, put on a blouse and a workman's cap, and went down into the dark streets. Before the end of the day he had made arrangements with four associations—the gas-fitters, the last-makers, the shawl-makers, and the hatters.

In this manner he spent the day of the 2d of December.

The day of the 3d was occupied in goings and comings "almost useless." So Biscarrat told Versigny, and he added, "However I have succeeded in this much, that the placards of the *coup d'état* have been everywhere torn down, so much so that in order to render the tearing down more difficult the police have ultimately posted them in the public conveniences—their proper place."

On Thursday, the 4th, early in the morning, Georges Biscarrat went to Ledouble's restaurant, where four Representatives of the People usually took their meals, Brives, Bertlhelon, Antoine Bard, and Viguier, nicknamed "Father Viguier." All four were there. Viguier related what we had done on the preceding evening, and shared my opinion that the closing catastrophe should be hurried on, that the Crime should be precipitated into the abyss which befitted it. Biscarrat came in. The Representatives did not know hire, and stared at him. "Who are you?" asked one of them. Before he could answer, Dr. Petit entered, unfolded a paper, and said,—

"Does anyone know Victor Hugo's handwriting?"

"I do," said Biscarrat. He looked at the paper. It was my proclamation to the army. "This must be printed," said Petit. "I will undertake it," said Biscarrat. Antoine Bard asked him, "Do you know Victor Hugo?" "He saved my life," answered Biscarrat. The Representatives shook hands with him.

Guilgot arrived. Then Versigny. Versigny knew Biscarrat. He had seen him at my house. Versigny said, "Take care what you do. There is a man outside the door." "It is a shawl-maker," said Biscarrat. "He has come with me. He is following me." "But," resumed Versigny, "he is wearing a blouse, beneath which he has a handkerchief. He seems to be hiding this, and he has something in the handkerchief."

"Sugar-plums," said Biscarrat.

They were cartridges.

Versigny and Biscarrat went to the office of the *Siècle*; at the *Siècle* thirty workmen, at the risk of being shot, offered to print my Proclamation. Biscarrat left it with them, and said to Versigny, "Now I want my barricade."

The shawl-maker walked behind them. Versigny and Biscarrat turned their steps towards the top of the Saint Denis quarter. When they drew near to she Porte Saint Denis they heard the hum of many voices. Biscarrat laughed and said to Versigny, "Saint Denis is growing angry, matters are improving." Biscarrat recruited forty combatants on the way, amongst whom was Moulin, head of the association of leather-dressers. Chapuis, sergeant-major of the National Guard, brought them four muskets and ten swords. "Do you know where there are anymore?" asked Biscarrat. "Yes, at the Saint Sauveur Baths." They went there, and found forty muskets. They gave them swords and cartridge-pouches. Gentlemen well dressed, brought tin boxes containing powder and balls. Women, brave and light-hearted, manufactured cartridges. At the first door adjoining the Rue du Hasard-Saint-Sauveur they requisitioned iron bars and hammers from a large courtyard belonging to a locksmith. Having the arms, they had the men. They speedily numbered a hundred. They began to tear up the pavements. It was half-past ten. "Quick! quick!" cried Georges Biscarrat, "the barricade of my dreams!" It was in the Rue Thévenot. The barrier was constructed high and formidable. To abridge. At eleven o'clock Georges Biscarrat had completed his barricade. At noon he was killed there.

XIV

OSSIAN AND SCIPIO

A rrests grew more numerous.

Towards noon a Commissary of Police, named Boudrot, appeared at the divan of the Rue Lepelletier. He was accompanied by the police agent Delahodde. Delahodde was that traitorous socialist writer, who, upon being unmasked, had passed from the Secret Police to the Public Police Service. I knew him, and I record this incident. In 1832 he was a master in the school at which were my two sons, then boys, and he had addressed poetry to me. At the same time he was acting the spy upon me. The Lepelletier divan was the place of meeting of a large number of Republican journalists. Delahodde knew them all. A detachment of the Republican Guard occupied the entrances to the café. Then ensued an inspection of all the ordinary customers, Delahodde walking first, with the Commissary behind him. Two Municipal Guards followed them. From time to time Delahodde looked round and said, "Lay hold of this man." In this manner some score of writers were arrested, among whom were Hennett de Kesler.[1] On the preceding evening Kesler had been on the Saint Antoine barricade. Kesler said to Delahodde, "You are a miserable wretch." "And you are an ungrateful fellow," replied Delahodde; "*I am saving your life.*" Curious words; for it is difficult to believe that Delahodde was in the secret of what was to happen on the fatal day of the Fourth.

At the head-quarters of the Committee encouraging information was forwarded to us from every side. Testelin, the Representative of Lille, is not only a learned man, but a brave man. On the morning of the 3d he had reached, shortly after me, the Saint Antoine barricade, where Baudin had just been killed. All was at an end in that direction. Testelin was accompanied by Charles Gambon, another dauntless man.[2] The two Representatives wandered through the agitated and dark streets, little followed, in no way understood, seeking a ferment of insurgents,

---

1. Died in exile in Guernsey. See the "Pendant l'Exil," under the heading *Actes et Paroles*, vol. ii.

2. Died in exile at Termonde.

and only finding a swarming of the curious. Testelin, nevertheless, having come to the Committee, informed us of the following:—At the corner of a street of the Faubourg Saint Antoine Gambon and himself had noticed a crowd. They had gone up to it. This crowd was reading a bill placarded on a wall. It was the Appeal to Arms signed "Victor Hugo." Testelin asked Gambon, "Have you a pencil?" "Yes," answered Gambon. Testelin took the pencil, went up to the placard, and wrote his name beneath mine, then he gave the pencil to Gambon, who in turn wrote his name beneath that of Testelin. Upon this the crowd shouted, "Bravo! these are true-hearted men!" "Shout 'Long live the Republic!'" cried Testelin. All shouted "Long live the Republic!" "And from above, from the open windows," added Gambon, "women clapped their hands."

"The little hands of women applauding are a good sign," said Michel de Bourges.

As has been seen, and we cannot lay too much stress upon the fact, what the Committee of Resistance wished was to prevent the shedding of blood as much as possible. To construct barricades, to let them be destroyed, and to reconstruct them at other points, to avoid the army, and to wear it out, to wage in Paris the war of the desert, always retreating, never yielding, to take time for an ally, to add days to days; on the one hand to give the people time to understand and to rise, on the other, to conquer the *coup d'état* by the weariness of the army; such was the plan discussed and adopted.

The order was accordingly given that the barricades should be but slightly defended.

We repeated in every possible form to the combatants,—

"Shed as little blood as possible! Spare the blood of the soldiers and husband your own."

Nevertheless, the struggle once begun, it became impossible in many instances, during certain excited hours of fighting, to moderate their ardor. Several barricades were obstinately defended, particularly those in the Rue Rambuteau, in the Rue Montorgueil, and in the Rue Neuve Saint Eustache.

These barricades were commanded by daring leaders.

Here, for the sake of history, we will record a few of these brave men fighting outlines who appeared and disappeared in the smoke of the combat. Radoux, an architect, Deluc, Mallarmet, Félix Bony, Luneau, an ex-Captain of the Republican Guard, Camille Berru, editor of the

Avénement, gay, warmhearted, and dauntless, and that young Eugène Millelot, who was destined to be condemned at Cayenne to receive 200 lashes, and to expire at the twenty-third stroke, before the very eyes of his father and brother, proscribed and convicts like himself.

The barricade of the Rue Aumaire was amongst those which were not carried without resistance. Although raised in haste, it was fairly constructed. Fifteen or sixteen resolute men defended it; two were killed.

The barricade was carried with the bayonet by a battalion of the 16th of the line. This battalion, hurled on the barricade at the double, was received by a brisk fusillade; several soldiers were wounded.

The first who fell in the soldiers' ranks was an officer. He was a young man of twenty-five, lieutenant of the first company, named Ossian Dumas; two balls broke both of his legs as though by a single blow.

At that time there were in the army two brothers of the name of Dumas, Ossian and Scipio. Scipio was the elder. They were near relatives of the Representative, Madier de Montjau.

These two brothers belonged to a poor but honored family. The elder had been educated at the Polytechnic School, the other at the School of Saint Cyr.

Scipio was four years older than his brother. According to that splendid and mysterious law of ascent, which the French Revolution has created, and which, so to speak, has placed a ladder in the centre of a society hitherto caste-bound and inaccessible, Scipio Dumas' family had imposed upon themselves the most severe privations in order to develop his intellect and secure his future. His relations, with the touching heroism of the poor of the present era, denied themselves bread to afford him knowledge. In this manner he attained to the Polytechnic School, where he quickly became one of the best pupils.

Having concluded his studies, he was appointed an officer in the artillery, and sent to Metz. It then became his turn to help the boy who had to mount after him. He held out his hand to his younger brother. He economized the modest pay of an artillery lieutenant, and, thanks to him, Ossian became an officer like Scipio. While Scipio, detained by duties belonging to his position, remained at Metz, Ossian was incorporated in an infantry regiment, and went to Africa. There he saw his first service.

Scipio and Ossian were Republicans. In October, 1851, the 16th of the line, in which Ossian was serving, was summoned to Paris. It was one of the regiments chosen by the ill-omened hand of Louis Bonaparte, and on which the *coup d'état* counted.

The 2d of December arrived.

Lieutenant Ossian Dumas obeyed, like nearly all his comrades, the order to take up arms; but everyone round him could notice his gloomy attitude.

The day of the 3d was spent in marches and counter-marches. On the 4th the combat began. The 16th, which formed part of the Herbillon Brigade, was told off to capture the barricades of the Rues Beaubourg, Trausnonain, and Aumaire. This battle-field was formidable; a perfect square of barricades had been raised there.

It was by the Rue Aumaire, and with the regiment of which Ossian formed part, that the military leaders resolved to begin action.

At the moment when the regiment, with arms loaded, was about to march upon the Rue Aumaire, Ossian Dumas went up to his captain, a brave and veteran officer, with whom he was a favorite, and declared that he would not march a step farther, that the deed of the 2d of December was a crime, that Louis Bonaparte was a traitor, that it was for them, soldiers, to maintain the oath which Bonaparte violated; and that, as for himself, he would not lend his sword to the butchery of the Republic.

A halt was made. The signal of attack was awaited; the two officers, the old captain and the young lieutenant, conversed in a low tone.

"And what do you want to do?" asked the captain.

"Break my sword."

"You will be taken to Vincennes."

"That is all the same to me."

"Most certainly dismissed."

"Possibly."

"Perhaps shot."

"I expect it."

"But there is no longer anytime; you should have resigned yesterday."

"There is always time to avoid committing a crime."

The captain, as may be seen, was simply one of those professional heroes, grown old in the leather stock, who know of no country but the flag, and no other law but military discipline. Iron arms and wooden heads. They are neither citizens nor men. They only recognize honor in the form of a general's epaulets. It is of no use talking to them of political duties, of obedience to the laws, of the Constitution. What do they know about all this? What is a Constitution; what are the most holy laws, against three words which a corporal may murmur into the ear of a sentinel? Take a pair of scales, put in one side the Gospels, in the other the official instructions; now weigh them. The corporal turns the balance; the Deity kicks the beam.

God forms a portion of the order of the day of Saint Bartholomew. "Kill all. He will recognized his own."

This is what the priests accept, and at times glorify.

Saint Bartholomew has been blessed by the Pope and decorated with the Catholic medal.[3]

Meanwhile Ossian Dumas appeared determined. The captain made a last effort.

"You will ruin yourself," said he.

"I shall save my honor."

"It is precisely your honor that you are sacrificing."

"Because I am going away?"

"To go away is to desert."

This seemed to impress Ossian Dumas. The captain continued,—

"They are about to fight. In a few minutes the barricade will be attacked. Your comrades will fall, dead or wounded. You are a young officer—you have not yet been much under fire."

"At all events," warmly interrupted Ossian Dumas, "I shall not have fought against the Republic; they will not say I am a traitor."

"No, but they will say that you are a coward."

Ossian made no reply.

A moment afterwards the command was given to attack.

The regiment started at the double. The barricade fired.

Ossian Dumas was the first who fell.

He had not been able to bear that word "coward," and he had remained in his place in the first rank.

They took him to the ambulance, and from thence to the hospital.

Let us at once state the conclusion of this touching incident.

Both of his legs were broken. The doctors thought that it would be necessary to amputate them both.

General Saint-Arnaud sent him the Cross of Honor.

As is known, Louis Bonaparte hastened to discharge his debt to his praetorian accomplices. After having massacred, the sword voted.

---

3. Pro Hugonotorum strage. Medal struck at Rome in 1572.

The combat was still smoking when the army was brought to the ballot-box.

The garrison of Paris voted "Yes." It absolved itself.

With the rest of the army it was otherwise. Military honor was indignant, and roused the civic virtue. Notwithstanding the pressure which was exercised, although the regiments deposited their votes in the shakos of their colonels, the army voted "No" in many districts of France and Algeria.

The Polytechnic School voted "No" in a body. Nearly everywhere the artillery, of which the Polytechnic School is the cradle, voted to the same effect as the school.

Scipio Dumas, it may be remembered, was at Metz.

By some curious chance it happened that the feeling of the artillery, which everywhere else had pronounced against the *coup d'état*, hesitated at Metz, and seemed to lean towards Bonaparte.

Scipio Dumas, in presence of this indecision set an example. He voted in a loud voice, and with an open voting paper, "No."

Then he sent in his resignation. At the same time that the Minister at Paris received the resignation of Scipio Dumas, Scipio Dumas at Metz, received his dismissal, signed by the Minister.

After Scipio Dumas' vote, the same thought had come at the same time to both the Government and to the officer, to the Government that the officer was a dangerous man, and that they could no longer employ him, to the officer that the Government was an infamous one, and that he ought no longer to serve it.

The resignation and the dismissal crossed on the way. By this word "dismissal" must be understood the withdrawal of employment.

According to our existing military laws it is in this manner that they now "break" an officer. Withdrawal of employment, that is to say, no more service, no more pay; poverty.

Simultaneously with his dismissal, Scipio Dumas learnt the news of the attack on the barricade of the Rue Aumaire, and that his brother had both his legs broken. In the fever of events he had been a week without news of Ossian. Scipio had confined himself to writing to his brother to inform him of his vote and of his dismissal, and to induce him to do likewise.

His brother wounded! His brother at the Val-de. Grâce! He left immediately for Paris.

He hastened to the hospital. They took him to Ossian's bedside. The poor young fellow had had both his legs amputated on the preceding day.

At the moment when Scipio, stunned, appeared at his bedside, Ossian held in his hand the cross which General Saint-Arnaud had just sent him.

The wounded man turned towards the aide-de-camp who had brought it, and said to him,—

"I will not have this cross. On my breast it would be stained with the blood of the Republic."

And perceiving his brother, who had just entered, he held out the cross to him, exclaiming,—

"You take it. You have voted "No," and you have broken your sword! It is you who have deserved it!"

XV

The Question Presents Itself

I t was one o'clock in the afternoon.

Bonaparte had again become gloomy.

The gleams of sunshine on such countenances as these last very short time.

He had gone back to his private room, had seated himself before the fire, with his feet on the hobs, motionless, and no one any longer approached him except Roquet.

What was he thinking of?

The twistings of the viper cannot be foreseen.

What this man achieved on this infamous day I have told at length in another book. See "Napoleon the Little."

From time to time Roquet entered and informed him of what was going on. Bonaparte listened in silence, deep in thought, marble in which a torrent of lava boiled.

He received at the Elysée the same news that we received in the Rue Richelieu; bad for him, good for us. In one of the regiments which had just voted, there were 170 "Noes:" This regiment has since been dissolved, and scattered abroad in the African army.

They had counted on the 14th of the line which had fired on the people in February. The Colonel of the 14th of the line had refused to recommence; he had just broken his sword.

Our appeal had ended by being heard. Decidedly, as we have seen, Paris was rising. The fall of Bonaparte seemed to be foreshadowed. Two Representatives, Fabvier and Crestin, met in the Rue Royale, and Crestin, pointing to the Palace of the Assembly, said to Fabvier, "We shall be there tomorrow."

One noteworthy incident. Mazes became eccentric, the prison unbent itself; the interior experienced an undefinable reverberation from the outside. The warders, who the preceding evening had been insolent to the Representatives when going for their exercise in the courtyard, now saluted them to the ground. That very morning of Thursday, the 4th, the governor of the prison had paid a visit to the prisoners, and had said to them, "It is not my fault." He brought them books and writing-paper, a thing which up to that time he had refused. The Representative Valentin was in solitary confinement; on the morning of the 4th his warder suddenly became amiable, and offered to obtain for him news from outside, through his wife, who, he said, had been a servant in General Leflô's household. These were significant signs. When the jailer smiles it means that the jail is half opening.

We may add, what is not a contradiction, that at the same time the garrison at Mazas was being increased. 1200 more men were marched in, in detachments of 100 men each, spacing out their arrivals in "little doses" as an eye-witness remarked to us. Later on 400 men. 100 litres of brandy were distributed to them. One litre for every sixteen men. The prisoners could hear the movement of artillery round the prison.

The agitation spread to the most peaceable quarters. But the centre of Paris was above all threatening. The centre of Paris is a labyrinth of streets which appears to be made for the labyrinth of riots. The Ligue, the Fronde, the Revolution—we must unceasingly recall these useful facts—the 14th of July, the 10th of August, 1792, 1830, 1848, have come out from thence. These brave old streets were awakened. At eleven o'clock in the morning from Notre Dame to the Porte Saint Martin there were seventy-seven barricades. Three of them, one in the Rue Maubuée, another in the Rue Bertin-Poirée, another in the Rue Guérin-Boisseau, attained the height of the second stories; the barricade of the Porte Saint Denis was almost as bristling and as formidable as the barrier of the Faubourg Saint Antoine in June, 1848. The handful of the Representatives of the People had swooped down like a shower of sparks on these famous and inflammable crossroads. The beginning of the fire. The fire had caught. The old central market quarter, that city which is contained in the city, shouted, "Down with Bonaparte!" They hooted the police, they hissed the troops. Some regiments seemed stupefied. They cried, "Throw up your butt ends in the air!" From the windows above, women encouraged the construction of the barricades. There was powder there, there were muskets. Now, we were no longer alone. We saw rising up in the gloom behind us the enormous head of the people. Hope at the present time was on our side. The oscillation of uncertainty had at length become steady, and we were, I repeat, almost perfectly confident.

There had been a moment when, owing to the good news pouring in upon us, this confidence had become so great that we who had staked our lives on this great contest, seized with an irresistible joy in the presence of a success becoming hourly more certain, had risen from our seats, and had embraced each other. Michel de Bourges was particularly angered against Bonaparte, for he had believed his word, and had even gone so far as to say, "He is my man." Of the four of us, he was the most indignant. A gloomy flash of victory shone in him. He struck the table with his fist, and exclaimed, "Oh! the miserable wretch! Tomorrow—" and he struck the table a second time, "tomorrow his head shall fall in the Place de Grève before the Hôtel de Ville."

I looked at him.

"No," said I, "this man's head shall not fall."

"What do you mean?"

"I do not wish it."

"Why?"

"Because," said I, "if after such a crime we allow Louis Bonaparte to live we shall abolish the penalty of death."

This generous Michel de Bourges remained thoughtful for a moment, then he pressed my hand.

Crime is an opportunity, and always gives us a choice, and it is better to extract from it progress than punishment. Michel de Bourges realized this.

Moreover this incident shows to what a pitch our hopes had been raised.

Appearances were on our side, actual facts not so. Saint-Arnaud had his orders. We shall see them.

Strange incidents took place.

Towards noon a general, deep in thought, was on horseback in the Place de la Madeleine, at the head of his wavering troops. He hesitated.

A carriage stopped, a woman stepped out and conversed in a low tone with the general. The crowd could see her. The Representative Raymond, who lived at No 4, Place de la Madeleine, saw her from his window. This woman was Madame K. The general stooping down on his horse, listened, and finally made the dejected gesture of a vanquished man. Madame K. got back into her carriage. This man, they said, loved that woman. She could, according to the side of her beauty which fascinated her victim, inspire either heroism or crime. This strange beauty was compounded of the whiteness of an angel, combined with the look of a spectre.

It was the look which conquered.

This man no longer hesitated. He entered gloomily into the enterprise.

From twelve to two o'clock there was in this enormous city given over to the unknown an indescribable and fierce expectation. All was calm and awe-striking. The regiments and the limbered batteries quitted the faubourg and stationed themselves noiselessly around the boulevards. Not a cry in the ranks of the soldiery. An eye-witness said, "The soldiers march with quite a jaunty air." On the Quai de la Ferronnerie, heaped up with regiments ever since the morning of the 2d of December, there now only remained a post of Municipal Guards. Everything ebbed back to the centre, the people as well as the army; the silence of the army had ultimately spread to the people. They watched each other.

Each soldier had three days' provisions and six packets of cartridges.

It has since transpired that at this moment 10,000 francs were daily spent in brandy for each brigade.

Towards one o'clock, Magnan went to the Hôtel de Ville, had the reserve limbered under his own eyes, and did not leave until all the batteries were ready to march.

Certain suspicious preparations grew more numerous. Towards noon the State workmen and the hospital corps had established a species of huge ambulance at No. 2, Faubourg Montmartre. A great heap of litters was piled up there. "What is all this for?" asked the crowd.

Dr. Deville, who had attended Espinasse when he had been wounded, noticed him on the boulevard, and asked him, "Up to what point are you going?"

Espinasse's answer is historical.

He replied, "To the end."

At two o'clock five brigades, those of Cotte, Bourgon, Canrobert, Dulac, and Reybell, five batteries of artillery, 16,400 men,[1] infantry and cavalry, lancers, cuirassiers, grenadiers, gunners, were echelloned without any ostensible reason between the Rue de la Paix and the Faubourg Poissonnière. Pieces of cannon were pointed at the entrance of every street; there were eleven in position on the Boulevard Poissonnière alone. The foot soldiers had their guns to their shoulders, the officers their swords drawn. What did all this mean? It was a curious sight, well worth the trouble of seeing, and on both sides of the pavements, on all the thresholds of the shops, from all the stories of the houses, an astonished, ironical, and confiding crowd looked on.

---

1. 16,410 men, the figures taken from the Ministry of War.

Little by little, nevertheless, this confidence diminished, and irony gave place to astonishment; astonishment changed to stupor. Those who have passed through that extraordinary minute will not forget it. It was evident that there was something underlying all this. But what? Profound obscurity. Can one imagine Paris in a cellar? People felt as though they were beneath a low ceiling. They seemed to be walled up in the unexpected and the unknown. They seemed to perceive some mysterious will in the background. But after all they were strong; they were the Republic, they were Paris; what was there to fear! Nothing. And they cried, "Down with Bonaparte!" The troops continued to keep silence, but the swords remained outside their scabbards, and the lighted matches of the cannon smoldered at the corners of the streets. The cloud grew blacker every minute, heavier and more silent. This thickening of the darkness was tragical. One felt the coming crash of a catastrophe, and the presence of a villain; snake-like treason writhed during this night, and none can foresee where the downward slide of a terrible design will stop when events are on a steep incline.

What was coming out of this thick darkness?

XVI

The Massacre

S uddenly a window was opened.

Upon Hell.

Dante, had he leaned over the summit of the shadow, would have been able to see the eighth circle of his poem; the funereal Boulevard Montmartre.

Paris, a prey to Bonaparte; a monstrous spectacle. The gloomy armed men massed together on this boulevard felt an appalling spirit enter into them; they ceased to be themselves, and became demons.

There was no longer a single French soldier, but a host of indefinable phantoms, carrying out a horrible task, as though in the glimmering light of a vision.

There was no longer a flag, there was no longer law, there was no longer humanity, there was no longer a country, there was no longer France; they began to assassinate.

The Schinderhannes division, the brigades of Mandrin, Cartouche, Poulailler, Trestaillon, and Tropmann appeared in the gloom, shooting down and massacring.

No; we do not attribute to the French army what took place during this mournful eclipse of honor.

There have been massacres in history, abominable ones assuredly, but they have possessed some show of reason; Saint Bartholomew and the Dragonnades are explained by religion, the Sicilian Vespers and the butcheries of September are explained by patriotism; they crush the enemy or annihilate the foreigner; these are crimes for a good cause; but the carnage of the Boulevard Montmartre is a crime without an ostensible reason.

The reason exists, however. It is hideous.

Let us give it.

Two things stand erect in a State, the Law and the People.

A man murders the Law. He feels the punishment approaching, there only remains one thing for him to do, to murder the People. He murders the People.

The Second of December was the Risk, the Fourth was the Certainty.

Against the indignation which arose they opposed the Terror.

The Fury, Justice, halted petrified before the Fury, Extermination. Against Erinnyes they set up Medusa.

To put Nemesis to flight, what a terrifying triumph!

To Louis Napoleon pertains this glory, which is the summit of his shame.

Let us narrate it.

Let us narrate what History had never seen before.

The assassination of a people by a man.

Suddenly, at a given signal, a musket shot being fired, no matter where, no matter by whom, the shower of bullets poured upon the crowd. A shower of bullets is also a crowd; it is death scattered broadcast. It does not know whither it goes, nor what it does; it kills and passes on.

But at the same time it has a species of soul; it is premeditated, it executes a will. This was an unprecedented moment. It seemed as though a handful of lightnings was falling upon the people. Nothing simpler. It formed a clear solution to the difficulty; the rain of lead overwhelmed the multitude. What are you doing there? Die! It is a crime to be passing by. Why are you in the street? Why do you cross the path of the Government? The Government is a cut-throat. They have announced a thing, they must certainly carry it out; what is begun must assuredly be achieved; as Society is being saved, the People must assuredly be exterminated.

Are there not social necessities? Is it not essential that Béville should have 87,000 francs a year and Fleury 95,000 francs? Is it not essential that the High Chaplain, Menjaud, Bishop of Nancy, should have 342 francs a day, and that Bassano and Cambacérès should each have 383 francs a day, and Vaillant 468 francs, and Saint-Arnaud 822 francs? Is it not necessary that Louis Bonaparte should have 76,712 francs a day? Could one be Emperor for less?

In the twinkling of an eye there was a butchery on the boulevard a quarter of a league long. Eleven pieces of cannon wrecked the Sallandrouze carpet warehouse. The shot tore completely through twenty-eight houses. The baths of Jouvence were riddled. There was a massacre at Tortoni's. A whole quarter of Paris was filled with an immense flying mass, and with a terrible cry. Everywhere sudden death. A man is expecting nothing. He falls. From whence does this come? From above, say the Bishops' *Te Deum*; from below, says Truth.

From a lower place than the galleys, from a lower place than Hell.

It is the conception of a Caligula, carried out by a Papavoine.

Xavier Durrieu comes upon the boulevard. He states,—

"I have taken sixty steps, I have seen sixty corpses."

And he draws back. To be in the street is a Crime, to be at home is a Crime. The butchers enter the houses and slaughter. In slaughter-house slang the soldiers cry, "Let us pole-axe the lot of them."

Adde, a bookseller, of 17, Boulevard Poissonnière, is standing before his door; they kill him. At the same moment, for the field of murder is vast, at a considerable distance from there, at 5, Rue de Lancry, M. Thirion de Montauban, owner of the house, is at his door; they kill him. In the Rue Tiquetonne a child of seven years, named Boursier, is passing by; they kill him. Mdlle. Soulac, 196, Rue du Temple, opens her window; they kill her. At No. 97, in the same street, two women, Mesdames Vidal and Raboisson, sempstresses, are in their room; they kill them. Belval, a cabinet-maker, 10, Rue de la Lune, is at home; they kill him. Debaëcque, a merchant, 45, Rue du Sentier, is in his own house; Couvercelle, florist, 257, Rue Saint Denis, is in his own house; Labitte, a jeweller, 55, Boulevard Saint Martin, is in his own house; Monpelas, perfumer, 181, Rue Saint Martin, is in his own house; they kill Monpelas, Labitte, Couvercelle, and Debaëcque. They sabre at her own home, 240, Rue Saint Martin, a poor embroideress, Mdlle. Seguin, who not having sufficient money to pay for a doctor, died at the Beaujon hospital, on the 1st of January, 1852, on the same day that the Sibour *Te Deum* was chanted at Notre Dame. Another, a waistcoat-maker, Françoise Noël, was shot down at 20, Rue du Faubourg Montmartre, and died in the Charité. Another, Madame Ledaust, a working housekeeper, living at 76, Passage du Caire, was shot down before the Archbishop's palace, and died at the Morgue. Passers-by, Mdlle. Gressier, living at 209, Faubourg Saint Martin; Madame Guilard, living at 77, Boulevard Saint Denis; Madame Gamier, living at 6, Boulevard Bonne Nouvelle, who had fallen, the first named beneath the volleys on the Boulevard Montmartre, the two others on the Boulevard Saint Denis, and who were still alive, attempted to rise, and became targets for the soldiers, bursting with laughter, and this time fell back again dead. Deeds of gallantry ware performed. Colonel Rochefort, who was probably created General for this, charged in the Rue do la Paix at the head of his Lancers a flock of nurses, who were put to flight.

Such was this indescribable enterprise. All the men who took part in it were instigated by hidden influences; all had something which urged them forward; Herbillon had Zaatcha behind him; Saint-Arnaud had Kabylia; Renault had the affair of the Saint-André and Saint Hippolyte villages; Espinasse, Rome and the storming of the 30th of June; Magnan, his debts.

Must we continue? We hesitate. Dr. Piquet, a man of seventy, was killed in his drawing-room by a ball in his stomach; the painter Jollivart, by a ball in the forehead, before his easel, his brains bespattered his painting. The English captain, William Jesse, narrowly escaped a ball which pierced the ceiling above his head; in the library adjoining the Magasins du Prophète, a father, mother, and two daughters were sabred. Lefilleul, another bookseller, was shot in his shop on the Boulevard Poissonnière; in the Rue Lepelletier, Boyer, a chemist, seated at his counter, was "spitted" by the Lancers. A captain, killing all before him, took by storm the house of the Grand Balcon. A servant was killed in the shop of Brandus. Reybell through the volleys said to Sax, "And I also am discoursing sweet music." The Café Leblond was given over to pillage. Billecoq's establishment was bombarded to such a degree that it had to be pulled down the next day. Before Jouvain's house lay a heap of corpses, amongst them an old man with his umbrella, and a young man with his eye-glass. The Hôtel de Castille, the Maison Dorée, the Petite Jeannette, the Café de Paris, the Café Anglais became for three hours the targets of the cannonade. Raquenault's house crumbled beneath the shells; the bullets demolished the Montmartre Bazaar.

None escaped. The guns and pistols were fired at close quarters.

New Year's-day was not far off, some shops were full of New Year's gifts. In the passage du Saumon, a child of thirteen, flying before the platoon-firing, hid himself in one of these shops, beneath a heap of toys. He was captured and killed. Those who killed him laughingly widened his wounds with their swords. A woman told me, "The cries of the poor little fellow could be heard all through the passage." Four men were shot before the same shop. The officer said to them, "This will teach you to loaf about." A fifth named Mailleret, who was left for dead, was carried the next day with eleven wounds to the Charité. There he died.

They fired into the cellars by the air-holes.

A workman, a currier, named Moulins, who had taken refuge in one of these shot-riddled cellars, saw through the cellar air-hole a passer-by, who had been wounded in the thigh by a bullet, sit down on the pavement with the death rattle in his throat, and lean against a shop. Some soldiers who heard this rattle ran up and finished off the wounded man with bayonet thrusts.

One brigade killed the passer-by from the Madeleine to the Opera, another from the Opera to the Gymnase; another from the Boulevard Bonne Nouvelle to the Porte Saint Denis; the 75th of the line having carried the barricade of the Porte Saint Denis, it was no longer a fight, it was a slaughter. The massacre radiated—a word horribly true—from the boulevard into all the streets. It was a devil-fish stretching out its feelers. Flight? Why? Concealment? To what purpose? Death ran after you quicker than you could fly. In the Rue Pagevin a soldier said to a passer-by, "What are you doing here?" "I am going home." The soldier kills the passer-by. In the Rue des Marais they kill four young men in their own courtyard. Colonel Espinasse exclaimed, "After the bayonet, cannon!" Colonel Rochefort exclaimed, "Thrust, bleed, slash!" and he added, "It is an economy of powder and noise." Before Barbedienne's establishment an officer was showing his gun, an arm of considerable precision, admiringly to his comrades, and he said, "With this gun I can score magnificent shots between the eyes." having said this, he aimed at random at someone, and succeeded. The carnage was frenzied. While the butchering under the orders of Carrelet filled the boulevard, the Bourgon brigade devastated the Temple, the Marulaz brigade devastated the Rue Rambuteau; the Renault division distinguished itself on the "other side of the water." Renault was that general, who, at Mascara, had given his pistols to Charras. In 1848 he had said to Charras, "Europe must be revolutionized." And Charras had said, "Not quite so fast!" Louis Bonaparte had made him a General of Division in July, 1851. The Rue aux Ours was especially devastated. Morny that evening said to Louis Bonaparte, "The 15th Light Infantry have scored a success. They have cleaned out the Rue aux Ours."

At the corner of the Rue du Sentier an officer of Spahis, with his sword raised, cried out, "This is not the sort of thing! You do not understand at all. Fire on the women." A woman was flying, she was with child, she falls, they deliver her by the means of the butt-ends of their muskets. Another, perfectly distracted, was turning the corner of a street. She was carrying a child. Two soldiers aimed at her. One said, "At the woman!" And he brought down the woman. The child rolled on the pavement. The other soldier said, "At the child!" And he killed the child.

A man of high scientific repute, Dr. Germain Sée, declares that in one house alone, the establishment of the Jouvence Baths, there were at six o'clock, beneath a shed in the courtyard, about eighty wounded, nearly all of whom (seventy, at least) were old men, women, and children. Dr. Sée was the first to attend to them.

In the Rue Mandar, there was, stated an eye-witness, "a rosary of corpses," reaching as far as the Rue Neuve Saint Eustache. Before the house of Odier twenty-six corpses. Thirty before the hotel Montmorency. Fifty-two before the Variétés, of whom eleven were women. In the Rue Grange-Batelière there were three naked corpses. No. 19, Faubourg Montmartre, was full of dead and wounded.

A woman, flying and maddened, with dishevelled hair and her arms raised aloft, ran along the Rue Poissonnière, crying, "They kill! they kill! they kill! they kill! they kill!"

The soldiers wagered. "Bet you I bring down that fellow there." In this manner Count Poninsky was killed whilst going into his own house, 52, Rue de la Paix.

I was anxious to know what I ought to do. Certain treasons, in order to be proved, need to be investigated. I went to the field of murder.

In such mental agony as this, from very excess of feeling one no longer thinks, or if one thinks, it is distractedly. One only longs for some end or other. The death of others instills in you so much horror that your own death becomes an object of desire; that is to say, if by dying, you would be in some degree useful! One calls to mind deaths which have put an end to angers and to revolts. One only retains this ambition, to be a useful corpse.

I walked along terribly thoughtful.

I went towards the boulevards; I saw there a furnace; I heard there a thunderstorm.

I saw Jules Simon coming up to me, who during these disastrous days bravely risked a precious life. He stopped me. "Where are you going?" he asked me. "You will be killed. What do you want?" "That very thing," said I.

We shook hands.

I continued to go on.

I reached the boulevard; the scene was indescribable. I witnessed this crime, this butchery, this tragedy. I saw that reign of blind death, I saw the distracted victims fall around me in crowds. It is for this that I have signed myself in this book An Eye-Witness.

Destiny entertains a purpose. It watches mysteriously over the future historian. It allows him to mingle with exterminations and carnages, but it does not permit him to die, because it wishes him to relate them.

In the midst of this inexpressible Pandemonium, Xavier Durrieu met me as I was crossing the bullet-swept boulevard. He said to me, "Ah, here you are. I have just met Madame D. She is looking for you." Madame D.[1] and Madame de la R.,[2] two noble and brave women, had promised Madame Victor Hugo, who was ill in bed, to ascertain where I was, and to give her some news of me. Madame D. had heroically ventured into this carnage. The following incident happened to her. She stopped before a heap of bodies, and had had the courage to manifest her indignation; at the cry of horror to which she gave vent, a cavalry soldier had run up behind her with a pistol in his hand, and had it not been for a quickly opened door through which she threw herself, and which saved her, she would have been killed.

It is well known that the total slaughter in this butchery is unrecorded. Bonaparte has kept these figures hidden in darkness. Such is the habit of those who commit massacres. They are scarcely likely to allow history to certify the number of the victims. These statistics are an obscure multitude which quickly lose themselves in the gloom. One of the two colonels of whom we have had a glimpse in pages 223–225 of this work, has stated that his regiment alone had killed "at least 2,500 persons." This would be more than one person per soldier. We believe that this zealous colonel exaggerates. Crime sometimes boasts of its blackness.

Lireux, a writer, arrested in order to be shot, and who escaped by a miracle, declares that he saw "more than 800 corpses."

Towards four o'clock the post-chaises which were in the courtyard of the Elysée were unhorsed and put up.

This extermination, which an English witness, Captain William Jesse, calls "a wanton fusillade," lasted from two till five o'clock. During these three terrible hours, Louis Bonaparte carried out what he had been premeditating, and completed his work. Up to that time the poor little "middle-class" conscience was almost indulgent. Well, what of it? It was a game at Prince, a species of state swindling, a conjuring feat on a large scale; the sceptics and the knowing men said, "It is a good joke played upon those idiots." Suddenly Louis Bonaparte grew uneasy and

---

1. No. 20, Cité Rodier.
2. Rue Caumartin. See pages 142, 145–148.

revealed all his policy. "Tell Saint-Arnaud to execute my orders." Saint-Arnaud obeyed, the *coup d'état* acted according to its own code of laws, and from that appalling moment an immense torrent of blood began to flow across this crime.

They left the corpses lying on the pavements, wild-looking, livid, stupefied, with their pockets turned inside out. The military murderer is thus condemned to mount the villainous scale of guilt. In the morning an assassin, in the evening a thief.

When night came enthusiasm and joy reigned at the Elysée. These men triumphed. Conneau has ingeniously related the scene. The familiar spirits were delirious with joy. Fialin addressed Bonaparte in hail-fellow-well-met style. "You had better break yourself of that," whispered Vieillard. In truth this carnage made Bonaparte Emperor. He was now "His Majesty." They drank, they smoked like the soldiers on the boulevards; for having slaughtered throughout the day, they drank throughout the night; wine flowed upon the blood. At the Elysée they were amazed at the result. They were enraptured; they loudly expressed their admiration. "What a capital idea the Prince had had! How well the thing had been managed! This was much better than flying the country, by Dieppe, like D'Haussez; or by Membrolle, like Guernon-Ranville; or being captured, disguised as a footboy, and blacking the boots of Madame de Saint Fargeau, like poor Polignac!" "Guizot was no cleverer than Polignac," exclaimed Persigny. Fleury turned to Morny: "Your theorists would not have succeeded in a *coup d'état*." "That is true, they were not particularly vigorous," answered Morny. He added, "And yet they were clever men,—Louis Philippe, Guizot, Thiers—" Louis Bonaparte, taking his cigarette from his lips, interrupted, "If such are clever men, I would rather be an ass—"

"A hyena in an ass's skin," says History.

XVII

THE APPOINTMENT MADE WITH THE
WORKMEN'S SOCIETIES

What had become of our Committee during these tragic events, and what was it doing? It is necessary to relate what took place. Let us go back a few hours.

At the moment when this strange butchery began, the seat of the Committee was still in the Rue Richelieu. I had gone back to it after the exploration which I had thought it proper to make at several of the quarters in insurrection, and I gave an account of what I had seen to my colleagues. Madier de Montjau, who also arrived from the barricades, added to my report details of what he had seen. For sometime we heard terrible explosions, which appeared to be close by, and which mingled themselves with our conversation. Suddenly Versigny came in. He told us that horrible events were taking place on the Boulevards; that the meaning of the conflict could not yet be ascertained, but that they were cannonading, and firing volleys of musket-balls, and that the corpses bestrewed the pavement; that, according to all appearances, it was a massacre,—a sort of Saint Bartholomew improvised by the coup d'état; that they were ransacking the houses at a few steps from us, and that they were killing everyone. The murderers were going from door to door, and were drawing near. He urged us to leave Grévy's house without delay. It was manifest that the Insurrectionary Committee would be a "find" for the bayonets. We decided to leave, whereupon M. Dupont White, a man distinguished for his noble character and his talent, offered us a refuge at his house, 11, Rue Monthabor. We went out by the back-door of Grévy's house, which led into 1, Rue Fontaine Molière, but leisurely, and two by two, Madier de Montjau with Versigny, Michel de Bourges with Carnot, myself arm-in-arm with Jules Favre. Jules Favre, dauntless and smiling as ever, wrapped a comforter over his mouth, and said, "I do not much mind being shot, but I do mind catching cold."

Jules Favre and I reached the rear of Saint Roch, by the Rue des Moulins. The Rue Veuve Saint Roch was thronged with a mass of affrighted passers-by, who came from the Boulevards flying rather than walking. The men were talking in a loud voice, the women screaming.

We could hear the cannon and the ear-piercing rattle of the musketry. All the shops were being shut. M. de Falloux, arm-in-arm with M. Albert de Rességuier, was striding down the Rue de Saint Roch and hurrying to the Rue Saint Honoré. The Rue Saint Honoré presented a scene of clamorous agitation. People were coming and going, stopping, questioning one another, running. The shopkeepers, at the threshold of their half-opened doors, asked the passers-by what was taking place, and were only answered by this cry, "Oh, my God!" People came out of their houses bareheaded and mingled with the crowd. A fine rain was falling. Not a carriage in the street. At the corner of the Rue Saint Roch and Rue Saint Honoré we heard voices behind us saying, "Victor Hugo is killed."

"Not yet," said Jules Favre, continuing to smile, and pressing my arm.

They had said the same thing on the preceding day to Esquiros and to Madier de Montjau. And this rumor, so agreeable to the Reactionaries, had even reached my two sons, prisoners in the Concièrgerie.

The stream of people driven back from the Boulevards and from the Rue Richelieu flowed towards the Rue de la Paix. We recognized there some of the Representatives of the Right who had been arrested on the 2d, and who were already released. M. Buffet, an ex-minister of M. Bonaparte, accompanied by numerous other members of the Assembly, was going towards the Palais Royal. As he passed close by us he pronounced the name of Louis Bonaparte in a tone of execration.

M. Buffet is a man of some importance; he is one of the three political advisers of the Right; the two others are M. Fould and M. Molé.

In the Rue Monthabor, two steps from the Rue Saint Honoré, there was silence and peace. Not one passer-by, not a door open, not a head out of window.

In the apartment into which we were conducted, on the third story, the calm was not less perfect. The windows looked upon an inner courtyard. Five or six red arm-chairs were drawn up before the fire; on the table could be seen a few books which seemed to me works on political economy and executive law. The Representatives, who almost immediately joined us and who arrived in disorder, threw down at random their umbrellas and their coats streaming with water in the corner of this peaceful room. No one knew exactly what was happening; everyone brought forward his conjectures.

The Committee was hardly seated in an adjoining little room when our ex-colleague, Leblond, was announced. He brought with him King the delegate of the working-men's societies. The delegate told us that the committee of the societies were sitting in permanent session, and had sent him to us. According to the instructions of the Insurrectionary Committee, they had done what they could to lengthen the struggle by evading too decisive encounters. The greater part of the associations had not yet given battle; nevertheless the plot was thickening. The combat had been severe during the morning. The Association of the Rights of Man was in the streets; the ex-constituent Beslay had assembled, in the Passage du Caire, six or seven hundred workmen from the Marais, and had posted them in the streets surrounding the Bank. New barricades would probably be constructed during the evening, the forward movement of the resistance was being precipitated, the hand-to-hand struggle which the Committee had wished to delay seemed imminent, all was rushing forward with a sort of irresistible impulse. Should we follow it, or should we stop? Should we run the risk of bringing matters to an end with one blow, which should be the last, and which would manifestly leave one adversary on the ground—either the Empire or the Republic? The workmen's societies asked for our instructions; they still held in reserve their three or four thousand combatants; and they could, according to the order which the Committee should give them, either continue to restrain them or send them under fire without delay. They believed themselves curtain of their adherents; they would do whatever we should decide upon, while not hiding from us that the workmen wished for an immediate conflict, and that it would be somewhat hazardous to leave them time to become calm.

The majority of the members of the Committee were still in favor of a certain slackening of action which should tend to prolong the struggle; and it was difficult to say that they were in the wrong. It was certain that if they could protract the situation in which the *coup d'état* had thrown Paris until the next week, Louis Bonaparte was lost. Paris does not allow herself to be trampled upon by an army for a whole week. Nevertheless, I was for my own part impressed with the following:—The workmen's societies offered us three or four thousand combatants, a powerful assistance;—the workman does not understand strategy, he lives on enthusiasm, abatements of ardor discourage him; his zeal is not extinguished, but it cools:—three thousand today would be five hundred tomorrow. And then some serious incident had just taken place on the Boulevards. We were still ignorant of what it actually was: we could not foresee what consequences it might bring about; but seemed to me impossible that the still unknown, but yet violent event, which had just taken place would not modify the situation, and consequently change our plan of battle. I began to speak to this effect. I stated that we ought to accept the offer of the associations, and to throw them at once into the struggle; I added that revolutionary warfare often necessitates sudden changes of tactics, that a general in the open country and before the enemy operates as he wishes; it is all clear around him; he knows the effective strength of his soldiers, the number of his regiments; so many men, so many horses, so many cannons, he knows his strength, and the strength of his enemy, he chooses his hour and his ground, he has a map under his eyes, he sees what he is doing. He is sure of his reserves, he possesses them, he keeps them back, he utilizes them when he wishes, he always has them by him. "But for ourselves," cried I, "we are in an undefined and inconceivable position. We are stepping at a venture upon unknown risks. Who is against us? We hardly know. Who is with us? We are ignorant. How many soldiers? How many guns? How many cartridges? Nothing! but the darkness. Perhaps the entire people, perhaps no one. Keep a reserve! But who would answer for this reserve? It is an army today, it will be a handful of dust tomorrow. We only can plainly distinguish our duty, as regards all the rest it is black darkness. We are guessing at everything. We are ignorant of everything. We are fighting a blind battle! Let us strike all the blows that can be struck, let us advance straight before us at random, let us rush upon the danger! And let us have faith, for as we are Justice and the Law, God must be with us in this obscurity. Let us accept this glorious and gloomy enterprise of Right disarmed yet still fighting."

The ex-constituent Leblond and the delegate King being consulted by the Committee, seconded my advice. The Committee decided that the societies should be requested in our name to come down into the streets immediately, and to call out their forces. "But we are keeping nothing for tomorrow," objected a member of the Committee, "what ally shall we have tomorrow?" "Victory," said Jules Favre. Carnot and Michel de Bourges remarked that it would be advisable for those members of the association who belonged to the National Guard to wear their uniforms. This was accordingly settled.

The delegate King rose,—"Citizen Representatives," said he, "these orders will be immediately transmitted, our friends are ready, in a few hours they will assemble. Tonight barricades and the combat!"

VICTOR HUGO

I asked him, "Would it be useful to you if a Representative, a member of the Committee, were with you tonight with his sash girded?"

"Doubtless," he answered.

"Well, then," resumed I, "here I am! Take me."

"We will all go," exclaimed Jules Favre.

The delegate observed that it would suffice for one of us to be there at the moment when the societies should make their appearance, and that he could then notify the other members of the Committee to come and join him. It was settled that as soon as the places of meeting and the rallying-points should be agreed upon, he would send someone to let me know, and to take me wherever the societies might be. "Before an hour's time you shall hear from me," said he on leaving us.

As the delegates were going away Mathieu de la Drôme arrived. On coming in he halted on the threshold of the door, he was pale, he cried out to us, "You are no longer in Paris, you are no longer under the Republic; you are in Naples and under King Bomba."

He had come from the boulevards.

Later on I again saw Mathieu de la Drôme. I said to him, "Worse than Bomba,—Satan."

XVIII

The Verification of Moral Laws

The carnage of the Boulevard Montmartre constitutes the originality of the *coup d'état*. Without this butchery the 2d of December would only be an 18th Brumaire. Owing to the massacre Louis Bonaparte escapes the charge of plagiarism.

Up to that time he had only been an imitator. The little hat at Boulogne, the gray overcoat, the tame eagle appeared grotesque. What did this parody mean? people asked. He made them laugh; suddenly he made them tremble.

He who becomes detestable ceases to be ridiculous.

Louis Bonaparte was more than detestable, he was execrable.

He envied the hugeness of great crimes; he wished to equal the worst. This striving after the horrible has given him a special place to himself in the menagerie of tyrants. Petty rascality trying to emulate deep villainy, a little Nero swelling himself to a huge Lacénaire; such is this phenomenon. Art for art, assassination for assassination.

Louis Bonaparte has created a special genus.

It was in this manner that Louis Bonaparte made his entry into the Unexpected. This revealed him.

Certain brains are abysses. Manifestly for a long time past Bonaparte had harbored the design of assassinating in order to reign. Premeditation haunts criminals, and it is in this manner that treason begins. The crime is a long time present in them, but shapeless and shadowy, they are scarcely conscious of it; souls only blacken gradually. Such abominable deeds are not invented in a moment; they do not attain perfection at once and at a single bound; they increase and ripen, shapeless and indecisive, and the centre of the ideas in which they exist keeps them living, ready for the appointed day, and vaguely terrible. This design, the massacre for a throne, we feel sure, existed for a long time in Louis Bonaparte's mind. It was classed among the possible events of this soul. It darted hither and thither like a *larva* in an aquarium, mingled with shadows, with doubts, with desires, with expedients, with dreams of one knows not what Caesarian socialism, like a Hydra dimly visible in a transparency of chaos. Hardly was he aware that he was fostering this hideous idea. When he needed it, he found it, armed and ready to serve him. His unfathomable brain had darkly nourished it. Abysses are the nurseries of monsters.

Up to this formidable day of the 4th December, Louis Bonaparte did not perhaps quite know himself. Those who studied this curious Imperial animal did not believe him capable of such pure and simple ferocity. They saw in him an indescribable mongrel, applying the talents of a swindler to the dreams of an Empire, who, even when crowned, would be a thief, who would say of a parricide, What roguery! Incapable of gaining a footing on any height, even of infamy, always remaining half-way uphill, a little above petty rascals, a little below great malefactors. They believed him clever at effecting all that is done in gambling-hells and in robbers' caves, but with this transposition, that he would cheat in the caves, and that he would assassinate in the gambling-hells.

The massacre of the Boulevards suddenly unveiled this spirit. They saw it such as it really was: the ridiculous nicknames "Big-beak," "Badinguet," vanished; they saw the bandit, they saw the true *contraffatto* hidden under the false Bonaparte.

There was a shudder! It was this then which this man held in reserve!

Apologies have been attempted, they could but fail. It is easy to praise Bonaparte, for people have praised Dupin; but it is an exceedingly complicated operation to cleanse him. What is to be done with the 4th of December? How will that difficulty be surmounted? It is far more troublesome to justify than to glorify; the sponge works with greater difficulty than the censer; the panegyrists of the *coup d'état* have lost their labor. Madame Sand herself, although a woman of lofty intellect, has failed miserably in her attempt to rehabilitate Bonaparte, for the simple reason that whatever one may do, the death-roll reappears through this whitewashing.

No! no! no extenuation whatever is possible. Unfortunate Bonaparte. The blood is drawn. It must be drunk.

The deed of the 4th of December is the most colossal dagger-thrust that a brigand let loose upon civilization has ever effected, we will not say upon a people, but upon the entire human race. The stroke was most monstrous, and struck Paris to the ground. Paris on the ground is Conscience, is Reason, is all human liberty on the ground; it is the progress of centuries lying on the pavement; it is the torch of Justice, of Truth, and of Life reversed and extinguished. This is what Louis Bonaparte effected the day when he effected this.

The success of the wretch was complete. The 2d of December was lost; the 4th of December saved the 2d of December. It was something like Erostratus saving Judas. Paris understood that all had not yet been told as regards deeds of horror, and that beneath the oppressor there was the garbage-picker. It was the case of a swindler stealing César's mantle. This man was little, it is true, but terrifying. Paris consented to this terror, renounced the right to have the last word, went to bed and simulated death. Suffocation had its share in the matter. This crime resembled, too, no previous achievements. Even after centuries have passed, and though he should be an Aeschylus or a Tacitus, anyone raising the cover would smell the stench. Paris resigned herself, Paris abdicated, Paris surrendered; the novelty of the treason proved its chief strength; Paris almost ceased to be Paris; on the next day the chattering of this terrified Titan's teeth could be heard in the shadows.

Let us lay a stress upon this, for we must verify the laws of morality. Louis Bonaparte remained, even after the 4th of December, Napoleon the Little. This enormity still left him a dwarf. The size of the crime does not change the stature of the criminal, and the pettiness of the assassin withstands the immensity of the assassination.

Be that as it may, the Pigmy had the better of the Colossus. This avowal, humiliating as it is, cannot be evaded.

Such are the blushes to which History, that greatly dishonored one, is condemned.

THE FOURTH DAY
THE VICTORY

I

What Happened During the Night—The Rue Tiquetonne

Just as Mathieu de la Drôme had said, "You are under King Bomba," Charles Gambon entered. He sank down upon a chair and muttered, "It is horrible." Bancel followed him. "We have come from it," said Bancel. Gambon had been able to shelter himself in the recess of a doorway. In front of Barbedienne's alone he had counted thirty-seven corpses. What was the meaning of it all? To what purpose was this monstrous promiscuous murder? No one could understand it. The Massacre was a riddle.

We were in the Sphinx's Grotto.

Labrousse came in. It was urgently necessary that we should leave Dupont White's house. It was on the point of being surrounded. For some moments the Rue Monthabor, ordinarily so deserted, was becoming thronged with suspicious figures. Men seemed to be attentively watching number Eleven. Some of these men, who appeared to be acting in concert, belonged to the ex-"Club of Clubs," which, owing to the manoeuvres of the Reactionists, exhaled a vague odor of the police. It was necessary that we should disperse. Labrousse said to us, "I have just seen Longe-pied roving about."

We separated. We went away one by one, and each in his own direction. We did not know where we should meet again, or whether we should meet again. What was going to happen and what was about to become of us all? No one knew. We were filled with a terrible dread.

I turned up towards the Boulevards, anxious to see what was taking place.

What was taking place I have just related.

Bancel and Versigny had rejoined me.

As I left the Boulevards, mingled with the whirl of the terrified crowd, not knowing where I was going, returning towards the centre of Paris, a voice suddenly whispered in my ear, "There is something over there which you ought to see." I recognized the voice. It was the voice of E.P.

E.P. is a dramatic author, a man of talent, for whom under Louis Philippe I had procured exemption from military service. I had not seen him for four or five years. I met him again in this tumult. He spoke to me as though we had seen each other yesterday. Such are these times of bewilderment. There is no time to greet each other "according to the rules of society." One speaks as though all were in full flight.

"Ah! it is you!" I exclaimed. "What do you want with me?"

He answered me, "I live in a house over there."

And he added,—

"Come."

He drew me into a dark street. We could hear explosions. At the bottom of the street could be seen the ruins of a barricade. Versigny and Bancel, as I have just said, were with me. E.P. turned to them.

"These gentlemen can come," said he.

I asked him,—

"What street is this?"

"The Rue Tiquetonne."

We followed him.

I have elsewhere told this tragical event.[1]

E.P. stopped before a tall and gloomy house. He pushed open a street-door which was not shut, then another door and we entered into a parlor perfectly quiet and lighted by a lamp.

This room appeared to adjoin a shop. At the end could be distinguished two beds side by side, one large and one small. Above the little bed hung a woman's portrait, and above the portrait a branch of holy box-tree.

The lamp was placed over the fireplace, where a little fire was burning.

Near the lamp upon a chair there was an old woman leaning forward, stooping down, folded in two as though broken, over something which was in the shadow, and which she held in her arms. I drew near. That which she held in her arms was a dead child.

The poor woman was silently sobbing.

E.P., who belonged to the house, touched her on the shoulder, and said,—

"Let us see it."

The old woman raised her head, and I saw on her knees a little boy, pale, half-undressed, pretty, with two red holes in his forehead.

---

1. "Les Châtiments."

The old woman stared at me, but she evidently did not see me, she muttered, speaking to herself,—

"And to think that he called me 'Granny' this morning!"

E.P. took the child's hand, the hand fell back again.

"Seven years old," he said to me.

A basin was on the ground. They had washed the child's face; two tiny streams of blood trickled from the two holes.

At the end of the room, near a half-opened clothes-press, in which could be seen some linen, stood a woman of some forty years, grave, poor, clean, fairly good-looking.

"A neighbor," E.P. said to me.

He explained to me that a doctor lived in the house, that the doctor had come down and had said, "There is nothing to be done." The child had been hit by two balls in the head while crossing the street to "get out of the way." They had brought him back to his grandmother, who "had no one left but him."

The portrait of the dead mother hung above the little bed.

The child had his eyes half open, and that inexpressible gaze of the dead, where the perception of the real is replaced by the vision of the infinite. The grandmother spoke through her sobs by snatches: "God! is it possible? Who would have thought it?—What brigands!"

She cried out,—

"Is this then the Government?"

"Yes," I said to her.

We finished undressing the child. He had a top in his pocket. His head rolled from one shoulder to the other; I held him and I kissed him on the brow; Versigny and Bancel took off his stockings. The grandmother suddenly started up.

"Do not hurt him!" she cried.

She took the two little white and frozen feet in her old hands, trying to warm them.

When the poor little body was naked, they began to lay it out. They took a sheet from the clothes-press.

Then the grandmother burst into bitter lamentation.

She cried out,—

"They shall give him back to me!"

She drew herself up and gazed at us, and began to pour forth incoherent utterances, in which were mingled Bonaparte, and God, and her little one, and the school to which he went, and her daughter whom she had lost, and even reproaches to us. She was livid, haggard, as though seeing a vision before her, and was more of a phantom than the dead child.

Then she again buried her face in her hands, placed her folded arms on her child, and once more began to sob.

The woman who was there came up to me, and without saying a word, wiped my mouth with a handkerchief. I had blood upon my lips.

What could be done? Alas! We went out overwhelmed.

It was quite dark. Bancel and Versigny left me.

II

What Happened During the Night—The Market Quarter

I came back to my lodging, 19, Rue Richelieu.

The massacre seemed to be at an end; the fusillades were heard no longer. As I was about to knock at the door I hesitated for a moment; a man was there who seemed to be waiting. I went straight up to this man, and I said to him,—

"You seem to be waiting for somebody?"

He answered,—

"Yes."

"For whom?"

"For you."

And he added, lowering his voice, "I have come to speak to you."

I looked at this man. A street-lamp shone on him. He did not avoid the light.

He was a young man with a fair beard, wearing a blue blouse, and who had the gentle bearing of a thinker and the robust hands of a workman.

"Who are you?" I asked him.

He answered,—"I belong to the Society of the Last-makers. I know you very well, Citizen Victor Hugo."

"From whom do you come?" I resumed.

He answered still in a whisper,—

"From Citizen King."

"Very good," said I.

He then told me his name. As he has survived the events of the night of the 4th, and as he since escaped the denunciations, it can be understood that we will not mention his name here, and that we shall confine ourselves to terming him throughout the course of this story by his trade, calling him the "last-maker."[1]

"What do you want to say to me?" I asked him.

---

1. We may now, after twenty-six years, give the name of this loyal and courageous man. His name was Galoy (and not Galloix, as certain historians of the *coup d'état* have printed it while recounting, after their fashion, the incidents which we are about to read).

He explained that matters were not hopeless, that he and his friends meant to continue the resistance, that the meeting-places of the Societies had not yet been settled, but that they would be during the evening, that my presence was desired, and that if I would be under the Colbert Arcade at nine o'clock, either himself or another of their men would be there, and would serve me as guide. We decided that in order to make himself known, the messenger, when accosting me, should give the password, "What is Joseph doing?"

I do not know whether he thought he noticed any doubt or mistrust on my part. He suddenly interrupted himself, and said,—

"After all, you are not bound to believe me. One does not think of everything: I ought to have asked them to give me a word in writing. At a time like this one distrusts everybody."

"On the contrary," I said to him, "one trusts everybody. I will be in the Colbert Arcade at nine o'clock."

And I left him.

I re-entered my asylum. I was tired, I was hungry, I had recourse to Charamaule's chocolate and to a small piece of bread which I had still left. I sank down into an arm-chair, I ate and I slept. Some slumbers are gloomy. I had one of those slumbers, full of spectres; I again saw the dead child and the two red holes in his forehead, these formed two mouths: one said "Morny," and the other "Saint-Arnaud." History is not made, however, to recount dreams. I will abridge. Suddenly I awoke. I started: "If only it is not past nine o'clock!" I had forgotten to wind up my watch. It had stopped. I went out hastily. The street was lonely, the shops were shut. In the Place Louvos I heard the hour striking (probably from Saint Roch); I listened. I counted nine strokes. In a few moments I was under the Colbert Arcade. I peered into the darkness. No one was under the Arcade.

I felt that it was impossible to remain there, and have the appearance of waiting about; near the Colbert Arcade there is a police-station, and the patrols were passing every moment. I plunged into the street. I found no one there. I went as far as the Rue Vivienne. At the corner of the Rue Vivienne a man was stopping before a placard and was trying to deface it or to tear it down. I drew near this man, who probably took me for a police agent, and who fled at the top of his speed. I retraced my steps. Near the Colbert Arcade, and just as I reached the point in the street where they post the theatrical bills, a workman passed me, and said quickly, "What is Joseph doing?"

I recognized the last-maker.

"Come," he said to me.

We set out without speaking and without appearing to know each other, he walking some steps before me.

We first went to two addresses, which I cannot mention here without pointing out victims for the proscription. In these two houses we got no news; no one had come there on the part of the societies.

"Let us go to the third place," said the last-maker, and he explained to me that they had settled among them three successive meeting-places, in case of need, so as to be always sure of finding each other if, perchance, the police discovered the first or even the second meeting-place, a precaution which for our part we adopted as much as possible with regard to our meetings of the Left end of the Committee.

We had reached the market quarter. Fighting had been going on there throughout the day. There were no longer any gas-lamps in the streets. We stopped from time to time, and listened so as not to run headlong into the arms of a patrol. We got over a paling of planks almost completely destroyed, and of which barricades had probably been made, and we crossed the extensive area of half-demolished houses which at that epoch encumbered the lower portions of the Rue Montmartre and Rue Montorgueil. On the peaks of the high dismantled gables could be seen a flickering red glow, doubtless the reflection of the bivouac-fires of the soldiers encamped in the markets and in the neighborhood of Saint Eustache. This reflection lighted our way. The last-maker, however, narrowly escaped falling into a deep hole, which was no less than the cellar of a demolished house. On coming out of this region, covered with ruins, amongst which here and there a few trees might be perceived, the remains of gardens which had now disappeared, we entered into narrow, winding, and completely dark streets, where it was impossible to recognize one's whereabouts. Nevertheless the last-maker walked on as much at his ease as in broad daylight, and like a man who is going straight to his destination. Once he turned round to me, and said to me,—

"The whole of this quarter is barricaded; and if, as I hope, our friends come down, I will answer that they will hold it for a long time."

Suddenly he stopped. "Here is one," said he. In truth, seven or eight paces before us was a barricade entirely constructed of paving-stones, not exceeding a man's height, and which in the darkness appeared like a ruined wall. A narrow passage had been formed at one end. We passed through it. There was no one behind the barricade.

"There has already been fighting here a short time ago," said the last-maker in a low voice; and he added, after a pause, "We are getting near."

The unpaving had left holes, of which we had to be careful. We strode, and sometimes jumped, from paving-stone to paving-stone. Notwithstanding the intense darkness, there yet hovered about an indefinable glimmer; on our way we noticed before us on the ground, close to the foot-pavement, something which looked like a stretched-out form. "The devil!" muttered my guide, "we were just going to walk upon it." He took a little wax match from his pocket and struck it on his sleeve; the flame flashed out. The light fell upon a pallid face, which looked at us with fixed eyes. It was a corpse lying there; it was an old man. The last-maker rapidly waved the match from his head to his feet. The dead man was almost in the attitude of a crucified man; his two arms were stretched out; his white hair, red at the ends, was soaking in the mud; a pool of blood was beneath him; a large blackish patch on his waistcoat marked the place where the ball had pierced his breast; one of his braces was undone; he had thick laced boots on his feet. The last-maker lifted up one of his arms, and said, "His collar-bone is broken." The movement shook the head, and the open mouth turned towards us as though about to speak to us. I gazed at this vision; I almost listened. Suddenly it disappeared.

This face re-entered the gloom; the match had just gone out.

We went away in silence. After walking about twenty paces, the last-maker, as though talking to himself, said in a whisper, "Don't know him."

We still pushed forward. From the cellars to the roofs, from the ground-floors to the garrets, there was not a light in the house. We appeared to be groping in an immense tomb.

A man's voice, firm and sonorous, suddenly issued out of the darkness, and shouted to us, "Who goes there?"

"Ah, there they are!" said the last-maker, and he uttered a peculiar whistle.

"Come on," resumed the voice.

It was another barricade. This one, a little higher than the first, and separated from it by a distance of about a hundred paces, was, as far as could be seen, constructed of barrels filled with paving-stones. On the top could be seen the wheels of a truck entangled between the barrels; planks and beams were intermingled. A passage had been contrived still narrower than the gangway of the other barricade.

"Citizens," said the last-maker, as he went into the barricade, "how many of you are there here?"

The voice which had shouted, "Who goes there?" answered,—

"There are two of us."

"Is that all?"

"That is all."

They were in truth two,—two men who alone during that night, in that solitary street, behind that heap of paving-stones, awaited the onslaught of a regiment.

Both wore blouses; they were two workmen; with a few cartridges in their pockets, and a musket upon each of their shoulders.

"So then," resumed the last-maker, in an impatient tone, "our friends have not yet come!"

"Well, then," I said to him, "let us wait for them."

The last-maker spoke for a short time in a low tone, and probably told my name to one of the two defenders of the barricade, who came up to me and saluted me. "Citizen Representative," said he, "it will be very warm here shortly."

"In the meantime," answered I laughingly, "it is cold."

It was very cold, in truth. The street which was completely unpaved behind the barricade, was nothing better than a sewer, ankle deep in water.

"I say that it will be warm," resumed the workman, "and that you would do well to go farther off."

The last-maker put his hand on his shoulder: "Comrade, it is necessary that we should remain here. The meeting-place is close by, in the ambulance."

"All the same," resumed the other workman, who was very short, and who stood up on a paving-stone; "the Citizen Representative would do well to go farther off."

"I can very well be where you are," said I to him.

The street was quite dark, nothing could be seen of the sky. Inside the barricade on the left, on the side where the passage was, could be seen a high paling of badly joined planks, through which shone in places a feeble light. Above the paling rose out, lost in the darkness, a house of six or seven storys; the ground floor, which was being repaired, and which was under-pinned, being closed in by these planks. A ray of light issuing from between the planks fell on the opposite wall, and lighted up an old torn placard, on which could be read, "Asnières. Water tournaments. Grand ball."

"Have you another gun?" asked the last-maker of the taller of the two workmen.

"If we had three guns we should be three men," answered the workman.

The little one added, "Do you think that the good will is wanting? There are plenty of musicians, but there are no clarionets."

By the side of the wooden paling could be seen a little, narrow and low door, which looked more like the door of a stall than the door of a shop. The shop to which this door belonged was hermetically sealed. The door seemed to be equally closed. The last-maker went up to it and pushed it gently. It was open.

"Let us go in," he said.

I went in first, he followed me, and shut the door behind me. We were in a room on the ground floor. At the end, on the left, a half-opened door emitted the reflection of a light. The room was only lighted by this reflection. A counter and a species of stove, painted in black and white, could be dimly distinguished.

A short, half-suffocated, intermittent gurgling could be heard, which seemed to come from an adjoining room on the same side as the light. The last-maker walked quickly to the half-opened door. I crossed the room after him, and we found ourselves in a sort of vast shed, lighted by one candle. We were on the other side of the plank paling. There was only the plank paling between ourselves and the barricade.

This species of shed was the ground floor in course of demolition. Iron columns, painted red, and fixed into stone sockets at short distances apart, supported the joists of the ceiling; facing the street, a huge framework standing erect, and denoting the centre of the surrounding paling, supported the great cross-beam of the first story, that is to say, supported the whole house. In a corner were lying some masons' tools, a heap of rubbish, and a large double ladder. A few straw-bottomed chairs were scattered here and there. The damp ground served for the flooring. By the side of a table, on which stood a candle in the midst of medicine bottles, an old woman and a young girl of about eight years old—the woman seated, the child squatting before a great basketful of old linen—were making lint. The end of the room, which was lost in the darkness, was carpeted with a litter of straw, on which three mattresses had been thrown. The gurgling noise came from there.

"It is the ambulance," said the last-maker.

The old woman turned her head, and seeing us, shuddered convulsively, and then, reassured probably by the blouse of the last-maker, she got up and came towards us.

The last-maker whispered a few words in her ear. She answered, "I have seen nobody."

Then she added, "But what makes me uneasy is that my husband has not yet come back. They have done nothing but fire muskets the whole evening."

Two men were lying on two of the mattresses at the end of the room. A third mattress was unoccupied and was waiting.

The wounded man nearest to me had received a musket ball in his stomach. He it was who was gurgling. The old woman came towards the mattress with a candle, and whispered to us, showing us her fist, "If you could only see the hole that that has made! We have stuffed lint as large as this into his stomach."

She resumed, "He is not above twenty-five years old. He will be dead tomorrow morning."

The other was still younger. He was hardly eighteen. "He has a handsome black overcoat," said the woman. "He is most likely a student." The young man had the whole of the lower part of his face swathed in blood-stained linen. She explained to us that he had received a ball in the mouth, which had broken his jaw. He was in a high fever, and gazed at us with lustrous eyes. From time to time he stretched his right arm towards a basin full of water in which a sponge was soaking; he took the sponge, carried it to his face, and himself moistened his bandages.

It seemed to me that his gaze fastened upon me in a singular manner. I went up to him, I stooped down, and I gave him my hand, which he took in his own. "Do you know me?" I asked him. He answered "Yes," by a pressure of the hand which went to my heart.

The last-maker said to me, "Wait a minute for me here, I shall be back directly; I want to see in this neighborhood, if there is any means of getting a gun."

He added,—

"Would you like one for yourself?"

"No," answered I. "I shall remain here without a gun. I only take a half share in the civil war; I am willing to die, I am not willing to kill."

I asked him if he thought his friends were going to come. He declared that he could not understand it, that the men from the societies ought to have arrived already, that instead of two men in the barricade there should be twenty, that instead of two barricades in the street there should have been ten, and that something must have happened; he added,—

"However, I will go and see; promise to wait for me here."

"I promise you," I answered, "I will wait all night if necessary."

He left me.

The old woman had reseated herself near the little girl, who did not seem to understand much of what was passing round her, and who from time to time raised great calm eyes towards me. Both were poorly clad, and it seemed to me that the child had stockingless feet. "My man has not yet come back," said the old woman, "my poor man has not yet come back. I hope nothing has happened to him!" With many heart-rending "My God's," and all the while quickly picking her lint, she wept. I could not help thinking with anguish of the old man we had seen stretched on the pavement at a few paces distant.

A newspaper was lying on the table. I took it up, and I unfolded it. It was the *P*——, the rest of the title had been torn off. A blood-stained hand was plainly imprinted on it. A wounded man on entering had probably placed his hand on the table on the spot where the newspaper lay. My eyes fell upon these lines:—

"M. Victor Hugo has just published an appeal to pillage and assassination."

In these terms the journal of the Elysée described the proclamation which I had dictated to Baudin, and which may be read in page 103 of this History.

As I threw back the paper on the table one of the two defenders of the barricade entered. It was the short man.

"A glass of water," said he. By the side of the medicine bottles there was a decanter and a glass. He drank, greedily. He held in his hand a morsel of bread and a sausage, which he was biting.

Suddenly we heard several successive explosions, following one after another, and which seemed but a short distance off. In the silence of this dark night it resembled the sound of a load of wood being shot on to the pavement.

The calm and serious voice of the other combatant shouted from outside, "It is beginning."

"Have I time to finish my bread?" asked the little one.

"Yes," said the other.

The little one then turned to me.

"Citizen Representative," said he to me, "those are volleys. They are attacking the barricades over there. Really you must go away."

I answered him, "But you yourselves are going to stay here."

"As for us, we are armed," resumed he; "as for you, you are not. You will only get yourself killed without benefiting anyone. If you had a gun, I should say nothing. But you have not. You must go away."

"I cannot," I answered him. "I am waiting for someone."

He wished to continue and to urge me. I pressed his hand.

"Let me do as I like," said I.

He understood that my duty was to remain, and no longer persisted. There was a pause. He again began to bite his bread. The gurgling of the dying man alone was audible. At that moment a sort of deep and hollow booming reached us. The old woman started from her chair, muttering, "It is the cannon!"

"No," said the little man, "it is the slamming of a street-door." Then he resumed, "There now! I have finished my bread," and he dusted one hand against the other, and went out.

In the meantime the explosions continued, and seemed to come nearer. A noise sounded in the shop. It was the last-maker who was coming back. He appeared on the threshold of the ambulance. He was pale.

"Here I am," said he, "I have come to fetch you. We must go home. Let us be off at once."

I arose from the chair where I had seated myself. "What does this mean? Will they not come?"

"No," he answered, "no one will come. All is at an end."

Then he hastily explained that he had gone through the whole of the quarter in order to find a gun, that it was labor lost, that he had spoken to "two or three," that we must abandon all hope of the societies, *that they would not come down*, that what had been done during the day had appalled everyone, that the best men were terrified, that the boulevards were "full of corpses," that the soldiers had committed "horrors," that the barricade was about to be attacked, that on his arrival he had heard the noise of footsteps in the direction of the crossway, that it was the soldiers who were advancing, that we could do nothing further there, that we must be off, that this house was "stupidly chosen," that there was no outlet in the rear, that perhaps we should already find it difficult to get out of the street, and that we had only just time.

He told this all panting, briefly, jerkily, and interrupted at every moment with this exclamation, "And to think that they have no arms, and to think that I have no gun!"

As he finished we heard from the barricade a shout of "Attention!" and almost immediately a shot was fired.

A violent discharge replied to this shot.

Several balls struck the paling of the ambulance, but they were too obliquely aimed, and none pierced it. We heard the glass of several broken windows falling noisily into the street.

"There is no longer time," said the last-maker calmly; "the barricade is attacked."

He took a chair and sat down. The two workmen were evidently excellent marksmen. Two volleys assailed the barricade, one after the other. The barricade answered with animation. Then the fire ceased. There was a pause.

"Now they are coming at us with the bayonet! They are coming at the double!" said a voice in the barricade.

The other voice said, "Let us be off." A last musket-shot was fired. Then a violent blow which we interpreted as a warning shook our wooden wall. It was in reality one of the workmen who had thrown down his gun when going away; the gun in falling had struck the paling of the ambulance. We heard the rapid steps of the two combatants, as they ran off.

Almost at the same moment a tumult of voices, and of butt ends of muskets striking the paving-stones, filled the barricade.

"It is taken," said the last-maker, and he blew out the candle.

To the silence which enveloped this street a moment before succeeded a sort of ill-omened tumult. The soldiers knocked at the doors of the houses with the butt-ends of their muskets. It was by a miracle that the shop-door escaped them. If they had merely pushed against it, they would have seen that it was not shut, and would have entered.

A voice, probably the voice of an officer, cried out, "Light up the windows!" The soldiers swore. We heard them say, "Where are those blackguard Reds? Let us search the houses." The ambulance was plunged in darkness. Not a word was spoken, not a breath could be heard; even the dying man, as though he divined the danger, had ceased to gurgle. I felt the little girl pressing herself against my legs.

A soldier struck the barrels, and said laughingly,—

"Here is something to make a fire with tonight."

Another resumed,—

"Which way have they gone? They were at least thirty. Let us search the houses."

We heard one raising objections to this,—

"Nonsense! What do you want to do on a night like this? Enter the houses of the 'middle classes' indeed! There is some waste ground over yonder. They have taken refuge there."

"All the same," repeated the others, "let us search the houses."

At this moment a musket-shot was fired from the end of the street. This shot saved us.

In fact, it was probably one of the two workmen who had fired in order to draw off their attention from us.

"That comes from over there," cried the soldiers, "They are over there!" and all starting off at once in the direction from which the shot had been fired, they left the barricade and ran down the street at the top of their speed.

The last-maker and myself got up.

"They are no longer there," whispered he. "Quick! let us be off."

"But this poor woman," said I. "Are we going to leave her here?"

"Oh," she said, "do not be afraid, I have nothing to fear; as for me, I am an ambulance. I am taking care of the wounded. I shall even relight my candle when you are gone. What troubles me is that my poor husband has not yet come back!"

We crossed the shop on tiptoe. The last-maker gently opened the door and glanced out into the street. Some inhabitants had obeyed the order to light up their windows, and four or five lighted candles here and there flickered in the wind upon the sills of the windows. The street was no longer completely dark.

"There is no one about now," said the last-maker; "but let us make haste, for they will probably come back."

We went out: the old woman closed the door behind us, and we found ourselves in the street. We got over the barricade and hurried away as quickly as possible. We passed by the dead old man. He was still there, lying on the pavement indistinctly revealed by the flickering glimmer from the windows; he looked as though he was sleeping. As we reached the second barricade we heard behind us the soldiers, who were returning.

We succeeded in regaining the streets in course of demolition. There we were in safety. The sound of musketry still reached us. The last-maker said, "They are fighting in the direction of the Rue de Cléry." Leaving the streets in course of demolition, we went round the markets, not without risk of falling into the hands of the patrols, by a number of zigzags, and from one little street to another little street. We reached the Rue Saint Honoré.

At the corner of the Rue de l'Arbre Sec the last-maker and I separated, "For in truth," said he to me, "two run more danger than one." And I regained No. 19, Rue Richelieu.

While crossing the rue des Bourdonnais we had noticed the bivouac of the Place Saint Eustache. The troops who had been dispatched for the attack had not yet come back. Only a few companies were guarding it. We could hear shouts of laughter. The soldiers were warming themselves at large fires lighted here and there. In the fire which was nearest to us we could distinguish in the middle of the brazier the wheels of the vehicles which had served for the barricades. Of some there only remained a great hoop of red-hot iron.

III

What Happened During the Night—The Petit Carreau

On the same night, almost at the same moment, at a few paces distant, a villainous deed was being perpetrated.

After the taking of the barricade, where Pierre Tissié was killed, seventy or eighty combatants had retired in good order by the Rue Saint Sauveur. They had reached the Rue Montorgueil, and had rejoined each other at the junction of the Rue du Petit Carreau and the Rue du Cadran. At this point the street rises. At the corner of the Rue du Petit Carreau and the Rue de Cléry there was a deserted barricade, fairly high and well built. There had been fighting there during the morning. The soldiers had taken it, but had not demolished it. Why? As we have said, there were several riddles of this nature during this day.

The armed band which came from the Rue Saint Denis had halted there and had waited. These men were astonished at not being pursued. Had the soldiers feared to follow them into the little narrow streets, where each corner of the houses might conceal an ambuscade? Had a counter order been given? They hazarded various conjectures. Moreover they heard close by, evidently on the boulevard, a terrific noise of musketry, and a cannonade which resembled continuous thunder. Having no more ammunition, they were reduced to listen. If they had known what was taking place there, they would have understood why they were not pursued. The butchery of the boulevard was beginning. The generals employed in the massacre had suspended fighting for awhile.

The fugitives of the boulevard streamed in their direction, but when they perceived the barricade they turned back. Some, however, joined them indignant, and crying out for vengeance. One who lived in the neighborhood ran home and brought back a little tin barrel full of cartridges.

These were sufficient for an hour's fighting. They began to construct a barricade at the corner of the Rue du Cadran. In this manner the Rue du Petit Carreau, closed by two barricades, one towards the Rue de Cléry, the other at the corner of the Rue du Cadran, commanded the whole of the Rue Montorgueil. The space between these two barricades formed a perfect citadel. The second barricade was stronger than the first.

These men nearly all wore coats. Some of them rolled the paving-stones with gloves on.

Few workmen were amongst them, but those who were there were intelligent and energetic. These workmen were what might be termed the "pick of the crowd."

Jeanty Sarre had rejoined them; he at once became their leader.

Charpentier accompanied him, too brave to abandon the enterprise, but too much a dreamer to become a commander.

Two barricades, enclosing in the same manner some forty yards of the Rue Montorgueil, had just been constructed at the top of the Rue Mauconseil.

Three other barricades, extremely feebly constructed, again intersected the Rue Montorgueil in the space which separates the Rue Mauconseil from Saint Eustache.

Evening was closing in. The fusillade was ceasing upon the boulevard. A surprise was possible. They established a sentry-post at the corner of the Rue du Cadran, and sent a main-guard in the direction of the Rue Montmartre. Their scouts came in to report some items of information. A regiment seemed to be preparing to bivouac in the Place des Victoires.

Their position, to all appearance strong, was not so in reality. There were too few in number to defend at the same time the two barricades on the Rue de Cléry and the Rue Montorgueil, and the soldiers arriving in the rear hidden by the second barricade would have been upon them without being even noticed. This determined them to establish a post in the Rue de Cléry. They put themselves in communication with the barricades of the Rue du Cadran and with the two Mauconseil barricades. These two last barricades were only separated from them by a space of about 150 paces. They were about six feet high, fairly solid, but only guarded by six workmen who had built them.

Towards half-past four, in the twilight—the twilight begins early in December—Jeanty Sarre took four men with him and went out to reconnoitre. He thought also of raising an advanced barricade in one of the little neighboring streets. On the way they found one which had been abandoned, and which had been built with barrels. The barrels, however, were empty, only one contained any paving-stones, and the barricade could not have been held for two minutes. As they left this barricade they were assailed by a sharp discharge of musketry. A company of infantry, hardly visible in the dusk, was close upon them.

They fell back hastily; but one of them, who was a shoemaker of the Faubourg du Temple, was hit, and had remained on the pavement. They went back and brought him away. He had the thumb of the right hand smashed. "Thank God!" said Jeanty Sarre, "they have not killed him." "No," said the poor man, "it is my bread which they have killed."

And he added, "I can no longer work; who will maintain my children?"

They went back, carrying the wounded man. One of them, a medical student, bound up his wound.

The sentries, whom it was necessary to post in every direction, and who were chosen from the most trustworthy men, thinned and exhausted the little central land. There were scarcely thirty in the barricade itself.

There, as in the Quarter of the Temple, all the streetlamps were extinguished; the gas-pipes cut; the windows closed and unlighted; no moon, not even stars. The night was profoundly dark.

They could hear distant fusillades. The soldiers were firing from around Saint Eustache, and every three minutes sent a ball in their direction, as much as to say, "We are here." Nevertheless they did not expect an attack before the morning.

Dialogues like the following took place amongst them:—

"I wish I had a truss of straw," said Charpentier; "I have a notion that we shall sleep here tonight."

"Will you be able to get to sleep?" asked Jeanty Sarre.

"I? Certainly I shall go to sleep."

He did go to sleep, in fact, a few moments later.

In this gloomy network of narrow streets, intersected with barricades, and blockaded by soldiers, two wine-shops had remained open. They made more lint there, however, than they drank wine; the orders of the chiefs were only to drink reddened water.

The doorway of one of these wine-shops opened exactly between the two barricades of the Petit Cancan. In it was a clock by which they regulated the sentries' relief. In a back room they had locked up two suspicious-looking persons who had intermingled with the combatants. One of these men at the moment when he was arrested said, "I have come to fight for Henri V." They kept them under lock and key, and placed a sentry at the door.

An ambulance had been established in an adjoining room. There the wounded shoemaker was lying upon a mattress thrown upon the ground.

They had established, in case of need, another ambulance in the Rue du Cadran. An opening had been effected at the corner of the barricade on this side, so that the wounded could be easily carried away.

Towards half-past nine in the evening a man came up to the barricade.

Jeanty Sarre recognized him.

"Good day, Denis," said he.

"Call me, Gaston," said the man.

"Why?"

"Because—"

"Are you your brother?"

"Yes, I am my brother. For today."

"Very well. Good-day, Gaston."

They heartily shook hands.

It was Denis Dussoubs.

He was pale, calm, and bleeding; he had already been fighting during the morning. At the barricade of the Faubourg Saint Martin a ball had grazed his breast, but had been turned off by some money in his pocket, and had only broken the skin. He had had the rare good fortune of being scratched by a ball. It was like the first touch from the claws of death. He wore a cap, his hat having been left behind in the barricade where he had fought: and he had replaced his bullet-pierced overcoat, which was made of Belleisle cloth, by a pea-jacket bought at a slop-shop.

How had he reached the barricade of the Petit Carreau? He could not say. He had walked straight before him. He had glided from street to street. Chance takes the predestined by the hand, and leads them straight to their goal through the thick darkness.

At the moment when he entered the barricade they cried out to him, "Who goes there?" He answered, "The Republic!"

They saw Jeanty Sarre shake him by the hand. They asked Jeanty Sarre,—

"Who is he?"

Jeanty Sarre answered,—

"It is someone."

And he added,—

"We were only sixty a short time since. We are a hundred now."

All pressed round the new-comer. Jeanty Sarre offered him the command.

"No," said he, "I do not understand the tactics of barricade fighting. I should be a bad chief, but I am a good soldier. Give me a gun."

They seated themselves on the paving-stones. They exchanged their experiences of what had been done. Denis described to them the fighting on the Faubourg Saint Martin. Jeanty Sarre told Denis of the fighting in the Rue Saint Denis.

During all this time the generals were preparing a final assault,—what the Marquis of Clermont-Tonnerre, in 1822, called the "Coup de Collier," and what, in 1789, the Prince of Lambese had called the "Coup de Bas." Throughout all Paris there was now only this point which offered any resistance. This knot of barricade, this labyrinth of streets, embattled like a redoubt, was the last citadel of the People and of Right. The generals invested it leisurely, step by step, and on all sides. They concentrated their forces. They, the combatants of this fateful hour, knew nothing of what was being done. Only from time to time they interrupted their recital of events and they listened. From the right and from the left, from the front, from the rear, from every side, at the same time, an unmistakable murmur, growing every moment louder, and more distinct, hoarse, piercing, fear-inspiring, reached them through the darkness. It was the sound of the battalions marching and charging at the trumpet-command in all the adjoining streets. They resumed their gallant conversation, and then in another moment they stopped again and listened to that species of ill-omened chant, chanted by Death, which was approaching.

Nevertheless some still thought that they would not be attacked till the next morning. Night combats are rare in street-warfare. They are more "risky" than all the other conflicts. Few generals venture upon them. But amongst the old hands of the barricade, from certain never-failing signs, they believed that an assault was imminent.

In fact, at half-past ten at night, and not at eight o'clock as General Magnan has said in the despicable document which he calls his report—a special movement was heard in the direction of the markets. This was the marching of the troops. Colonel de Lourmel had determined to make the attack. The 51st of the Line, posted at Saint Eustache, entered the Rue Montorgueil. The 2d battalion formed the advanced guard. The Grenadiers and the Light Infantry, hurled forward at the double, quickly carried the three little barricades which were on the other side of the vacant space of the Rue Mauconseil, and the feebly defended barricades of the adjoining streets. It was at that very moment that the barricade near which I was happened to be carried.

From the barricade of the Petit Carreau they heard the night-strife draw near through the darkness, with a fitful noise, strange and appalling. First a great tumult, then volleys, then silence, and then all began again. The flashing of the fusillades suddenly delineated in the darkness the outlines of the houses, which appeared as though they themselves were affrighted.

The decisive moment drew near.

The outpost had fallen back upon the barricades. The advanced posts of the Rue de Cléry and the Rue du Cadran had come back. They called over the roll. Not one of those of the morning was missing.

They were, as we have said, about sixty combatants, and not a hundred, as the Magnan report has stated.

From the upper extremity of the street where they were stationed it was difficult to ascertain what was happening. They did not exactly know how many barricades they were in the Rue Montorgueil between them and Saint Eustache, whence the troops were coming. They only knew that their nearest point of resistance was the double Mauconseil barricade, and that, when all was at an end there, it would be their turn.

Denis had posted himself on the inner side of the barricade in such a manner that half his body was above the top, and from there he watched. The glimmer which came from the doorway of the wine-shop rendered his gestures visible.

Suddenly he made a sign. The attack on the Mauconseil redoubt was beginning.

The soldiers, in fact, after having sometime hesitated before this double wall of paving-stones, lofty, well-built, and which they supposed was well defended, had ended by rushing upon it, and attacking it with blows of their guns.

They were not mistaken. It was well defended. We have already said that there were only six men in this barricade, the six workmen who had built it. Of the six one only had three cartridges, the others had only two shots to fire. These six men heard the regiment advancing and the roll of the battery which was followed on it, and did not stir. Each remained silent at his post of battle, the barrel of his gun between two paving-stones. When the soldiers were within range they fired, and the battalion replied.

"That is right. Rage away, Red Breeches," said, laughingly, the man who had three shots to fire.

Behind them, the men of the Petit Carreau were crowded round Denis and Jeanty Sarre, and leaning on the crest of their barricade, stretching their necks towards the Mauconseil redoubt, they watched them like the gladiators of the next combat.

The six men of this Mauconseil redoubt resisted the onslaught of the battalion for nearly a quarter of an hour. They did not fire together, "in order," one of them said, "to make the pleasure last the longer." The pleasure of being killed for duty; a noble sentence in this workman's mouth. They did not fall back into the adjoining streets until after having exhausted their ammunition. The last, he who had three cartridges, did not leave until the soldiers were actually scaling the summit of the barricade.

In the barricade of the Petit Carreau not a word was spoken; they followed all the phases of this struggle, and they pressed each other's hands.

Suddenly the noise ceased, the last musket-shot was fired. A moment afterwards they saw the lighted candles being placed in all the windows which looked on on the Mauconseil redoubt. The bayonets and the brass ornaments on the shakos sparkled there. The barricade was taken.

The commander of the battalion, as is always the custom in similar circumstances, had sent orders into the adjoining houses to light up all the windows.

This was done at the Mauconseil redoubt.

Seeing that their hour had come, the sixty combatants of the barricade of the Petit Carreau mounted their heap of paving-stones, and shouted with one voice, in the midst of the darkness, this piercing cry, "Long live the Republic!"

No one answered them.

They could only hear the battalion loading their guns.

This acted upon them as a species of signal for action. They were all worn out with fatigue, having been on their feet since the preceding day, carrying paving-stones or fighting, the greater part had neither eaten nor slept.

Charpentier said to Jeanty Sarre,—

"We shall all be killed."

"Shall we really!" said Jeanty Sarre.

Jeanty Sarre ordered the door of the wine-shop to be closed, so that their barricade, completely shrouded in darkness, would give them some advantage over the barricade which was occupied by the soldiers and lighted up.

In the meantime the 51st searched the streets, carried the wounded into the ambulances, and took up their position in the double barricade of the Rue Mauconseil. Half an hour thus elapsed.

Now, in order to clearly understand what is about to follow, the reader must picture to himself in this silent street, in this darkness of the night, at from sixty to eighty yards apart, within speaking distance, these two redoubts facing each other, and able as in an Iliad to address each other.

On one side the Army, on the other side the People, the darkness over all.

The species of truce which always precedes decisive encounters drew to a close. The preparations were completed on both sides. The soldiers could be heard forming into order of battle, and the captains giving out their commands. It was evident that the struggle was at hand.

"Let us begin," said Charpentier; and he raised his gun.

Denis held his arm back. "Wait," he said.

Then an epic incident was seen.

Denis slowly mounted the paving-stones of the barricade, ascended to the top, and stood there erect, unarmed and bareheaded.

Thence he raised his voice, and, facing the soldiers, he shouted to them, "Citizens!"

At this word a sort of electric shudder ensued which was felt from one barricade to the other. Every sound was hushed, every voice was silent, on both sides reigned a deep religious and solemn silence. By the distant glimmer of a few lighted windows the soldiers could vaguely distinguish a man standing above a mass of shadows, like a phantom who was speaking to them in the night.

Denis continued,—

"Citizens of the Army! Listen to me!"

The silence grew still more profound.

He resumed,—

"What have you come to do here? You and ourselves, all of us who are in this street, at this hour, with the sword or gun in hand, what are we about to do? To kill each other! To kill each other, citizens! Why? Because they have raised a misunderstanding between us! Because we obey—you your discipline—we our Right! You believe that you are carrying out your instructions; as for us, we know that we are doing our duty. Yes! it is Universal Suffrage, it is the Right of the Republic, it is our Right that we are defending, and our Right, soldiers, is your Right. The Army is the People, as the People is the Army. We are the same nation, the some country, the same men. My God! See, is there any Russian blood in my veins, in me who am speaking to you? Is there any Prussian blood in your veins, in you who are listening to me? No! Why then should we fight? It is always an unfortunate thing for a man to fire upon a man. Nevertheless, a gun-shot between a Frenchman and an Englishman can be understood; but between a Frenchman and a Frenchman, ah! that wounds Reason, that wounds France, that wounds our mother!"

All anxiously listened to him. At this moment from the opposite barricade a voice shouted to him,—

"Go home, then!"

At this coarse interruption an angry murmur ran through Denis's companions, and several guns could be heard being loaded. Denis restrained them by a sign.

This sign possessed a strange authority.

"Who is this man?" the combatants behind the barricade asked each other. Suddenly they cried out,—

"He is a Representative of the People!"

Denis had, in fact, suddenly assumed his brother Gaston's sash.

What he had premeditated was about to be accomplished; the hour of the heroic falsehood had arrived. He cried out,—

"Soldiers, do you know what the man is who is speaking to you at this moment? He is not only a citizen, he is a Legislator! He is a Representative chosen by Universal Suffrage! My name is Dussoubs, and I am a Representative of the People. It is in the name of the National Assembly, it is in the name of the Sovereign Assembly, it is in the name of the People, and in the name of the Law, that I summon you to hear me. Soldiers, you are the armed force. Well, then, when the Law speaks, the armed force listens."

This time the silence was not broken.

We reproduce these words almost literally; such as they are, and such as they have remained graven on the memory of those who heard them; but what we cannot reproduce, and what should be added to these words, in order to realize the effect, is the attitude, the accent, the thrill of emotion, the vibration of the words issuing from this noble breast, the intense impression produced by the terrible hour and place.

Denis Dussoubs continued: "He spoke for some twenty minutes," an eye-witness has told me. Another has said, "He spoke with a loud voice; the whole street heard him." He was vehement, eloquent, earnest; a judge for Bonaparte, a friend for the soldiers. He sought to rouse them by everything which could still vibrate in them; he recalled to them their true wars, their true victories, the national glory, the ancient military honor, the flag. He told them that all this was about to be slain by the bullets from their guns. He adjured them, he ordered them to join themselves to the People and to the Law; and then suddenly coming back to the first words which he had pronounced, carried away by that fraternity with which his soul overflowed, he interrupted himself in the middle of a half-completed sentence, and cried out:—

"But to what purpose are all these words? It is not all this that is wanted, it is a shake of the hand between brothers! Soldiers, you are there opposite us, at a hundred paces from us, in a barricade, with the sword drawn, with guns pointed; you are aiming directly at me; well then, all of us who are here love you! There is not one of us who would not give his life for one of you. You are the peasants of the fields of France; we are the workmen of Paris. What, then, is in question? Simply to see each other, to speak to each other, and not to cut each other's throats. Shall we try this? Say! Ah! as for myself in this frightful battle-field of civil war, I would rather die than kill. Look now, I am going to get off this barricade and come to you. I am unarmed; I only know that you are my brothers. I am confident, I am calm; and if one of you presents his bayonet at me, I will offer him my hand."

He finished speaking.

A voice cried out from the opposite barricade, "Advance in order!"

Then they saw him slowly descend the dimly-lighted crest of the barricade, paving-stone by paving-stone, and plunge with head erect into the dark street.

From the barricade all eyes followed him with an inexpressible anxiety. Hearts ceased beating, mouths no longer breathed.

No one attempted to restrain Denis Dussoubs. Each felt that he was going where he ought to go. Charpentier wished to accompany him.

"Would you like me to go with you?" he cried out to him. Dussoubs refused, with a shake of the head.

Dussoubs, alone and grave, advanced towards the Mauconseil Barricade. The night was so dark that they lost sight of him immediately. They could distinguish only for a few seconds his peaceable and intrepid bearing. Then he disappeared. They could no longer see anything. It was an inauspicious moment. The night was dark and dumb. There could only be heard in this thick darkness the sound of a measured and firm step dying away in the distance.

After sometime, how long no one could reckon, so completely did emotion eclipse thought amongst the witnesses of this marvellous scene, a glimmer of light appeared in the barricade of the soldiers; it was probably a lantern which was being brought or taken away. By the flash they again saw Dussoubs, he was close to the barricade, he had almost reached it, he was walking towards it with his arms stretched out like Christ.

Suddenly the word of command, "Fire!" was heard.

A fusillade burst forth.

They had fired upon Dussoubs when he was at the muzzles of their guns.

Dussoubs fell.

Then he raised himself and cried, "Long live the Republic!"

Another bullet struck him, he fell again. Then they saw him raise himself once more, and heard him shout in a loud voice, "I die with the Republic."

These were his last words.

In this manner died Denis Dussoubs.

It was not vainly that he had said to his brother, "Your sash will be there."

He was anxious that this sash should do its duty. He determined in the depths of his great soul that this sash should triumph either through the law or through death.

That is to say, in the first case it would save Right, in the second save Honor.

Dying, he could say, "I have succeeded."

Of the two possible triumphs of which he had dreamed, the gloomy triumph was not the less splendid.

The insurgent of the Elysée thought that he had killed a Representative of the People, and boasted of it. The sole journal published by the *coup d'état* under these different titles *Patrie*, *Univers*, *Moniteur*, *Parisien*, etc., announced on the next day, Friday, the 5th, "that the ex-Representative Dussoubs (Gaston) had been killed at the barricade of the Rue Neuve Saint Eustache, and that he bore 'a red flag in his hand.'"

IV

What Was Done During the Night—The Passage Du Saumon

When those on the barricade of the Petit Carreau saw Dussoubs fall, so gloriously for his friends, so shamefully for his murderers, a moment of stupor ensued. Was it possible? Did they really see this before them? Such a crime committed by our soldiers? Horror filled every soul.

This moment of surprise did not last long. "Long live the Republic!" shouted the barricade with one voice, and it replied to the ambuscade by a formidable fire.

The conflict began. A mad conflict on the part of the *coup d'état*, a struggle of despair on the side of the Republic. On the side of the soldiers an appalling and cold blooded resolution, a passive and ferocious obedience, numbers, good arms, absolute chiefs, pouches filled with cartridges. On the side of the People no ammunition, disorder, weariness, exhaustion, no discipline, indignation serving for a leader.

It appears that while Dussoubs was speaking, fifteen grenadiers, commanded by a sergeant named Pitrois, had succeeded in gliding in the darkness along the houses, and, unperceived and unheard, had taken up their position close to the barricade. These fifteen men suddenly formed themselves together with lowered bayonets at twenty paces from the barricade ready to scale it. A volley received them. They fell back, leaving several corpses in the gutter. Major Jeannin cried out, "Finish them off." The entire battalion which occupied the Mauconseil barricade, then appeared with raised bayonets upon the uneven crest of this barricade, and from there without breaking their line, with a sudden, but regulated and inexorable movement, sprang into the street. The four companies, in close order, and as though mingled and hardly visible, seemed like a wave precipitating itself with a great noise from the height of the barricade.

At the barricade of the Petit Carreau they noted the manoeuvre, and had paused in their fire. "Present," cried Jeanty Sarre, "but do not fire; wait for the order."

Each put his gun to his shoulder, then placed the barrels between the paving-stones, ready to fire, and waited.

As soon as it had quitted the Mauconseil redoubt, the battalion rapidly formed itself into an attacking column, and a moment afterwards they heard the intermittent sound of an advance at the double. It was the battalion which was coming upon them.

"Charpentier," said Jeanty Sarre, "you have good eyes. Are they midway?"

"Yes," said Charpentier.

"Fire," said Jeanty Sarre.

The barricade fired. The whole street was filled with smoke. Several soldiers fell. They could hear the cries of the wounded. The battalion, riddled with balls, halted and replied by platoon firing.

Seven or eight combatants whose bodies reached above the barricade, which had been made hastily and was too low were hit. Three were killed on the spot. One fell wounded by a ball in his stomach, between Jeanty Sarre and Charpentier. He shrieked out with pain.

"Quick, to the ambulance:" said Jeanty Sarre.

"Where?"

"In the Rue du Cadran."

Jeanty Sarre and Charpentier picked up the wounded man, the one by the feet, the other by the head, and carried him to the du Cadran through the passage in the barricade.

During all this time there was continued file firing. There no longer seemed anything in the street but smoke, the balls whistling and crossing each other, the brief and repeated commands, some plaintive cries, and the flash of the guns lighting up the darkness.

Suddenly a loud void died out, "Forwards!" The battalion resumed its double-quick march and threw itself upon the barricade.

Then ensued a horrible scene. They fought hand to hand, four hundred on the one side, fifty on the other. They seized each other by the collar, by the throat, by the mouth, by the hair. There was no longer a cartridge in the barricade, but there remained despair. A workman, pierced through and through, snatched the bayonet from his belly, and stabbed a soldier with it. They did not see each other, but they devoured each other. It was a desperate scuffle in the dark.

The barricade did not hold out for two minutes. In several places, it may be remembered, it was low. It was rather stridden over than scaled. That was all the more heroic. One of the survivors[1] told the writer of

---

1. February 18. Louvain.

these lines, "The barricade defended itself very badly, but the men died very well."

All this took place while Jeanty Sarre and Charpentier were carrying the wounded man to the ambulance in the Rue du Cadran. His wounds having been attended to, they came back to the barricade. They had just reached it when they heard themselves called by name. A feeble voice close by said to them, "Jeanty Sarre! Charpentier!" They turned round and saw one of their men who was dying leaning against a wall, and his knees giving way beneath him. He was a combatant who had left the barricade. He had only been able to take a few steps down the street. He held his hand over his breast, where he had received a ball fired at close quarters. He said to them in a scarcely audible voice, "The barricade is taken, save yourselves."

"No," said Jeanty Sarre, "I must unload my gun." Jeanty Sarre re-entered the barricade, fired a last shot and went away.

Nothing could be more frightful than the interior of the captured barricade.

The Republicans, overpowered by numbers, no longer offered any resistance. The officers cried out, "No prisoners!" The soldiers billed those who were standing, and despatched those who had fallen. Many awaited their death with their heads erect. The dying raised themselves up, and shouted, "Long live the Republic!" Some soldiers ground their heels upon the faces of the dead, so that they should not be recognized. There, stretched out amongst the corpses, in the middle of the barricade, with his hair in the gutter, was seen the all-but namesake of Charpentier, Carpentier, the delegate of the committee of the Tenth Arrondissement, who had been killed, and had fallen backwards, with two balls in his breast. A lighted candle which the soldiers had taken from the wine-shop was placed on a paving stone.

The soldiers were infuriated. One would say that they were revenging themselves. On whom? A workman, named Paturel, received three balls and six bayonet-thrusts, four of which were in the head. They thought that he was dead, and they did not renew the attack. He felt them search him. They took ten francs which he had about him. He did not die till six days later, and he was able to relate the details which are given here. We may note, by the way, that the name of Paturel does not figure upon any of the lists of the corpses published by M. Bonaparte.

Sixty Republicans were shut up in this redoubt of the Petit Carreau. Forty-six were killed there. These men had come there that morning free, proud to fight, and joyous to die. At midnight all was at an end. The night wagons carried away on the next day nine corpses to the hospital cemetery, and thirty-seven to Montmartre.

Jeanty Sarre escaped by a miracle, as well as Charpentier, and a third whose name we have not been able to ascertain. They glided along the houses and reached the Passage du Saumon. The grated doors which closed the Passage during the night only reached to the centre of the archway. They climbed it and got over the spikes, at the risk of tearing themselves. Jeanty Sarre was the first to climb it; having reached the summit, one of the spikes pierced his trousers, hooked them, and Jeanty Sarre fell headforemost upon the pavement. He got up again, he was only stunned. The other two followed him, and gliding along the bars, all three found themselves in the Passage. It was dimly lighted by a lamp which shone at one end. In the meanwhile, they heard the soldiers, who were pursuing them, coming up. In order to escape by the Rue Montmartre, they would have to climb the grated gateway at the other end of the Passage; their hands were grazed, their knees were bleeding; they were dying of weariness; they were in no condition to recommence a similar ascent.

Jeanty Sarre knew where the keeper of the Passage lived. He knocked at his window, and begged him to open. The keeper refused.

At this moment the detachment which had been sent in pursuit of them reached the grated gateway which they had just climbed. The soldiers, hearing a noise in the Passage, passed the barrels of their guns through the bars. Jeanty Sarre squeezed himself against the wall behind one of those projecting columns which decorate the Passage; but the column was very thin, and only half covered him. The soldiers fired, and smoke filled the Passage. When it cleared away, Jeanty Sarre saw Charpentier stretched on the stones, with his face to the ground. He had been shot through the heart. Their other companion lay a few paces from him, mortally wounded.

The soldiers did not scale the grated gateway, but they posted a sentinel before it. Jeanty Sarre heard them going away by the Rue Montmartre. They would doubtless come back.

No means of flight. He felt all the doors round his prison successively. One of them at length opened. This appeared to him like a miracle. Whoever could have forgotten to shut the door? Providence, doubtless. He hid himself behind it, and remained there for more than an hour, standing motionless, scarcely breathing. He no longer heard any sound; he ventured out. The sentinel was no longer there. The detachment had rejoined the battalion.

One of his old friends, a man to whom he had rendered services such as are not forgotten, lived in this very Passage du Saumon. Jeanty Sarre looked for the number, woke the porter, told him the name of his friend, was admitted, went up the stairs, and knocked at the door. The door was opened, his friend appeared in his nightshirt, with a candle in his hand.

He recognized Jeanty Sarre, and cried out, "You here! What a state you are in! Where hove you come from? From what riot? from what madness? And then you come to compromise us all here? To have us murdered? To have us shot? Now then, what do you want with me?"

"I want you to give me a brush down," said Jeanty Sarre.

His friend took a brush and brushed him, and Jeanty Sarre went away. While going down the stairs, Jeanty Sarre cried out to his friend, "Thanks!"

Such is the kind of hospitality which we have since received in Belgium, in Switzerland, and even in England.

The next day, when they took up the bodies they found on Charpentier a note-book and a pencil, and upon Denis Dussoubs a letter. A letter to a woman. Even these stoic souls love.

On the 1st of December, Denis Dussoubs began this letter. He did not finish it. Here it is:—

My Dear Marie,

"Have you experienced that sweet pain of feeling regret for him who regrets you? For myself since I left you I have known no other affliction than that of thinking of you. Even in my affliction itself there was something sweet and tender, and although I was troubled, I was nevertheless happy to feel in the depths of my heart how greatly I loved you by the regret which you cost me. Why are we separated? Why have I been forced to fly from you? For we were so happy! When I think of our little evenings so free from constraint, of our gay country chats with your sisters, I feel myself seized with a bitter regret. Did we not love each other clearly, my darling? We had no secret from each other because we had no need to have one, and our lips uttered the thoughts of our hearts without our thinking to keep anything back.

"God has snatched away from us all these blessings, and nothing will console me for having lost them; do you not lament with me the evils of absence?

"How seldom we see those whom we love! Circumstances take us far from them, and our soul tormented and attracted out of ourselves lives in a perpetual anguish. I feel this sickness of absence. I imagine myself wherever you are. I follow your work with my eyes, or I listen to your words, seated beside you and seeking to divine the word which you are about to utter; your sisters sew by our side. Empty dreams—illusions of a moment—my hand seeks yours; where are you, my beloved one?

"My life is an exile. Far from those whom I love and by whom I am loved, my heart calls them and consumes away in its grief. No, I do not love the great cities and their noise, towns peopled with strangers where no one knows you and where you know no one, where each one jostles and elbows the other without ever exchanging a smile. But I love our quiet fields, the peace of home, and the voice of friends who greet you. Up to the present I have always lived in contradiction with my nature; my fiery blood, my nature so hostile to injustice, the spectacle of unmerited miseries have thrown me into a struggle of which I do not foresee the issue, a struggle in which will remain to the end without fear and without reproach, that which daily breaks me down and consumes my life.

"I tell you, my much-loved darling, the secret miseries of my heart; no, I do not blush for what my hand has just written, but my heart is sick and suffering, and I tell it to you. I suffer. . . I wish to blot out these lines, but why? Could they offend you? What do they contain that could wound my darling? Do I not know your affection, and do I not know that you love me? Yes, you have not deceived me, I did not kiss a lying mouth; when seated on my knees you lulled me with the charm of your words, I believed you. I wished to bind myself to a burning iron bar; weariness preys upon me and devours me. I feel a maddening desire to recover life. Is it Paris that produces this effect upon me? I always yearn to be in places where I am not. I live here to a complete solitude. I believe you, Marie. . ."

Charpentier's note-book only contained this line, which he had written in the darkness at the foot of the barricade while Denis Dussoubs was speaking:—

Admonet et magna testatur voce per umbras.

V

OTHER DEEDS OF DARKNESS

Yvan had again seen Conneau. He corroborated the information given in the letter of Alexandre Dumas to Bocage; with the fact we had the names. On the 3d of December at M. Abbatucci's house, 31, Rue Caumartin, in the presence of Dr. Conneau and of Piétri, a Corsican, born at Vezzani, named Jacques François Criscelli,[1] a man attached to the secret and personal service of Louis Bonaparte, had received from Piétri's own mouth the offer of 25,000 francs "to take or kill Victor Hugo." He had accepted, and said, "That is all very well if I am alone. But suppose there are two of us?"

Piétri had answered,—

"Then there will be 50,000 francs."

This communication, accompanied by urgent prayers, had been made to me by Yvan in the Rue de Monthabor, while we were still at Dupont White's.

This said, I continue my story.

The massacre of the 4th did not produce the whole of its effect until the next day, the 5th. The impulse given by us to the resistance still lasted for some hours, and at nightfall, in the labyrinth of houses ranging from the Rue du Petit Carreau to the Rue du Temple, there was fighting. The Pagevin, Neuve Saint Eustache, Montorgueil, Rambuteau, Beaubourg, and Transnonain barricades were gallantly defended. There, there was an impenetrable network of streets and crossways barricaded by the People, surrounded by the Army.

The assault was merciless and furious.

The barricade of the Rue Montorgueil was one of those which held out the longest. A battalion and artillery was needed to carry it. At the last moment it was only defended by three men, two shop-clerks and a lemonade-seller of an adjoining street. When the assault began the night was densely dark, and the three combatants escaped. But they

---

1. It was this same Criscelli, who later on at Vaugirard in the Rue du Trancy, killed by special order of the Prefect of Police a man named Kech, "suspected of plotting the assassination of the Emperor."

were surrounded. No outlets. Not one door was open. They climbed the grated gateway of the Passage Verdeau as Jeanty Sarre and Charpentier had scaled the Passage du Saumon, had jumped over, and had fled down the Passage. But the other grated gateway was closed, and like Jeanty Sarre and Charpentier they had no time to climb it. Besides, they heard the soldiers corning on both sides. In a corner at the entrance of the Passage there were a few planks which had served to close a stall, and which the stall-keeper was in the habit of putting there. They hid themselves beneath these planks.

The soldiers who had taken the barricade, after having searched the streets, bethought themselves of searching the Passage. They also climbed over the grated gateway, looked about everywhere with lanterns, and found nothing They were going away, when one of them perceived the foot of one of these three unfortunate men which was projecting from beneath the planks.

They killed all three of them on the spot with bayonet-thrusts. They cried out, "Kill us at once! Shoot us! Do not prolong our misery."

The neighboring shop-keepers heard these cries, but dared not open their doors or their windows, for fear, as one of them said the next day, "that they should do the same to them."

The execution at an end, the executioners left the three victims lying in a pool of blood on the pavement of the Passage. One of those unfortunate men did not die until eight o'clock next morning.

No one had dared to ask for mercy; no one had dared to bring any help. They left them to die there.

One of the combatants of the Rue Beaubourg was more fortunate. They were pursuing him. He rushed up a staircase, reached a roof, and from there a passage, which proved to be the top corridor of an hotel. A key was in the door. He opened it boldly, and found himself face to face with a man who was going to bed. It was a tired-out traveller who had arrived at the hotel that very evening. The fugitive said to the traveller, "I am lost, save me!" and explained him the situation in three words.

The traveller said to him, "Undress yourself, and get into my bed." And then he lit a cigar, and began quietly to smoke. Just as the man of the barricade had got into bed a knock came at the door. It was the solders who were searching the house. To the questions which they asked him the traveller answered, pointing to the bed, "We are only two here. We have just arrived here. I am smoking my cigar, and my brother is asleep." The waiter was questioned, and confirmed the traveller's statement. The soldiers went away, and no one was shot.

We will say this, that the victorious soldiers killed less than on the preceding day. They did not massacre in all the captured barricades. The order had been given on that day to make prisoners. It might also be believed that a certain humanity existed. What was this humanity? We shall see.

At eleven o'clock at night all was at an end.

They arrested all those whom they found in the streets which had been surrounded, whether combatants or not, they had all the wine-shops and the *cafés* opened, they closely searched the houses, they seized all the men whom they could find, only leaving the women and the children. Two regiments formed in a square carried away all these prisoners huddled together. They took them to the Tuileries, and shut them up in the vast cellar situated beneath the terrace at the waterside.

On entering this cellar the prisoners felt reassured. They called to mind that in June, 1848, a great number of insurgents had been shut up there, and later on had been transported. They said to themselves that doubtless they also would be transported, or brought before the Councils of War, and that they had plenty of time before them.

They were thirsty. Many of them had been fighting since that morning, and nothing parches tire mouth so much as biting cartridges. They asked for drink. Three pitchers of water were brought to them.

A sort of security suddenly fell upon them. Amongst them were several who had been transported in June, 1848, and who had already been in that cellar, and who said, "In June they were not so humane. They left us for three days without food or drink." Some of them wrapped themselves up in their overcoats or cloaks, lay down, and slept. At one o'clock in the morning a great noise was heard outside. Soldiers, carrying torches, appeared in the cellars, the prisoners who were sleeping woke with a start, an officer ordered them to get up.

They made them go out anyhow as they had come in. As they went out they coupled them two by two at random, and a sergeant counted them in a loud voice. They asked neither their names, nor their professions, nor their families, nor who they were, nor whence they came; they contented themselves with the numbers. The numbers sufficed for what they were about to do.

In this manner they counted 337. The counting having come to an end, they ranged them in close columns, still two by two and arm-in-arm. They were not tied together, but on each side of the column, on the right and on the left, there were three files of soldiers keeping them within their ranks, with guns loaded; a battalion was at their head, a battalion in their rear. They began to march, pressed together and enclosed in this moving frame of bayonets.

At the moment when the column set forward, a young law-student, a fair pale Alsatian, of some twenty years, who was in their ranks, asked a captain, who was marching by him with his sword drawn,—

"Where are we going?"

The officer made no reply.

Having left the Tuileries, they turned to the right, and followed the quay as far as the Pont de la Concorde. They crossed the Pont de la Concorde, and again turned to the right. In this manner they passed before the esplanade of the Invalides, and reached the lonely quay of Gros-Caillou.

As we have just said, they numbered 337, and as they walked two by two, there was one, the last, who walked alone. He was one of the most daring combatants of the Rue Pagevin, a friend of Lecomte the younger. By chance the sergeant, who was posted in the inner file by his side, was a native of the same province. On passing under a street-lamp they recognized each other. They exchanged quickly a few words in a whisper.

"Where are we going?" asked the prisoner.

"To the military school," answered the sergeant. And he added, "Ah! my poor lad!"

And then he kept at a distance from the prisoner.

As this was the end of the column, there was a certain space between the last rank of the soldiers who formed the line, and the first rank of the company which closed the procession.

As they reached the lonely boulevard of Gros-Caillon, of which we have just spoken, the sergeant drew near to the prisoner, and said to him in a rapid and low tone,—

"One can hardly see here. It is a dark spot. On the left there are trees. Be off!"

"But," said the prisoner, "they will fire at me."

"They will miss you."

"But suppose they kill me?"

"It will be no worse than what awaits you."

The prisoner understood, shook the sergeant's hand, and taking advantage of the space between the line of soldiers and rear-ground, rushed with a single bound outside the column, and disappeared in the darkness beneath the trees.

"A man is escaping!" cried out the officer who commanded the last company. "Halt! Fire!"

The column halted. The rear-guard company fired at random in the direction taken by the fugitive, and, as the sergeant had foreseen, missed him. In a few moments the fugitive had reached the streets adjoining the tobacco manufactory, and had plunged into them. They did not pursue him. They had more pressing work on hand.

Besides, confusion might have arisen in their ranks, and to recapture one they risked letting the 336 escape.

The column continued its march. Having reached the Pont d'Iéna, they turned to the left, and entered into the Champ de Mars.

There they shot them all.

These 336 corpses were amongst those which were carried to Montmartre Cemetery, and which were buried there with their heads exposed.

In this manner their families were enabled to recognize them. The Government learned who they were after killing them.

Amongst these 336 victims were a large number of the combatants of the Rue Pagevin and the Rue Rambuteau, of the Rue Neuve Saint Eustache and the Porte Saint Denis. There were also 100 passers-by, whom they had arrested because they happened to be there, and without any particular reason.

Besides, we will at once mention that the wholesale executions from the 3d inst. were renewed nearly every night. Sometimes at the Champ de Mars, sometimes at the Prefecture of Police, sometimes at both places at once.

When the prisons were full, M. de Maupas said "Shoot!" The fusillades at the Prefecture took place sometimes in the courtyard, sometimes in the Rue de Jérusalem. The unfortunate people whom they shot were placed against the wall which bears the theatrical notices. They had chosen this spot because it is close by the sewer-grating of the gutter, so that the blood would run down at once, and would leave fewer traces. On Friday, the 5th, they shot near this gutter of the Rue de Jérusalem 150 prisoners. Someone[2] said to

---

2. The Marquis Sarrazin de Montferrier, a relative of my eldest brother. I can now mention his name.

me, "On the next day I passed by there, they showed the spot; I dug between the paving-stones with the toe of my boot, and I stirred up the mud. I found blood."

This expression forms the whole history of the *coup d'état*, and will form the whole history of Louis Bonaparte. Stir up this mud, you will find blood.

Let this then be known to History:—

The massacre of the boulevard had this infamous continuation, the secret executions. The *coup d'état* after having been ferocious became mysterious. It passed from impudent murder in broad day to hidden murder at night.

Evidence abounds.

Esquiros, hidden in the Gros-Caillou, heard the fusillades on the Champ de Mars every night.

At Mazas, Chambolle, on the second night of his incarceration, heard from midnight till five o'clock in the morning, such volleys that he thought the prison was attacked.

Like Montferrier, Desmoulins bore evidence to blood between the paving-stones of the Rue de Jérusalem.

Lieutenant-Colonel Cailland, of the ex-Republican Guard, is crossing the Pont Neuf; he sees some *sergents de ville* with muskets to their shoulders, aiming at the passers-by; he says to them, "You dishonor the uniform." They arrest him. They search him. A *sergent de ville* says to him, "If we find a cartridge upon you, we shall shoot you." They find nothing. They take him to the Prefecture of Police, they shut him up in the station-house. The director of the station-house comes and says to him, "Colonel, I know you well. Do not complain of being here. You are confided to my care. Congratulate yourself on it. Look here, I am one of the family, I go and I come, I see, I listen; I know what is going on; I know what is said; I divine what is not said. I hear certain noises during the night; I see contain traces in the morning. As for myself I am not a bad fellow. I am taking care of you. I am keeping you out of the way. At the present moment be contented to remain with me. If you were not here you would be underground."

An ex-magistrate, General Leflô's brother-in-law, is conversing on the Pont de la Concorde with some officers before the steps of the Chamber; some policemen come up to him: "You are tampering with the army." He protests, they throw him into a vehicle, and they take him to the Prefecture of Police. As he arrives there he sees a young man, in a blouse and a cap, passing on the quay, who is being shoved along by three municipal guards with the butt-ends of their muskets. At an opening of the parapet, a guard shouts to him, "Go in there." The man goes in. Two guards shoot him in the back. He falls. The third guard despatches him with a shot in his ear.

On the 13th the massacres were not yet at an end. On the morning of that day, in the dim light of the dawn, a solitary passer-by, going along the Rue Saint Honoré, saw, between two lines of horse-soldiers, three wagons wending their way, heavily loaded. These wagons could be traced by the stains of blood which dripped from them. They came from the Champ de Mars, and were going to the Montmartre Cemetery. They were full of corpses.

VI

The Consultative Committee

A l danger being over, all scruples vanished. Prudent and wise people could now give their adherence to the *coup d'état*, they allowed their names to be posted up.

Here is the placard:

Fɴᴇɴᴄʜ Rᴇᴘᴜʙʟɪᴄ.
In the name of the French People.

"The President of the Republic,

"Wishing, until the reorganization of the Legislative Body and the Council of State, to be surrounded by men who justly possess the esteem and the confidence of the country,

"Has created a Consultative committee, which is composed of MM.—

"Abbatucci, ex-Councillor of the Court of Cassation (of the Loiret).

General Achard (of the Moselle).

André, Ernest (of the Seine).

André (of the Charente).

D'Argout, Governor of the Bank, ex-Minister.

General Arrighi of Padua (of Corsica).

General de Bar (of the Seine).

General Baraguay-d'Hilliers (of Doubs).

Barbaroux, ex-Procureur-General (of the Réunion).

Baroche, ex-Minister of the Interior and of Foreign Affairs, Vice-President of the Committee (of the Charente-Inférieure).

Barret (Ferdinand), ex-Minister (of the Seine).

Barthe, ex-Minister, first President (of the Cour de Comptes).

Bataille (of the Haute-Vienne).

Bavoux (Evariste) (of the Seine-et-Marne).

De Beaumont (of the Somme).

Bérard (of the Lot-et-Garonne).

Berger, Prefect of the Seine (of Puy-de-Dôme).

Bertrand (of the Yonne).

Bidault (of the Cher).

Bigrel (of the Côtes-du-Nord).

Billault, barrister.

Bineau, ex-Minister (of the Maine-et-Loire).

Boinvilliers, ex-President of the body of barristers (of the Seine).

Bonjean, Attorney-General of the Court of Cassation (of the Drome).

Boulatignier.

Bourbousson (of Vaucluse).

Bréhier (of the Manche).

De Cambacérès (Hubert).

De Cambacérès (of the Aisne).

Carlier, ex-Prefect of Police.

De Casabianca, ex-Minister (of Corsica).

General de Castellane, Commander-in-Chief at Lyons.

De Caulaincourt (of Calvados).

Vice-Admiral Cécile (of the Seine-Inférieure).

Chadenet (of the Meuse).

Charlemagne (of the Indre).

Chassaigne-Goyon (of Puy de Dôme).

General de Chasseloup-Laubat (of the Seine-Inférieure).

Prosper de Chasseloup-Laubat (Charente-Inférieure).

Chaix d'Est-Ange, Barrister of Paris (of the Marne).

De Chazelles, Mayor of Clermont-Ferrand (of Puy-de-Dôme).

Collas (of the Gironde).

De Crouseilhes, ex-Councillor of the Court of Cassation, ex-Minister (of the Basses-Pyrénées).

Curial (of the Orne).

De Cuverville (of the Côtes-du-Nord).

Dabeaux (of the Haute-Garonne).

Dariste (of the Basses-Pyrénées).

Daviel, ex-Minister.

Delacoste, ex-Commissary-General (of the Rhône).

Delajus (of the Charente-Inférieure).

Delavau (of the Indre).

Deltheil (of the Lot).

Denjoy (of the Gironde).

Desjobert (of the Seine-Inférieure).

Desmaroux (of the Allier).

Drouyn de Lhuys, ex-Minister (of the Seine-et-Marne).

Théodore Ducos, Minister of the Marine and of the Colonies (of the Seine).

Dumas (of the Institut) ex-Minister (of the Nord).

Charles Dupin, of the Institut (of the Seine-Inférieure).

General Durrieu (of the Landes).

Maurice Duval, ex-Prefect.

Eschassériaux (of the Charente-Inférieure).

Marshal Excelmans, Grand Chancellor of the Legion of Honor.

Ferdinand Favre (of the Loire-Inférieure) General de Flahaut, ex-Ambassador.

Fortoul, Minister of Public Instruction (of the Basses-Alpes).

Achille Fould, Minister of Finance (of the Seine).

De Fourment (of the Somme).

Fouquier-d'Hérouël (of the Aisne).

Fremy (of the Yonne).

Furtado (of the Seine).

Gasc (of the Haute Garonne).

Gaslonde (of the Manche).

De Gasparin (ex-Minister).

Ernest de Girardin (of the Charente).

Augustin Giraud (of Maine-et-Loire).

Charles Giraud, of the Institut, member of the Court of Public Instruction, ex-Minister.

Godelle (of the Aisne).

Goulhot de Saint-Germain (of the Manche).

General de Grammont (of the Loire).

De Grammont (of the Haute-Saône).

De Greslan (of the Réunion).

General de Grouchy (of the Gironde).

Kallez Claparède (of the Bas-Rhin).

General d'Hautpoul, ex-Minister (of the Aude).

Hébert (of the Aisne).

De Heeckeren (of the Haut-Rhin).

D'Hérembault (of the Pas-de-Calais).

Hermann.

Heurtier (of the Loire).

General Husson (of the Aube).
Janvier (of the Tarn-et-Garonne).
Lacaze (of the Hautes-Pyrénées).
Lacrosse, ex-Minister (of Finistère).
Ladoucette (of the Moselle).
Frédéric de Lagrange (of the Gers).
De Lagrange (of the Gironde).
General de La Hitte, ex-Minister.
Delangle, ex-Attorney-General.
Lanquetin, President of the Municipal Commission.
De la Riboissière (of Ille-et-Vilaine).
General Lawoestine.
Lebeuf (of the Seine-et-Marne).
Genéral Lebreton (of the Eure-et-Loir).
Le Comte (of the Yonne).
Le Conte (of the Côtes-du-Nord).
Lefebvre-Duruflé, Minister of Commerce (of the Eure).
Lélut (of the Haute-Saône).
Lemarois (of the Manche).
Lemercier (of the Charente). Lequien (of the Pas-de-Calais).
Lestiboudois (of the Nord).
Levavasseur (of the Seine-Inférieure).
Le Verrier (of the Manche).
Lezay de Marnésia (of Loir-et-Cher).
General Magnan, Commander-in-chief of the Army of Paris.
Magne, Minister of Public Works (of the Dordogne).
Edmond Maigne (of the Dordogne).
Marchant (of the Nord).
Mathieu Bodet, Barrister at the Court of Cassation.
De Maupas, Prefect of Police.
De Mérode (of the Nord).
Mesnard, President of the Chamber of the Court of Cassation.
Meynadier, ex-Prefect (of the Lozère).
De Montalembert (of the Doubs).
De Morny (of the Puy-de-Dôme).
De Mortemart (of the Seine-Inférieure).
De Mouchy (of the Oise).
De Moustiers (of the Doubs).
Lucien Murat (of the Lot).

General d'Ornano (of the Indre-et-Loire).

Pepin Lehalleur (of the Seine-et-Marne).

Joseph Périer, Governor of the Bank.

De Persigny (of the Nord).

Pichon, Mayor of Arras (of the Pas de Calais).

Portalis, First President of the Court of Cassation.

Pongerard, Mayor of Pennes (of the Ille-et-Vilaine).

General de Préval.

De Rancé (of Algeria).

General Randon, ex-Minister, Governor-General of Algeria.

General Regnauld de Saint-Jean-d'Angély, ex-Minister (of the Charente-Inférieure).

Renouard de Bussière (of the Bas-Rhin).

Renouard (of the Lozère).

General Rogé.

Rouher, Keeper of the Seals, Minister of Justice (of the Puy-de-Dôme).

De Royer, ex-Minister, Attorney-General at the Court of Appeal of Paris.

General de Saint-Arnaud, Minister of War.

De Saint-Arnaud, Barrister at the Court of Appeal of Paris.

De Salis (of the Moselle).

Sapey (of the Isère).

Schneider, ex-Minister.

De Ségur d'Aguesseau (of the Hautes-Pyréneés).

Seydoux (of the Nord).

Amédée Thayer.

Thieullen (of the Côtes-du-Nord).

De Thorigny, ex-Minister.

Toupot de Béveaux (of the Haute-Marne).

Tourangin, ex-Prefect. Troplong, First President of the Court of Appeal.

De Turgot, Minister for Foreign Affairs.

Vaillant, Marshal of France.

Vaisse, ex-Minister (of the Nord).

De Vandeul (of the Haute-Marne).

General Vast-Vimeux (of the Charente-Inférieure).

Vauchelle, Mayor of Versailles.

Viard (of the Meurthe).

Vieillard (of the Manche).

Vuillefroy.

Vuitry, Under-Secretary of State at the Ministry of Finance De Wagram.

The President of the Republic,

LOUIS NAPOLEON BONAPARTE

Minister of the Interior, DE MORNY

The name of Bourbousson is found on this list.

It would be a pity if this name were lost.

At the same time as this placard appeared the protest of M. Daru, as follows:—

"I approve of the proceedings of the National Assembly at the Mairie of the Tenth Arrondissement on the 2d of December, 1851, in which I was hindered from participating by force.

DARU

Some of these members of the Consultative Committee came from Mazas or from Mount Valerien. They had been detained in a cell for four-and-twenty hours, and then released. It may be seen that these legislators bore little malice to the man who had made them undergo this disagreeable taste of the law.

Many of the personages comprised in this menagerie possessed no other renown but the outcry caused by their debts, clamoring around them. Such a one had been twice declared bankrupt, but this extenuating circumstance was added, "not under his own name:" Another who belonged to a literary or scientific circle was reputed to have sold his vote. A third, who was handsome, elegant, fashionable, dandified, polished, gilded, embroidered, owed his prosperity to a connection which indicated a filthiness of soul.

Such people as these gave their adherence with little hesitation to the deed which "saved society."

Some others, amongst those who composed this mosaic, possessed no political enthusiasm, and merely consented to figure in this list in order to keep their situations and their salaries; they were under the Empire what they had been before the Empire, neuters, and during the nineteen years of the reign, they continued to exercise their military, judicial, or administrative functions unobtrusively, surrounded with the right and proper respect due to inoffensive idiots.

Others were genuine politicians, belonging to that learned school which begins with Guizot, and does not finish with Parieu, grave physicians of social order, who reassure the frightened middle-classes, and who preserve dead things.

> *"Shall I lose my eye?" asked Messer Pancrace.*
> *"Not at all, my friend, I hold it in my hand."*

In this quasi Council of State there were a goodly number of men of the Police, a race of beings then held in esteem, Carlier, Piétri, Maupas, etc.

Shortly after the 2d of December under the title of Mixed Commissions, the police substituted itself for justice, drew up judgments, pronounced sentences, violated every law judicially without the regular magistracy interposing the slightest obstacle to this irregular magistracy: Justice allowed the police to do what it liked with the satisfied look of a team of horses which had just been relieved.

Some of the men inscribed on the list of this commission refused: Léon Faucher Goulard, Mortemart, Frédéric Granier, Marchand, Maillard Paravay, Beugnot. The newspapers received orders not to publish these refusals.

M. Beugnot inscribed on his card: "Count Beugnot, who does not belong to the Consultative Committee."

M. Joseph Périer went from corner to corner of the streets, pencil in hand, scratching out his name from all the placards, saying, "I shall take back my name wherever I find it."

General Baraguay d'Hilliers did not refuse. A brave soldier nevertheless; he had lost an arm in the Russian war. Later on, he has been Marshall of France; he deserved better than to have been created a Marshal by Louis Bonaparte. It did not appear likely that he would have come to this. During the last days of November General Baraguay d'Hilliers, seated in a large arm-chair before the high fireplace of the Conference Hall of the National Assembly, was warming himself; someone, one of his colleagues, he who is writing these lines, sat down near him on the other side of the fireplace. They did not speak to each other, one belonging to the Right, the other to the Left; but M. Piscatory came in, who belonged a little to the Right and a little to the Left. He addressed himself to Baraguay d'Hilliers: "Well, general, do you know what they are saying?"

"What?"

"That one of these days the President will shut the door in our faces."

General Baraguay d'Hilliers answered, and I heard the answer,— "If M. Bonaparte should close the door of the Assembly against us, France will fling it wide open again."

Louis Bonaparte at one moment thought of entitling this committee the "Executive Commission." "No," said Morny to him, "that would be to credit them with courage. They will willingly be supporters; they will not be proscribers."

General Rulhière was dismissed for having blamed the passive obedience of the army.

Let us here mention an incident. Some days after the 4th of December, Emmanuel Arago met M. Dupin, who was going up the Faubourg Saint Honoré.

"What!" said Arago, "are you going to the Elysée?"

M. Dupin answered, "I never go to disreputable houses."

Yet he went there.

M. Dupin, it may be remembered, was appointed Attorney-General at the Court of Cessation.

VII

The Other List

O pposite to the list of adherents should be placed the list of the proscribed. In this manner the two sides of the *coup d'état* can be seen at a glance.

Decree.

"Article I.—The ex-Representatives of the Assembly, whose names are found beneath, are expelled from French territory, from Algeria, and from the Colonies, for the sake of public safety:—

"Edmond Valentine.
Paul Racouchot.
Agricol Perdiguier.
Eugène Cholat.
Louis Latrade.
Michel Renaud.
Joseph Benoist (du Rhône).
Joseph Burgard.
Jean Colfavru.
Joseph Faure (du Rhone).
Pierre-Charles Gambon.
Charles Lagrange.
Martin Nadaud.
Barthélemy Terrier.
Victor Hugo.
Cassal.
Signard.
Viguier.
Esquiros.
Madier de Montjau.
Noël Parfait.
Emile Péan.

Charrassin.
Bandsept.
Savoye.
Joly.
Combier.
Boysset.
Duché.
Ennery.
Guilgot.
Hochstuhl.
Michot Boutet.
Baune.
Bertholon.
Schoelcher.
De Flotte.
Joigneaux.
Laboulaye.
Bruys.
Gaston Dussoubs.
Guiter.
Lafon.
Lamarque.

Pelletier.

Raspail.

Théodore Bac.

Bancel.

Belin (Drôme).

Bosse.

Bourzat.

Brive.

Chavoix.

Clément Dulac.

Dupout (de Bussac).

Pierre Lafranc.

Jules Leroux.

Francisque Maigne.

Malardier.

Mathieu (de la Drôme).

Millotte.

Roselli-Mollet.

Charras.

Saint-Ferreol.

Sommier.

Testelin (Nord).

"ARTICLE II.—In the event, contrary to the present decree, of one of the persons named in Article I. re-entering the prohibited limits, he may be transported for the sake of public safety.

"Given at the Palace of the Tuileries, at the Cabinet Council assembled, January 9th, 1852.

LOUIS BONAPARTE

DE MORNY, Minister of the Interior

There was besides a list of the "provisionally exiled," on which figured Edward Quinet, Victor Chauffour, General Laidet, Pascal Duprat, Versigny, Antony Thouret, Thiers, Girardin, and Rémusat. Four Representatives, Mathé, Greppo, Marc-Dufraisse, and Richardet, were added to the list of the "expelled." Representative Miot was reserved for the tortures of the casemates of Africa. Thus in addition to the massacres, the victory of the *coup d'état* was paid for by these figures: eighty-eight Representatives proscribed, one killed.

I usually dined at Brussels in a café, called the Café des Mille Colonnes, which was frequented by the exiles. On the 10th of January I had invited Michel de Bourges to lunch, and we were sitting at the same table. The waiter brought me the *Moniteur Français*; I glanced over it.

"Ah," said I, "here is the list of the proscribed." I ran my eye over it, and I said to Michel de Bourges, "I have a piece of bad news to tell you." Michel de Bourges turned pale. I added, "You are not on the list." His face brightened.

Michel de Bourges, so dauntless in the face of death, was faint-hearted in the face of exile.

VIII

DAVID D'ANGERS

Brutalities and ferocities were mingled together. The great sculptor, David d'Angers, was arrested in his own house, 16, Rue d'Assas; the Commissary of Police on entering, said to him,—

"Have you any arms in your house?"

"Yes," Said David, "for my defence."

And he added,—

"If I had to deal with civilized people."

"Where are these arms?" rejoined the Commissary. "Let us see them."

David showed him his studio full of masterpieces.

They placed him in a *fiacre*, and drove him to the station-house of the Prefecture of Police.

Although there was only space for 120 prisoners, there were 700 there. David was the twelfth in a dungeon intended for two. No light nor air. A narrow ventilation hole above their heads. A dreadful tub in a corner, common to all, covered but not closed by a wooden lid. At noon they brought them soup, a sort of warm and stinking water, David told me. They stood leaning against the wall, and trampled upon the mattresses which had been thrown on the floor, not having room to lie down on them. At length, however, they pressed so closely to each other, that they succeeded in lying down at full length. Their jailers had thrown them some blankets. Some of them slept. At day break the bolts creaked, the door was half-opened and the jailers cried out to them, "Get up!" They went into the adjoining corridor, the jailer took up the mattresses, threw a few buckets of water on the floor, wiped it up anyhow, replaced the mattresses on the damp stones, and said to them, "Go back again." They locked them up until the next morning. From time to time they brought in 100 new prisoners, and they fetched away 100 old ones (those who had been there for two or three days). What became of them?—At night the prisoners could hear from their dungeon the sound of explosions, and in the morning passers-by could see, as we have stated, pools of blood in the courtyard of the Prefecture.

The calling over of those who went out was conducted in alphabetical order.

One day they called David d'Angers. David took up his packet, and was getting ready to leave, when the governor of the jail, who seemed to be keeping watch over him, suddenly came up and said quickly, "Stay, M. David, stay."

One morning he saw Buchez, the ex-President of the Constituent Assembly, coming into his cell "Ah!" said David, "good! you have come to visit the prisoners?"—"I am a prisoner," said Buchez.

They wished to insist on David leaving for America. He refused. They contented themselves with Belgium. On the 19th December he reached Brussels. He came to see me, and said to me, "I am lodging at the Grand Monarque, 89, Rue des Fripiers."[1]

And he added laughing, "The Great Monarch—the King. The old clothesmen—the Royalists, '89. The Revolution." Chance occasionally furnishes some wit.

---

1. *Anglice*, "old clothes men."

IX

OUR LAST MEETING

On the 3d of December everything was coming in in our favor. On the 5th everything was receding from us. It was like a mighty sea which was going out. The tide had come in gloriously, it went out disastrously. Gloomy ebb and flow of the people.

And who was the power who said to this ocean, "Thou shalt go no farther?" Alas! a pigmy.

These hiding-places of the abyss are fathomless.

The abyss is afraid. Of what?

Of something deeper than itself. Of the Crime.

The people drew back. They drew back on the 5th; on the 6th they disappeared.

On the horizon there could be seen nothing but the beginning of a species of vast night.

This night has been the Empire.

We found ourselves on the 5th what we were on the 2d. Alone.

But we persevered. Our mental condition was this—desperate, yes; discouraged, no.

Items of bad news came to us as good news had come to us on the evening of the 3d, one after another. Aubry du Nord was at the Concièrgerie. Our dear and eloquent Crémieux was at Mazas. Louis Blanc, who, although banished, was coming to the assistance of France, and was bringing to us the great power of his name and of his mind, had been compelled, like Ledru Rollin, to halt before the catastrophe of the 4th. He had not been able to get beyond Tournay.

As for General Neumayer, he had not "marched upon Paris," but he had come there. For what purpose? To give in his submission.

We no longer possessed a refuge. No. 15, Rue Richelieu, was watched, No. 11, Rue Monthabor, had been denounced. We wandered about Paris, meeting each other here and there, and exchanging a few words in a whisper, not knowing where we should sleep, or whether we should get a meal; and amongst those heads which did not know what pillow they should have at night there was at least one upon which a price was set.

They accosted each other, and this is the sort of conversation they held:—

"What has became of So-and-So?"

"He is arrested."

"And So-and-So?"

"Dead."

"And So-and-So?"

"Disappeared."

We held, however, one other meeting. This was on the 6th, at the house of the Representative Raymond, in the Place de la Madeleine. Nearly all of us met there. I was enabled to shake the hands of Edgar Quinet, of Chauffour, of Clément Dulac, of Bancel, of Versigny, of Emile Péan, and I again met our energetic and honest host of the Rue Blanche, Coppens, and our courageous colleague, Pons Stande, whom we had lost sight of in the smoke of the battle. From the windows of the room where we were deliberating we could see the Place de la Madeleine and the Boulevards militarily occupied, and covered with a fierce and deep mass of soldiers drawn up in battle order, and which still seemed to face a possible combat. Charamaule came in.

He drew two pistols from his great cloak, placed them on the table, and said, "All is at an end. Nothing feasible and sensible remains, except a deed of rashness. I propose it. Are you of my opinion, Victor Hugo?"

"Yes," I answered.

I did not know what he was going to say, but I knew that he would only say that which was noble.

This was his proposition.

"We number," resumed he, "about fifty Representatives of the People, still standing and assembled together. We are all that remains of the National Assembly, of Universal Suffrage, of the Law, of Right. Tomorrow, where shall we be? We do not know. Scattered or dead. The hour of today is ours; this hour gone and past, we have nothing left but the shadow. The opportunity is unique. Let us profit by it."

He stopped, looked at us fixedly with his steadfast gaze, and resumed,—

"Let us take the advantage of this chance of being alive and the good fortune of being together. The group which is here is the whole of the Republic. Well, then; let us offer in our persons all the Republic to the army, and let us make the army fall back before the Republic, and Might fall back before Right. In that supreme moment one of the two must tremble, Might or Right, and if Right does not tremble Might will tremble. If we do not tremble the soldiers will tremble. Let us march upon the Crime. If the Law advances, the Crime will draw back. In either case we shall have done our duty. Living, we shall be preservers, dead, we shall be heroes. This is what I propose."

A profound silence ensued.

"Let us put on our sashes, and let us all go down in a procession, two by two, into the Place de la Madeleine. You can see that Colonel before that large flight of steps, with his regiment in battle array; we will go to him, and there, before his soldiers, I will summon him to come over to the side of duty, and to restore his regiment to the Republic. If he refuses. . ."

Charamaule took his two pistols in his hands.

". . . I will blow out his brains."

"Charamaule," said I, "I will be by your side."

"I knew that well," Charamaule said to me.

He added,—

"This explosion will awaken the people."

"But," several cried out, "suppose it does not awaken them?"

"We shall die."

"I am on your side," said I to him.

We each pressed the other's hand. But objections burst forth.

No one trembled, but all criticised the proposal. Would it not be madness? And useless madness? Would it not be to play the last card of the Republic without any possible chance of success? What good fortune for Bonaparte! To crush with one blow all that remained of those who were resisting and of those who were combating! To finish with them once for all! We were beaten, granted, but was it necessary to add annihilation to defeat? No possible chance of success. The brains of an army cannot be blown out. To do what Charamaule advised would be to open the tomb, nothing more. It would be a magnificent suicide, but it would be a suicide. Under certain circumstances it is selfish to be merely a hero. A man accomplishes it at once, he becomes illustrious, he enters into history, all that is very easy. He leaves to others behind him the laborious work of a long protest, the immovable resistance of the exile, the bitter, hard life of the conquered who continues to combat the victory. Some degree of patience forms a part of politics. To know how to await revenge is sometimes more difficult than to hurry on its catastrophe. There are two kinds of courage—bravery and perseverance;

the first belongs to the soldier, the second belongs to the citizen. A haphazard end, however dauntless, does not suffice. To extricate oneself from the difficulty by death, it is only too easily done: what is required, what is the reverse of easy, is to extricate one's country from the difficulty. No, said those high-minded men, who opposed Charamaule and myself, this today which you propose to us is the suppression of tomorrow; take care, there is a certain amount of desertion in suicide. . .

The word "desertion" grievously wounded Charamaule. "Very well," said he, "I abandon the idea."

This scene was exceedingly grand, and Quinet later on, when in exile, spoke to me of it with deep emotion.

We separated. We did not meet again.

I wandered about the streets. Where should I sleep? That was the question. I thought that No. 19, Rue Richelieu would probably be as much watched as No. 15. But the night was cold, and I decided at all hazards to re-enter this refuge, although perhaps a hazardous one. I was right to trust myself to it. I supped on a morsel of bread, and I passed a very goodnight. The next morning at daybreak on waking I thought of the duties which awaited me. I thought that I was abut to go out, and that I should probably not come back to the room; I took a little bread which remained, and I crumbled it on the window-sill for the birds.

X

DUTY CAN HAVE TWO ASPECTS

Had it been in the power of the Left at any moment to prevent the *coup d'état*?

We do not think so.

Nevertheless here is a fact which we believe we ought not to pass by in silence. On the 16th November, 1851, I was in my study at home at 37, Rue de la Tour d'Auvergne; it was about midnight. I was working. My servant opened the door.

"Will you see M. ——, sir?"

And he mentioned a name.

"Yes," I said.

Someone came in.

I shall only speak reservedly of this eminent and distinguished man. Let it suffice to state that he had the right to say when mentioning the Bonapartes "my family."

It is known that the Bonaparte family is divided into two branches, the Imperial family and the private family. The Imperial family had the tradition of Napoleon, the private family had the tradition of Lucien: a shade of difference which, however, had no reality about it.

My midnight visitor took the other corner of the fireplace.

He began by speaking to me of the memoirs of a very highminded and virtuous woman, the Princess ——, his mother, the manuscript of which he had confided to me, asking my advice as to the utility or the suitability of their publication; this manuscript, besides being full of interest, possessed for me a special charm, because the handwriting of the Princess resembled my mother's handwriting. My visitor, to whom I gave it back, turned over the leaves for a few moments, and then suddenly interrupting himself, he turned to me and said,—

"The Republic is lost."

I answered,—

"Almost."

He resumed,—

"Unless you save it."

"I?"

"You."

"How so?"

"Listen to me."

Then he set forth with that clearness, complicated at times with paradoxes, which is one of the resources of his remarkable mind, the situation, at the same time desperate and strong, in which we were placed.

This situation, which moreover I realized as well as he himself, was this:—

The Right of the Assembly was composed of about 400 members, and the Left of about 180. The four hundred of the majority belonged by thirds to three parties, the Legitimist party, the Orleanist party, the Bonapartist party, and in a body to the Clerical party. The 180 of the minority belonged to the Republic. The Right mistrusted the Left, and had taken a precaution against the minority.

A Vigilance Committee, composed of sixteen members of the Right, charged with impressing unity upon this trinity of parties, and charged with the task of carefully watching the Left, such was this precaution. The Left at first had confined itself to irony, and borrowing from me a word to which people then attached, though wrongly, the idea of decrepitude, had called the sixteen Commissioners the "Burgraves." The irony subsequently turning into suspicion, the Left had on its side ended by creating a committee of sixteen members to direct the Left, and observe the Right; these the Right had hastened to name the "Red Burgraves." A harmless rejoinder. The result was that the Right watched the Left, and that the Left watched the Right, but that no one watched Bonaparte. They were two flocks of sheep so distrustful of one another that they forgot the wolf. During that time, in his den at the Elysée, Bonaparte was working. He was busily employing the time which the Assembly, the majority and the minority, was losing in mistrusting itself. As people feel the loosening of the avalanche, so they felt the catastrophe tottering in the gloom. They kept watch upon the enemy, but they did not turn their attention in the true direction. To know where to fix one's mistrust is the secret of a great politician. The Assembly of 1851 did not possess this shrewd certainty of eyesight, their perspective was bad, each saw the future after his own fashion, and a sort of political short-sightedness blinded the Left as well as the Right; they were afraid, but not where fear was advisable; they were in the presence of a mystery, they had an ambuscade before them, but they sought it where it did not exist, and they did not perceive where it really lay. Thus it was that these two flocks of sheep, the majority, and the minority faced each other affrightedly, and while the leaders on one side and the guides on the other, grave and attentive, asked themselves anxiously what could be the mewing of the grumbling, of the Left on the one side, of the bleatings of the Right on the other, they ran the risk of suddenly feeling the four claws of the *coup d'état* fastened in their shoulders.

My visitor said to me,—

"You are one of the Sixteen!"

"Yes," answered I, smiling; "a 'Red Burgrave.'"

"Like me, a 'Red Prince.'"

And his smile responded to mine.

He resumed,—

"You have full powers?"

"Yes. Like the others."

And I added,—

"Not more than the others. The Left has no leaders."

He continued,—

"Yon, the Commissary of Police, is a Republican?'

"Yes."

"He would obey an order signed by you?"

"Possibly."

"*I* say, without doubt."

He looked at me fixedly.

"Well, then, have the President arrested this night."

It was now my turn to look at him.

"What do you mean?"

"What I say."

I ought to state that his language was frank, resolute, and self-convinced, and that during the whole of this conversation, and now, and always, it has given me the impression of honesty.

"Arrest the President!" I cried.

Then he set forth that this extraordinary enterprise was an easy matter; that the Army was undecided; that in the Army the African Generals counterpoised the President; that the National Guard favored the Assembly, and in the Assembly the Left; that Colonel Forestier answered for the 8th Legion; Colonel Gressier for the 6th, and Colonel Howyne for the 5th; that at the order of the Sixteen of the Left there would be an immediate taking up of arms; that my signature would suffice; that, nevertheless, if I preferred to call together the Committee, in Secret Session, we could wait till the next day; that on the order from the Sixteen, a battalion would march upon the Elysée; that the Elysée apprehended nothing, thought only of offensive, and not of defensive measures, and accordingly would be taken by surprise; that the soldiers would not resist the National Guard; that the thing would be done without striking a blow; that Vincennes would open and close while Paris slept; that the President would finish his night there, and that France, on awakening, would learn the twofold good tidings: that Bonaparte was out of the fight, and France out of danger.

He added,—

"You can count on two Generals: Neumayer at Lyons, and Lawoëstyne at Paris."

He got up and leaned against the chimney-piece; I can still see him there, standing thoughtfully; and he continued:

"I do not feel myself strong enough to begin exile all over again, but I feel the wish to save my family and my country."

He probably thought he noticed a movement of surprise in me, for he accentuated and italicized these words.

"I will explain myself. Yes; I wish to save my family and my country. I bear the name of Napoleon; but as you know without fanaticism. I am a Bonaparte, but not a Bonapartist. I respect the name, but I judge it. It already has one stain. The Eighteenth Brumaire. Is it about to have another? The old stain disappeared beneath the glory; Austerlitz covered Brumaire. Napoleon was absolved by his genius. The people admired him so greatly that it forgave him. Napoleon is upon the column, there is an end of it, let them leave him there in peace. Let them not resuscitate him through his bad qualities. Let them not compel France to remember too much. This glory of Napoleon is vulnerable. It has a wound; closed, I admit. Do not let them reopen it. Whatever apologists may say and do, it is none the less true that by the Eighteenth of Brumaire Napoleon struck himself a first blow."

"In truth," said I, "it is ever against ourselves that we commit a crime."

"Well, then," he continued, "his glory has survived a first blow, a second will kill it. I do not wish it. I hate the first Eighteenth Brumaire; I fear the second. I wish to prevent it."

He paused again, and continued,—

"That is why I have come to you tonight. I wish to succor this great wounded glory. By the advice which I am giving you, if you can carry it out, if the Left carries it out, I save the first Napoleon; for if a second crime is superposed upon his glory, this glory would disappear. Yes, this name would founder, and history would no longer own it. I will go farther and complete my idea. I also save the present Napoleon, for he who as yet has no glory will only have come. I save his memory from an eternal pillory. Therefore, arrest him."

He was truly and deeply moved. He resumed,—

"As to the Republic, the arrest of Louis Bonaparte is deliverance for her. I am right, therefore, in saying that by what I am proposing to you I am saving my family and my country."

"But," I said to him, "what you propose to me is a *coup d'état*."

"Do you think so?"

"Without doubt. We are the minority, and we should commit an act which belongs to the majority. We are a part of the Assembly. We should be acting as though we were the entire Assembly. We who condemn all usurpation should ourselves become usurpers. We should put our hands upon a functionary whom the Assembly alone has the right of arresting. We, the defenders of the Constitution, we should break the Constitution. We, the men of the Law, we should violate the Law. It is a *coup d'état*."

"Yes, but a *coup d'état* for a good purpose."

"Evil committed for a good purpose remains evil."

"Even when it succeeds?"

"Above all when it succeeds."

"Why?"

"Because it then becomes an example."

"You do not then approve of the Eighteenth Fructidor?"

"No."

"But Eighteenth Fructidors prevent Eighteenth Brumaires."

"No. They prepare the way for them."

"But reasons of State exist?"

"No. What exists is the Law."

"The Eighteenth Fructidor has been accepted by exceedingly honest minds."

"I know that."

"Blanqui is in its favor, with Michelet."

"I am against it, with Barbès."

From the moral aspect I passed to the practical aspect.

"This said," resumed I, "let us examine your plan."

This plan bristled with difficulties. I pointed them out to him.

"Count on the National Guard! Why, General Lawoëstyne had not yet got command of it. Count on the Army? Why, General Neumayer was at Lyons, and not at Paris. Would he march to the assistance of the Assembly? What did we know about this? As for Lawoëstyne, was he not double-faced? Were they sure of him? Call to arms the 8th Legion? Forestier was no longer Colonel. The 5th and 6th? But Gressier and Howyne were only lieutenant-colonels, would these legions follow them? Order the Commissary Yon? But would he obey the Left alone? He was the agent of the Assembly, and consequently of the majority, but not of the minority. These were so many questions. But these questions, supposing them answered, and answered in the sense of success, was success itself the question? The question is never Success, it is always Right. But here, even if we had obtained success, we should not have Right. In order to arrest the President an order of the Assembly was necessary; we should replace the order of the Assembly by an act of violence of the Left. A scaling and a burglary; an assault by scaling-ladders on the constituted authority, a burglary on the Law. Now let us suppose resistance; we should shed blood. The Law violated leads to the shedding of blood. What is all this? It is a crime."

"No, indeed," he exclaimed, "it is the *salus populi*."

And he added,—

"*Suprema Lex*."

"Not for me," I said.

I continued,—

"I would not kill a child to save a people."

"Cato did so."

"Jesus did not do so."

And I added,—

"You have on your side all ancient history, you are acting according to the uprightness of the Greeks, and according to the uprightness of the Romans; for me, I am acting according to the uprightness of Humanity. The new horizon is of wider range than the old."

There was a pause. He broke it.

"Then he will be the one to attack!"

"Let it be so."

"You are about to engage in a battle which is almost lost beforehand."

"I fear so."

"And this unequal combat can only end for you, Victor Hugo, in death or exile."

"I believe it."

"Death is the affair of a moment, but exile is long."

"It is a habit to be learned."

 He continued,—

"You will not only be proscribed. You will be calumniated."

"It is a habit already learned."

 He continued,—

"Do you know what they are saying already?"

"What?"

"They say that you are irritated against him because he has refused to make you a Minister."

"Why you know yourself that—"

"I know that it is just the reverse. It is he who has asked you, and it is you who have refused."

"Well, then—"

"They lie."

"What does it matter?"

 He exclaimed,—

"Thus, you will have caused the Bonapartes to re-enter France, and you will be banished from France by a Bonaparte!"[1]

"Who knows," said I, "if I have not committed a fault? This injustice is perhaps a justice."

 We were both silent. He resumed,—

"Could you bear exile?"

"I will try."

"Could you live without Paris?"

"I should have the ocean."

"You would then go to the seaside?"

"I think so."

"It is sad."

"It is grand."

 There was another pause. He broke it.

"You do not know what exile is. I do know it. It is terrible. Assuredly, I would not begin it again. Death is a bourne whence no one comes back, exile is a place whither no one returns."

"If necessary," I said to him, "I will go, and I will return to it."

"Better die. To quit life is nothing, but to quit one's country—"

---

1. 14th of June, 1847. Chamber of Peers. See the work "Avant l'Exile."

"Alas!" said I, "that is everything."

"Well, then, why accept exile when it is in your power to avoid it? What do you place above your country?"

"Conscience."

This answer made him thoughtful. However, he resumed.

"But on reflection your conscience will approve of what you will have done."

"No."

"Why?"

"I have told you. Because my conscience is so constituted that it puts nothing above itself. I feel it upon me as the headland can feel the lighthouse which is upon it. All life is an abyss, and conscience illuminates it around me."

"And I also," he exclaimed—and I affirm that nothing could be more sincere or more loyal than his tone—"and I also feel and see my conscience. It approves of what I am doing. I appear to be betraying Louis; but I am really doing him a service. To save him from a crime is to save him. I have tried every means. There only remains this one, to arrest him. In coming to you, in acting as I do, I conspire at the same time against him and for him, against his power, and for his honor. What I am doing is right."

"It is true," I said to him. "You have a generous and a lofty aim."

And I resumed,—

"But our two duties are different. I could not hinder Louis Bonaparte from committing a crime unless I committed one myself. I wish neither for an Eighteenth Brumaire for him, nor for an Eighteenth Fructidor for myself. I would rather be proscribed than be a proscriber. I have the choice between two crimes, my crime and the crime of Louis Bonaparte. I will not choose my crime."

"But then you will have to endure his."

"I would rather endure a crime than commit one."

He remained thoughtful, and said to me,—

"Let it be so."

And he added,—

"Perhaps we are both in the right."

"I think so," I said.

And I pressed his hand.

He took his mother's manuscript and went away. It was three o'clock in the morning. The conversation had lasted more than two hours. I did not go to bed until I had written it out.

XI

The Combat Finished, The Ordeal Begins

I did not know where to go.

On the afternoon of the 7th I determined to go back once more to 19, Rue Richelieu. Under the gateway someone seized my arm. It was Madame D. She was waiting for me.

"Do not go in," she said to me.

"Am I discovered?"

"Yes."

"And taken."

"No."

She added,—

"Come."

We crossed the courtyard, and we went out by a backdoor into the Rue Fontaine Molière; we reached the square of the Palais Royal. The *fiacres* were standing there as usual. We got into the first we came to.

"Where are we to go?" asked the driver.

She looked at me.

I answered,—

"I do not know."

"I know," she said.

Women always know where Providence lies.

An hour later I was in safety.

From the 4th, everyday which passed by consolidated the *coup d'état*. Our defeat was complete, and we felt ourselves abandoned. Paris was like a forest in which Louis Bonaparte was making a *battue* of the Representatives; the wild beast was hunting down the sportsmen. We heard the indistinct baying of Maupas behind us. We were compelled to disperse. The pursuit was energetic. We entered into the second phase of duty—the catastrophe accepted and submitted to. The vanquished became the proscribed. Each one of us had his own concluding adventures. Mine was what it should have been—exile; death having missed me. I am not going to relate it here, this book is not my biography, and I ought not to divert to myself any of the attention which it may excite. Besides, what concerns me personally is told in a narrative which is one of the testaments of exile.[1]

Notwithstanding the relentless pursuit which was directed against us, I did not think it my duty to leave Paris as long as a glimmer of hope remained, and as long as an awakening of the people seemed possible. Malarmet sent me word in my refuge that a movement would take place at Belleville on Tuesday the 9th. I waited until the 12th. Nothing stirred. The people were indeed dead. Happily such deaths as these, like the deaths of the gods, are only for a time.

I had a last interview with Jules Favre and Michel de Bourges at Madame Didier's in the Rue de la Ville-Lévêque. It was at night. Bastide came there. This brave man said to me,—

"You are about to leave Paris; for myself, I remain here. Take me as your lieutenant. Direct me from the depths of your exile. Make use of me as an arm which you have in France."

"I will make use of you as of a heart," I said to him.

On the 14th, amidst the adventures which my son Charles relates in his book, I succeeded in reaching Brussels.

The vanquished are like cinders, Destiny blows upon them and disperses them. There was a gloomy vanishing of all the combatants for Right and for Law. A tragical disappearance.

---

1. "Les Hommes de l'Exile," by Charles Hugo.

XII

The Exiled

The Crime having succeeded, all hastened to join it. To persist was possible, to resist was not possible. The situation became more and more desperate. One would have said that an enormous wall was rising upon the horizon ready to close in. The outlet: Exile.

The great souls, the glories of the people, emigrated. Thus there was seen this dismal sight—France driven out from France.

But what the Present appears to lose, the Future gains, the hand which scatters is also the hand which sows.

The Representatives of the Left, surrounded, tracked, pursued, hunted down, wandered for several days from refuge to refuge. Those who escaped found great difficulty in leaving Paris and France. Madier de Montjan had very black and thick eyebrows, he shaved off half of them, cut his hair, and let his beard grow. Yvan, Pelletier, Gindrier, and Doutre shaved off their moustaches and beards. Versigny reached Brussels on the 14th with a passport in the name of Morin. Schoelcher dressed himself up as a priest. This costume became him admirably, and suited his austere countenance and grave voice. A worthy priest helped him to disguise himself, and lent him his cassock and his band, made him shave off his whiskers a few days previously, so that he should not be betrayed by the white trace of his freshly-cut beard, gave him his own passport, and only left him at the railway station.[1]

De Flotte disguised himself as a servant, and in this manner succeeded in crossing the frontier at Mouscron. From there he reached Ghent, and thence Brussels.

On the night of December 26th, I had returned to the little room, without a fire, which I occupied (No. 9) on the second story of the Hôtel de la Porte-Verte; it was midnight; I had just gone to bed and was falling asleep, when a knock sounded at my door. I awoke. I always left the key outside. "Come in," I said. A chambermaid entered with a light, and brought two men whom I did not know. One was a lawyer, of

---

1. See "Les Hommes de l'Exile."

Ghent, M. ——; the other was De Flotte. He took my two hands and pressed them tenderly. "What," I said to him, "is it you?"

At the Assembly De Flotte, with his prominent and thoughtful brow, his deep-set eyes, his close-shorn head, and his long beard, slightly turned back, looked like a creation of Sebastian del Piombo wandering out of his picture of the "Raising of Lazarus"; and I had before my eyes a short young man, thin and pallid, with spectacles. But what he had not been able to change, and what I recognized immediately, was the great heart, the lofty mind, the energetic character, the dauntless courage; and if I did not recognize him by his features, I recognized him by the grasp of his hand.

Edgar Quinet was brought away on the 10th by a noble-hearted Wallachian woman, Princess Cantacuzène, who undertook to conduct him to the frontier, and who kept her word. It was a troublesome task. Quinet had a foreign passport in the name of Grubesko, he was to personate a Wallachian, and it was arranged that he should not know how to speak French, he who writes it as a master. The journey was perilous. They ask for passports along all the line, beginning at the terminus. At Amiens they were particularly suspicious. But at Lille the danger was great. The gendarmes went from carriage to carriage; entered them lantern in hand, and compared the written descriptions of the travellers with their personal appearance. Several who appeared to be suspicious characters were arrested, and were immediately thrown into prison. Edgar Quinet, seated by the side of Madame Cantacuzène awaited the turn of his carriage. At length it came. Madame Cantacuzène leaned quickly forward towards the gendarmes, and hastened to present her passport, but the corporal waved back Madame Cantacuzène's passport saying, "It is useless, Madame. We have nothing to do with women's passports," and he asked Quinet abruptly, "Your papers?" Quinet held out his passport unfolded. The gendarmes said to him, "Come out of the carriage, so that we can compare your description." It happened, however, that the Wallachian passport contained no description. The corporal frowned, and said to his subordinates, "An irregular passport! Go and fetch the Commissary."

All seemed lost, but Madame Cantacuzène began to speak to Quinet in the most Wallachian words in the world, with incredible assurance and volubility, so much so that the gendarme, convinced that he had to deal with all Wallachia in person, and seeing the train ready to start, returned the passport to Quinet, saying to him, "There! be off with you!"—a few hours afterwards Edgar Quinet was in Belgium.

Arnauld de l'Ariège also had his adventures. He was a marked man, he had to hide himself. Arnauld being a Catholic, Madame Arnauld went to the priest; the Abbé Deguerry slipped out of the way, the Abbé Maret consented to conceal him; the Abbé Maret was honest and good. Arnauld d'Ariège remained hidden for a fortnight at the house of this worthy priest. He wrote from the Abbé Maret's a letter to the Archbishop of Paris, urging him to refuse the Pantheon, which a decree of Louis Bonaparte took away from France and gave to Rome. This letter angered the Archbishop. Arnauld, proscribed, reached Brussels, and there, at the age of eighteen months, died the "little Red," who on the 3d of December had carried the workman's letter to the Archbishop— an angel sent by God to the priest who had not understood the angel, and who no longer knew God.

In this medley of incidents and adventures each one had his drama. Cournet's drama was strange and terrible.

Cournet, it may be remembered, had been a naval officer. He was one of those men of a prompt, decisive character, who magnetized other men, and who on certain extraordinary occasions send an electric shock through a multitude. He possessed an imposing air, broad shoulders, brawny arms, powerful fists, a tall stature, all of which give confidence to the masses, and the intelligent expression which gives confidence to the thinkers. You saw him pass, and you recognized strength; you heard him speak, and you felt the will, which is more than strength. When quite a youth he had served in the navy. He combined in himself in a certain degree—and it is this which made this energetic man, when well directed and well employed, a means of enthusiasm and a support—he combined the popular fire and the military coolness. He was one of those natures created for the hurricane and for the crowd, who have begun their study of the people by their study of the ocean, and who are at their ease in revolutions as in tempests. As we have narrated, he took an important part in the combat. He had been dauntless and indefatigable, he was one of those who could yet rouse it to life. From Wednesday afternoon several police agents were charged to seek him everywhere, to arrest him wherever they might find him, and to take him to the Prefecture of the Police, where orders had been given to shoot him immediately.

Cournet, however, with his habitual daring, came and went freely in order to carry on the lawful resistance, even in the quarters occupied by the troops, shaving off his moustaches as his sole precaution.

On the Thursday afternoon he was on the boulevards at a few paces from a regiment of cavalry drawn up in order. He was quietly conversing with two of his comrades of the fight, Huy and Lorrain. Suddenly, he perceives himself and his companions surrounded by a company of *sergents de ville*; a man touches his arm and says to him, "You are Cournet; I arrest you."

"Bah!" answers Cournet; "My name is Lépine."

The man resumes,—

"You are Cournet. Do not you recognize me? Well, then, I recognize you; I have been, like you, a member of the Socialist Electoral Committee."

Cournet looks him in the face, and finds this countenance in his memory. The man was right. He had, in fact, formed part of the gathering in the Rue Saint Spire. The police spy resumed, laughing,—

"I nominated Eugène Sue with you."

It was useless to deny it, and the moment was not favorable for resistance. There were on the spot, as we have said, twenty *sergents de ville* and a regiment of Dragoons.

"I will follow you," said Cournet.

A *fiacre* was called up.

"While I am about it," said the police spy, "come in all three of you."

He made Huy and Lorrain get in with Cournet, placed them on the front seat, and seated himself on the back seat by Cournet, and then shouted to the driver,—

"To the Prefecture!"

The *sergents de ville* surrounded the *fiacre*. But whether by chance or through confidence, or in the haste to obtain the payment for his capture, the man who had arrested Cournet shouted to the coachman, "Look sharp, look sharp!" and the *fiacre* went off at a gallop.

In the meantime Cournet was well aware that on arriving he would be shot in the very courtyard of the Prefecture. He had resolved not to go there.

At a turning in the Rue St Antoine he glanced behind, and noticed that the *sergents de ville* only followed the *fiacre* at a considerable distance.

Not one of the four men which the *fiacre* was bearing away had as yet opened their lips.

Cournet threw a meaning look at his two companions seated in front of him, as much as to say, "We are three; let us take advantage of this to escape." Both answered by an imperceptible movement of the eyes, which pointed out the street full of passers-by, and which said, "No."

A few moments afterwards the *fiacre* emerged from the Rue St. Antoine, and entered the Rue de Fourcy. The Rue de Fourcy is usually deserted, no one was passing down it at that moment.

Cournet turned suddenly to the police spy, and asked him,—

"Have you a warrant for my arrest?"

"No; but I have my card."

And he drew his police agent's card out of his pocket, and showed it to Cournet. Then the following dialogue ensued between these two men,—

"This is not regular."

"What does that matter to me?"

"You have no right to arrest me."

"All the same, I arrest you."

"Look here; is it money that you want? Do you wish for any? I have some with me; let me escape."

"A gold nugget as big as your head would not tempt me. You are my finest capture, Citizen Cournet."

"Where are you taking me to?"

"To the Prefecture."

"They will shoot me there?"

"Possibly."

"And my two comrades?"

"I do not say 'No.'"

"I will not go."

"You will go, nevertheless."

"I tell you I will not go," exclaimed Cournet.

And with a movement, unexpected as a flash of lightning, he seized the police spy by the throat.

The police agent could not utter a cry, he struggled: a hand of bronze clutched him.

His tongue protruded from his mouth, his eyes became hideous, and started from their sockets. Suddenly his head sank down, and reddish froth rose from his throat to his lips. He was dead.

Huy and Lorrain, motionless, and as though themselves thunderstruck, gazed at this gloomy deed.

They did not utter a word. They did not move a limb. The *fiacre* was still driving on.

"Open the door!" Cournet cried to them.

They did not stir, they seemed to have become stone.

Cournet, whose thumb was closely pressed in the neck of the wretched police spy, tried to open the door with his left hand, but he did not succeed, he felt that he could only do it with his right hand, and he was obliged to loose his hold of the man. The man fell face forwards, and sank down on his knees.

Cournet opened the door.

"Off with you!" he said to them.

Huy and Lorrain jumped into the street and fled at the top of their speed.

The coachman had noticed nothing.

Cournet let them get away, and then, pulling the check string, stopped the *fiacre*, got down leisurely, reclosed the door, quietly took forty sous from his purse, gave them to the coachman, who had not left his seat, and said to him, "Drive on."

He plunged into Paris. In the Place des Victoires he met the ex-Constituent Isidore Buvignier, his friend, who about six weeks previously had come out of the Madelonnettes, where he had been confined for the matter of the *Solidarité Républicaine*. Buvignier was one of the noteworthy figures on the high benches of the Left; fair, close-shaven, with a stern glance, he made one think of the English Roundheads, and he had the bearing rather of a Cromwellian Puritan than of a Dantonist Man of the Mountain. Cournet told his adventure, the extremity had been terrible.

Buvignier shook his head.

"You have killed a man," he said.

In "Marie Tudor," I have made Fabiani answer under similar circumstances,—

"No, a Jew."

Cournet, who probably had not read "Marie Tudor," answered,—

"No, a police spy."

Then he resumed,—

"I have killed a police spy to save three men, one of whom was myself."

Cournet was right. They were in the midst of the combat, they were taking him to be shot; the spy who had arrested him was, properly speaking, an assassin, and assuredly it was a case of legitimate defence.

I add that this wretch, a democrat for the people, a spy for the police, was a twofold traitor. Moreover, the police spy was the jackal of the *coup d'état*, while Cournet was the combatant for the Law.

"You must conceal yourself," said Buvignier; "come to Juvisy."

Buvignier had a little refuge at Juvisy, which is on the road to Corbeil. He was known and loved there; Cournet and he reached there that evening.

But they had hardly arrived when some peasants said to Buvignier, "The police have already been here to arrest you, and are coming again tonight."

It was necessary to go back.

Cournet, more in danger than ever, hunted, wandering, pursued, hid himself in Paris with considerable difficulty. He remained there till the 16th. He had no means of procuring himself a passport. At length, on the 16th, some friends of his on the Northern Railway obtained for him a special passport, worded as follows:—

"Allow M. ——, an Inspector on the service of the Company, to pass."

He decided to leave the next day, and take the day train, thinking, perhaps rightly, that the night train would be more closely watched.

On the 17th, at daybreak, favored by the dim dawn, he glided from street to street, to the Northern Railway Station. His tall stature was a special source of danger. He, however, reached the station in safety. The stokers placed him with them on the tender of the engine of the train, which was about to start. He only had the clothes which he had worn since the 2d; no clean linen, no trunk, a little money.

In December, the day breaks late and the night closes in early, which is favorable to proscribed persons.

He reached the frontier at night without hindrance. At Neuvéglise he was in Belgium; he believed himself in safety. When asked for his papers he caused himself to be taken before the Burgomaster, and said to him, "I am a political refugee."

The Burgomaster, a Belgian but a Bonapartist—this breed is to be found—had him at once reconducted to the frontier by the gendarmes, who were ordered to hand him over to the French authorities.

Cournet gave himself up for lost.

The Belgian gendarmes took him to Armentières. If they had asked for the Mayor it would have been all at an end with Cournet, but they asked for the Inspector of Customs.

A glimmer of hope dawned upon Cournet.

He accosted the Inspector of Customs with his head erect, and shook hands with him.

The Belgian gendarmes had not yet released him.

"Now, sir," said Cournet to the Custom House officer, "you are an Inspector of Customs, I am an Inspector of Railways. Inspectors do not eat inspectors. The deuce take it! Some worthy Belgians have taken fright and sent me to you between four gendarmes. Why, I know not. I am sent by the Northern Company to relay the ballast of a bridge somewhere about here which is not firm. I come to ask you to allow me to continue my road. Here is my pass."

He presented the pass to the Custom House officer, the Custom House officer read it, found it according to due form, and said to Cournet,—

"Mr. Inspector, you are free."

Cournet, delivered from the Belgian gendarmes by French authority, hastened to the railway station. He had friends there.

"Quick," he said, "it is dark, but it does not matter, it is even all the better. Find me someone who has been a smuggler, and who will help me to pass the frontier."

They brought him a small lad of eighteen; fair-haired, ruddy, hardy, a Walloon[2] and who spoke French.

"What is your name?" said Cournet.

"Henry."

"You look like a girl."

"Nevertheless I am a man."

"Is it you who undertake to guide me?"

"Yes."

"You have been a smuggler?"

"I am one still."

"Do you know the roads?"

"No. I have nothing to do with the roads."

"What do you know then?"

"I know the passes."

"There are two Custom House lines."

"I know that well."

---

2. The name given to a population belonging to the Romanic family, and more particularly to those of French descent, who occupy the region along the frontiers of the German-speaking territory in the South Netherlands from Dunkirk to Malmedy in Rhenish Prussia.

"Will you pass me across them?"

"Without doubt."

"Then you are not afraid of the Custom House officers?"

"I'm afraid of the dogs."

"In that case," said Cournet, "we will take sticks."

They accordingly armed themselves with big sticks. Cournet gave fifty francs to Henry, and promised him fifty more when they should have crossed the second Custom House line.

"That is to say, at four o'clock in the morning," said Henry.

It was midnight.

They set out on their way.

What Henry called the "passes" another would have called the "hindrances." They were a succession of pitfalls and quagmires. It had been raining, and all the holes were pools of water.

An indescribable footpath wound through an inextricable labyrinth, sometimes as thorny as a heath, sometimes as miry as a marsh.

The night was very dark.

From time to time, far away in the darkness, they could hear a dog bark. The smuggler then made bends or zigzags, turned sharply to the right or to the left, and sometimes retraced his steps.

Cournet, jumping hedges, striding over ditches, stumbling at every moment, slipping into sloughs, laying hold of briers, with his clothes in rags, his hands bleeding, dying with hunger, battered about, wearied, worn out, almost exhausted, followed his guide gaily.

At every minute he made a false step; he fell into every bog, and got up covered with mud. At length he fell into a pond. It was several feet deep. This washed him.

"Bravo!" he said. "I am very clean, but I am very cold."

At four o'clock in the morning, as Henry had promised him, they reached Messine, a Belgian village. The two Custom House lines had been cleared. Cournet had nothing more to fear, either from the Custom House nor from the *coup d'état*, neither from men nor from dogs.

He gave Henry the second fifty francs, and continued his journey on foot, trusting somewhat to chance.

It was not until towards evening that he reached a railway station. He got into a train, and at nightfall he arrived at the Southern Railway Station at Brussels.

He had left Paris on the preceding morning, had not slept an hour, had been walking all night, and had eaten nothing. On searching in his pocket he missed his pocket book, but found a crust of bread. He was more delighted at the discovery of the crust than grieved at the loss of his pocket-book. He carried his money in a waistband; the pocket-book, which had probably disappeared in the pond, contained his letters, and amongst others an exceedingly useful letter of introduction from his friend M. Ernest Koechlin, to the Representatives Guilgot and Carlos Forel, who at that moment were refugees at Brussels, and lodged at the Hôtel de Brabant.

On leaving the railway station he threw himself into a cab, and said to the coachman,—

"Hôtel de Brabant."

He heard a voice repeat, "Hôtel de Brabant." He put out his head and saw a man writing something in a notebook with a pencil by the light of a street-lamp.

It was probably some police agent.

Without a passport, without letters, without papers, he was afraid of being arrested in the night, and he was longing for a good sleep. A good bed tonight, he thought, and tomorrow the Deluge! At the Hôtel de Brabant he paid the coachman, but did not go into the hotel. Moreover, he would have asked in vain for the Representatives Forel and Guilgot; both were there under false names.

He took to wandering about the streets. It was eleven o'clock at night, and for a long time he had begun to feel utterly worn out.

At length he saw a lighted lamp with the inscription "Hôtel de la Monnaie."

He walked in.

The landlord came up, and looked at him somewhat askance.

He then thought of looking at himself.

His unshaven beard, his disordered hair, his cap soiled with mud, his blood-stained hands, his clothes in rags, he looked horrible.

He took a double louis out of his waistband, and put it on the table of the parlor, which he had entered and said to the landlord,—

"In truth, sir, I am not a thief, I am a proscript; money is now my only passport. I have just come from Paris, I wish to eat first and sleep afterwards."

The landlord was touched, took the double louis, and gave him bed and supper.

Next day, while he was still sleeping, the landlord came into his room, woke him gently, and said to him,—

"Now, sir, if I were you, I should go and see Baron Hody."

"Who and what is Baron Hody?" asked Cournet, half asleep.

The landlord explained to him who Baron Hody was. When I had occasion to ask the same question as Cournet, I received from three inhabitants of Brussels the three answers as follows:—

"He is a dog."

"He is a polecat."

"He is a hyena."

There is probably some exaggeration in these three answers.

A fourth Belgian whom I need not specify confined himself to saying to me,—

"He is a beast."

As to his public functions, Baron Hody was what they call at Brussels "The Administrator of Public Safety"; that is to say, a counterfeit of the Prefect of Police, half Carlier, half Maupas.

Thanks to Baron Hody, who has since left the place, and who, moreover, like M. de Montalembert, was a "mere Jesuit," the Belgian police at that moment was a compound of the Russian and Austrian police. I have read strange confidential letters of this Baron Hody. In action and in style there is nothing more cynical and more repulsive than the Jesuit police, when they unveil their secret treasures. These are the contents of the unbuttoned cassock.

At the time of which we are speaking (December, 1851), the Clerical party had joined itself to all the forms of Monarchy; and this Baron Hody confused Orleanism with Legitimate right. I simply tell the tale. Nothing more.

"Baron Hody. Very well, I will go to him," said Cournet.

He got up, dressed himself, brushed his clothes as well as he could, and asked the landlord, "Where is the Police office?"

"At the Ministry of Justice."

In fact this is the case in Brussels; the police administration forms part of the Ministry of Justice, an arrangement which does not greatly raise the police and somewhat lowers justice.

Cournet went there, and was shown into the presence of this personage.

Baron Hody did him the honor to ask him sharply,—

"Who are you?"

"A refugee," answered Cournet; "I am one of those whom the *coup d'état* has driven from Paris.

"Your profession?"

"Ex-naval officer."

"Ex-naval officer!" exclaimed Baron Hody in a much gentler tone, "did you know His Royal Highness the Prince de Joinville?"

"I have served under him."

It was the truth. Cournet had served under M. de Joinville, and prided himself on it.

At this statement the administrator of Belgian safety completely unbent, and said to Cournet, with the most gracious smile that the police can find, "That's all right, sir; stay here as long as you please; we close Belgium to the Men of the Mountain, but we throw it widely open to men like you."

When Cournet told me this answer of Hody's, I thought that my fourth Belgian was right.

A certain comic gloom was mingled at times with these tragedies. Barthelémy Terrier was a Representative of the people, and a proscript. They gave him a special passport for a compulsory route as far as Belgium for himself and his wife. Furnished with this passport he left with a woman. This woman was a man. Préveraud, a landed proprietor at Donjon, one of the most prominent men in the Department of Allier, was Terrier's brother-in-law. When the *coup d'état* broke out at Donjon, Préveraud had taken up arms and fulfilled his duty, had combated the outrage and defended the law. For this he had been condemned to death. The justice of that time, as we know. Justice executed justice. For this crime of being an honest man they had guillotined Charlet, guillotined Cuisinier, guillotined Cirasse. The guillotine was an instrument of the reign. Assassination by the guillotine was one of the means of order of that time. It was necessary to save Préveraud. He was little and slim: they dressed him as a woman. He was not sufficiently pretty for them not to cover his face with a thick veil. They put the brave and sturdy hands of the combatant in a muff. Thus veiled and a little filled out with padding, Préveraud made a charming woman. He became Madame Terrier, and his brother-in-law took him away. They crossed Paris peaceably, and without any other adventure than an imprudence committed by Préveraud, who, seeing that the shaft-horse of a wagon had fallen down, threw aside his muff, lifted his veil and his petticoat, and if Terrier, in dire alarm, had not stopped him, he would have helped the carter to raise his horse. Had a *sergent de ville* been there, Préveraud would have been captured. Terrier hastened to thrust Préveraud into a carriage, and at nightfall they left for Brussels. They were alone in the carriage, each in a corner and face to face. All went well as far as Amiens. At Amiens station the door was opened, and a gendarme entered and seated himself by the side of Préveraud. The gendarme asked for his passport, Terrier showed it him; the little woman in her corner, veiled and silent, did not stir, and the gendarme found all in due form. He contented himself with saying, "We shall travel together, I am on duty as far as the frontier."

The train, after the ordinary delay of a few minutes, again started. The night was dark. Terrier had fallen asleep. Suddenly Préveraud felt a knee press against his, it was the knee of the policeman. A boot placed itself softly on his foot, it was a horse-soldier's boot. An idyll had just germinated in the gendarme's soul. He first tenderly pressed Préveraud's knee, and then emboldened by the darkness of the hour and by the slumbering husband, he ventured his hand as far as her dress, a circumstance foreseen by Molière, but the fair veiled one was virtuous. Préveraud, full of surprise and rage, gently pushed back the gendarme's hand. The danger was extreme. Too much love on the part of the gendarme, one audacious step further, would bring about the unexpected, would abruptly change the eclogue into an official indictment, would reconvert the amorous satyr into a stony-hearted policeman, would transform Tircis into Vidocq; and then this strange thing would be seen, a passenger guillotined because a gendarme had committed an outrage. The danger increased every moment. Terrier was sleeping. Suddenly the train stopped. A voice cried, "Quièvrain!" and the door was opened. They were in Belgium. The gendarme, obliged to stop here, and to re-enter France, rose to get out, and at the moment when he stepped on to the ground he heard behind him these expressive words coming from beneath the lace veil, "Be off, or I'll break your jaw!"

XIII

The Military Commissions and the Mixed Commissions

J ustice sometime meets with strange adventures.

This old phrase assumed a new sense.

The code ceased to be a safeguard. The law became something which had sworn fealty to a crime. Louis Bonaparte appointed judges by whom one felt oneself stopped as in the corner of a wood. In the same manner as the forest is an accomplice through its density, so the legislation was an accomplice by its obscurity. What it lacked at certain points in order to make it perfectly dark they added. How? By force. Purely and simply. By decree. *Sic jubeo*. The decree of the 17th of February was a masterpiece. This decree completed the proscription of the person, by the proscription of the name. Domitian could not have done better. Human conscience was bewildered; Right, Equity, Reason felt that the master had over them the authority that a thief has over a purse. No reply. Obey. Nothing resembles those infamous times.

Every iniquity was possible. Legislative bodies supervened and instilled so much gloom into legislation that it was easy to achieve a baseness in this darkness.

A successful *coup d'état* does not stand upon ceremony. This kind of success permits itself everything.

Facts abound. But we must abridge, we will only present them briefly.

There were two species of Justice; the Military Commissions and the Mixed Commissions.

The Military Commissions sat in judgment with closed doors. A colonel presided.

In Paris alone there were three Military Commissions: each received a thousand bills of indictment. The Judge of Instruction sent these accusations to the Procureur of the Republic, Lascoux, who transmitted them to the Colonel President. The Commission summoned the accused to appear. The accused himself was his own bill of indictment. They searched him, that is to say, they "thumbed" him. The accusing document was short. Two or three lines. Such as this, for example,—

Name. Christian name. Profession. A sharp fellow. Goes to the Café. Reads the papers. Speaks. Dangerous.

The accusation was laconic. The judgment was still less prolix. It was a simple sign.

The bill of indictment having been examined, the judges having been consulted, the colonel took a pen, and put at the end of the accusing line one of three signs:—

-     +   o

- signified consignment to Lambessa.

+ signified transportation to Cayenne. (The dry guillotine. Death.)

o signified acquittal.

While this justice was at work, the man on whose case they were working was sometimes still at liberty, he was going and coming at his ease; suddenly they arrested him, and without knowing what they wanted with him, he left for Lambessa or for Cayenne.

His family was often ignorant of what had become of him.

People asked of a wife, of a sister, of a daughter, of a mother,—

"Where is your husband?"

"Where is your brother?"

"Where is your father?"

"Where is your son?"

The wife, the sister, the daughter, the mother answered,—"I do not know."

In the Allier eleven members of one family alone, the Préveraud family of Donjon, were struck down, one by the penalty of death, the others by banishment and transportation.

A wine-seller of the Batignolles, named Brisadoux, was transported to Cayenne for this line in his deed of accusation: *his shop is frequented by Socialists*.

Here is a dialogue, word for word, and taken from life, between a colonel and his convicted prisoner:—

"You are condemned."

"Indeed! Why?"

"In truth I do not exactly know myself. Examine your conscience. Think what you have done."

"I?"

"Yes, you."

"How I?"

"You must have done something."

"No. I have done nothing. I have not even done my duty. I ought to have taken my gun, gone down into the street, harangued the people, raised barricades; I remained at home stupidly like a sluggard" (the accused laughs); "that is the offence of which I accuse myself."

"You have not been condemned for that offence. Think carefully."

"I can think of nothing."

"What! You have not been to the *café*?"

"Yes, I have breakfasted there."

"Have you not chatted there?"

"Yes, perhaps."

"Have you not laughed?"

"Perhaps I have laughed."

"At whom? At what?"

"At what is going on. It is true I was wrong to laugh."

"At the same time you talked?"

"Yes."

"Of whom?"

"Of the President."

"What did you say?"

"Indeed, what may be said with justice, that he had broken his oath."

"And then?"

"That he had not the right to arrest the Representatives."

"You said that?"

"Yes. And I added that he had not the right to kill people on the boulevard. . ."

Here the condemned man interrupted himself and exclaimed,—

"And thereupon they send me to Cayenne!"

The judge looks fixedly at the prisoner, and answers,—"Well, then?"

Another form of justice:—

Three miscellaneous personages, three removable functionaries, a Prefect, a soldier, a public prosecutor, whose only conscience is the sound of Louis Bonaparte's bell, seated themselves at a table and judged. Whom? You, me, us, everybody. For what crimes? They invented crimes. In the name of what laws? They invented laws. What penalties did they inflict? They invented penalties. Did they know the accused? No. Did they listen to him? No. What advocates did they listen to?

None. What witnesses did they question? None. What deliberation did they enter upon? None. What public did they call in? None. Thus, no public, no deliberation, no counsellors, no witnesses, judges who are not magistrates, a jury where none are sworn in, a tribunal which is not a tribunal, imaginary offences, invented penalties, the accused absent, the law absent; from all these things which resembled a dream there came forth a reality: the condemnation of the innocent.

Exile, banishment, transportation, ruin, home-sickness, death, and despair for 40,000 families.

That is what History calls the Mixed Commissions.

Ordinarily the great crimes of State strike the great heads, and content themselves with this destruction; they roll like blocks of stone, all in one piece, and break the great resistances; illustrious victims suffice for them. But the Second of December had its refinements of cruelty; it required in addition petty victims. Its appetite for extermination extended to the poor and to the obscure, its anger and animosity penetrated as far as the lowest class; it created fissures in the social subsoil in order to diffuse the proscription there; the local triumvirates, nicknamed "mixed mixtures," served it for that. Not one head escaped, however humble and puny. They found means to impoverish the indigent, to ruin those dying of hunger, to spoil the disinherited; the *coup d'état* achieved this wonderful feat of adding misfortune to misery. Bonaparte, it seems, took the trouble to hate a mere peasant; the vine-dresser was torn from his vine, the laborer from his furrow, the mason from his scaffold, the weaver from his loom. Men accepted this mission of causing the immense public calamity to fall, morsel by morsel, upon the humblest walks of life. Detestable task! To crumble a catastrophe upon the little and on the weak.

XIV

A Religious Incident

A little religion can be mingled with this justice. Here is an example. Frederick Morin, like Arnauld de l'Ariège, was a Catholic Republican. He thought that the souls of the victims of the 4th of December, suddenly cast by the volleys of the *coup d'état* into the infinite and the unknown, might need some assistance, and he undertook the laborious task of having a mass said for the repose of these souls. But the priests wished to keep the masses for their friends. The group of Catholic Republicans which Frederick Morin headed applied successively to all the priests of Paris; but met with a refusal. They applied to the Archbishop: again a refusal. As many masses for the assassin as they liked, but far the assassinated not one. To pray for dead men of this sort would be a scandal. The refusal was determined. How should it be overcome? To do without a mass would have appeared easy to others, but not to these staunch believers. The worthy Catholic Democrats with great difficulty at length unearthed in a tiny suburban parish a poor old vicar, who consented to mumble in a whisper this mass in the ear of the Almighty, while begging Him to say nothing about it.

XV

How They Came Out of Ham

On the night of the 7th and 8th of January, Charras was sleeping. The noise of his bolts being drawn awoke him.

"So then!" said he, "they are going to put us in close confinement." And he went to sleep again.

An hour afterwards the door was opened. The commandant of the fort entered in full uniform, accompanied by a police agent carrying a torch.

It was about four o'clock in the morning.

"Colonel," said the Commandant, "dress yourself at once."

"What for?"

"You are about to leave."

"Some more rascality, I suppose!"

The Commandant was silent. Charras dressed himself.

As he finished dressing, a short young man, dressed in black, came in. This young man spoke to Charras.

"Colonel, you are about to leave the fortress, you are about to quit France. I am instructed to have you conducted to the frontier."

Charras exclaimed,—

"If I am to quit France I will not leave the fortress. This is yet another outrage. They have no more the right to exile me than they had the right to imprison me. I have on my side the Law, Right, my old services, my commission. I protest. Who are you, sir?"

"I am the Private Secretary of the Minister of the Interior."

"Ah! it is you who are named Léopold Lehon."

The young man cast down his eyes.

Charras continued,—

"You come on the part of someone whom they call 'Minister of the Interior,' M. de Morny, I believe. I know M. de Morny. A bald young man; he has played the game where people lose their hair; and now he is playing the game where people risk their heads."

The conversation was painful. The young man was deeply interested in the toe of his boot.

After a pause, however, he ventured to speak,—

"M. Charras, I am instructed to say that if you want money—"

Charras interrupted him impetuously.

"Hold your tongue, sir! not another word. I have served my country five-and-twenty years as an officer, under fire, at the peril of my life, always for honor, never for gain. Keep your money for your own set!"

"But, sir—"

"Silence! Money which passes through your hands would soil mine."

Another pause ensued, which the private secretary again broke,—

"Colonel, you will be accompanied by two police agents who have special instructions, and I should inform you that you are ordered to travel with a false passport, and under the name of Vincent."

"Good heavens!" said Charras; "this is really too much. Who is it imagines that they will make me travel by order with a false passport, and under a false name?" And looking steadily at M. Léopold Lehon, "Know, sir, that my name is Charras and not Vincent, and that I belong to a family whose members have always borne the name of their father."

They set out.

They journeyed by carriage as far as Creil, which is on the railway.

At Creil station the first person whom Charras saw was General Changarnier.

"Ah! it is you, General."

The two proscripts embraced each other. Such is exile.

"What the deuce are they doing with you?" asked the General.

"What they are probably doing with you. These vagabonds are making me travel under the name of Vincent."

"And me," said Changarnier, "under the name of Leblanc."

"In that case they ought at least to have called me Lerouge," said Charras, with a burst of laughter.

In the meantime a group, kept at a distance by the police agents, had formed round them. People had recognized them and saluted them. A little child, whose mother could not hold him back, ran quickly to Charras and took his hand.

They got into the train apparently as free as other travellers. Only they isolated them in empty compartments, and each was accompanied by two men, who sat one at the side and the other facing him, and who never took their eyes off him. The keepers of General Changarnier were of ordinary strength and stature. Those of Charras were almost giants. Charras is exceedingly tall; they topped him by an entire head. These men who were galley sergeants, had been carabineers; these spies had been heroes.

Charras questioned them. They had served when quite young, from 1813. Thus they had shared the bivouac of Napoleon; now they ate the same bread as Vidocq. The soldier brought to such a sorry pass as this is a sad sight.

The pocket of one of them was bulged out with something which he was hiding there.

When this man crossed the station in company with Charras, a lady traveller said,—

"Has he got M. Thiers in his pocket?"

What the police agent was hiding was a pair of pistols. Under their long, buttoned-up and doubled-breasted frock coats these men were armed. They were ordered to treat "those gentlemen" with the most profound respect, but in certain circumstances to blow out their brains.

The prisoners had each been informed that in the eyes of the different authorities whom they would meet on the road they would pass for foreigners, Swiss or Belgians, expelled on account of their political opinions, and that the police agents would keep their title of police agents, and would represent themselves as charged with reconducting these foreigners to the frontier.

Two-thirds of the journey were accomplished without any hindrance. At Valenciennes an incident occurred.

The *coup d'état* having succeeded, zeal reigned paramount. No task was any longer considered despicable. To denounce was to please; zeal is one of the forms of servitude towards which people lean the most willingly. The general became a common soldier, the prefect became a commissary of police, the commissary of police became a police spy.

The commissary of police at Valenciennes himself superintended the inspection of passports. For nothing in the world would he have deputed this important office to a subordinate inspector. When they presented him the passport of the so-called Leblanc, he looked the so-called Leblanc full in the face, started, and exclaimed,—

"You are General Changarnier!"

"That is no affair of mine," said the General.

Upon this the two keepers of the General protested and exhibited their papers, perfectly drawn up in due form.

"Mr. Commissary, we are Government agents. Here are our proper passports."

"Improper ones," said the General.

The Commissary shook his head. He had been employed in Paris, and had been frequently sent to the headquarters of the staff at the Tuileries, to General Changarnier. He knew him very well.

"This is too much!" exclaimed the police agents. They blustered, declared that they were police functionaries on a special service, that they had instructions to conduct to the frontier this Leblanc, expelled for political reasons, swore by all the gods, and gave their word of honor that the so-called Leblanc was really named Leblanc.

"I do not much believe in words of honor," said the Commissary.

"Honest Commissary," muttered Changarnier, "you are right. Since the 2d of December words of honor and oaths are no more than worthless paper money."

And then he began to smile.

The Commissary became more and more perplexed. The police agents ended by invoking the testimony of the prisoner himself.

"Now, sir, tell him your name yourself."

"Get out of the difficulty yourselves," answered Changarnier.

All this appeared most irregular to the mind of a provincial alguazil.

It seemed evident to the Commissary of Valenciennes that General Changarnier was escaping from Ham under a false name with a false passport, and with false agents of police, in order to mislead the authorities, and that it was a plot to escape which was on the point of succeeding.

"Come down, all three of you!" exclaimed the Commissary.

The General gets down, and on putting foot to the ground notices Charras in the depths of his compartment between his two bullies.

"Oho! Charras, you are there!" he cries.

"Charras!" exclaimed the Commissary. "Charras there! Quick! the passports of these gentlemen!" And looking Charras in the face,—

"Are you Colonel Charras?"

"Egad!" said Charras.

Yet another complication. It was now the turn of Charras's bullies to bluster. They declared that Charras was the man called Vincent, displayed passports and papers, swore and protested. The Commissary's suspicions were fully confirmed.

"Very well," said he, "I arrest everybody."

And he handed over Changarnier, Charras, and the four police agents to the gendarmes. The Commissary saw the Cross of Honor shining in the distance. He was radiant.

The police arrested the police. It happens sometimes that the wolf thinks he has seized a victim and bites his own tail.

The six prisoners—for now there were six prisoners—were taken into a parlor at the railway station. The Commissary informed the town authorities. The town authorities hastened hither, headed by the sub-prefect.

The sub-prefect, who was named Censier, comes in, and does not know whether he ought to salute or to question, to grovel in the dust or to keep his hat on his head. These poor devils of magistrates and local officials were very much exercised in their minds. General Changarnier had been too near the Dictatorship not to make them thoughtful. Who can foresee the course of events? Everything is possible. Yesterday called itself Cavaignac, today calls itself Bonaparte, tomorrow may call itself Changarnier. Providence is really cruel not to let sub-prefects have a peep at the future.

It is sad for a respectable functionary, who would ask for nothing better than to be servile or arrogant according to circumstances, to be in danger of lavishing his platitudes on a person who is perhaps going to rot forever in exile, and who is nothing more than a rascal, or to risk being insolent to a vagabond of a postscript who is capable of coming back a conqueror in six months' time, and of becoming the Government in his turn. What was to be done? And then they were spied upon. This takes place between officials. The slightest word would be maliciously interpreted, the slightest gesture would be laid to their discredit. How should he keep on good terms at the same time this Cabbage, which is called Today, and that Goat, which is called Tomorrow? To ask too many questions would offend the General, to render to many salutations would annoy the President. How could he be at the same time very much a sub-prefect, and in some degree a lacquey? How could he combine the appearance of obsequiousness, which would please Changarnier, with the appearance of authority, which would please Bonaparte?

The sub-prefect thought to get out of the difficulty by saying, "General, you are my prisoner," and by adding, with a smile, "Do me the honor of breakfasting with me?" He addressed the same words to Charras.

The General refused curtly.

Charras looked at him fixedly, and did not answer him.

Doubts regarding the identity of the prisoners came to the mind of the sub-prefect. He whispered to the Commissary "Are you quite sure?" "Certainly," said the Commissary.

The sub-prefect decided to address himself to Charras, and dissatisfied with the manner in which his advances had been received, asked him somewhat sharply, "But, in short, who are you?"

Charras answered, "We are packages."

And turning to his keepers who were now in their turn in keeping:—

"Apply to our exporters. Ask our Custom House officers. It is a mere matter of goods traffic."

They set the electric telegraph to work. Valenciennes, alarmed, questioned Paris. The sub-prefect informed the Minister of the Interior that, thanks to a strict supervision, which he had trusted to no one but himself, he had just effected an important capture, that he had just discovered a plot, had saved the President, had saved society, had saved religion, etc., that in one word he had just arrested General Changarnier and Colonel Charras, who had escaped that morning from the fort of Ham with false passports, doubtless for the purpose of heading a rising, etc., and that, in short, he asked the Government what was to be done with the two prisoners.

At the end of an hour the answer arrived:—"Let them go on their way."

The police perceived that in a burst of zeal they had pushed profundity to the point of stupidity. That sometimes happens.

The next train carried away the prisoners, restored, not to liberty, but to their keepers.

They passed Quiévrain.

They got down from the carriage, and got in again.

When the train again started Charras heaved the deep, joyous sigh of a freed man, and said, "At last!"

He raised his eyes, and perceived his two jailers by his side.

They had got up behind him into the carriage.

"Ah, indeed!" he said to them; "you there!"

Of these two men there was only one who spoke, that one answered,—

"Yes, Colonel."

"What are you doing here?"

"We are keeping watch over you."

"But we are in Belgium."

"Possibly."

"Belgium is not France."

"Ah, that may be."

"But suppose I put my head out of the carriage? Suppose I call out? Suppose I had you arrested? Suppose I reclaimed my liberty?"

"You will not do all that, Colonel."

"How will you prevent me?"

The police agent showed the butt-end of his pistol and said "Thus."

Charras burst out laughing, and asked them, "Where then are you going to leave me?"

"At Brussels."

"That is to say, that at Brussels you will salute me with your cap; but that at Mons you will salute me with your pistol."

"As you say, Colonel."

"In truth," said Charras, "it does not matter to me. It is King Leopold's business. The Bonaparte treats countries as he has treated the Representatives. He has violated the Assembly, he violates Belgium. But all the same, you are a medley of strange rascals. He who is at the top is a madman, those who are beneath are blockheads. Very well, my friends, let me go to sleep."

And he went to sleep.

Almost the same incident happened nearly at the same moment to Generals Changarnier and Lamoricière and to M. Baze.

The police agents did not leave General Changarnier until they had reached Mons. There they made him get down from the train, and said to him, "General, this is your place of residence. We leave you free."

"Ah!" said he, "this is my place of residence, and I am free? Well, then, goodnight."

And he sprang lightly back into the carriage just as the train was starting, leaving behind him two galley sergeants dumfounded.

The police released Charras at Brussels, but did not release General Lamoricière. The two police agents wished to compel him to leave immediately for Cologne. The General, who was suffering from rheumatism which he had caught at Ham, declared that he would sleep at Brussels.

"Be it so," said the police agents.

They followed him to the Hôtel de Bellevue. They spent the night there with him. He had considerable difficulty to prevent them from sleeping in his room. Next day they carried him off, and took him to Cologne-violating Prussian territory after having violated Belgian territory.

The *coup d'état* was still more impudent with M. Baze.

They made M. Baze journey with his wife and his children under the name of Lassalle. He passed for the servant of the police agent who accompanied him.

They took him thus to Aix-la-Chapelle.

There, in the middle of the night, in the middle of the street, the police agents deposited him and the whole of his family, without a passport, without papers, without money. M. Baze, indignant, was obliged to have recourse to threats to induce them to take him and identify him before a magistrate. It was, perhaps, part of the petty joys of Bonaparte to cause a Questor of the Assembly to be treated as a vagrant.

On the night of the 7th of January, General Bedeau, although he was not to leave till the next day, was awakened like the others by the noise of bolts. He did not understand that they were shutting him in, but on the contrary, believed that they were releasing M. Baze, his neighbor in the adjoining cell. He cried through the door, "Bravo, Baze!"

In fact, everyday the Generals said to the Questor, "You have no business here, this is a military fortress. One of these fine mornings you will be thrust outside like Roger du Nord."

Nevertheless General Bedeau heard an unusual noise in the fortress. He got up and "knocked" for General Leflô, his neighbor in the cell on the other side, with whom he exchanged frequent military dialogues, little flattering to the *coup d'état*. General Leflô answered the knocking, but he did not know anymore than General Bedeau.

General Bedeau's window looked out on the inner courtyard of the prison. He went to this window and saw lanterns flashing hither and thither, species of covered carts, horsed, and a company of the 48th under arms. A moment afterwards he saw General Changarnier come into the courtyard, get into a carriage, and drive off. Some moments elapsed, then he saw Charras pass. Charras noticed him at the window, and cried out to him, "Mons!"

In fact he believed he was going to Mons, and this made General Bedeau, on the next day, choose Mons as his residence, expecting to meet Charras there.

Charras having left, M. Léopold Lehon came in accompanied by the Commandant of the fort. He saluted Bedeau, explained his business, and gave his name. General Bedeau confined himself to saying, "They banish us; it is an illegality, and one more indignity added to the others. However, with the people who send you one is no longer surprised at anything."

They did not send him away till the next day. Louis Bonaparte had said, "We must 'space out' the Generals."

The police agent charged with escorting General Bedeau to Belgium was one of those who, on the 2d of December, had arrested General Cavaignac. He told General Bedeau that they had had a moment of uneasiness when arresting General Cavaignae: the picket of fifty men, which had been told off to assist the police having failed them.

In the compartment of the railway carriage which was taking General Bedeau into Belgium there was a lady, manifestly belonging to good society, of very distinguished appearance, and who was accompanied by three little children. A servant in livery, who appeared to be a German, had two of the children on his knees, and lavished a thousand little attentions on them. However, the General, hidden by the darkness, and muffled up, like the police agents, in the collar of his mantle, paid little attention to this group. When they reached Quièvrain, the lady turned to him and said, "General, I congratulate you, you are now in safety."

The General thanked her, and asked her name.

"Baroness Coppens," she answered.

It may be remembered that it was at M. Coppens's house, 70, Rue Blanche, that the first meeting of the Left had taken place on December 2d.

"You have charming children there, madam," said the General, "and," he added, "an exceedingly good servant."

"It is my husband," said Madame Coppens.

M. Coppens, in fact, had remained five weeks buried in a hiding-place contrived in his own house. He had escaped from France that very night under the cover of his own livery. They had carefully taught their children their lesson. Chance had made them get into the same carriage as General Bedeau and the two bullies who were keeping guard over him, and throughout the night Madame Coppens had been in terror lest, in the presence of the policeman, one of the little ones awakening, should throw its arms around the neck of the servant and cry "Papa!"

XVI

A Retrospect

Louis Bonaparte had tested the majority as engineers test a bridge; he had loaded it with iniquities, encroachments, enormities, slaughters on the Place du Havre, cries of "Long live the Emperor," distributions of money to the troops, sales of Bonapartist journals in the streets, prohibition of Republican and parliamentary journals, reviews at Satory, speeches at Dijon; the majority bore everything.

"Good," said he, "It will carry the weight of the *coup d'état*."

Let us recall the facts. Before the 2d of December the *coup d'état* was being constructed in detail, here and there, a little everywhere, with exceeding impudence, and yet the majority smiled. The Representative Pascal Duprat had been violently treated by police agents. "That is very funny," said the Right. The Representative Dain was seized. "Charming." The Representative Sartin was arrested. "Bravo." One fine morning when all the hinges had been well tested and oiled, and when all the wires were well fixed, the *coup d'état* was carried out all at once, abruptly. The majority ceased to laugh, but the trick, was done. It had not perceived that for a long time past, while it was laughing at the strangling of others, the cord was round its own neck.

Let us maintain this, not to punish the past, but to illuminate the future. Many months before being carried out, the *coup d'état* had been accomplished. The day having come, the hour having struck, the mechanism being completely wound up, it had only to be set going. It was bound not to fail, and nothing did fail. What would have been an abyss if the majority had done its duty, and had understood its joint responsibility with the Left, was not even a ditch. The inviolability had been demolished by those who were inviolable. The hand of gendarmes had become as accustomed to the collar of the Representatives as to the collar of thieves: the white tie of the statesman was not even rumpled in the grasp of the galley sergeants, and one can admire the Vicomte de Falloux—oh, candor!—for being dumfounded at being treated like Citizen Sartin.

The majority, going backwards, and ever applauding Bonaparte, fell into the hole which Bonaparte had dug for it.

XVII

CONDUCT OF THE LEFT

The conduct of the Republican Left in this grave crisis of the 2d of December was memorable.

The flag of the Law was on the ground, in the mire of universal treason, under the feet of Louis Bonaparte; the Left raised this flag, washed away the mire with its blood, unfurled it, waved it before the eyes of the people, and from the 2d to the 5th of December held Bonaparte at bay.

A few men, a mere handful, 120 Representatives of the people escaped by chance from arrest, plunged in darkness and in silence, without even possessing that cry of the free press which sounds the tocsin to human intellects, and which encourages the combatants, without generals under their orders, without soldiers, without ammunition, went down into the streets, resolutely barred the way against the *coup d'état*, and gave battle to this monstrous crime, which had taken all its precautions, which was mail-clad in every part, armed to the teeth, crowding round it forests of bayonets, and making a pack of mortars and cannons give tongue in its favor.

They had that presence of mind, which is the most practical kind of courage; they had, while lacking everything else, the formidable improvisation of duty, which never loses heart. They had no printing-offices, they obtained them; they had no guns, they found them; they had no balls, they cast them; they had no powder, they manufactured it; they had nothing but paving-stones, and from thence they evolved combatants.

It is true that these paving-stones were the paving-stones of Paris, stones which change themselves into men.

Such is the power of Right, that, during four days these hundred and twenty men, who had nothing in their favor but the goodness of their cause, counterbalanced an army of 100,000 soldiers. At one moment the scale turned on their side. Thanks to them, thanks to their resistance, seconded by the indignation of honest hearts, there came an hour when the victory of the law seemed possible, and even certain. On Thursday, the 4th, the *coup d'état* tottered, and was obliged to support itself by assassination. We seen that without the butchery of the boulevards, if he had not saved his perjury by a massacre, if he had not sheltered his crime by another crime, Louis Bonaparte was lost.

During the long hours of this struggle, a struggle without a truce, a struggle against the army during the day and against the police during the night,—an unequal struggle, where all the strength and all the rage was on one side, and, as we have just said, nothing but Right on the other, not one of these hundred and twenty Representatives, not a single one failed at the call of duty, not one shunned the danger, not one drew back, not one wearied,—all these heads placed themselves resolutely under the axe, and for four days waited for it to fall.

Today captivity, transportation, expatriation, exile, the axe has fallen on nearly all these heads.

I am one of those who have had no other merit in this struggle than to rally into one unique thought the courage of all; but let me here heartily render justice to those men amongst whom I pride myself with having for three years served the holy cause of human progress, to this Left, insulted, calumniated, unappreciated, and dauntless, which was always in the breach, and which did not repose for a single day, which recoiled none the more before the military conspiracy than before the parliamentary conspiracy, and which, entrusted by the people with the task of defending them, defended them even when abandoned by themselves; defended them in the tribune with speech, and in the street with the sword.

When the Committee of Resistance in the sitting at which the decree of deposition and of outlawry was drawn up and voted, making use of the discretionary power which the Left had confided to it, decided that all the signatures of the Republican Representatives remaining at liberty should be placed at the foot of the decree, it was a bold stroke; the Committee did not conceal from itself that it was a list of proscription offered to the victorious *coup d'état* ready drawn up, and perhaps in its inner conscience it feared that some would disavow it, and protest against it. As a matter of fact, the next day we received two letters, two complaints. They were from two Representatives who had been omitted from the list, and who claimed the honor of being reinstated there. I reinstate these two Representatives here, in their right of being proscripts. Here are their names—Anglade and Pradié.

From Tuesday, the 2d, to Friday, the 5th of December, the Representatives of the Left and the Committee, dogged, worried, hunted down, always on the point of being discovered and taken, that is to say—massacred; repaired for the purpose of deliberating, to twenty-seven different houses, shifted twenty-seven times their place of meeting, from their first gathering in the Rue Blanche to their last conference at Raymond's. They refused the shelters which were offered them on the left bank of the river, wishing always to remain in the centre of the combat. During these changes they more than once traversed the right bank of Paris from one end to the other, most of the time on foot, and making long circuits in order not to be followed. Everything threatened them with danger; their number, their well-known faces, even their precautions. In the populous streets there was danger, the police were permanently posted there; in the lonely streets there was danger, because the goings and comings were more noticed there.

They did not sleep, they did not eat, they took what they could find, a glass of water from time to time, a morsel of bread here and there. Madame Landrin gave us a basin of soup, Madame Grévy the remainder of a cold pie. We dined one evening on a little chocolate which a chemist had distributed in a barricade. At Jeunesse's, in the Rue de Grammont, during the night of the 3rd, Michel de Bourges took a chair, and said, "This is my bed." Were they tired? They did not feel it. The old men, like Ronjat, the sick, like Boysset, all went forward. The public peril, like a fever, sustained them.

Our venerable colleague, Lamennais, did not come, but he remained three days without going to bed, buttoned up in his old frock coat, his thick boots on his feet, ready to march. He wrote to the author these three lines, which it is impossible not to quote:—"You are heroes without me. This pains me greatly. I await your orders. Try, then, to find me something to do, be it but to die."

In these meetings each man preserved his usual demeanor. At times one might have thought it an ordinary sitting in one of the bureaux of the Assembly. There was the calm of everyday, mingled with the firmness of decisive crises. Edgar Quinet retained all his lofty judgment, Noël Parfait all his mental vivacity, Yvan all his vigorous and intelligent penetration, Labrousse all his animation. In a corner Pierre Lefranc, pamphleteer and ballad-writer, but a pamphleteer like Courier, and a ballad-writer like Béranger smiled at the grave and stern words of Dupont de Bussac. All that brilliant group of young orators of the Left, Baneel with his powerful ardor, Versigny and Victor Chauffour with their youthful daring. Sain with his coolheadedness which reveals strength, Farconnet with his gentle voice and his energetic inspiration, lavishing his efforts in resisting the *coup d'état*, sometimes taking part in the deliberations, at others amongst the people, proving that to be an orator one must possess all the qualifications of a combatant. De Flotte, indefatigable, was ever ready to traverse all Paris. Xavier Durrieu was courageous, Dulac dauntless, Charamaule fool-hardy. Citizens and Paladins. Courage! who would have dared to exhibit none amongst all these men, of whom not one trembled? Untrimmed beards, torn coats, disordered hair, pale faces, pride glistening in every eye. In the houses where they were received they installed themselves as best they could. If there were no sofas or chairs, some, exhausted in strength, but not in heart, seated themselves on the floor. All became copyists of the decrees and proclamations; one dictated, ten wrote. They wrote on tables, on the corners of furniture, on their knees. Frequently paper was lacking, pens were wanting. These wretched trifles created obstacles at the most critical times. At certain moments in the history of peoples an inkstand where the ink is dried up may prove a public calamity. Moreover, cordiality prevailed among all, all shades of difference were effaced. In the secret sittings of the Committee Madier de Montjau, that firm and generous heart, De Flotte, brave and thoughtful, a fighting philosopher of the Devolution, Carnot, accurate, cold, tranquil, immovable, Jules Favre, eloquent, courageous, admirable through his simplicity and his strength, inexhaustible in resources as in sarcasms, doubled, by combining them, the diverse powers of their minds.

Michel de Bourges, seated in a corner of the fireplace, or leaning on a table enveloped in his great coat, his black silk cap on his head, had an answer for every suggestion, gave back to occurrences blow for blow, was on his guard for danger, difficulty, opportunity, necessity, for his is one of those wealthy natures which have always something ready either in their intellect or in their imagination. Words of advice crossed without jostling each other. These men entertained no illusion. They knew that they had entered into a life-and-death struggle. They had no quarter to expect. They had to do with the Man who had said, "Crush everything." They knew the bloody words of the self-styled Minister, Merny. These words the placards of Saint-Arnaud interpreted by decrees, the Praetorians let loose in the street interpreted them by murder. The members of the Insurrectionary Committee and the Representatives assisting at the meetings were not ignorant that wherever they might be taken they would be killed on the spot by bayonet-thrusts. It was the fortune of this war. Yet the prevailing expression on every face was serenity; that profound serenity which comes from a happy conscience. At times this serenity rose to gaiety. They laughed willingly and at everything. At the torn trousers of one, at the hat which another had brought back from the barricade instead of his own, at the comforter of a third. "Hide your big body," they said to him. They were children, and everything amused them. On the morning of the 4th Mathien de la Drôme came in. He had organized for his part a committee which communicated with the Central Committee, he came to tell us of it. He had shaved off his fringe of beard so as not to be recognized in the streets. "You look like an Archbishop," said Michel de Bourges to him, and there was a general laugh. And all this, with this thought which every moment brought back; the noise which is heard at the door, the key which turns in the lock is perhaps Death coming in.

The Representatives and the Committee were at the mercy of chance. More than once they could have been captured, and they were not; either owing to the scruples of certain police agents (where the deuce will scruples next take up their abode?) or that these agents doubted the final result, and feared to lay their hand heedlessly upon possible victors. If Vassal, the Commissary of Police, who met us on the morning of the 4th, on the pavement of the Rue des Moulins, had wished, we might have been taken that day. He did not betray us. But these were exceptions. The pursuit of the police was none the less ardent and implacable. At Marie's, it may be remembered that the *sergents de ville* and the gendarmes arrived ten minutes after we had left the house, and that they even ransacked under the beds with their bayonets.

Amongst the Representatives there were several Constituents, and at their head Bastide. Bastide, in 1848, had been Minister for Foreign Affairs. During the second night, meeting in the Rue Popincourt, they reproached him with several of his actions. "Let me first get myself killed," he answered, "and then you can reproach me with what you like." And he added, "How can you distrust me, who am a Republican up to the hilt?" Bastide would not consent to call our resistance the "insurrection," he called it the "counter-insurrection." he said, "Victor Hugo is right. The insurgent is at the Elysée." It was my opinion, as we have seen, that we ought to bring the battle at once to an issue, to defer nothing, to reserve nothing; I said, "We must strike the *coup d'état* while it is hot." Bastide supported me. In the combat he was impassive, cold, gay beneath his coldness. At the Saint Antoine barricade, at the moment when the guns of the *coup d'état* were leveled at the Representatives of the people, he said smilingly to Madier de Montjau, "Ask Schoelcher what he thinks of the abolition of the penalty of death." (Schoelcher, like myself, at this supreme moment, would have answered, "that it ought to be abolished") In another barricade Bastide, compelled to absent himself for a moment, placed his pipe on a paving-stone. They found Bastide's pipe, and they thought him dead. He came back, and it was hailing musket-balls; he said, "My pipe?" he relighted it and resumed the fight. Two balls pierced his coat.

When the barricades were constructed, the Republican Representatives spread themselves abroad; and distributed themselves amongst them. Nearly all the Representatives of the Left repaired to the barricades, assisting either to build them or to defend them. Besides the great exploit at Saint Antoine barricade, where Schoelcher was so admirable, Esquiros went to the barricade of the Rue de Charonne, De Flotte to those of the Pantheon and of the Chapelle Saint Denis, Madier de Montjau to those of Belleville and the Rue Aumaire, Doutre and Pelletier to that of the Mairie of the Fifth Arrondissement, Brives to that of Rue Beaubourg, Arnauld de l'Ariège to that of Rue de Petit-Repîsoir, Viguier to that of the Rue Pagevin, Versigny to that of the Rue Joigneaux; Dupont de Bussac to that of the Carré Saint Martin; Carlos Forel and Boysset to that of the Rue Rambuteau. Doutre received a sword-cut on his head, which cleft his hat; Bourzat had four balls in his overcoat; Baudin was killed; Gaston Dussoubs was ill and could not come; his brother, Denis Dussoubs, replaced him. Where? In the tomb.

Baudin fell on the first barricade, Denis Dussoubs on the last.

I was less favored than Bourzat; I only had three balls in my overcoat, and it is impossible for me to say whence they came. Probably from the boulevard.

After the battle was lost there was no general helter-skelter, no rout, no flight. All remained hidden in Paris ready to reappear, Michel in the Rue d'Alger, myself in the Rue de Navarin. The Committee held yet another sitting on Saturday, the 6th, at eleven o'clock at night. Jules Favre, Michel de Bourges, and myself, we came during the night to the house of a generous and brave woman, Madame Didier. Bastide came there and said to me, "If you are not killed here, you are going to enter upon exile. For myself, I am going to remain in Paris. Take me for your lieutenant." I have related this incident.

They hoped for the 9th (Tuesday) a resumption of arms, which did not take place. Malarmet had announced it to Dupont de Bussac, but the blow of the 4th had prostrated Paris. The populace no longer stirred. The Representatives did not resolve to think of their safety, and to quit France through a thousand additional dangers until several days afterwards, when the last spark of resistance was extinguished in the heart of the people, and the last glimmer of hope in heaven.

Several Republican Representatives were workmen; they have again become workmen in exile. Nadaud has resumed his trowel, and is a mason in London. Faure (du Rhône), a cutler, and Bansept, a shoemaker, felt that their trade had become their duty, and practise it in England. Faure makes knives, Bansept makes boots. Greppo is a weaver, it was he who when a proscript made the coronation robe of Queen Victoria. Gloomy smile of Destiny. Noël Parfait is a proof-reader at Brussels; Agricol Perdiguier, called Avignonnais-la-Vertu, has girded on his leathern apron, and is a cabinet-maker at Antwerp. Yesterday these men sat in the Sovereign Assembly. Such things as these are seen in Plutarch.

The eloquent and courageous proscript, Emile Deschanel, has created at Brussels, with a rare talent of speech, a new form of public instruction, the Conferences. To him is due the honor of this foundation, so fruitful and so useful.

Let us say in conclusion that the National Legislative Assembly lived badly but died well.

At this moment of the fall, irreparable for the cowards, the Right was worthy, the Left was great.

Never before has History seen a Parliament fall in this manner.

February had blown upon the Deputies of the legal country, and the Deputies had vanished. M. Sauzet had sunk down behind the tribune, and had gone away without even taking his hat.

Bonaparte, the other, the first, the true Bonaparte, had made the "Five Hundred" step out of the windows of the Orangery of Saint Cloud, somewhat embarrassed with their large mantles.

Cromwell, the oldest of the Bonapartes, when he achieved his Eighteenth Brumaire, encountered scarcely any other resistance than a few imprecations from Milton and from Ludlaw, and was able to say in his boorishly gigantic language, "I have put the King in my knapsack and the Parliament in my pocket."

We must go back to the Roman Senate in order to find true Curule chairs.

The Legislative Assembly, let us repeat, to its honor, did not lose countenance when facing the abyss. History will keep an account of it. After having betrayed so many things, it might have been feared that this Assembly would end by betraying itself. It did nothing of the kind. The Legislature, one is obliged to remember, had committed faults upon faults; the Royalist majority had, in the most odious manner, persecuted the Republican minority, which was bravely doing its duty in denouncing it to the people; this Assembly had had a very long cohabitation and a most fatal complicity with the Man of Crime, who had ended by strangling it as a robber strangles his concubine in his bed; but whatever may be said of this fateful Assembly, it did not exhibit that wretched vanishing away which Louis Bonaparte hoped for; it was not a coward.

This is due to its having originated from universal suffrage. Let us mention this, for it is an instructive lesson. The virtue of this universal suffrage, which had begotten the Assembly and which the Assembly had wished to slay, it felt in itself to its last hour.

The sap of a whole people does not spread in vain throughout an Assembly, even throughout the most decrepit. On the decisive day this sap asserts itself.

The Legislative Assembly, laden as it may be with formidable responsibilities, will, perhaps, be less overwhelmed than it deserves by the reprobation of posterity.

Thanks to universal suffrage, which it had deceived, and which constituted its faith and its strength at the last moment, thanks to the Left, which it had oppressed, scoffed at, calumniated, and decimated, and which cast on it the glorious reflection of its heroism, this pitiful Assembly died a grand death.

XVIII

Page Written at Brussels

W ell then, yes, I will kick open the door of this Palace, and I will enter with you, History! I will seize by the collar all the perpetrators, continually caught red-handed in the commission of all these outrages! I will suddenly illuminate this cavern of night with the broad daylight of truth!

Yes, I will bring in the daylight! I will tear down the curtain, I will open the window, I will show to every eye such as it really is, infamous, horrible, wealthy, triumphant, joyous, gilded, besmirched— this Elysée! this Court! this group! this heap! call it what you will! this galley-crew! where writhe and crawl, and pair and breed every baseness, every indignity, every abomination: filibusters, buccaneers, swearers of oaths, Signers of the Cross, spies, swindlers, butchers, executioners, from the brigand who vends his sword, to the Jesuit who sells his God second-hand! This sink where Baroche elbows Teste! where each brings his own nastiness! Magnan his epaulets; Montalembert his religion, Dupin his person!

And above all the innermost circle, the Holy of Holies, the private Council, the smug den where they drink—where they eat—where they laugh—where they sleep—where they play—where they cheat— where they call Highnesses "Thou,"—where they wallow! Oh! what ignominies! It is them! It is there! Dishonor, baseness, shame, and opprobrium are there! Oh History! A hot iron for all these faces.

It is there that they amuse themselves, and that they jest, and that they banter, and that they make sport of France! It is there that they pocket hap-hazard, amid great shouts of laughter, the millions of louis and the millions of votes! See them, look at them! They have treated the Law like a girl, they are content! Right is slaughtered, Liberty is gagged, the flag is dishonored, the people are under their feet. They are happy! And who are they? What are these men? Europe knows not. One fine morning it saw them come out of a crime. Nothing more. A parcel of rascals who vainly tried to become celebrated, and who have remained anonymous. Look! they are all there! See them, I tell you! Look at them, I tell you! Recognize them if you can. Of what sex are they? To what species do they belong? Who is this one? Is he a writer? No; he is a dog. He gobbles human flesh. And that one? Is he a dog? No, he is a courtier—he has blood on his paw.

New men, that is what they term them. New, in truth! Unlooked-for, strange, unprecedented, monstrous! Perjury, iniquity, robbery, assassination, erected into ministerial departments, swindling applied to universal suffrage, government under false pretences, duty called crime, crime called duty, cynicism laughing in the midst of atrocity,—it is of all this that their newness is compounded.

Now, all is well, they have succeeded, they have a fair wind, they enjoy themselves to the full. They have cheated France, they are dividing the spoil. France is a bag, and they put their hand in it. Rummage, for Heaven's sake! Take, while you are there; help yourselves, draw out, plunder, steal! One wants money, another wants situations, another wants a decorative collar round his neck, another a plume in his hat, another embroidery on his sleeve, another women, another power; another news for the Bourse, another a railway, another wine. I should think, indeed, that they are well satisfied. Picture to yourself a poor devil who, three years ago, borrowed ten sous of his porter, and who today, leaning voluptuously on the *Moniteur*, has only to sign a decree to take a million. To make themselves perfectly happy, to be able to devour the finances of the State, to live at the expense of the Treasury like a son of the family, this is what is called their policy. Their ambition has a true name, it is gluttony.

They ambitious? Nonsense! They are gluttons. To govern is to gamble. This does not prevent betrayal. On the contrary, they spy upon each other, they betray each other. The little traitors betray the great traitors. Pietri looks askance at Maupas, and Maupas at Carlier. They all lie in the same reeking sewer! They have achieved the *coup d'état* in common. That is all. Moreover they feel sure of nothing, neither of glances, nor of smiles, nor of hidden thoughts, nor of men, nor of women, nor of the lacquey, nor of the prince, nor of words of honor, nor of birth certificates. Each feels himself fraudulent, and knows himself suspected. Each has his secret aims. Each alone knows why he has done this. Not one utters a word about his crime, and no one bears the name of his father. Ah! may God grant me life, and may Jesus pardon me, I will raise a gibbet a hundred yards high, I will take hammer and nails, and I will crucify this Beauharnais called Bonaparte, between this Leroy called Saint-Arnoud, and this Fialin called Persigny!

And I would drag you there also, all of you accomplices! This Morny, this Romieu, this Fould, the Jew senator, this Delangle, who bears on his back this placard: JUSTICE! and this Troplong, this judicial glorifier of the violation of the laws, this lawyer apologist of the *coup d'état*, this magistrate flatterer of perjury, this judge panegyrist of murder, who will go down to posterity with a sponge filled with mud and with blood in his hand.

I begin the battle therefore. With whom? With the present ruler of Europe. It is right that this spectacle should be given to the world. Louis Bonaparte is the success, is the intoxicated triumph, is the gay and ferocious despotism, opening out under the victory, he is the mad fulness of power, seeking limits and finding none, neither in things nor in men; Louis Bonaparte holds France, *Urbem Roman habit*; and whoever holds France holds the world; he is master of the votes, master of the consciences, master of the people; he nominates his successor, reigns forever over future electoral scrutinies, disposes of eternity, and places futurity in an envelope; his Senate, his Legislative Body, his Council of State, with heads lowered and mingled confusedly behind him, lick his feet; he drags along in a leash the bishops and cardinals; he tramples on the justice which curses him, and on the judges who adore him, thirty correspondents inform the Continent that he has frowned, and every electric telegraph vibrates if he raises his little finger; around him is heard the rustling of sabres, and the drums beat the salute; he sits under the shadow of the eagle in the midst of bayonets and of citadels, the free nations tremble and hide their liberties for fear that he should steal them, the great American Republic herself falters in his presence, and dares not withdraw her Ambassador from him; the kings, surrounded by their armies, look at him smilingly, with their hearts full of fear. Where will he begin? With Belgium? With Switzerland? With Piedmont? Europe expects to be overrun. He is capable of all, and he dreams of all.

Well, then! Before this master, this triumpher, this conqueror, this dictator, this Emperor, this all-powerful, there rises a solitary man, a wanderer, despoiled, ruined, prostrate, proscribed, and attacks him. Louis Napoleon has ten thousand cannons, and five hundred thousand soldiers; the writer has his pen and his ink-stand. The writer is nothing, he is a grain of dust, he is a shadow, he is an exile without a refuge, he is a vagrant without a passport, but he has by his side and fighting with him two powers, Right, which is invincible, and Truth, which is immortal.

Assuredly, for this struggle to the death, for this formidable duel, Providence could have chosen a more illustrious champion, a grander athlete. But what matter men, there, where it is the idea with combats! Such as it is, it is good, let us repeat, that this spectacle should be given to the world. What is this in truth? It is intellect, an atom which resists strength—a colossus.

I have only one stone in my sling, but that stone is a good one; that stone is justice.

I attack Louis Bonaparte at this hour, when he is erect; at this hour, when he is master. He is in his zenith. So much the better; it is that which suits me.

Yes, I attack Louis Bonaparte. I attack him before the world; I attack him in the presence of God and men; I attack him resolutely, desperately; for the love of the people and of France. He is about to be Emperor, let it be so. Let there be at least one brow which resists. Let Louis Bonaparte know that an Empire may be taken, but that a Conscience cannot be taken.

XIX

The Infallible Benediction

The Pope approved.

When the mails brought to Rome intelligence of the event of the 2d of December, the Pope went to a review held by General Gémeau, and begged him to congratulate Prince Louis Napoléon for him.

There was a precedent for this.

On the 12th December, 1572, Saint-Goard, Ambassador of Charles the Ninth, King of France, to Philip the Second, King of Spain, wrote from Madrid to his master, Charles the Ninth, "The news of the events of the day of Saint Bartholomew have reached the Catholic King. Contrary to his wont and custom, he has shown so much joy, that he has manifested it more openly than he has ever done for all the happy events and good fortune which have previously befallen him. So that I went to him on Sunday morning at Saint Hieronimus, and having approached him, he burst out laughing, and with every demonstration of extreme pleasure and contentment, began to praise your Majesty."[1]

The hand of Pius IX. remained extended over France, when it had become the Empire.

Then, under the shadow of this benediction, began an era of prosperity.

---

1. "Archives of the house of Orange," page 125, Supplement.

CONCLUSION
THE FALL

I

I was coming back from my fourth exile—an exile in Belgium, a small matter. It was one of the last days of September, 1871. I was re-entering France by the Luxembourg frontier. I had fallen asleep in the carriage. Suddenly the jolt of the train coming to a standstill awoke me. I opened my eyes.

The train had stopped in the middle of a charming landscape.

I was in the half-consciousness of an interrupted sleep; and ideas, as yet half-dreams, hazy and diffuse, hovered between myself and reality. I experienced the undefinable and confused sensation of awakening.

A river flowed by the side of the railway, clear, around a bright and verdant island. This vegetation was so thick that the moor-hens, on reaching it, plunged beneath it and disappeared. The river wound through a valley, which appeared like a huge garden. Apple-trees were there, which reminded one of Eve, and willows, which made one think of Galatea. It was, as I have said, in one of those equinoctial months when may be felt the peculiar charm of a season drawing to a close. If it be winter which is passing away, you hear the song of approaching spring; if it be summer which is vanishing, you see glimmering on the horizon the undefinable smile of autumn. The wind lulled and harmonized all those pleasant sounds which compose the murmur of the fields; the tinkling of the sheep-bells seemed to soothe the humming of the bees; the last butterflies met together with the first grapes; this hour of the year mingles the joy of being still alive with the unconscious melancholy of fast approaching death; the sweetness of the sun was indescribable. Fertile fields streaked with furrows, honest peasants' cottages; under the trees a turf covered with shade, the lowing of cattle as in Virgil, and the smoke of hamlets penetrated by rays of sunshine; such was the complete picture. The clanging of anvils rang in the distance, the rhythm of work amidst the harmony of nature. I listened, I mused vaguely. The valley was beautiful and quiet, the blue heavens seemed as though resting upon a lovely circle of hills; in the distance were the voices of birds, and close to me the voices of children, like two songs of angels mingled together; the universal purity enshrouded me: all this grace and all this grandeur shed a golden dawn into my soul. . .

Suddenly a fellow-traveller asked,—

"What place is this?"

Another answered,—

"Sedan."

I shuddered.

This paradise was a tomb.

I looked around. The valley was circular and hollow, like the bottom of a crater; the winding river resembled a serpent; the high hills, ranged one behind the other, surrounded this mysterious spot like a triple line of inexorable walls; once there, there is no means of exit. It reminded me of the amphitheatres. An indescribable disquieting vegetation which seemed to be an extension of the Black Forest, overran all the heights, and lost itself in the horizon like a huge impenetrable snare; the sun shone, the birds sang, carters passed by whistling; sheep, lambs, and pigeons were scattered about, leaves quivered and rustled; the grass, a densely thick grass, was full of flowers. It was appalling.

I seemed to see waving over this valley the flashing of the avenging angel's sword.

This word "Sedan" had been like a veil abruptly torn aside. The landscape had become suddenly filled with tragedy. Those shapeless eyes which the bark of trees delineates on the trunks were gazing—at what? At something terrible and lost to view.

In truth, that was the place! And at the moment when I was passing by thirteen months all but a few days had elapsed. That was the place where the monstrous enterprise of the 2d of December had burst asunder. A fearful shipwreck.

The gloomy pathways of Fate cannot be studied without profound anguish of the heart.

II

O n the 31st of August, 1870, an army was reassembled, and was, as it were, massed together under the walls of Sedan, in a place called the Givonne Valley. This army was a French army—twenty-nine brigades, fifteen divisions, four army corps—90,000 men. This army was in this place without anyone being able to divine the reason; without order, without an object, scattered about—a species of heap of men thrown down there as though with the view of being seized by some huge hand.

This army either did not entertain, or appeared not to entertain, for the moment any immediate uneasiness. They knew, or at least they thought they knew, that the enemy was a long way off. On calculating the stages at four leagues daily, it was three days' march distant. Nevertheless, towards evening the leaders took some wise strategic precautions; they protected the army, which rested in the rear on Sedan and the Meuse, by two battle fronts, one composed of the 7th Corps, and extending from Floing to Givonne, the other composed of the 12th Corps, extending from Givonne to Bazeilles; a triangle of which the Meuse formed the hypothenuse. The 12th Corps, formed of the three divisions of Lacretelle, Lartigue, and Wolf, ranged on the right, with the artillery, between the brigades formed a veritable barrier, having Bazeilles and Givonne at each end, and Daigny in its centre; the two divisions of Petit and Lhéritier massed in the rear upon two lines supported this barrier. General Lebrun commanded the 12th Corps. The 7th Corps, commanded by General Douay, only possessed two divisions—Dumont's division and Gilbert's division—and formed the other battle front, covering the army of Givonne to Floing on the side of Illy; this battle front was comparatively weak, too open on the side of Givonne, and only protected on the side of the Meuse by the two cavalry divisions of Margueritte and Bonnemains, and by Guyomar's brigade, resting in squares upon Floing. Within this triangle were encamped the 5th Corps, commanded by General Wimpfen, and the 1st Corps, commanded by General Ducrot. Michel's cavalry division covered the 1st Corps on the side of Daigny; the 5th supported itself upon Sedan. Four divisions, each disposed upon two lines—the divisions of Lhéritier, Grandchamp, Goze, and Conseil-Duménil—formed a sort of horseshoe, turned towards Sedan, and uniting the first battle front with the second. The cavalry division of Ameil and the brigade of Fontanges served as a reserve for these four divisions. The whole of the artillery was upon the two battle fronts. Two portions of the army were in confusion, one to the right of Sedan beyond Balan, the other to the left of Sedan, on this side of Iges. Beyond Balan were the divisions of Vassoigne and the brigade of Reboul, on this side of Iges were the two cavalry divisions of Margueritte and Bonnemains.

These arrangements indicated a profound feeling of security. In the first place the Emperor Napoleon III would not have come there if he had not been perfectly tranquil. This Givonne Valley is what Napoleon I called a "washhand basin." There could not be a more complete enclosure. An army is so much at home there that it is too much so; it runs the risk of no longer being able to get out. This disquieted some brave and prudent leaders such as Wimpfen, but they were not listened to. If absolutely necessary, said the people of the Imperial circle, they could always be sure of being able to reach Mézières, and at the worst the Belgian frontier. Was it, however, needful to provide for such extreme eventualities? In certain cases foresight is almost an offence. They were all of one mind, therefore, to be at their ease.

If they had been uneasy they would have cut the bridges of the Meuse; but they did not even think of it. To what purpose? The enemy was a long way off. The Emperor, who evidently was well informed, affirmed it.

The army bivouacked somewhat in confusion, as we have said, and slept peaceably throughout this night of August 31, having, whatever might happen, or believing that they had, the retreat upon Mézières open behind it. They disdained to take the most ordinary precautions, they made no cavalry reconnaissances, they did not even place outposts. A German military writer has stated this.[1] Fourteen leagues at least separated them from the German army, three days' march; they did not exactly know where it was; they believed it scattered, possessing little unity, badly informed, led somewhat at random upon several points at once, incapable of a movement converging upon one single point, like Sedan; they believed that the Crown Prince of Saxony was marching on Chalons, and that the Crown Prince of Prussia was marching on Metz; they were ignorant of everything appertaining to this army, its leaders, its plan, its armament, its effective force. Was it still following

---

1. M. Harwik.

the strategy of Gustavus Adolphus? Was it still following the tactics of Frederick II? No one knew. They felt sure of being at Berlin in a few weeks. What nonsense! The Prussian army! They talked of this war as of a dream, and of this army as of a phantom.

During this very night, while the French army was sleeping, this is what was taking place.

III

A t a quarter to two in the morning, at his headquarters at Mouzon, Albert, Crown Prince of Saxony, set the Army of the Meuse in motion; the Royal Guard were beat to arms, and two divisions marched, one upon Villers-Cernay, by Escambre and Fouru-aux-Bois, the other upon Francheval by Suchy and Fouru-Saint-Remy. The Artillery of the Guard followed.

At the same moment the 12th Saxon Corps was beaten to arms, and by the high road to the south of Douzy reached Lamécourt, and marched upon La Moncelle; the 1st Bavarian Corps marched upon Bazeilles, supported at Reuilly-sur-Meuse by an Artillery Division of the 4th Corps. The other division of the 4th Corps crossed the Meuse at Mouzon, and massed itself in reserve at Mairy, upon the right bank. These three columns maintained close communication with each other. The order was given to the advanced guards to begin no offensive movement before five o'clock, and silently to occupy Fouru-aux-Bois, Fouru-Saint-Remy, and Douay. They had left their knapsacks behind them. The baggage-wagons did not stir. The Crown Prince of Saxony was on horseback on the heights of Amblimont.

At the same time, at his headquarters at Chémery, Blumenthal was having a bridge built over the Meuse by the Wurtemburg division. The 11th Corps, astir before daylight, crossed the Meuse at Dom-le-Mesnil and at Donchery, and reached Vrigne-sur-Bois. The artillery followed, and held the road from Vrigne to Sedan. The Wurtemburg division kept the bridge which it had built, and held the road from Sedan to Mézières. At five o'clock, the 2d Bavarian Corps, with the artillery at its head, detached one of its divisions, and sent it by Bulson upon Frénois; the other division passed by Noyers, and drew up before Sedan, between Frénois and Wadelincourt. The artillery of the Reserve was drawn up on the heights of the left bank, opposite Donchery.

At the same time the 6th Cavalry Division was sent from Mazeray, and passing by Boutancourt and Bolzicourt, reached the Meuse at Flize; the 2d Cavalry Division quitted its encampment, and took up its position to the south of Boutancourt; the 4th Cavalry Division took up its position to the south of Frénois; the 1st Bavarian Corps installed itself at Remilly; the 5th Cavalry Division and the 6th Corps were posted to observe, and all in line, and order, massed upon the heights waited for the dawn to appear. The Crown Prince of Prussia was on horseback on the hill of Frénois.

At the same moment, upon every point of the horizon, other and similar movements were taking place from every side. The high hills were suddenly overrun by an immense black army. Not one shout of command. Two hundred and fifty thousand men came silently to encircle the Givonne Valley.

This is what the circle consisted of,—

The Bavarians, the right wing, at Bazeilles on the Meuse; next to the Bavarians the Saxons, at La Moncelle and Daigny; opposite Givonne, the Royal Guard; the 5th Corps at Saint Menges; the 2d at Flaigneux; the Wurtemburgers at the bend of the Meuse, between Saint Menges and Donchery; Count Stolberg and his cavalry at Donchery; in front, towards Sedan, the 2d Bavarian Army.

All this was carried out in a ghostly manner, in order, without a whisper, without a sound, through forests, ravines, and valleys. A tortuous and ill-omened march. A stealthy gliding onwards of reptiles.

Scarcely could a murmur be heard beneath the thick foliage. The silent battle swarmed in the darkness awaiting the day.

The French army was sleeping.

Suddenly it awoke.

It was a prisoner.

The sun rose, brilliant on the side of God—terrible on the side of man.

IV

L et us review the situation.

The Germans have numbers on their side; they are three against one, perhaps four; they own to 250,000 men, and it is certain that their attacking front extended for 30 kilomètres; they have on their side the positions, they crown the heights, they fill the forests, they are covered by all these escarpments, they are masked by all this shade; they possess an incomparable artillery. The French army is in a valley, almost without artillery and without supplies, utterly naked beneath their hail of lead. The Germans have on their side the ambuscade, and the French have only on their side heroism. Death is glorious, but surprise is profitable.

A surprise, that is the true description of this brilliant exploit.

Is it fair warfare? Yes. But if this is fair, what is unfair warfare? It is the same thing.

This said, the story of the Battle of Sedan has been told.

I should have wished to stop there. But I cannot. Whatever horror the historian may feel, History is a duty, and this duty must be fulfilled. There is no incline more inexorable than this: to tell the truth; he who ventures on it rolls to the very bottom. It must be so. The guardian of Justice is doomed to justice.

The Battle of Sedan is more than a battle which has been fought; it is a syllogism which is completed; a formidable premeditation of destiny. Destiny never hurries, but it always comes. At its hour, there it is. It allows years to pass by, and at the moment when men are least thinking of it, it appears. Of this character is the fatal, the unexpected catastrophe named Sedan. From time to time in History, Divine logic makes an onslaught. Sedan is one of those onslaughts.

Thus on the 1st of September, at five o'clock in the morning the world awoke under the sun, and the French army under the thunderbolt.

V

Bazeilles takes fire, Givonne takes fire, Floing takes fire; the battle begins with a furnace. The whole horizon is aflame. The French camp is in this crater, stupefied, affrighted, starting up from sleeping,—a funereal swarming. A circle of thunder surrounds the army. They are encircled by annihilation. This mighty slaughter is carried on on all sides simultaneously. The French resist, and they are terrible, having nothing left but despair. Our cannon, almost all old-fashioned and of short range, are at once dismounted by the fearful and exact aim of the Prussians. The density of the rain of shells upon the valley is so great, that "the earth is completely furrowed," says an eye-witness, "as though by a rake." How many cannon? Eleven hundred at least. Twelve German batteries upon La Moncelle alone; the 3d and 4th *Abtheilung*, an awe-striking artillery, upon the crests of Givonne, with the 2d horse battery in reserve; opposite Doigny ten Saxon and two Wurtemburg batteries; the curtain of trees of the wood to the north of Villers-Cernay masks the mounted *Abtheilung*, which is there with the 3d Heavy Artillery in reserve, and from this gloomy copse issues a formidable fire; the twenty-four pieces of the 1st Heavy Artillery are ranged in the glade skirting the road from La Moncelle to La Chapelle; the battery of the Royal Guard sets fire to the Garenne Wood; the shells and the balls riddle Suchy, Francheval, Fouru-Saint-Remy, and the valley between Heibes and Givonne; and the third and fourth rank of cannon extend without break of continuity as far as the Calvary of Illy, the extreme point of the horizon. The German soldiers, seated or lying before the batteries, watch the artillery at work. The French soldiers fall and die. Amongst the bodies which cover the plain there is one, the body of an officers on which they will find, after the battle, a sealed note, containing this order, signed NAPOLEON: "Today, September 1st, rest for the whole army."

The gallant 35th of the Line almost completely disappears under the overwhelming shower of shells; the brave Marine Infantry holds at bay for a moment the Saxons, joined by the Bavarians, but outflanked on every side, draws back; all the admirable cavalry of the Targueritte Division hurled against the German infantry, halts and sinks down midway, "annihilated," says the Prussian Report, "by well-aimed and cool firing."[1] This field of carnage has three outlets; all three barred: the Bouillon road by the Prussian Guard, the Carignan road by the Bavarians, the Mézières road by the Wurtemburgers. The French have not thought of barricading the railway viaduct; three German battalions have occupied it during the night. Two isolated houses on the Balan road could be made the pivot of a long resistance; but the Germans are there. The wood from Monvilliers to Bazeilles, bushy and dense, might prevent the junction of the Saxons, masters of La Moncelle, and the Bavarians, masters of Bazeilles; but the French have been forestalled: they find the Bavarians cutting the underwood with their bill-hooks. The German army moves in one piece, in one absolute unity; the Crown Prince of Saxony is on the height of Mairy, whence he surveys the whole action; the command oscillates in the French army; at the beginning of the battle, at a quarter to six, MacMahon is wounded by the bursting of a shell; at seven o'clock Ducrot replaces him; at ten o'clock Wimpfen replaces Ducrot. Every instant the wall of fire is drawing closer in, the roll of the thunder is continuous, a dismal pulverization of 90,000 men! Never before has anything equal to this been seen; never before has an army been overwhelmed beneath such a downpour of lead and iron! At one o'clock all is lost. The regiments fly helter-skelter into Sedan. But Sedan begins to burn; Dijonval burns, the ambulances burn, there is nothing now possible but to cut their way out. Wimpfen, brave and resolute, proposes this to the Emperor. The 3d Zouaves, desperate, have set the example. Cut off from the rest of the army, they have forced a passage, and have reached Belgium. A flight of lions!

Suddenly, above the disaster, above the huge pile of dead and dying, above all this unfortunate heroism, appears disgrace. The white flag is hoisted.

Turenne and Vauban were both present, one in his statue, the other in his citadel.

The statue and the citadel witnessed the awe-striking capitulation. These two virgins, one of bronze, the other of granite, felt themselves prostituted. O noble face of our country! Oh, eternal blushes!

---

1. The Franco-German War of 1870–71. Report of the Prussian Staff, page 1087.

VI

This disaster of Sedan was easy of avoidance by any other man, but impossible of avoidance for Louis Bonaparte. He avoided it so little that he sought it. *Lex fati*.

Our army seemed expressly arranged for the catastrophe. The soldier was uneasy, ignorant of his whereabouts, famished. On the 31st of August, in the streets of Sedan, soldiers were seeking their regiments, and going from door to door asking for bread. We have seen the Emperor's order announcing the next day, September 1st, as a day of rest. In truth the army was worn out with fatigue. And yet it had only marched by short stages. The soldier was almost losing the habit of marching. One corps, the 1st, for example, only accomplished two leagues per day (on the 29th of August from Stonne to Raucourt).

During that time the German army, inexorably commanded and driven at the stick's end like the army of the Xerxes, achieved marches of fourteen leagues in fifteen hours, which enabled it to arrive unexpectedly, and to surround the French army while asleep. It was customary to allow oneself to be surprised. General Failly allowed himself to be surprised at Beaumont; during the day the soldiers took their guns to pieces to clean them, at night they slept, without even cutting the bridges which delivered them to the enemy; thus they neglected to blow up the bridges of Mouzon and Bazeilles. On September 1st, daylight had not yet appeared, when an advance guard of seven battalions, commanded by General Schultz, captured La Rulle, and insured the junction of the army of the Meuse with the Royal Guard. Almost at the same minute, with German precision, the Wurtemburgers seized the bridge of La Platinerie, and hidden by the Chevalier Wood, the Saxon battalions, spread out into company columns, occupied the whole of the road from La Moncelle to Villers-Cernay.

Thus, as we have seen, the awakening of the French Army was horrible. At Bazeilles a fog was added to the smoke. Our soldiers, attacked in this gloom, knew not what death required of them; they fought from room to room and from house to house.[1]

It was in vain that the Reboul brigade came to support the Martin des Pallières brigade; they were obliged to yield. At the same time Ducrot

---

1. "The French were literally awakened from sleep by our attack."—Helvic.

was compelled to concentrate his forces in the Garenne Wood, before the Calvary of Illy; Douay, shattered, fell back; Lebrun alone stood firm on the plateau of Stenay. Our troops occupied a line of five kilomètres; the front of the French army faced the east, the left faced the north, the extreme left (the Guyomar brigade) faced the west; but they did not know whether they faced the enemy, they did not see him; annihilation struck without showing itself; they had to deal with a masked Medusa. Our cavalry was excellent, but useless. The field of battle, obstructed by a large wood, cut up by clumps of trees, by houses and by farms and by enclosure walls, was excellent for artillery and infantry, but bad for cavalry. The rivulet of Givonne, which flows at the bottom of the valley and crosses it, for three days ran with more blood than water. Among other places of carnage, Saint-Menges was appalling. For a moment it appeared possible to cut a way out by Carignan towards Montmédy, and then this outlet reclosed. This refuge only remained, Sedan; Sedan encumbered with carts, with wagons, with carriages, with hospital huts; a heap of combustible matter. This dying agony of heroes lasted ten hours. They refused to surrender, they grew indignant, they wished to complete their death, so bravely begun. They were delivered up to it.

As we have said, three men, three dauntless soldiers, had succeeded each other in the command, MacMahon, Ducrot, Wimpfen; MacMahon had only time to be wounded, Ducrot had only time to commit a blunder, Wimpfen had only time to conceive an heroic idea, and he conceived it; but MacMahon is not responsible for his wound, Ducrot is not responsible for his blunder, and Wimpfen is not responsible for the impossibility of his suggestion to cut their way out. The shell which struck MacMahon withdrew him from the catastrophe; Ducrot's blunder, the inopportune order to retreat given to General Lebrun, is explained by the confused horror of the situation, and is rather an error than a fault. Wimpfen, desperate, needed 20,000 soldiers to cut his way out, and could only get together 2000. History exculpates these three men; in this disaster of Sedan there was but one sole and fatal general, the Emperor. That which was knitted together on the 2d December, 1851, came apart on the 2d September, 1870; the carnage on the Boulevard Montmartre, and the capitulation of Sedan are, we maintain, the two parts of a syllogism; logic and justice have the same balance; it was Louis Bonaparte's dismal destiny to begin with the black flag of massacres and to end with the white flag of disgrace.

VII

There was no alternative between death and opprobrium; either soul or sword must be surrendered. Louis Bonaparte surrendered his sword.

He wrote to William:

SIRE, MY BROTHER,

"Not having been able to die in the midst of my troops, it only remains for me to place my sword in your Majesty's hands.

"I am, your Majesty,

Your good Brother,
NAPOLEON
Sedan, 1st September, 1870

William answered, "Sire, my Brother, I accept your sword."

And on the 2d of September, at six o'clock in the morning, this plain, streaming with blood, and covered with dead, saw pass by a gilded open carriage and four, the horses harnessed after Daumont fashion, and in this carriage a man, cigarette in mouth. It was the Emperor of the French going to surrender his sword to the King of Prussia.

The King kept the Emperor waiting. It was too early. He sent M. de Bismarck to Louis Bonaparte to say that he "would not" receive him yet awhile. Louis Bonaparte entered into a hovel by the side of the road. A table and two chairs were there. Bismarck and he leant their arms on the table and conversed. A mournful conversation. At the hour which suited the King, towards noon, the Emperor got back into his carriage, and went to the castle of Bellevue, half way to the castle of Vandresse. There he waited until the King came. At one o'clock William arrived from Vandresse, and consented to receive Bonaparte. He received him badly. Attila has not a light hand. The King, a blunt, straightforward man, showed the Emperor a pity involuntarily cruel. There are pities which overwhelm. The conqueror upbraided the conquered with the victory. Bluntness handles an open wound badly. "Whatever was your reason for declaring this war?" The conquered excused himself, accusing France. The distant hurrahs of the victorious German army cut short this dialogue.

The King caused the Emperor to be reconducted by a detachment of the Royal Guard. This excess of ignominy is called "an escort of honor."

After the sword the Army.

On the 3d of September, Louis Bonaparte handed over to Germany 88,000 French soldiers.

"In addition" (says the Prussian report):—

"One eagle and two flags.

"419 field-guns and mitrailleuses.

"139 heavy pieces.

"1079 vehicles of all kinds.

"60,000 muskets.

"6000 horses, still good for service."

These German figures are not wholly to be depended upon. According to what seems useful at the moment, the Aulic chancellors swell or reduce the disaster. There were about 13,000 wounded amongst the prisoners. The numbers vary in the official documents. A Prussian report, reckoning up the French soldiers killed and wounded in the battle of Sedan, publishes this total: *Sixteen thousand four hundred* men. This number causes a shudder. For it is that very number, *Sixteen thousand four hundred* men, which Saint Arnaud had set to work on the Boulevard Montmartre upon the 4th of December, 1851.

Half a league to the north-west of Sedan, near Iges, the bend of the Meuse almost forms an island. A canal crosses the isthmus, so that the peninsula becomes an island. It was there that there were penned, under the stick of the Prussian corporals, 83,000 French soldiers. A few sentinels watched over this army.

They placed but few, insolently. These conquered men remained there ten days, the wounded almost without care, the able-bodied almost without nourishment. The German army sneered around them. The heavens took part against them. The weather was fearful. Neither huts nor tents. Not a fire, not a truss of straw. For ten days and ten nights these 83,000 prisoners bivouacked with their heads beneath the rain, their feet in the mud. Many died of fever, regretting the hail of bullets.

At length ox-wagons came and took them away.

The King placed the Emperor in some place or other. Wilhelmshöhe. What a thing of rags and tatters, an Emperor "drawn" like a fowl!

VIII

I was there, thoughtful. I looked on these fields, these ravines, these hills, shuddering. I would willingly have insulted this terrible place.

But sacred horror held me back.

The station-master of Sedan came to my carriage, and explained to me what I had before my eyes. I seemed to see, through his words, the pale lightnings of the battle. All these distant cottages, scattered about and charming in the sun, had been burnt; they were rebuilt; Nature, so quickly diverted, had repaired everything, had cleaned everything, had swept everything, had replaced everything. The ferocious convulsion of men had vanished, eternal order had resumed its sway. But, as I have said, the sun was there in vain, all this valley was smoke and darkness. In the distance, upon an eminence to my left, I saw a huge castle; it was Vandresse. There lodged the King of Prussia. Halfway up this height, along the road, I distinguished above the trees three pointed gables; it was another castle, Bellevue; there Louis Bonaparte surrendered to William; there he had given and delivered up our army; it was there that, not being immediately admitted, and requested to exercise a little patience, he had remained for nearly an hour silent and wan before the door, bringing his disgrace, and waiting until it should please William to open the door to him; it was there that before receiving it the King of Prussia had made the sword of France dangle about in an ante-chamber. Lower down, nearer, in the valley, at the beginning of a road leading to Vandresse, they pointed out to me a species of hovel. There they told me, while waiting for the King of Prussia, the Emperor Napoleon III had got down, livid; he had gone into a little courtyard, which they pointed out to me, and where a dog growled on the chain; he had seated himself on a stone close by a dunghill, and he had said, "I am thirsty." A Prussian soldier had brought him a glass of water.

Terrible end of the *coup d'état*! Blood when it is drunk does not quench the thirst. An hour was to come when the unhappy one should utter the cry of fever and of agony. Disgrace reserved for him this thirst, and Prussia this glass of water.

Fearful dregs of Destiny.

Beyond the road, at a few steps from me, five trembling and pale poplars sheltered the front of the house, the single story of which was surmounted by a sign. On this sign was written in great letters this name: DROUET. I became haggard. *Drouet* I read *Varennes*. Tragical Chance, which mingled Varennes with Sedan, seemed to wish to bring the two catastrophes face to face, and to couple in a manner with the same chain the Emperor a prisoner of the foreigner, to the King a prisoner of his people.

The mist of reverie veiled this plain from me. The Meuse appeared to me to wear a ruddy reflection, the neighboring isle, whose verdure I had admired, had for its subsoil a tomb: Fifteen hundred horses, and as many men, were buried there: thence the thick grass. Here and there, as far as could be seen, mounds, covered with ill-favored vegetation, dotted the valley; each of these patches of vegetation marked the place of a buried regiment. There Guyomar's Brigade had been annihilated; there, the Lhéritier Division had been exterminated; here the 7th Corps had perished; there, without having even reached the enemy's infantry, had fallen "beneath the cool and well-aimed firing," as the Prussian report states, the whole of General Margueritte's cavalry. From these two heights, the most elevated of this circle of hills, Daigny, opposite Givonne, which is 266 mètres high, Fleigneux, opposite Illy, 296 mètres high, the batteries of the Prussian Royal Guard had crushed the French Army. It was done from above, with the terrible authority of Destiny. It seemed as though they had come there purposely, these to kill, the others to die. A valley for a mortar, the German Army for a pestle, such is the battle of Sedan. I gazed, powerless to avert my eyes, at this field of disaster, at this undulating country which had proved no protection to our regiments, at this ravine where all our cavalry were demolished, at all this amphitheatre where the catastrophe was spread out, at the gloomy escarpments of La Marphée, at these thickets, at these declivities, at these precipices, at these forests filled with ambushes, and in this terrible shadow, O Thou the Invisible! I saw Thee.

IX

N ever was there a more dismal fall.
　　No expiation can be compared with this. The unprecedented drama was in five acts, so fierce that Aeschylus himself would not have dared to dream of them. "The Ambush!" "The Struggle!" "The Massacre!" "The Victory!" "The Fall!" What a tangle and what an unwinding! A poet who would have predicted it would have seemed a traitor. God alone could permit Himself Sedan.

Everything in proportion, such is His law. Far worse than Brumaire, it needed a more crushing retribution than Waterloo.

The first Napoleon, as we have said elsewhere,[1] had faced his destiny; he had not been dishonored by his punishment, he fell while steadfastly regarding God. He came back to Paris, appraising the deserts of those men who overthrew him, proudly distinguishing amongst them, esteeming Lafayette and despising Dupin. He had at the last moment wished to see clearly into his destiny, he had not allowed his eyes to be bandaged; he had accepted the catastrophe while making his conditions with it. Here there is nothing of the kind. One might almost say that the traitor is struck treacherously. In this case there is a bad man who feels himself in the grasp of Destiny, and who does not know what it is doing to him. He was at the summit of his power, the blind master of an idiot world. He had wished for a *plebiscitum*, he had had one. He had at his feet this very William. It was at this moment that his crime suddenly seized him. He did not struggle against it; he was the condemned man who obeys his sentence. He submitted to everything which terrible Fate exacted from him. Never was there a more docile patient. He had no army, he made war; he had only Rouher, he provoked Bismarck; he had only Leboeuf, he attacked Moltke. He confided Strasburg to Uhrich; he gave Metz to Bazaine to guard. He had 120,000 men at Châlons; he had it in his power to cover Paris. He felt that his crime rose up there, threatening and erect; he fled, not daring to face Paris. He himself led—purposely, and yet despite himself; willing and yet unwilling, knowingly and yet unknowingly, a miserable mind, a prey to the abyss—he led his army into a place of annihilation; he made that terrible choice, a battle-field without an outlet; he was no longer conscious of anything,

---

1. "L'Année Terrible."

no more of his blunder of today than of his crime of former days; he must finish, but he could only finish as a fugitive; this condemned one was not worthy to look his end in the face; he lowered his head, he turned his back. God executed him in degrading him. Napoleon III as an Emperor had a right to thunder, but for this man the thunder was ignominious—he was thunderstruck in the back.

X

L et us forget this man, and let us look at Humanity.

The invasion of France by Germany, in 1870, was a night effect. The world was astonished that so much gloom could come forth from a people. Five black months—such was the siege of Paris. To create night may prove Power, but Glory consists in the creation of daylight. France creates daylight. Thence her immense human popularity. To her Civilization owes the dawn. The human mind in order to see clearly turns in the direction of France. Five months of darkness, that is what, in 1870, Germany succeeded in giving to the Nations; France has given to them four centuries of light.

Today the civilized world more than ever feels the need which it has of France. France has proved this by her danger. The ungrateful apathy of Governments only increased the anxiety of nations. At the sight of Paris threatened, there arose among the peoples dread that their own heads were in danger. Would they allow Germany to go on? But France saved herself quite alone. She had only to rise. *Patuit dea*.

Today she is greater than ever. What would have killed another nation has hardly wounded her. The darkening of her horizon has rendered her light more visible. What she has lost in territory she has gained in radiancy. Moreover, she is fraternal without an effort. Above her misfortune there is her smile. It is not on her that the Gothic Empire weighs. She is a nation of citizens and not a flock of subjects. Frontiers? Will there be any frontiers in twenty years? Victories? France counts in her past victories of war, and in her future victories of peace. The future belongs to Voltaire, and not to Krupp; the future belongs to the book, and not to the sword. The future belongs to life, and not to death. There is in the policy opposed to France a certain amount of the tomb; to seek life in the old institutions is a vain task, and to feed upon the past is to bite the dust. France has the faculty of giving light; no catastrophe, political or military, will deprive her of this mysterious supremacy. The cloud passes away, the star is seen once more.

The star possesses no anger; the dawn bears no malice. Light is satisfied in being light. Light is everything; the human race has no other love. France knows herself beloved because she is good, and the greatest of all powers is to be loved. The French revolution is for all the world. It is a battle perpetually waged for Right, and perpetually gained

for Truth. Right is the innermost part of man; Truth is the innerm
part of God. What can be done against a revolution which has
much right on its side? Nothing. To love it. That is what the nations do
France offers herself, the world accepts her. The whole phenomenon lies
in these few words. An invasion of armies can be resisted; an invasion
of ideas cannot be resisted. The glory of barbarians is to be conquered
by humanity; the glory of savages is to be conquered by civilization; the
glory of darkness is to be conquered by the torch. This is why France is
desired and assented to by all. This is why, having no hatred, she has no
fear; this is why she is fraternal and maternal; this is why it is impossible
to lessen her, impossible to humiliate her, impossible to irritate her; this
is why, after so many ordeals, after so many catastrophes, after so many
disasters, after so many calamities, after so many falls, incorruptible and
invulnerable she holds out her hand to all the peoples from above.

When our glance rests on this old continent, stirred today by a new
breath, certain phenomena appear, and we seem to gain a glimpse
of that august and mysterious problem, the formation of the future.
It may be said, that in the same manner as light is compounded of
seven colors, civilization is compounded of seven peoples. Of these
peoples, three, Greece, Italy, and Spain, represent the South; three,
England, Germany, and Russia, represent the north; the seventh, or
the first, France, is at the same time North and South, Celtic and
Latin, Gothic and Greek. This country owes to its heaven this sublime
good fortune, the crossing of two rays of light; the crossing of two
rays of light is as though we were to say the joining of two hands, that
is to say Peace. Such is the privilege of this France, she is at the same
time solar and starry. In her heaven she possesses as much dawn as the
East, and as many stars as the North. Sometimes her glimmer rises
in the twilight, but it is in the black night of revolutions and of wars
that her resplendence blazes forth, and her aurorean dawn becomes
the Aurora Borealis.

One day, before long, the seven nations, which combine in themselves
the whole of humanity, will join together and amalgamate like the seven
colors of the prism, in a radiant celestial arch; the marvel of Peace will
appear eternal and visible above civilization, and the world, dazzled,
will contemplate the immense rainbow of the United Peoples of Europe.

THE END

VICTOR HUGO

A NOTE ABOUT THE AUTHOR

Victor Hugo (1802–1885) was a French poet and novelist. Born in Besançon, Hugo was the son of a general who served in the Napoleonic army. Raised on the move, Hugo was taken with his family from one outpost to the next, eventually setting with his mother in Paris in 1803. In 1823, he published his first novel, launching a career that would earn him a reputation as a leading figure of French Romanticism. His Gothic novel *The Hunchback of Notre-Dame* (1831) was a bestseller throughout Europe, inspiring the French government to restore the legendary cathedral to its former glory. During the reign of King Louis-Philippe, Hugo was elected to the National Assembly of the French Second Republic, where he spoke out against the death penalty and poverty while calling for public education and universal suffrage. Exiled during the rise of Napoleon III, Hugo lived in Guernsey from 1855 to 1870. During this time, he published his literary masterpiece *Les Misérables* (1862), a historical novel which has been adapted countless times for theater, film, and television. Towards the end of his life, he advocated for republicanism around Europe and across the globe, cementing his reputation as a defender of the people and earning a place at Paris' Panthéon, where his remains were interred following his death from pneumonia. His final words, written on a note only days before his death, capture the depth of his belief in humanity: "To love is to act."

A NOTE FROM THE PUBLISHER

Spanning many genres, from non-fiction essays to literature classics to children's books and lyric poetry, Mint Edition books showcase the master works of our time in a modern new package. The text is freshly typeset, is clean and easy to read, and features a new note about the author in each volume. Many books also include exclusive new introductory material. Every book boasts a striking new cover, which makes it as appropriate for collecting as it is for gift giving. Mint Edition books are only printed when a reader orders them, so natural resources are not wasted. We're proud that our books are never manufactured in excess and exist only in the exact quantity they need to be read and enjoyed.

Discover more of your favorite classics with Bookfinity™.

- Track your reading with custom book lists.
- Get great book recommendations for your personalized Reader Type.
- Add reviews for your favorite books.
- AND MUCH MORE!

Visit **bookfinity.com** and take the fun Reader Type quiz to get started.

Enjoy our classic and modern companion pairings!

Printed in the USA
CPSIA information can be obtained
at www.ICGtesting.com
JSHW022203140824
68134JS00018B/843